Please send S.A.S.E. when writing to Bud Hastin for book

1991 - 1992 Edition

This book is updated and the latest information on Avon collecting is released to the public about every 2 to 3 years. Send your name and address to Bud Hastin to be first to know when the next book will be released. Be sure to say what edition is your last book purchased.

Bud Hastin's

Avon Collectible's Price Guide™

The official Guide For Avon Bottle Collectors

1st Edition

Published, Written, Photographed and Researched by
Bud Hastin
P.O. Box 9868 Kansas City, MO 64134

Bud Hastin is in no way responsible for buying, selling or trading Avon bottles at the prices quoted in this guide book. It is published only as a guide and prices vary from state to state as much as 90%. Most prices quoted are top prices in mint condition and it is not uncommon for prices to be quoted differently, usually being lower. Bud Hastin does not solicit Avon bottles to buy or sell. The current values in this book should be used only as a guide. They are not intended to set prices, which vary from one section of the country to another. Auction prices as well as dealer prices vary greatly and are affected by condition as well as demand. Neither the Author nor the Publisher assumes responsibility for any losses that might be incurred as a result of consulting this guide.

*The Bud Hastin's Avon Collectible's Price Guide™ is recognized by
Avon Collectors and Avon Representatives as the official
Avon collector's guide in print.*

Acknowledgments & Credits

Bud Hastin personally thanks all the Avon collectors across the nation who have permitted him to photograph their collection to update this book. Much credit goes to all the following people for their assistance and help, be it big or small. For without them there would never have been an Avon Collectible's Price Guide.

Dwight & Vera Young, MO

Jim & Sally Herrema, MI

Jerry Fink, IL

Jenny Stanley, OH

Grace Powers, GA

Mary Rhoads, CA

Anna & Evans Briedenbach, PA

Mary Lou Bussy, NY

Jane Wendt, NY

Marlene Gruenwald, MI

Marcy & Nick Latoff, NJ

Jackie Hoffman, CA

Gladys Dwyer, NJ

Mary Ann Morganello, NY

David Holmberg, MI

Jerry Graham, IA

Catherin Hopkins, IN

About This Book

In 1969 Bud Hastin published his 1st Book on Avon Collecting. That 1st Book was similar to this book. It featured only the original Avon Collectibles. As the years passed Collector interest expanded to include every single item that had the name Avon on it.

Now 22 years later, the majority of new Avon Collectors are going back to the basic's. This includes all the contents of this 1st Edition of Avon Collectibles. This covers Mens & Womens Decanters, & Figurines. All soaps, Mens, Womens & Kids, Kids Toys, Plates, Candles & Avon Representative Awards. These are the items in Avon Collecting that are hot in the 1990s. All items must be in new condition as originally sold, this includes the box, to bring top dollar on resale of Avon Collectibles.

Any Avon Collectible that is damaged in any way should not be bought or sold.

If you do, I suggest not paying more than 10% of Current Market Value. Lets weed out the junk in Avon Collecting and only collect what will be desirable in the future to other collectors.

The 1987 11th Edition Avon Encyclopedia

(will not be revised till 1993.)

Bud Hastin's Avon Encyclopedia is in its 11th Edition and covers all California Perfume Company & Avon Products 1886 to 1987. If you are looking for information on the older Avon products then you should write to Bud Hastin, Box 9868, Kansas City, MO 64134. You can call Vera Young at (816)763-2022 for information on the cost of the Avon Encyclopedia. Please send S.A.S.E.

Vera Young is also the owner & publisher of Avon Times, the nations largest Avon Collectors Club and can give you information on subscribing to Avon Times. See order forms in back of this book.

No.1 Rule in Avon Collecting: "Set a goal for your hobby and collect only what you want to collect." You rule the hobby, it doesn't rule you. Decide what part of the overall hobby appeals to you, set your goal and work hard toward that goal. Ask yourself some questions. How much room do I have? How much can I spend each month? What do I enjoy most about Avon Collecting? Base your goal on the answer.

Since 1969 Bud has sold over 655,000 copies of his Avon Collectors book.

NATIONAL ASSOCIATION OF AVON COLLECTORS

Bud was chairman of the Board of the National Association of Avon Collectors Clubs, and was the founder of the National Organization in 1971 to 1986. The N.A.A.C. is not a club, but an organization to help promote Avon collecting in the United States. The N.A.A.C. is run by an elected board of Directors. The N.A.A.C. is ready to help anyone start a new Avon collectors club in your area. For information on starting a new Avon Collectors Club, write to N.A.A.C. in care of Bud Hastin and we will see all N.A.A.C. material is sent to you. At present there are 100 active Avon Collectors Clubs in the N.A.A.C. A National Convention is held each year along with a National Avon Bottle Show. Each year it is held in a different section of the U.S. The N.A.A.C. is a non-profit organization. See the N.A.A.C. section of this book for N.A.A.C. collectibles.

Grading Condition of Avons

MINT CONDITION means items must be in new condition as originally sold, with all labels bright and correct, and cap and/or stopper. Items need not be full or boxed, but will bring a higher price in most cases if they are in the box.

If any Avon is damaged in any way - I would not buy it.
Collect only mint Avons and throw away the less than mint ones
in the Avon Line.

TO BUY AND SELL AVONS. Garage sales, flea markets, antique shops, bottle shops are the best places to buy and sell Avon bottles locally. To sell Avons in your own town, place a small ad in your local paper and say Avon bottles for sale with your address or phone number. Have a garage sale and put Avon bottles on your sign. People will come to you. If you have no luck locally, **The Avon Times is the number one spot in the U.S. to sell those extra Avons.** The Avon Times is the largest in the world and Avon ads get the best result anywhere. Write Avon Times, P.O. Box 9868, Kansas City, MO 64134, for a sample copy of this club magazine. Send $1.00 to cover postage.

There are several reasons for pricing all items empty. After Shave bottles are known to explode in sun light or heat. Full bottles sitting on glass shelves increase the chance of the shelves breaking. After a few years, the contents become spoiled or unsafe to skin and dangerous in the hands of children. I feel if you buy the item new, use the contents and you will still have the pretty bottles.

IF ANYTHING IS TOO BADLY DAMAGED, DON'T BUY IT OR SELL IT!

PRICING CURRENT MARKET VALUE

All pricing in this book for CMV has been set by several qualified Avon bottle dealers and collectors across the United States. The prices reflected are what the item is actually selling for in their respective areas. All items are priced empty unless otherwise stated. Remember, the price paid to the Avon Representative is not a collector's price, but a new product price. You are paying for the contents. After you use the product, the price usually goes down and it becomes a used item. After you buy the item from Avon it is a used item. It takes some time for the item to become scarce on the collector's market before you see a true collector's price.

WHAT IS CMV?

Current Market Value - Definition: A willing buyer and a willing seller with neither under duress to make the transaction.

What makes an Avon valuable? Shape, color, unusual design, scarcity and how well it will display:

      a. Too big - takes too much room

      b. Too small - gets lost in collection

      c. Odd shapes - doesn't fit shelves, also takes too much room

Condition: Refer to coin collectors. Mint means perfect condition, unused, exceptional and undamaged.

Mint means Mint, commands top dollar:

      a. Boxes were made to protect the container, keeping it clean and brilliant. Boxes advertise the product and instruct the user. Boxes tell a story. When you say original condition, that was with a box. Boxes (especially men's) were usually thrown away immediately. A good clean, crisp box will help make the item bring a premium.

      b. Grading and condition become even more important for an item with a CMV over $25.00.

      c. Example: 1966-67 Tall Pony Post. The box is probably the hardest to find of the modern figures. Box should have a premium price.

MEN'S DECANTERS CERAMICS & FIGURINES

COLLECTORS
**All Containers are
Priced Empty**

BO means .... Bottle Only (empty)
CMV means ...... Current Market Value (mint)
SSP means .... Special Selling Price
OSP means .... Original Selling Price
MB means .... Mint and Boxed
DP means .... Avon Rep Cost

EXTRA SPECIAL MALE 1977-79
(Left) 3 oz. blue glass, dark blue cap and white plastic roof. Separate American eagle and red striped stick on decals. Came in Deep Woods or Everest After Shave. SSP $4.44 **BO $5., MB $8.**

MUSTANG '64 1976-78
(Right) 2 oz. size blue glass and blue tail cap. Came in Spicy or Tai Winds. SSP $3. **CMV $5 . BO, $7. MB.**

WINNEBAGO MOTOR HOME 1978-79
(Top) 5 oz. white painted over clear glass. Stick on trim decals. Holds Wild Country or Deep Woods After Shave. SSP $7 CMV $9.

STANLEY STEAMER 1978
(Bottom) Silver, 5 oz. silver paint over clear glass. Came in Tai Winds or Deep Woods After Shave. SSP $9 **CMV $12 MB.**

BIG MACK 1973-75
6 oz. green glass with beige bed. Holds Oland or Windjammer After Shave. SSP $5 **CMV $8 MB $5 BO.**

RED SENTINAL "FIRE TRUCK" 1978-79
4 piece decanter. Engine is 3 1/2 oz. clear glass painted red. Holds Wild Country or Deep Woods After Shave. Plastic hook and ladder center section and 6 oz. rear red plastic section holds talc. Comes with stick on decals. SSP $12 **CMV $13 MB.**

FERRARI '53' 1974-75
(Left) 2 oz. dark amber glass with plastic closure. Came in Wild Country After Shave or Avon Protein Hair Lotion for Men. OSP $3 **CMV $6. BO, $8 MB.**

THUNDERBIRD '55 1974-75
(Right) 2 oz. blue glass with blue plastic closure. Came in Wild Country or Deep Woods After Shave. OSP $3 **CMV $6. BO, $8 MB.**

FOUR WHEEL DRIVE DECANTER 1987
3 oz. black glass. Stick on decals. Holds After Shave. SSP $8, **CMV $8 MB.**

GREYHOUND BUS '31 1976-77
5 oz. blue painted over clear glass. Blue plastic front cap. White plastic roof will pop off. Came in Avon Spicy or Everest. SSP $6 **CMV $6 BO, $8 MB.**

PIERCE ARROW '33 1975-77
(Left) 5 oz. dark blue sprayed glass with beige plastic cap. Came in Wild Country or Deep Woods After Shave. OSP $6 **CMV $8. BO $10 MB.**

STOCK CAR RACER 1974-75
(Right) 5 oz. blue glass with blue plastic cap. Holds Wild Country After Shave or Electric Pre-Shave Lotion. OSP $6 **CMV $7. BO, $8. MB.**

CHRYSLER TOWN & COUNTRY '48 1976
4.25 oz. off red painted over clear glass. Beige plastic top. Came in Everest or Wild COuntry. SSP $5 **CMV $8. BO, $10. MB.**

THE CAMPER 1972-74
5 oz. green glass truck with After Shave. 4 oz. Talc in beige plastic camper. Came in Deep Woods or Oland. SSP $8. **CMV $10. BO, $12. MB.**

1973 FORD RANGER PICK-UP 1978-79
5 oz. blue paint over clear glass, blue plastic bed cap. Stick on decals. Came in Wild Country or Deep woods. SSP $6 **CMV $7. BO, $9. MB.**

ROLLS ROYCE 1972-75
6 oz. beige painted over glass with dark brown and silver plastic parts. Came in Deep Woods or Tai Winds After Shave. SSP $7. **CMV $10. BO, $13. MB.**

TRIUMPH TR-3 '56 1975-76
(Left) 2 oz. blue-green glass with plastic cap. Came with Spicy or Wild Country After Shave. OSP $4 **CMV $6. BO, $8. MB.**
PORSCHE DECANTER '68 1976
(Right) 2 oz. amber glass with amber plastic cap. Holds Wild Country or Spicy After Shave. OSP $3 **CMV $6. BO, $8 MB.**

GOLD CADILLAC 1969-73
(Left) 6 oz. gold paint over clear glass. Came in Oland & wild Country After Shave. OSP $6. **CMV $10. BO. mint, $13. MB.**
SILVER DUESENBERG 1970-72
(Right) 6 oz. silver paint over clear glass. Came in Oland & Wild Country After Shave. OSP $6. **CMV $10 BO. mint, $13 MB.**

BUGATTI '27 1974-75
6.5 oz. black glass with chrome colored plastic trim. Came in Wild Country or Deep Woods Cologne or After Shave. OSP $6. **CMV $10., $12. MB.**

STUDEBAKER '51 1975-76
(Left) 2 oz. blue glass with blue plastic parts. Holds Avon Spicy or Wild Country. OSP $2.50 **CMV $6. BO, $8 MB.**
CORVETTE STINGRAY '65 1975
(Right) 2 oz. green glass with green plastic cap. Holds Wild Country, Deep Woods or Avon Spicy After Shave. OSP $3 **CMV $6. BO, $8 MB.**

SURE WINNER RACING CAR 1972-75
(Left) 5.5 oz. blue glass with blue cap. Came in Sure Winner Bracing Lotion and Wild Country. OSP $5 **CMV $8. MB, $7. BO.**
JAGUAR CAR DECANTER 1973-76
5 oz. jade green glass with green plastic trunk over cap. Holds Deep Woods or Wild Country After Shave. SSP $5 **CMV $8. MB, $10. BO.**

'37 CORD 1974-76
7 oz. yellow painted with yellow plastic cap and black plastic top. Came in Tai Winds or Wild Country After Shave. SSP $7. **CMV $12. MB, $10. BO.**

JEEP RENEGADE 1981-82
3 oz. black glass, stick on decals. Tan plastic top. Black cap. Sure Winner Bracing Lotion or Trazerra Cologne. SSP $9. **CMV $9. MB, $7. BO.**

10-FOUR TRUCK DECANTER 1989
2.1/2 oz. truck holds after shave. SSP $8. **CMV $8. MB.**
SPEEDBOAT DECANTER 1989
7" long blue glass boat with stick on decals. Holds after shave. SSP. $8. **CMV $8. MB.**

'36 FORD 1976-77
5 oz. orange paint over clear glass. Plastic stick on hub caps and grill. Came in Tai Winds or Oland. SSP $5. **CMV $8. BO, $10. MB.**

VOLKSWAGON RABBIT 1980-82
3 oz. blue glass and blue plastic cap. Comes with silver stick on windows and hub caps. Choice of Light Musk Cologne or Sure Winner Bracing Lotion. SSP $8. **CMV $8. MB, $6. BO.**

BUICK SKYLARK '53 1979-80
(Left) 4 oz. emerald green glass and cap. Stick on decals. Came in Clint or Everest After Shave. SSP $9. **CMV $11. MB, $9. BO.**

VANTASTIC 1979-80
(Right) 5 oz. burgandy color glass. Stick on decals. Comes in Wild Country or Everest After Shave. SSP $6. **CMV $8. MB, $6. BO.**

BLUE VOLKSWAGON 1973-74
(left) 4 oz. light blue painted with plastic cap. Holds Oland or Windjammer After Shave. SSP $3. **CMV $6. BO, $7. MB.**

BLACK VOLKSWAGON 1970-72
(Right) 4 oz. black glass with black plastic cap. Holds Wild Country, Spicy or Electric Pre-Shave Lotion. SSP $2. **CMV $7. MB, $6. BO.**

RED VOLKSWAGON 1972
(Center) 4 oz. painted red with red cap. Came in Oland or Wild Country After Shave or Sports Rally Bracing Lotion. SSP $3. **CMV $6. BO, $7. MB.**

MINI-BIKE 1972-73
(Left) 4 oz. light amber glass coated over clear glass with light amber plastic wheel and silver handlebars with yellow grips. Came in Wild Country After Shave, Sure Winner Bracing Lotion, or Protein Hair Lotion for Men. SSP $5. **CMV $8. MB, $7. BO.**

ROAD RUNNER DECANTER 1973-74
(Right) 5.5 oz. blue glass with blue plastic front wheel, silver handle bars with black grips. Holds Sure Winner Bracing Lotion or Wild Country After Shave. SSP. $6. **CMV $9. MB, $7. BO.**

SUPER CYCLE 1971-72
(Left) 4 oz. gray glass. Came in Wild Country, Island Lime or Sports Rally Bracing Lotion. SSP $5. **CMV $9. MB, $7. BO.**

SUPER CYCLE II 1974-75
(Right) Issued in blue glass. Came in Wild Country and Spicy After Shave. SSP $5. **CMV $7. BO, $9. MB.**

AVON OPEN GOLF CART 1972-75
(Left) 5 1/2" long, green glass bottle with green plastic front end, red plastic golf bags. Holds 5 oz. Wild Country or Windjammer After Shave. Came in light or darker green glass. OSP $6. **CMV $10. MB, $8. BO.**

SNOWMOBILE 1974-75
(Right) 4 oz. blue glass with yellow plastic front and back runners. Came in Oland or Windjammer After Shave. SSP $6. **CMV $8. BO, $9. MB.**

MAXWELL '23 DECANTER 1972-74
6 oz. green glass with beige plastic top and trunk over cap. Came in Deep Woods or Tribute Cologne or After Shave. SSP $5. **CMV $7., $9. MB.**

HARVESTER TRACTOR 1973-75
5.5 oz. amber glass with amber plastic front. Holds Wild Country After Shave or Protein Hair Lotion for men. OSP $5. **CMV $10. BO, $14. MB.**

'55 CHEVY 1975-76
5 oz. sprayed green glass with white plastic parts. Holds Wild Country or Electric Pre-Shave Lotion. SSP $5. **CMV $9. BO, $11. MB.**

TOURING T SILVER 1978
6 oz. silver plated over clear glass. May, 1978 on bottom. Came in Deep Woods or Everest. SSP $8. **CMV $10. BO, $12. MB.**

STERLING SIX SILVER 1978
7 oz. plated over clear glass. Came in Tai Winds or Deep Woods After Shave. May 1978 on Bottom. SSP $8. **CMV $9. BO, $11. MB.**

1914 STUTZ BEARCAT 1974-77
(Left) 6 oz. red painted with black plastic seats and cap. Came in Oland or Blend 7 After Shave. SSP $6. **CMV $9. MB, $7. BO.**

1936 MG DECANTER 1974-75
(Right) 5 oz. red painted with red plastic cap and white plastic top. Came in Avon Blend 7, Tai Winds or Wild Country After Shave. SSP $4. **CMV $8. BO, $10. MB.**

COVERED WAGON 1970-71
6 oz.. 4 1/2" long. Dark amber glass bottom, white painted top and gold cap. Came in Spicy and Wild Country After Shave. OSP $5. **CMV $8., MB. $10.**

SIDE WHEELER 1971-72
5 oz. dark amber glass, black plastic stacks, silver cap, brown label. Came in Wild Country and Spicy After Shave. OSP $6. **CMV $9. BO, $11. MB. Reissued 1976 in Tai Winds gold cap, white label, same CMV.**

COUNTRY VENDOR 1973
5 oz. brown glass with brown plastic top, has picture of fruits and vegetables on side. Holds Wild Country or Avon Spicy After Shave. SSP $7. **CMV $10. MB, $8. BO.**

STRAIGHT 8 1969-71
(Left) 5 oz. dark green glass with black trunk cap. No. 8 on hoood. Came in Wild Country, Windjammer, and Island Lime After Shave. Label says "Avon for Men" OSP $3.50. **CMV $10 MB, $8 BO.**

STRAIGHT 8 1973-75
(Left) 5 oz. green glass. Came in Wild Country and Island Lime After Shave. Label says Avon-Keep out of reach of children. OSP $3.50 **CMV $8. BO, $10 MB.**

DUNE BUGGY 1971-73
(Right) 5 oz. blue glass, silver motor cap. Came in Spicy After Shave, Liquid Hair Lotion and Sports Rally Bracing Lotion. OSP $5. **CMV $8., MB. $10.**

ARMY JEEP 1974-75
4 oz. olive drab green with plastic closure. Came with Wild Country or Avon Spicy After Shave. OSP $5. **CMV $8. BO, $10. MB.**

GOLDEN ROCKET 0-2-2 1974-76
(Right) 6 oz. smokey gold over clear glass with gold plastic cap. Came in Tai Winds or Wild Country After Shave. OSP $7. **CMV $10. MB, $8. BO.** Factory reject from factory is indented sides and gold coated. **CMV $20.**

1926 CHECKER CAB 1977-78
5 oz. yellow painted over clear glass. Black plastic trunk cap and top. Stick on decal hub caps, bumper and checker design. Came in Everest or Wild Country. SSP $6. **CMV $8. BO, $10. MB.**

TOURING T 1969-70
(Left) 6 1/2" long, 6 oz. black glass with black plastic top and tire cap. Came in Excalibur or Tribute After Shave. OSP $6. **CMV $10. BO, $12. MB.**

MODEL A 1972-74
(Right) 4 oz. yellow painted over clear glass, yellow cap. Holds Wild Country or Leather After Shave. SSP $4. **CMV $8. BO, $10. MB.**

STERLING SIX 1968-70
7 oz. came in 4 different shades of amber glass, black tire cap, rough top roof. Came in Spicy, Tribute, Leather After Shave. OSP $4. **CMV $8. BO, $10. MB.** Smooth top in very light amber glass. **CMV $45.**

STERLING SIX II 1973-74
7 oz. green glass with white tire cap. Came in Wild Country or Tai Winds After Shave. SSP. $4. **CMV $7. BO, $8. MB.**

FIRST VOLUNTEER 1971-72
6 oz. gold coated over clear glass. Oland or Tai Winds Cologne. OSP $8.50. **CMV $12. BO, $14. MB.**

ELECTRIC CHARGER 1970-72
(Left) 5 oz. black glass with red cap and red side decals. Came in Spicy, Leather or Wild Country After Shave. OSP $4. **CMV $8. BO, $10. MB.**

STAGE COACH 1970-77
(Right) 5 oz. dark amber glass with gold cap. Came in Wild Country, Tai Winds or Oland After Shave. 1977 issue has "R" on bottom for reissue, hard to find silver cap. **CMV $7 for reissue.** OSP $5. **CMV $8. BO, $10. MB.**

1910 FIRE FIGHTER 1975
6 oz. painted over glass with red plastic back. Came in Wild Country or Tai Winds After Shave. OSP $6. **CMV $9. MB, $7 BO.**

VOLKSWAGON BUS 1975-76
(Left) 5 oz. red painted glass with silver gray motorcycle plastic closure. Set of 4 "decorate-it-yourself" labels come with each decanter. Came with Tai Winds After Shave or Sure Winner Bracing Lotion. OSP $5. **CMV $8. BO, $10. MB.**

THE THOMAS FLYER 1908 1974-75
(Right) 6 oz. white painted glass with red and blue plastic parts with white tire cap on back. Came in Wild Country or Oland After Shave. OSP $6. **CMV $10. BO, $12. MB.**

REO DEPOT WAGON 1972-73
5" long, 5 oz. amber glass with black plastic top and cap. Holds Tai Winds and Oland After Shave Lotion. OSP $6. **CMV $10., MB $12.**

CEMENT MIXER 1979-80
3 piece bottle. Front section is dark amber glass. Comes in Wild Country or Everest After Shave. Center plastic section connects to 6 oz. pale yellow plastic rear section bottle. Holds talc. Has stick on decals. SSP $12. **CMV $12. BO., $13. MB.**

STATION WAGON 1971-73
6 oz. green glass car with tan plastic top. Came in Wild Country or Tai Winds After Shave. OSP $6. **CMV $10. BO, $12. MB.**

PACKARD ROADSTER 1970-72
6 oz. light amber glass and matching plastic rumble seat cap. Came in Oland and Leather Cologne. 6 1/2" long. OSP $6. **CMV $10., MB $12.**

TRAIN 1876 CENTENNIAL EXPRESS DECANTER 1978-86
5.5 oz. dark green glass with stick on trim decals. Holds Wild Country or Everest After Shave. SSP $12. **CMV $10. BO, $12. MB.** Reissues 1986.

STANLEY STEAMER 1971-72
5 oz. blue glass bottle with black plastic seats and tire cap. Came in Wild Country or Windjammer After Shave. OSP $5. **CMV $8. BO, $10. MB.**

HIGHWAY KING 1977-79
4 oz. green glass bottle with white plastic center connection piece and rear section is 6.5 oz. white plastic talc bottle. Came in Wild Country or Everest. OSP $12.50. **CMV $13. BO, $14. MB.**

CABLE CAR DECANTER 1974-75
4 oz. green painted over clear glass has plastic green and white top. Came in Wild Country or Avon Leather. SSP $7. **CMV $10. BO, $12. MB.**

HAYNES APPERSON 1902 1973-74
4.5 oz. green glass with green plastic front over cap. Has silver tiller steering rod. Holds Avon Blend 7 or Tai Winds After Shave. SSP $5. **CMV $10. MB, $8. BO.**

ATLANTIC 4-4-2 DECANTER 1973-75
5 oz. silver over clear glass with silver plastic parts. Holds Deep Woods or Leather After Shave or Cologne. SSP $8. **CMV $12. MB, $14. BO.**

BIG RIG 1975-76
3.5 oz. blue glass cab with 6 oz. white & blue plastic trailer. Cab holds After Shave, trailer holds Talc in Wild Country or Deep Woods. OSP $10. **CMV $14. BO, $16. MB.**

CANNONBALL EXPRESS 4-6-0 1976-77
3.25 oz. black glass, black cap. Came in Deep Woods or Wild Country or After Shave. SSP $6. **CMV $10. BO, $11. MB.**

GENERAL 4-4-0 1971-72
5 1/2 oz. dark blue glass and cap. Came in Tai Winds or Wild Country After Shave. OSP $7.50. **CMV $14., MB $12.**

GONE FISHING DECANTER 1973-74
5 oz. lt. blue boat with white plastic man, yellow fishing rod. Came in Tai Winds or Spicy. SSP $6. **CMV $10. MB, $12. BO.**

RAINBOW TROUT 1973-74
(Left) Plastic head over cap. Holds Deep Woods or Tai Winds. SSP $5. **CMV $10. MB, $8. BO.**
SEA TROPHY 1972
(Right) 5.5 oz. lt. blue with plastic blue head over cap. Came in Wild Country or Windjammer After Shave. SSP $5. **CMV $10. BO, $12. MB.**

AMERICAN SCHOONER 1972-73
4.5 oz. blue glass with blue plastic end over cap. Some are blue painted over clear glass. Came in Oland or Spicy After Shave. SSP $5. **CMV $12. MB, $10. BO.**

BLOOD HOUND PIPE 1976
5 oz. lt. tan paint over clear glass, brown & silver cap. Came in Wild Country or Deep Woods After Shave. OSP $7. **CMV $10. MB, $8. BO.**
CHIEF PONTIAC CAR ORNAMENT CLASSIC 1976
4 oz. black ribbed glass with silver Indian. Came in Tai Winds or Deep Woods After Shave. OSP $8. **CMV $10. BO, $11. MB.**

CAPTAINS PRIDE 1970
6 oz. bottle with ship decal, tan cap & blue neck label. Sits on black plastic stand. Came in Oland & Windjammer After Shave. OSP $5. **CMV $8. BO, $10. MB.**

VIKING DISCOVERER 1977-79
4 oz. blue-green glass & matching plastic cap. Red & white metal sail. Black plastic sail post. Came in Wild Country or Everest. SSP $9. **CMV $10. BO, $12. MB.**

PIPE DREAM 1967
6 oz. dark amber glass, black cap, tan plastic base. Came in Spicy, Tribute & Leather After Shave. OSP $5. **CMV $15. BO, $20. MB.**
PIPE DREAM CLEAR TEST 1967
6 oz. clear glass factory test bottle. Very rare. **CMV $250.**

COLLECTOR'S PIPE 1973-74
3 oz. brown glass with black stem. Holds Deep Woods or Windjammer After Shave or Cologne. SSP $3. **CMV $8. MB, $6. BO.**

AMERICAN EAGLE PIPE 1974-75
5 oz. dark amber glass with gold plastic top & black handle. Holds Wild Country or Tai Winds Cologne. OSP $5. **CMV $9. MB, $8. BO.**

CALABASH PIPE 1974-75
3 oz. yellow gold sprayed glass with yellow gold plastic cap & black plastic stand. Holds Wild Country or Deep Woods After Shave. OSP $5. **CMV $9. MB, $8. BO.**

BULL DOG PIPE 1972-73
6 oz. cream colored milk glass with black stem. Came in Wild Country or Oland After Shave or Cologne. SSP $4. **CMV $8. BO, $10. MB.**

DUTCH PIPE 1973-74
2 oz. white milk glass, blue design, silver handle & cap. Came in Tribute or Tai Winds Cologne. SSP $7. **CMV $7. BO, $9. MB.**

PONY POST MINIATURE 1973-74
1.5 oz. clear glass with gold cap & ring. Holds Oland or Spicy After Shave. OSP $3. **CMV $4. BO, $5. MB.**

PONY POST 1972-73
5 oz. bronze paint over clear glass with bronze cap & nose ring. Holds Tai Winds or Leather After Shave. OSP $5. **CMV $8. BO, $9. MB.**

PONY POST "TALL" 1966-67
8 oz. green glass with gold cap & nose ring. Holds Island Lime, Tribute or Leather After Shave. OSP $4. **CMV $15. MB, $10. BO.**

UNCLE SAM PIPE 1975-76
3 oz. white opal glass with blue band & blue plastic stem. Holds Wild Country or Deep Woods After Shave. OSP $5. **CMV $8. MB, $7. BO.**

PONY EXPRESS RIDER PIPE 1975-76
3 oz. white milk glass with black plastic stem. Holds Wild Country or Tai Winds Cologne. OSP $5. **CMV $8. MB, $7. BO.**

CORNCOB PIPE 1974-75
3 oz. amber glass with black plastic stem. Holds Wild Country or Avon Spicy. OSP $3. **CMV $5. BO, $6. MB.**

PIPE FULL DECANTER 1971-72
2 oz. brown glass with black stem. Holds Spicy, Oland, Tai Winds or Excalibur After Shave. SSP $2. **CMV $7. MB, $5. BO.**

PIPE FULL DECANTER 1972-74
2 oz. lt. green glass with brown plastic stem. Holds Tai Winds or Spicy After Shave. SSP $2. **CMV $4. BO, $5. MB.**

PEPPERBOX PISTOL 1850-1979
(Top) 3 oz. silver plated over clear glass barrel bottle with gold and brown plastic handle cap. Came in Everest or Tai Winds. SSP $7. **CMV $8. MB, $6. BO.**

PEPPERBOX PISTOL 1982-83
Reissued in gold tone instead of silver came in Clint and Wild Country. SSP $11. **CMV $11. MB.**

DERRINGER 1977
(Bottom) 2 oz. gold plated over amber glass. Came in Deep Woods or Wild Country. SSP $6. **CMV $8. BO, $9. MB.**

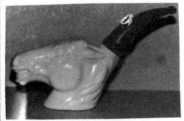

WILD MUSTANG PIPE 1976-77
3 oz. white paint over clear glass. Holds Wild Country or Deep Woods cologne. SSP $5. **CMV $8. MB, $7. BO.**

PHILADELPHIA DERRINGER 1980-82
2 oz. dark amber glass with gray stick on parts & gold trim. Came in Light Musk or Brisk Spice After Shave. SSP $10. **CMV $10. MB, $9. BO.**

MINIATURE VOLCANIC REPEATER PISTOL DECANTER 1986
1.4 oz. amber glass. SSP $10. **CMV $10. MB.**

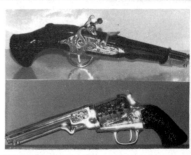

SHORT PONY DECANTER 1968-69
(Right) 4 oz. green glass, gold cap. Came in
Wild Country, Windjammer, Spicy, Leather or
Electric Pre-Shave. OSP $3.50. **CMV $7. BO,
$10. MB.**
**SHORT PONY, FOREIGN, DECANTER 1968-
69**
Gold cap, greenish amber color. $7. Bright
green from Germany. **CMV $15. MB.**

BLUNDERBUSS PISTOL 1780 1976
(Top) 12 1/2" long, 5.5 oz. dark amber glass,
gold cap & plastic trigger. Came in Everest &
Wild Country. OSP $12. **CMV $13. MB, $11.
BO.**
THOMAS JEFFERSON HAND GUN 1978-79
(Bottom) 10" long, 2.5 oz. dark amber glass
with gold & silver plastic cap. Holds Deep
Woods or Everest cologne. SSP $9. **CMV
$10. MB, $9. BO.**

DUELING PISTOL 1760 1973-74
(Top) 4 oz. brown glass with silver clamp on
parts, silver cap. Holds Deep Woods or Tai
Winds After Shave. SSP $8. **CMV $12. MB,
$10. BO.**
DUELING PISTOL II 1975
Same as above but black glass & gold plastic
parts. Came in Wild Country or Tai Winds.
SSP $8. **CMV $10. BO, $12. MB.**
COLT REVOLVER 1851 1975-76
(Bottom) 3 oz. amber glass with silver plastic
barrel. Holds Wild Country or Deep Woods
After Shave. OSP $9. **CMV $12. MB, $10.
BO.**

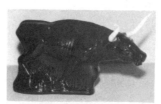

TWENTY PACES 1967-69
3 oz. each, 10" long. Gold paint over clear
glass, gold cap. Red paper labels on end of
barrel. Came in All Purpose Cologne, Wild
Country & Leather After Shave. OSP $11.95.
**CMV brown box lined with red $40, black
lined box $120, blue lined box $160.** Very
rare gun with raised sight did not break off in
glass mold. **CMV $100. Raised sight gun
only. Regular issue guns $10. each mint.**

LONGHORN STEER 1975-76
5 oz. dark amber glass with amber plastic
head, ivory colored horns. Holds Wild Country
or Tai Winds After Shave. OSP $6. **CMV $9.
BO, $10. MB.**

OLD FAITHFUL 1972-73
5 oz. brown glass with brown plastic head &
gold keg. Holds Wild Country or Spicy After
Shave. SSP $5. **CMV $9. BO, $10. MB.**

CLASSIC SPORTS CAR DECANTER 1990
2 oz. blue glass car with stick on decals. Holds
Wild Country After Shave. SSP $8. **CMV $8.
MB.**
CORVETTE DECANTER 1988
3 oz. black glass 1988 Corvette holds after
shave. SSP $8. **CMV $8. MB.**

**GAS PUMP - REMEMBER WHEN DE-
CANTER 1979-80**
4 oz. clear glass painted yellow, white top,
yellow cap. Came in Light Musk or Cool Sage.
SSP $6. **CMV $7. MB, $6. BO.**
**VOLCANIC REPEATING PISTOL DE-
CANTER 1979-80**
2 oz. silver coated over clear glass. Silver &
pearl plastic handle. Holds Wild Country or
Brisk Spice Cologne. SSP $10. **CMV $9. BO,
$10. MB.**

MAJESTIC ELEPHANT 1977
5.5 oz. gray painted over clear glass. Gray
head cap. Came in Wild Country or Deep
Woods. SSP $9. **CMV $9. BO, $11. MB.**

AT POINT DECANTER 1973-74
5 oz. reddish brown glass with reddish brown plastic head. Came in Deep Woods or Tribute. SSP $4. **CMV $8. MB, $7. BO.**
SNOOPY SURPRISE 1969-71
5 oz., 5 1/2" high. White glass with blue or yellow hat & black ears. Came in Wild Country, Excalibur After Shave & Sports Rally Bracing Lotion. OSP $4. **CMV $9., $11. MB.**

PHEASANT 1972-74
5 oz. brown glass with green plastic head. Holds Oland or Leather After Shave. OSP $6. **CMV $10. MB, $8. BO.**
CANADA GOOSE 1973-74
5 oz. brown glass with black plastic head. Holds Deep Woods, Wild Country or Everest After Shave or Cologne. OSP $6. **CMV $8. BO, $10. MB.** Reissued in 1976 in smaller box in After Shave only. **Same CMV.**

NOBLE PRINCE 1975-77
4 oz. brown glass with plastic head. Holds Wild Country After Shave or Electric Pre-Shave Lotion. OSP $3.25 **CMV $8 MB, $7 BO.**
CLASSIC LION 1973-75
8 oz. green glass with green plastic head. Holds Wild Country, Tribute After Shave or Deep Woods Emollient After Shave. OSP $6 **CMV $9 MB, $7 BO.**

FAITHFUL LADDIE 1977-79
4 oz. light amber glass & amber head cap. Came in Wild Country or Deep Woods. SSP $4.99. **CMV $8. MB, $7. BO.**
KODIAK BEAR 1977
6 oz. dark amber glass & head. Came in Wild Country or Deep Woods. SSP $5. **CMV $7. BO, $8. MB.**

PONY EXPRESS 1971-72
5 oz. brown glass with copper colored man on cap. Came in Avon Leather or Wild Country After Shave. SSP $4. **CMV $10. MB, $8. BO.**
BUCKING BRONCO 1971-72
6 oz. dark amber glass horse with bronze plastic cowboy cap. Came in Oland or Excalibur. OSP $6. **CMV $10. MB, $8. BO.**

SPORT OF KINGS DECANTER 1975
5 oz. amber glass with plastic head. Holds Wild Country, Avon Spicy or Avon Leather After Shave. OSP $5 **CMV $9. MB, $8. BO.**
AMERICAN BUFFALO 1975-76
5 oz. amber glass with amber plastic head & ivory colored horns. Holds Wild Country or Deep Woods After Shave. OSP $6. **CMV $8. BO, $9. MB.**

PHEASANT DECANTER 1977
Same bottle as 1972-74 issue only came in Deep Woods or Wild Country and box is smaller than early issue. SSP $6. **CMV $9. MB, $8. BO.**

WILDERNESS CLASSIC 1976-77
6 oz. silver plated over clear glass. Silver plastic head. Came in Sweet Honesty or Deep Woods. SSP $9. **CMV $11. MB, $10. BO.**

WESTERN BOOT 1973-75
5 oz. dark amber glass bottle, silver cap & clamp on spurs. Came in Wild Country or Leather. SSP $4. **CMV $7. MB, $6. BO.**

ALASKAN MOOSE 1974-75
8 oz. amber glass with cream colored plastic antlers. Holds Deep Woods or Wild COuntry After Shave. OSP $7. **CMV $8. BO, $10. MB.**

TEN-POINT BUCK 1973-74
6 oz. reddish brown glass with reddish brown plastic head & gold antlers. Holds Wild Country or Leather After Shave. OSP $7. **CMV $10. MB, $8. BO.**

DUCK AFTER SHAVE 1971
3 oz. glass bottles with gold caps & ducks painted on sides. Came in Collector's Organizer Set only in Tai Winds & Wild Country After Shave. **CMV $4. each.**

BIG GAME RHINO 1972-73
4 oz. green glass with green plastic head over cap. Came in Spicy or Tai Winds After Shave. SSP $4. **CMV $8. BO, $6. MB.**

BLACKSMITH'S ANVIL 1972-73
4 oz. black glass with silver cap. Came in Deep Woods or Avon Leather After Shave. SSP $4. **CMV $8. MB, $6. BO.**

MALLARD DUCK 1967-68
6 oz. green glass, silver head. Came in Spicy, Tribute, Blue Blazer, Windjammer After Shave. OSP $5. **CMV $10. BO, $13. MB.**

MALLARD-IN-FLIGHT 1974-76
5 oz. amber glass with green plastic head. Holds Wild Country or Tai Winds Cologne or After Shave. OSP $6. **CMV $9. MB, $7. BO.**

AMERICAN EAGLE 1971-72
6" high, dark amber glass with silver eagle head. Holds 5 oz. Oland or Windjammer After Shave. OSP $5. **CMV $10. MB, $8. BO.**

AMERICAN EAGLE 1973-75
Eagle is black glass with dark gold ead. **CMV $6. BO, $7. MB.**

CAPTAIN'S CHOICE 1964-65
(Right) 8 oz. green glass with green paper label, gold cap. Came in Spicy & Original After Shave Lotion, Electric Pre-Shave Lotion, Spicy After Shower Cologne for Men & Vigorate After Shave Lotion. OSP $2.50 **CMV $9., $15. MB.**

CAPITOL DECANTER 1976-77
4.5 oz. white milk glass with white cap & gold tip. Came in Spicy or Wild Country After Shave. OSP $4. **CMV $7. MB, $6. BO.**

CAPITOL DECANTER 1970-72
5 oz. amber glass or clear glass coated amber, gold cap. Came in Leather & Tribute After Shave. OSP $5. **CMV $10. MB, $8. BO.**

WILD TURKEY 1974-76
6 oz. amber glass with silver & red plastic head. Holds Wild Country or Deep Woods After Shave. OSP $5. **CMV $7. BO, $8. MB.**

QUAIL DECANTER 1973-75
5.5 oz. brown glass, gold cap. Came in Avon Blend 7, Deep Woods or Wild Country After Shave. OSP $6. **CMV $9. MB, $7. BO.**

REVOLUTIONARY CANNON 1975-76
2 oz. bronze spray over glass with plastic cap. Holds Avon Spicy or Avon Blend 7 After Shave. OSP $4. **CMV $7. MB, $6. BO.**

HOMESTEAD DECANTER 1973-74
4 oz. brown glass with gray plastic chimney over cap. Holds Wild Country After Shave or Electric Pre-Shave. OSP $3. **CMV $7. MB, $6. BO.**

WISE CHOICE OWL 1969-70
4 oz. silver top, light amber bottom. Came in Excalibur or Leather After Shave. OSP $4. **CMV $8., MB. $9.**

RADIO 1972-73
5" high dark amber glass with gold cap & paper dial on front. Holds 5 oz. liquid Hair Lotion, Wild Country or Spicy After Shave. OSP $4. **CMV $8., MB. $9.**

KING PIN 1969-70
(Left) 4 oz. 6 1/2" high. White glass & cap, red label. Came in Wild Country & Bravo After Shave. OSP $3. CMV $7. MB, $5. BO.

STRIKE DECANTER 1978-79
(Right) 4 oz. white milk glass, white cap. Red painted on AMF designs. Came in Sweet Honesty of Wild Country. SSP $3. CMV $5. MB, $4. BO.

RAM'S HEAD 1975-76
5 oz. white opal glass on brown plastic base. Holds Wild Country or Avon Blend 7 After Shave. OSP $5. CMV $7 MB, $5 BO.

MINUTEMAN 1975-76
4 oz. white opal glass with plastic top. Holds Wild Country or Tai Winds After Shave. OSP $7. CMV $8. BO, $9. MB.

LONG DRIVE 1973-75
4 oz. brown glass with black cap. Holds Deep Woods After Shave or Electric Pre-Shave Lotion. SSP $3. CMV $6 MB, $4. BO.

TEE-OFF DECANTER 1973-75
3 oz. white golf ball on a plastic yellow tee & fits into a green plastic green. Holds Protein Hair Lotion for Men. SSP $3. CMV $6. MB, $4. BO.

BOOT "SILVER TOP" 1965-66
8 oz. amber glass, silver cap with hook on cap. Came in Leather All Purpose Lotion for Men. OSP $5. CMV $7., $8. MB.

BOOT "GOLD TOP" 1966-71
8 oz. amber glass with hook on cap. Came in Leather All purpose Cologne for Men. OSP $5. CMV $5., MB. $7. Gold top boot with no hook on cap is 1971-72 with Leather Cologne. OSP $5. CMV $5. BO, $7. MB.

BOOT SPRAY COLOGNE 1967-70
3 oz. tan plastic coated with black cap. Came in Leather All Purpose Cologne in early issues. CMV $6. MB. & Leather Cologne Spray in later issues. OSP $4. CMV $4, MB. $5.

OPENING PLAY 1968-69
6 oz. each, 4" high. Gold caps, white plastic face guards. Came in Sports Rally Bracing Lotion, Spicy & Wild Country After Shave. OSP each $4. Shiny gold over blue glass was issued one campaign only, on last campaign Open Play was sold. CMV Shiny gold $25., BO $30. Dull gold over blue glass with bllue stripe CMV $10, $12 MB. Dull gold over blue glass, no stripe, CMV $14 BO, $16. MB.

MARINE BINOCULARS 1973-74
Black over clear glass with gold caps. One side holds 4 oz. Tai Winds or Tribute Cologne, other side holds 4 oz. Tai Winds or Tribute After Shave. SSP $8. CMV $11., MB. $9.

SURE WINNER BASEBALL 1973-74
White ball with dark blue lettering, blue blue base contains Liquid Hair Trainer. SSP $2. CMV $6 MB, $4. BO.

FIRST DOWN 1970
5 oz. brown glass, white plastic base. Came in Wild Country or Sports Rally Bracing Lotion. OSP $4. CMV $8. MB, $6. BO.

FIRST DOWN 1973-74
5 oz. brown glass, white base. Came in Deep Woods & Sure Winner Bracing Lotion. SSP $3. CMV $8. MB, $6. BO.

THEODORE ROOSEVELT 1975-76
(Left) 6 oz. white paint over clear glass. Came in Wild Country or Tai Winds After Shave. OSP $9. CMV $9. BO, $10. MB.

THOMAS JEFFERSON 1977-78
(Right) 5 oz. white paint over clear glass. White head cap. Came in Wild Country or Everest After Shave. SSP $8. CMV $8. BO, $9. MB.

PASS PLAY 1973-75
5 oz. blue glass with white soft plastic top over cap. Came in Sure Winner Bracing Lotion or Wild Country After shave. OSP $5. CMV $8. BO, $10. MB.

PERFECT DRIVE 1975-76
4 oz. green glass with white plastic top over cap. Holds Avon Spicy After Shave or Avon Protein Hair/Scalp Conditioner. OSP $6. CMV $8. BO, $10. MB.

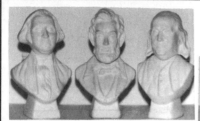

PRESIDENT WASHINGTON 1974-76
6 oz. white spray over clear glass, white plastic head. Holds Wild Country or Tai Winds After Shave. 1976 came in Deep Woods or Tai Winds After Shave. OSP $6. **CMV $7. BO, $8. MB.**

PRESIDENT LINCOLN 1973
6 oz. white spray over clear glass, white plastic head. Holds Wild Country or Tai Winds After Shave. OSP $5. **CMV $9. BO, $12. MB.**

BENJAMIN FRANKLIN 1974-76
6 oz. white spray over clear glass, white plastic head. Holds Wild Country or Tai Winds After Shave. OSP $6. **CMV $7. BO, $8. MB.**

PRESIDENT LINCOLN BRONZE 1979
6 oz. bronze tone over clear glass. Dated 1979 on bottom. Also came no date on bottom. Holds Deep Woods or Everest After Shave. SSP $11 **CMV $11 MB.**

PRESIDENT WASHINGTON BRONZE 1979
6 oz. bronze tone over clear glass. Dated 1979 on bottom. Holds Wild Country or Tai Winds After Shave. SSP $11 **CMV $11 MB.**

WASHINGTON BOTTLE 1970-72
5 1/2" high, 4 oz. bottle with gold eagle cap. Holds Spicy or Tribute After Shave. OSP $3.50 **CMV $5. MB, $3. BO.**

LINCOLN BOTTLE 1971-72
5 1/2" high, 4 oz. bottle with gold eagle cap. Holds Wild Country or Leather After Shave. OSP $3.50 **CMV $5. MB, $3. BO.**

CHESS PIECE "BROWN" (THE ORIGINAL SET)
3 oz. dark amber glass with silver toned tops. OSP $4. each.

SMART MOVE 1971-72
Came in Tribune & Oland Cologne. **CMV $8.** Smart move came in Wild Country After Shave or Protein Hair/Scalp Conditioner. **CMV $4. MB.**

THE KING 1972-73
Came in Tai Winds or Oland After Shave. **CMV $8. MB.**

THE KING 1973-78
The King came in Wild Country or Oland. **CMV $4 MB.**

THE QUEEN 1973-74
Came in Tai Winds or Oland After Shave. **CMV $7. MB.**

THE QUEEN 1974-78
The Queen came in Wild Country or Deep Woods After Shave. **CMV $4 MB.**

THE ROOK 1973-74
Came in Oland & Spicy After Shave. **CMV $7. MB.**

THE ROOK 1974-78
The rook came in Wild Country, Avon Blend 7 or Avon Protein Hair Lotion for Men. **CMV $4. MB.**

THE BISHOP 1974-78
Came in Wild Country, Avon Blend 7 or Avon Protein Hair Lotion for Men. **CMV $4 MB.**

THE PAWN 1974-78
Came in Wild Country, Oland or Electric Pre-Shave Lotion. **CMV $6. BO, $8. MB.** (Pieces needed for one side are 2 Smart Moves, 1 King, 1 Queen, 2 Rooks, 2 Bishops, 8 Pawns.) Early issues Chess Pieces do not have to have name on label.

COLLECTOR'S STEIN 1976-79
Hand made ceramic blue stein. Made in Brazil and numbered on bottom. Came with 8 oz. plastic bottle of Everest or Wild Country. SSP $25. **CMV $40. MB.**

CHESS PIECE DECANTER (THE OPPOSING SET)
3 oz. silver over clear or amber glass with amber plastic tips. OSP $3. **CMV $4. BO, $5. MB,** Pawns CMV $6. BO, $8. MB. **Silver over clear are hard to find.**

SMART MOVE II 1975-78
Came in Wild Country After Shave, Avon Protein Hair Lotion or Avon Protein Hair/Scalp Conditioner for Men.

THE KING II 1975-78
Came in Avon Spicy After Shave or Avon Protein Hair Lotion.

THE QUEEN II 1975-78
Came in Avon Spicy After Shave or Avon Protein Hair/Scalp Conditioner.

THE ROOK II 1975-78
Came in Wild Country After Shave or Protein Hair Lotion for Men.

THE BISHOP II 1975-78
Came in Avon Spicy After Shave or Avon Protein Hair Lotion for Men. **CMV $5. MB, $4. BO.**

THE PAWN II 1975-78
Came in Avon Spicy After Shave or Avon Protein Hair/Scalp Conditioner for Men. **(Pieces needed for one side are 2 Smart Moves, 1 King, 1 Queen, 2 Rooks, 2 Bishops, 8 Pawns.)**

AVON CALLING '1905 DECANTER 1973
7 oz. brown glass with brown plastic top, has gold bell & black plastic receiver. Holds 7 oz. After Shave and .75 oz. Talc. Came in Wild Country or Avon Spicy. SSP $9. **CMV $12. BO, $14. MB.**

AVON CALLING FOR MEN 1969-70
8 1/2" high, 6 oz. gold paint over clear glass, gold cap, black mouth piece, black plastic ear piece. Holds 1 1/4 oz. Talc. Came in Wild Country and Leather Cologne. OSP $8. **CMV $12., MB. $14.**

WESTERN SADDLE 1971-72
5 oz. brown glass with brown cap, sets on beige fence. Came in Wild Country or Avon Leather After Shave. SSP $6. **CMV $8. BO. and fence, $10. MB.**

MIXED DOUBLES TENNIS BALL 1977-78
(Left) 3 oz. light green flock over clear glass. Green cap base. Came in Sweet Honesty Body Splash or Avon Spicy. SSP $3. **CMV $5. BO, $6. MB.**
SURE CATCH 1977
(Right) 1 oz. white milk glass, with red cap, yellow tassel, black eyes. Came in Spicy or Wild Country. SSP $4. **CMV $5. BO, $6. MB.**

WHALE ORGANIZER BOTTLES 1973
3 oz. ivory milk glass with dark blue design. Holds After Shave & Cologne in Deep Woods or Avon Blend7. Sold only in Whale Organizer. **CMV $5. each.**

GOOD SHOT 1976-80
(Left) 2 oz. plastic bottle, gold cap. Red bottle in Wild Country or Brisk Spice After Shave and yellow bottle in Deep Woods or Cool Sage After Shave. SSP $2. **CMV $3. BO, $4. MB. Add $5. for cap on wrong end.**
WILD WEST" BULLET" 1977-78
(Right) 1.5 oz. bronze plated over clear glass. Silver top. Wild Country or Everest. SSP $2.50 **CMV $4. BO, $5. MB.**

FIRM GRIP 1977-78
(Left) 1.5 oz. silver plated clear glass. Came in Wild Country or Everest. SSP $3. **CMV $5. BO, $6. MB.**
WEATHER VANE 1977-78
(Right) 4 oz. red painted over clear glass. Silver top with black horse weather vane. Came in Wild Country or Deep Woods. SSP $4. **CMV $7. MB.**

EAGLE - PRIDE OF AMERICA 1982-83
7 3/4" high porcelain eagle figurine. SSP $29.50 **CMV $30. MB.**

GET THE MESSAGE DECANTER 1978-79
(Left) 3 oz. black glass with silver & black plastic top. Came in Clint or Sweet Honesty. SSP $5. **CMV $8. MB, $7. BO.**
NO CAUSE FOR ALARM DECANTER 1979-80
(Right) 4 oz. silver plated over clear glass. Silver plastic top. Came in Deep Woods, or Tai Winds. SSP $7. **CMV $8 MB, $7. BO.**

ARCTIC KING 1976-79
(Left) 5 oz. blue glass bottle, silver bear cap. Came in Everest only. SSP $5. **CMV $7. MB, $6. BO.**
BOLD EAGLE 1976-78
(Right) 3 oz. gold plated over clear glass, gold top. Came in Tai Winds or Wild Country. SSP $7. **CMV $8. MB, $7. BO.**

NBA DECANTER 1977-80
(Left) Came with your choice of individual NBA team labels. Came in Wild Country or Sure Winner Bracing Lotion. 6 oz. dark amber glass. Silver top. SSP $6. **CMV $8. MB, $7. BO.**
NFL DECANTER 1976-77
(Right) Came with your choice of NFL team emblem out of 28 member clubs of the National Football League. Came in Wild Country or Sure Winner Bracing Lotion. 6 oz. black glass with silver top. SSP $5. **CMV $8. MB, $7. BO.**

INDIAN CHIEFTAIN 1972-75
(Left) 4 oz. brown glass with gold cap. Came in Avon Spicy After Shave or Avon Protein Hair Lotion for Men. OSP $2.50 **CMV $6. MB.**
INDIAN TEPEE DECANTER 1974-75
(Right) 4 oz. amber glass with brown plastic cap. Holds Wild Country or Avon Spicy. OSP $3. **CMV $6. MB, $5. BO.**

MOTOCROSS HELMET 1976-78
6 oz. white plastic bottle with stick on decals, blue plastic face guard cap. Came in Wild Country or Avon Protein Hair Lotion for Men. SSP $3. **CMV $7. MB, $6. BO.**

BIG BOLT 1976-77
(Left) 2 oz. silver plated over clear glass. Silver cap. Came in Dep Woods or Wild Country. SSP $2. **CMV $4. MB.**
DURACELL SUPER CHARGE 1976-78
(Center) 1 1/2 oz. black glass with bronze & silver cap. Came in Spicy or Everest. SSP $2. **CMV $4. MB.**
RIGHT CONNECTION "FUSE" 1977
(Right) 1.5 oz. clear glass, with gold & brown cap. Came in Oland or Wild Country. SSP $2. **CMV $4. MB.**

LOVER BOY AFTER SHAVE 1980
3 oz. clear glass. Red letters and cap. Red box, SSP $3.49, **CMV $3 MB.**

REMEMBER WHEN GAS PUMP 1976-77
(Left) 4 oz. red painted over clear glass. Red & white plastic cap. Came in Deep Woods or Wild Country. SSP $5. **CMV $8. BO, $9. MB.**
ONE GOOD TURN "SCREWDRIVER" 1976
(Right) 4 oz. clear glass, silver cap. Came in Tai Winds or Avon Spicy. SSP $3. **CMV $7. MB, $6. BO.**

SUPER SLEUTH MAGNIFIER 1979
10" long. Bottom is dark amber glass and top is real magnifying glass. Came in Wild Country or Everest After Shave. SSP $8., **CMV $8. MB.**
COUNTRY LANTERN 1979
4 oz. clear glass painted red. Red wire handle. Holds Wild country or Deep Woods After Shave. SSP $6., **CMV $7. MB.**
GENTLEMEN'S TALC 1979
3.75 oz. green can. Holds Clint, Trazarra or Wild Country Talc. SSP $4., **CMV $2. mint, no box.**

STATUE OF LIBERTY DECANTER 1986
7 1/2" high. Dark amber glass base. Gold top. Holds men's or women's fragrance. SSP $10. **CMV $10. MB.**

PERFECT COMBO MUG & POPCORN 1982
Box holds 12. oz. clear glass mug with geese on side & 10 oz. gold foil wrapped can of popcorn. SSP $10. **CMV $10. MB set, mug only $5.**

IRON HORSE SHAVING MUG 1974-76
White milk glass mug holds 7 oz. plastic bottle with gold cap. Came in Avon Blend, Deep Woods or Avon Leather After Shave. SSP $6. **CMV $7. MB, $3. mug only.**

SCIMITAR 1968-69
10'long, 6 oz. gold paint with red windows over clear glass, gold cap. Came in Tribune & Windjammer After Shave Lotion. OSP $6. **CMV $15. mint, $20 MB.**

LITTLE BROWN JUG DECANTER 1978-79
Brown glass, tan plastic cap. Beige painted sides. Holds 2 oz. Deep Woods or Tai Winds After Shave. SSP $3., **CMV $3. MB.**

BABY BASSETT DECANTER 1978-79
1.25 oz. amber glass and matching plastic hear. Holds Topaze or sweet Honesty Cologne. SSP $3., **CMV $4 MB.**

QUAKER STATE POWERED HAND CLEANER 1978-79
12 oz. cardboard sides and gold plastic top and bottom. Holds heavy duty powedered hand cleaner. SSP $3. **CMV $3.**

ROOKIE COLOGNE FOR BOYS 1980-81
2.5 oz. clear glass. Red cap & label. SSP $2.80 **CMV $2. MB.**

AVON'S FINEST DECANTER 1980-81
2 oz. dark amber glass. Gold tone cap. Comes in Clint or Trazarra cologne. SSP. $5. **CMV $3. MB.**

BOOTS 'N SADDLE DECANTER 1980-81
7 1/2" high, 7 oz. dark amber glass. Silver label, brown leather look wrap around label. Choice of Wild Country or Weekend After Shave. SP $10. **CMV $4. MB.**

DESK CADDY 1977-80
Brown cork holder, silver top made in Spain. Holds 4 oz. clear glass bottle of Clint cologne, red letters, silver cap or Wild Country. **CMV $5. MB.**

DAD'S PRIDE & JOY PICTURE FRAME 1982-83
6 1/2" long clear glass. Holds pictures. SSP $8. **CMV $8. MB.**

SPIRIT OF ST. LOUIS 1970-72
6 oz. silver paint over clear glass. Came in Windjammer & Excalibur After Shave. 7 1/2" long. OSP $8.50 **CMV $12. MB, $10. BO.**

VIKING HORN 1966
7 oz. dark amber glass with gold cap & decoration. Came in Spicy, Blue Blazer & Original After Shave. OSP $5. **CMV $10. BO, $17. MB.**

DEFENDER CANNON 1966
6 oz. 9 1/2" long, amber glass, brown plastic stand, gold cap, & gold center band, small paper label. Came in Leather, Island Lime & Tribute After Shave. OSP $5. **CMV $10 bottle & stand mint, $17 MB.**

TRIBUTE SILVER WARRIOR 1967
6" high, 6 oz. silver & blue paint over clear glass, silver cap. Came in Tribute After Shave. OSP $4.50 **CMV $15 BO mint, $20. MB, All blue glass $30 mint.**

TRIBUTE RIBBED WARRIOR 1971-73
6" high, 6 oz. clear ribbed glass, silver cap. Came in Tribute Cologne. OSP $4. **CMV $8., MB $11.**

TRIBUTE RIBBED WARRIOR 1968-71
6" high, 6 oz. frosted glass, silver cap. Came in Tribute Cologne. OSP $4. **CMV $8. BO, $11. MB.**

WEATHER-OR-NOT 1969-71
5 oz. dark amber glass, regular issue on left, gold cap. Came in Leather & Oland, Tribute, Wild Country & Spicy After Shave. OSP $5. **There are 5 different Thermometers starting with 20 below, 10 below, 0, 10 above, & 20 above. All same price. CMV $10. BO, $13. MB.**

SUPER SHIFT 1978
4 oz. black glass bottle with silver & black shifter cap. Came in Sure Winner Bracing Lotion or Everest Cologne. 7" high. SSP $5. **CMV $7. MB, $6. BO.**

GAVEL 1967-68
5 oz. dark amber glass with brown plastic handle. 8" long. Came in Island Lime, Original, & Spicy. OSP $4. **CMV $12. BO, $17. MB.**

GOODYEAR BLIMP 1978
2 oz. silver gray paint over clear glass, blue letters. Came in Everest or Wild Country After Shave. SSP $5. **CMV $6. BO, $7. MB.**

WESTERN CHOICE (STEER HORNS) 1967
Brown plastic base with red center, Holds 2-3 bottles with silver caps. Came in Wild Country & Leather After Shave. OSP $6. **CMV $15. BO, $25. MB.**

PAID STAMP 1970-71
5" high, dark amber glass with black cap & red rubber paid stamp on bottom. Holds 4 oz. of Spicy or Windjammer After Shave. OSP $4. **CMV $8. BO, $10. MB.**

SWINGER GOLF BAG 1969-71
5 oz. black glass, red & silver clubs. Came in Wild Country & Bravo After Shave. OSP $5. **CMV $9. BO, $11. MB.**

INKWELL 1969-70
(Right) 6 oz. amber with purple tint, black cap with gold or silver pen. Came in Windjammer & Spicy After Shave. OSP $6. **CMV $10. BO, $12. MB.** (Left) Factory test. No value established.

POT BELLY STOVE 1970-71
5" high, 5 oz. black glass bottle with black cap. Came in Bravo or Excalibur After shave. OSP $4. **CMV $8. BO, $10. MB.**

BAY RUM KEG 1965-67
(Right) 6 oz. brown & silver paint over clear glass bottle. OSP $2.50 **CMV $15. BO, $22. MB.**

DECISIONS 1965
8 oz. red painted labels, black caps with red centers that say Panic Buttons. Came in Spicy After shave Lotion. OSP $2.50 **CMV $22. MB, $15. BO.**

TOWN PUMP 1968-69
8" high black glass bottle with gold cap & plastic shoe horn. Holds 6 oz. of Leather, Windjammer, Wild Country. OSP $5. **CMV $10. BO, $13. MB.**

FIRST CLASS MALE 1970-71
(Left) 4 1/2" high, 4 oz. blue glass with red cap. Came in Bravo or Wild Country after Shave or Liquid Hair Lotion. OSP $3. **CMV $8. MB, $6. BO.**

DAYLIGHT SHAVING TIME 1968-70
6 oz. gold paint over clear glass. Came in Spicy, Wild Country, Windjammer, Bravo & Leather After Shave. OSP $5. **CMV $10. BO, $12. MB.**

CASSEY'S LANTERN 1966-67
10 oz. gold paint on clear glass bottle gold caps. Came in Leather After Shave in red window & Island Lime in green window. OSP each. $6. **CMV amber & green $55. MB, Red $45 MB, BO $10 less each mint.**

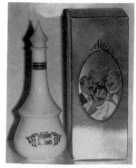

CLOSE HARMONY (BARBER BOTTLE) 1963
8 oz. white glass bottle, gold painted letter & neck band. White cap with tip. Came in Spicy & Original After Shave. OSP $2.25 Vigorate & After Shower Cologne. OSP $2.50 **CMV without tip $3., with tip $15 BO, $25 MB.**

DOLLARS 'N SCENTS 1966-67
8 oz. white glass bottle with green dollar painted on silver cap. Came in Spicy After Shave. Red rubber band around bottle. OSP $2.50 **CMV $17. MB, $10. BO.**

TOP DOLLAR SOAP ON A ROPE 1966-67
White 1886 dollar soap. OSP $1.75 **CMV $30 MB, $20 soap only mint.**

AVON CLASSICS 1969
6 oz. each OSP $3.50 Leather in clear & dark amber glass. Wild Country in light & dark amber glass & clear glass. Tribute After Shave in clear glass, light & dark amber glass. All bottle caps & labels must match color, gold or silver. **CMV $6. BO, $8. MB.**

FIRST EDITION 1967-68
6 oz. gold cap. Came in Bay Rum, **CMV $9 BO, $12. MB.** Wild Country & Leather After Shave. OSP $3.50 **CMV $7. BO, $9. MB.**

ROYAL ORB 1965-66
8 oz. round bottle, gold cap, red felt around neck. Came in Spicy & Original After Shave. Red letters painted on bottle common issue. OSP $3.50 **CMV $20., MB $27, White letter Orb $75.**

ALPINE FLASK 1966-67
8 oz. 8 3/4" high, brown glass, gold cap & neck chain. Came in Spicy, Original, Blue Blazer & Leather After Shave. OSP $4. **CMV $30. MB, $25. BO.**

GENTLEMAN'S REGIMENT COLLECTION 1982-83
Talc in beige tin can, SSP $5. No box, **CMV $1.**

SHAVING MUG AND SOAP
Beige in color glass mug and matching bar of soap. SSP $15. **CMV $15. MB.**

SHAVING BRUSH
Beige plastic brush. SSP $9. **CMV $3. MB.**

AFTER SHAVE DECANTER
4.5 oz. clear glass painted beige. Gold cap. SSP $10. **CMV $6. MB.** Fragrance choice was Wild Country or Black Suede.

KING OF HEARTS DECANTER 1990
Plain .9 oz. bottle of after shave in King of Hearts card box. SSP $4. **CMV $4. MB.**

JUST A TWIST 1977-78
2 oz. silver plated over clear glass. Came in Sweet Honesty or Deep Woods. SSP $3. **CMV $5 BO, $6. MB.**

HARD HAT 1977-78
4 oz. yellow paint over clear glass. Yellow plastic base. Came with seven decals. Came in Everest or Deep Woods. SSP $4. **CMV $5 BO, $6. MB.**

NO PARKING FIRE PLUG 1975-76
(Left) 6 oz. red painted glass with red cap. Came in Wild Country After Shave or Electric Pre-Shave. OSP $4. **CMV $7 BO, $8. MB.**

FIRE ALARM BOX 1975-76
(Right) 4 oz. red painted glass with black cap. Came in Avon Spicy After Shave, Avon Protein Hair Lotion or Electric Pre-Shave. OSP $3. **CMV $6. BO, $7. MB.**

ANGLER 1970
5 oz., 4 1/2" high blue glass with silver reel cap & trim. Came in Windjammer & Wild Country After Shave. OSP $5. **CMV $10. BO, $12. MB.**

EIGHT BALL DECANTER 1973
3 oz. black glass with black cap & white 8. Came in Spicy After Shave, Avon Protein Lotion for Men, or Electric Pre-Shave Lotion. SSP $2. **CMV $7. MB, $6. BO.**

BARBER POLE 1974-75
3 oz. white milk glass with red & blue paper striped label & white plastic cap. Holds Avon Protein Hair/Scalp Conditioner or Wild Country After shave. OSP $3. **CMV $6. BO, $7. MB.**

BARBER SHOP BRUSH 1976
1.5 oz. brown glass with black & white plastic brush cap. Came in Tai Winds or Wild Country Cologne. **CMV $6. BO, $7. MB.**

ELECTRIC GUITAR DECANTER 1974-75
6 oz. brown glass with silver plastic handle. Came in Avon Sure Winner Bracing Lotion or Wild Country After Shave. SSP $4. **CMV $10. BO, $12. MB.**

TOTEM POLE DECANTER 1975
6 oz. dark amber glass with plastic cap. Holds Wild Country, Deep Woods or Avon Spicy After Shave. OSP $5. **CMV $8. BO, $10. MB.**

SMOOTH GOING OIL CAN 1978
1.5 silver plated over clear glass. Came in Deep Woods or Everest After Shave. SSP $3. **CMV $6. MB, $5. BO.**

BUFFALO NICKEL 1971-72
5 oz. plated over clear glass with matching cap. Came in Spicy, Wild Country After Shave or Liquid Hair Lotion. SSP $4. **CMV $10. MB, $8. BO.**

INDIAN HEAD PENNY 1970-72
4 oz. 4" high. Bronze paint & cap over clear glass. Came in Bravo, Tribute, Excalibur After shave. OSP $4. **CMV $10. MB, $8. BO.**

LIBERTY DOLLAR 1970-72
(Left) 6 oz. silver paint over clear glass, silver cap with eagle. 6" high. Came in Oland, and Tribute After Shave. OSP $5. **CMV $10. MB, $8. BO. Same bottle only gold, Rare $40. MB.**

TWENTY DOLLAR GOLD PIECE 1971-72
(Right) 6 oz. gold paint over clear glass. Gold cap. Came in Windjammer After Shave & Electric Pre-Shave Lotion. OSP $5. **CMV $8. BO, $10. MB.**

LIBERTY BELL 1971-72
(Left) 5 oz. light amber glass coated over clear glass, brown cap. Came in Tribute or Oland After Shave or Cologne. OSP $5. **CMV $10. MB, $7. BO.**

LIBERTY BELL 1976
(Right) 5 oz. sprayed bronze with bronze cap. Came in Oland or Deep Woods After Shave. OSP $5. **CMV $9. MB, $6. BO.**

AFTER SHAVE ON TAP 1974-75
(Left) 5 oz. dark amber glass with gold plastic spigot cap. Holds Wild Country or Oland After Shave. OSP $3. **CMV $7. MB, $6. BO.**

AFTER SHAVE ON TAP 1976
5 oz. amber glass, red spigot cap. Holds Spicy or Wild Country. OSP $4. **CMV $7. MB, $6. BO.**

TRIPLE CROWN 1974-76
(Right) 4 oz. brown glass with red plastic cap. Holds Spicy After Shave or Avon Protein Hair/Scalp Conditioner. OSP $3. **CMV $6. MB, $5. BO.**

IT'S A BLAST 1970-71
(Left) 5 oz. 8 1/2" high, gold paint over clear glass, black rubber horn on cap. Came in Oland or Windjammer After Shave. OSP $7. **CMV $11. BO, $13. MB.**

MAN'S WORLD 1969-70
(Right) Brown plastic stand holds 6 oz. globe. Gold paint over clear glass, gold cap. Came in Bravo, Windjammer & Tribute After Shave. 4" high. OSP $5. **CMV $10. BO, $14. MB.**

BREAKER 19 1977-79
(Left) 2 oz. black glass with black & silver plastic cap. Wild Country or Sweet Honesty. SSP $3. **CMV $5. BO, $6. MB.**

COLEMAN LANTERN 1977-79
(Right) 5 oz. green painted over clear glass. Green cap, silver bail handle. Came in Wild Country or Deep Woods. SSP $5. **CMV $9. BO, $10. MB.**

AUBURN BOATTAIL SPEEDSTER 1983-84
1st in series. Black & red ceramic car figurine. 8 1/2" long. Dated 1983. SSP $29.50 **CMV $30. MB.**

CAPTAINS LANTERN 1864 1976-77
(Left) 7 oz. black glass with black plastic cap & gold ring. Came in Wild Country or Oland After Shave. OSP $5. **CMV $8. MB, $7. BO.**

WHALE OIL LANTERN 1974-75
(Right) 5 oz. green glass with silver toned plastic top & base. Holds Wild Country, Oland or Tai Winds. OSP $4. **CMV $8. MB, $7. BO.**

HISTORIC FLIGHT "1903 FLYER" 1986
3/3/4" high pewter plane. Wood base. DP $21. **CMV $21. MB.**

SPIRIT OF ST. LOIUS 1986
4 1/2" wide pewter plane with wood base. DP $21. **CMV $21. MB.**

PEWTER CAR COLLECTION 1984
Wood base with '63 Corvette, '63 Riviera, '55 Thunderbird, '57 Chrysler 300, and '64 Mustang. DP $15. **CMV $15. each MB.**

JUKE BOX 1977-78
4.5 oz. amber glass, silver top. Came in Sweet Honesty or Wild Country. Came with decals. SSP $4. **CMV $7. MB, $6. BO.**

AVON ON THE AIR 1975-76
3 oz. black glass with silver plastic stand. Holds Wild Country, Deep Woods or Spicy After Shave. OSP $4. **CMV $7. MB, $6. BO.**

JOHN WAYNE FIGURINE 1985
7 1/4" porcelain figurine. DP $18. **CMV $28. MB.**

BENJAMIN J BEARINGTON FIGURINES 1983-84
2" high pewter "First Day Back", "Hard At Work", "Report Card Day", "Schools Out". 4 in a series. DP $8 each. **CMV $10. each MB.**

"FATHER'S ARMS" FIGURINE 1984
Wood base. Pewter figurine. DP. $10. **CMV $12. MB.**

ALL AMERICAN SPORTS FAN MUG & POPCORN 1983
5 1/2" high clear glass mug with red white and blue design. Comes with red white and blue cannister of popcorn. SSP $8. **CMV $8. set MB., or $4 mug only.**

PIANO 1972
(Left) 4" high, 4 oz. dark amber glass piano with white music stack cap. Holds Tai Winds or Tribute After Shave Lotion. OSP $4. **CMV $8. BO, $10. MB.**

FIELDER'S CHOICE 1971-72
(Right) 5 oz. dark amber glass, black cap. Came in Sports Rally Bracing Lotion, Liquid Hair Trainer, or Wild Country After Shave. OSP $4. **CMV $8. BO, $10. MB.**

CORD CAR '1937' 1984
9" long car, yellow. DP. $18. **CMV $22. MB.**

DUCK SERIES 1983-84
6 different hand painted metal ducks. 4" long, 2" high. SSP $13. each. **CMV $13. each MB.**

DUCK DISPLAY RACK 1983-84
12 1/2 " long two tier wood rack to display all six duck figurines. SSP $15. **CMV $15. MB.**

SPORTING MINIATURE STEIN 1983-84
5" tall ceramic stein. Hunting scene on side. SSP $13. **CMV $13. MB.**

BLACKSMITH STEIN 1985
Ceramic stein, pewter top, Made in Brazil & numbered. DP $22. **CMV $35. MB.**

SHIP BUILDER STEIN 1986
Both ceramic steins 8 1/2" high, numbered on bottom. Pewter lids. DP. $24. **CMV $40. each MB.**

AGE OF THE IRON HORSE STEIN 1982-84
8 1/2" ceramic stein made in Brazil. Numbered and dated. Metal top. Has train design on side. Sold Empty. SSP $40. **CMV $40. MB.**

GREAT AMERICAN FOOTBALL STEIN 1982-83
9" high ceramic stein made in Brazil. Metal flip top. SSP $40. **CMV $40. MB.**

BIG SHOT MUG - TEST AREA 1983
Chrome plated brass jigger about 2 1/2" inches high. Comes with or without stick on initials. Sold only in Test area in Mid-West. OSP $13. **CMV $40. in white test box.**

WRIGHT BROTHERS MUG 1985
3" high. Hand painted porcelain mug. DP $12. **CMV $16. MB.**

LEWIS & CLARK MUG 1985
Hand painted porcelain mug. 3" high. DP. $12. **CMV $16. MB.**

MINIATURE STEINS 1982-83
4 1/2" to 5 1/2" high ceramic steins. Choice of Tall Ships, Vintage Cars or Flying Classics. Each numbered and dated 1982. SSP $13. **CMV $13. each MB.**

WESTERN ROUND UP MINI STEIN 1983-84
5" mini ceramic tan & white stein, made in Brazil and numbered on bottom. Cowboys on side. SSP $13. **CMV $13. MB.**

ENDANGERED SPECIES MINI STEIN 1983-84
Blue and white 5" mini stein, moose and goat on side. SSP $13. **CMV $13. MB.**

IRON HORSE MINI STEIN 1985
5 1/4" high ceramic stein. DP $6. **CMV $10. MB.**

GREAT AMERICAN BASEBALL STEIN 1984
Ceramic stein 8 3/4" high , Metal top, Made in Brazil. SSP $22. **CMV $40. MB.**

AUTO LANTERN DECANTER 1973
Shiny gold with amber windows. Left bottle holds 5 oz. Oland or Deep Woods After Shave. Right base holds 1.25 oz. Oland or Deep Woods Talc. SSP $12. **CMV $12 BO, $15 MB.**

SUPER SHAVER 1973
4 oz. blue glass with gray plastic top. Holds Sure Winner Bracing Lotion or Avon spicy After Shave. SSP $3. **CMV $7 MB, $5 BO.**

BOTTLED BY AVON 1973
(Right) 5 oz. clear glass with silver lift off cap, holds Oland or Windjammer After Shave. SSP $3. **CMV $7 MB, $5 BO.**

FUTURA 1969
5 oz., 7 1/2" high, silver paint over clear glass, silver cap. Came in Excalibur & Wild country Cologne. OSP $7. **CMV $12.50 MB, $10 BO.**

WORLD'S GREATEST DAD DECANTER 1971
4 oz. clear glass, red cap. Came in spicy or tribute After Shave or Electric Pre-Shave Lotion. OSP $3.50 **CMV $2 BO, $4 MB.**

STOP! DECANTER 1975
5 oz. red plastic with white plastic base. Holds Wild Country After Shave or Sweet Honesty After Bath Freshener. OSP $3. **CMV $4. no box.**

STOP 'N GO 1974
4 oz. green glass with green cap. Holds Wild Country or Avon Spicy After Shave. OSP $4, **CMV $7 MB, $5 BO.**

"HAMMER" ON THE MARK DECANTER 1978
8 1/2" long dark amber glass with silver top holds 2.5 oz. of everest or Wild Country After Shave. SSP $5. **CMV $5. BO, $7. MB.**

ON THE LEVEL DECANTER 1978
3 oz. silver coated over clear glass holds Everest or Deep Woods After Shave. SSP $4. **CMV $4. BO, $6. MB.**

ON TAP MUG DECANTER 1979
4 oz. clear glass with white plastic top. Holds Wild Country or Deep Woods After Shave. SSP $6. **CMV $7. MB.**

PAUL REVERE BELL DECANTER 1979
4 oz. clear glass painted gold. Brown and silver handle. 1979 stamped in bottom. Holds Clint After Shave or sweet Honesty Body Splash. SSP $8. **CMV $8. MB.**

STAR SIGNS DECANTER 1975
4 oz. black glass with gold cap. Came in Sweet Honesty Cologne or Wild Country After Shave. Came blank with choice of one of 12 Zodiac signs sticker to apply. OSP $3.50 **CMV $4 MB each,. $3 BO.**

SPARK PLUG DECANTER 1975
1.5 oz. white milk glass with gray cap. Holds Wild Country, Tai Winds or Avon Spicy After Shave. OSP $2. **CMV $3 MB, $2 BO.**

BIG WHISTLE DECANTER 1972
4 oz. blue glass with silver cap. Came in Tai Winds or Spicy After Shave or Electric Pre-Shave Lotion. SSP $3.50 **CMV $7. MB, $5. BO.**

#1 DAD DECANTER GIFT BOX 1989
.9 oz. bottle holds after shave in special box. SSP $4. **CMV $4. MB.**

DUCKS OF AMERICAN WILDERNESS STEIN 1988
8 3/4" high ceramic stein. Duck on top of lid. SSP $40. **CMV $40 MB.**

FLYING CLASSIC CERAMIC STEIN 1981
6th in series, 9 1/2" high blue ceramic stein made in Brazil and numbered on the bottom. Sold empty. Metal Top. SSP $38, **CMV $38 MB.**

SPORTING STEIN DECANTER 1978
9" tall, ceramic stein marked on bottom "Made in Brazil for Avon Products 1978". Came with choice of 8 oz. Trazarra or Wild Country cologne with gold cap in red plastic bottle. Each stein is numbered on the bottom. SSP $27 **CMV $35 MB.**

CAR CLASSIC STEIN 1979-80
9" high ceramic stein made in Brazil & numbered on the bottom. Comes with 8oz. plastic of Trazarra Cologne. SSP $33.00 **CMV $40.00 MB**

WESTERN ROUND-UP CERAMIC STEIN 1980
(Left) 8 1/2" high. Made in Brazil and numbered on the bottom. Metal top. Comes with 8 oz. plastic bottle of Wild Country or trazarra cologne. SSP $38, CMV $38 MB.

CASEY AT THE BAT TANKARD 1980
(Right) 6" high beige opaque glass. Comes with a 4 oz. Casey plastic bottle of Wild Country or Weekend After Shave. SSP $16, **CMV $16 MB.**

HUNTER'S STEIN 1972
8 oz. nickle plated over clear glass, has gray and black plastic bottle inside. Holds Deep Woods or Wild Country After Shave. SSP $9 **CMV $12 MB.**

STEIN – SILVER 1968
(Left) 6 oz. silver paint over clear glass, silver cap. Came in spicy, Windjammer & Tribute After Shave. OSP $4.50 **CMV $7, $10. MB.**
STEIN – SILVER 1965
(Right) 8 oz. silver paint over clear glass, silver cap. Came in Tribute. OSP $4, Spicy OSP $3.50, Blue Blazer & 4A After Shave OSP $3.75 each. **CMV $7 BO, $10 MB.**

TALL SHIPS STEIN 1977
Ceramic stein, pewter handle and lid. Came with 8 oz. red plastic bottle of Clint or brown plastic of Wild country cologne for men. Silver cap. Each stein was hand made in Brazil and numbered on the bottom. OSP $25 **CMV $35 MB.**

TALL SHIPS SHORT STEIN 1978
Smaller stein on right was sold in Trend Setter test area and was later changed to larger regular issue size on left. Both marked Avon on bottom and numbered. **CMV $60 small stein.**

AMERICAN ARMED FORCES STEIN 1990
9 1/4" high ceramic stein with pewter bald eagle lid. SSP $45. **CMV $45. MB.**

GOLD RUSH STEIN 1987
8 1/2" high ceramic stein - gold trim. SSP $40. **CMV $40.**

RACING CAR STEIN 1989
9 1/4" high ceramic stein. Has pewter race car on lid. SSP $43. **CMV $43. MB.**

ENDANGERED SPECIES MINI STEINS 1990
American Bald Eagle or Asian Elephant 5 1/4" ceramic mini steins with pewter lids. SSP. $20 ea. **CMV $20. MB.**

INDIANS OF THE AMERICAN FRONTIER STEIN 1988
9" high ceramic stein. Indian design. SSP $40. **CMV $40. MB.**

ELVIS PRESLEY FIGURINE 1987
6 1/2" high, hand painted porcelain. SSP $35. **CMV $35. MB.**

FISHING STEIN 1990
8 1/2" high ceramic Fish stein. SSP $40. **CMV $40. MB.**

FIRE FIGHTER'S STEIN 1989
9" high ceramic stein. Gold Bell lid & trim. SSP $45. **CMV $45. MB.**

NATIVE AMERICAN WOOD DUCK 1989
2 1/2" high, hand painted. SSP $13. **CMV $13 MB.**

NATIVE AMERICAN GOLDENEYE DUCK
Cold cast plaster duck figurine 3 3/4" wide.
SSP $13. **CMV $13. MB.**

AMERICAN WIDGEON DUCK 1989
3 1/2" long porcelain duck figurine. SSP $13.
CMV $13. MB.

NATIVE AMERICAN MALLARD DUCK 1989
Cold cast plaster duck 4 3/4" high. SSP $13.
CMV $13. MB.

NATIVE AMERICAN DUCK COLLECTION SHELVES 1989
2 wood shelves 12" long to hold 6 duck
figurines. SSP $15 set. **CMV $10. MB.**

DUTCH BOY HEAVY DUTY POWDER HAND CLEANER 1979-80
12 oz. blue and white paper sides. Yellow
plastic top, gray bottom. No box. SSP $4.
CMV $3. mint.

BATH BREW DECANTER 1979-80
4 oz. dark amber glass, gold cap. Brown box.
Holds Wild Country Bubble Bath. SSP $4.
CMV $4. MB.

HANKERCHIEF SAVINGS BANK 1988
Ben Franklin 4 1/2" high metal bank with white
hankerchief inside. SSP $9. **CMV $9. MB.**

TIME FOR DAD MINI COLOGNE 1990
.33 oz. bottle with Avon clock on face. SSP $2.
CMV $2. MB.

WEEKEND DECISION MAKER DECANTER 1978-79
3oz. green and white painted over clear glass.
Green top. Holds Wild Country or Tai Winds
After Shave. SSP $6.00 **CMV $6.00 MB**

THERMOS PLAID BRAND DECANTER 1978-79
3 oz. white milk glass. Red cap and plaid
design. Holds Wild Country After Shave or
Sweet Honesty Body Splash. SSP $4.00 **CMV $4.00 MB**

DOMINO DECANTER 1978-79
1.5 oz. black glass with white spots. Holds
Everest or Tai Winds After Shave. SSP $4.
CMV $4 MB

BE 1ST TO KNOW, BE INFORMED

If you want to be 1st to know when the next Bud Hastin Avon Collectors Encyclopedia will be for sale in the future, get on Bud's personal mailing list. PLUS you will get a bonus discount on his next book by ordering direct from Bud. <u>Please tell us what your last Avon Book from Bud Hastin is.</u> Please send SASE when requesting an answer to any question relating to Avon or Avon Books to Bud Hastin. Just PRINT your name and address and send it to:

BUD HASTIN
P.O. BOX 9868
KANSAS CITY, MO 64134
Just say: "Put me on your next book list."

COLOGNE ROYAL 1972-74
1 oz. clear glass, gold cap. Came in Field Flowers, Roses Roses, Bird of Paradise, Sonnet, Charisma, Unforgettable, Somewhere. SSP $1.75. **CMV $4. MB, $3. BO.**

COURTING CARRIAGE 1973-74
1 oz. clear glass, gold cap. Came in Moonwind, Sonnet, Field Flowers or Flower Talk. SSP $2. **CMV $5. MB, $4. BO.**

PINEAPPLE PETITE 1972-74
1 oz. clear glass, gold cap. Came in Roses Roses, Charisma, Elusive, Brocade or Regence. SSP $2. **CMV $4. MB, $3. BO.** Reissued in 1977 in Field Flowers & Unforgettable.

KEY NOTE PERFUME 1967
1/4 oz. glass key with gold plastic cap. 4A design on cap. Came in Here's My Heart, To A Wild Rose. OSP $5. Somewhere, Topaze, Cotillion. OSP $5.50. Unforgettable, Rapture, Occur!. OSP $6.50. **CMV $20. MB, $12. key only.**

LADY BUG PERFUME 1975-76
1/8 oz. frosted glass, gold cap. Came in Sonnet, Moonwind or Patchwork. OSP $4. **CMV $4. BO, $5. MB.**

SCENT WITH LOVE 1971-72
1/4 oz. frosted glass with gold pen cap, white and gold label around bottle. Came in Field Flowers, Moonwind, Bird of paradise, Charisma, Elusive, Moonwind. OSP $6. **CMV $12. MB, $8. BO.**

COLLECTORS
All containers are Priced Empty

BO means .... Bottle only (empty)

CMV means .... Current Market Value

SSP means .... Special Selling Price

OSP means .... Original Selling Price

MB means .... Mint and Boxed

DP means Demo Price .... Avon Rep Cost

PRECIOUS TURTLE 1975-76
.66 oz. gold jar with plastic lid. Came in Patchwork, or Roses Roses Cream Sachet. OSP $4. **CMV $5. MB, $4. BO.**

TREASURE TURTLE 1971-73
1 oz. brown glass turtle with gold head. Holds Field Flowers, Hana Gasa, Bird of Paradise, Elusive, Charisma, Brocade, Unforgettable, Rapture, Occur!, Somewhere, Topaze, Cotillion, Here's My Heart and Persian Wood. OSP $3.50. **CMV $6. MB, $4. BO.**

TRESAURE TURTLE 1977
1 oz. clear glass turtle with gold cap. Came in Sweet Honesty or Charisma cologne. Avon on bottom & 'R' for reissue on tail. OSP $4.50. **CMV $4. MB, $3. BO.**

EMERALD PRINCE FROG 1977-79
1 oz. green frosted paint over clear glass. Came in Sweet Honesty or Moonwind cologne. OSP $5. **CMV $4. MB, $3. BO.**

AUTUMN ASTER DECANTER 1978-80
(Left) .75 oz. clear glass, gold cap. Holds Topaze or Sun Blossoms cologne. SSP $2. **CMV $2. MB.**

DOGWOOD DEMI DECANTER 1978-80
(Right) .75 oz. flower shaped bottle, gold flower lid. Came in Apple Blossom, Moonwind or Topaze cologne. SSP $3. **CMV $2. MB.**

WHAT'S HOT AND WHAT'S NOT IN WOMEN'S FIGURINES

What's hot is any decanter or figurine that's made of glass or ceramic. It has to look like something. This is what collectors are after today. What's not hot is plain looking bottles of no particular shape. Almost all plastic bottles, wall tiles & wall decorations, plain tin can items, jars, fabric items such as sachet pillows etc., ceramic items not marked Avon on bottom & kitchen items that have no shape that would appeal to most collectors.

Avon collecting is 24 years old as we know it and the Avon product line has expanded well beyond most people's ability to collect everything in their product line. There are thousands of products to collect. Choose the one's that appeal to most collectors & you should have a market when you decide to sell your collection in years to come.

This book has been researched to include all products that are hot with most collectors.

Some new products not shown in this book fall in the catagory of new collectible. There are over 500,000 Avon Reps, we feel there are more than ample supplies to collectors. It will take several years for almost any new products to become scarce & start to rise in value due to supply & demand. Keep this in mind in buying new collectibles. Only the older products are true collectibles. This is why the CPC items, the first Avon products, are so scarce & have risen so high in price. We hope you find this information helpful in guiding your collecting.

Candy products from Avon are not in this book unless they come in a figurine type container. Boxes & cans of candy will not be considered collectible as it easily melts & is dangerous when it gets old & could cause harm to children. We suggest you buy this type of product to use and dispose of the box it came in.

DREAM GARDEN 1972-73
1/2 oz. pink frosted glass with gold cap. Came in Moonwind, Bird of Paradise, Charisma, Elusive or Unforgettable perfume oil. OSP $5. **CMV $15. MB, $12. BO.**
SNOW MAN PETITE PERFUME 1973
.25 oz. textured glass with pink eyes, mouth & scarf. Gold cap. Came in Cotillion, Bird of Paradise, Field Flowers. OSP $4. **CMV $6. BO, $8. MB.**
PRECIOUS SWAN PERFUME 1974-76
1/8 oz. frosted glass with gold cap. Came in Field Flowers, Bird of Paradise or Charisma. OSP $4. **CMV $6. BO, $7. MB.**

ICICLE PERFUME 1967-68
1 dram, gold cap. Came in Here's My Heart, To A Wild Rose, Somewhere, Topaz, Cotillion, Unforgettable, Rapture, Occur!, Regence. OSP $3. with gold neck label. **CMV $7. MB, $5. BO.**

PRECIOUS SLIPPER 1973-74
.25 oz. frosted glass bottle with gold cap. Came in Sonnet or Moonwind. OSP $4. **CMV $7. MB, $5. BO.**
LOVE BIRD PERFUME 1969-70
1/4 oz. frosted bird with silver cap. 2 1/2" long. Came in Charisma, Elusive, Brocade, Regence, Unforgettable, Rapture, Occur!. OSP $6.25. **CMV $9. MB, $5. BO.**
SMALL WONDER PERFUME 1972-73
1/8 oz. frosted glass with gold cap. Holds Field Flowers, Bird of Paradise, Charisma. OSP $2.50. **CMV $7. MB, $5. BO.**

BOW TIE PERFUME 1970
1/8 oz. clear glass. Shape of bow with gold cap. Came in Pink Slipper Soap in Charisma & Cotillion. CMV $4. mint.

ONE DRAM PERFUME 1974-76
Clear glass with gold cap. Came in Bird of Paradise, Charisma or Field Flowers. OSP $3.75. Sonnet, Moonwind or Imperial Garden. OSP $4.25. CMV $3. MB, $2. BO.

STRAWBERRY FAIR PERFUME 1974-75
1/8 oz. red glass, silver cap. Came in Moonwind, Charisma or Sonnet. OSP $4. CMV $6. MB, $4. BO.

FRISKY FRIENDS 1981
3 different frosted 1 oz. glass cats. With blue cap, Honeysuckle, yellow cap has Roses Roses & pink cap has Hawaiian White Ginger. SSP $5. CMV $5. MB each.

HEAVENLY ANGEL 1981
(Left) .5 oz. blue glass angel, silver cap. Choice of Ariane, Candid, Timeless. Red box dated 1981. SSP $2. CMV $2. MB.

WINGED PRINCESS 1981
(Center) .5 oz. swan shaped iridescent glass, gold cap. Choice of Occur!, Charisma, Sweet Honesty. Box dated 1981. SSP $2.25 CMV $3. MB

LOVE CHIMES 1981-82
(Right) .5 oz. clear glass bell shape, gold cap. Choice of Roses Roses, Charisma, Moonwind, Sweet Honesty. SSP $1.75. CMV $2. MB.

SEWING NOTIONS 1975
1 oz. pink and white glass with silver cap. Holds Sweet Honesty, To A Wild Rose or Cotillion. OSP $3. CMV $4. MB, $3. BO.

CRYSTALIER COLOGNE 1975
2 oz. clear glass. Filled with Field Flowers, Bird of Paradise or Roses Roses Cologne. OSP $4. CMV $4. MB, $3. BO.

BABY OWL 1975-77
1 oz. clear glass, goldc ap. Holds Sweet Honesty or Occur! Cologne. OSP $2. CMV $2. BO, $3. MB.

PERT PENGUIN 1975-76
1 oz. clear glass, gold cap. Holds Field Flowers or Cotillion Cologne. OSP $2. CMV $2. BO, $3. MB.

ROLLIN GREAT ROLLER SKATE 1980-81
2 oz. glass red top. Choice of Zany Cologne or Lover Boy Cologne. SSP $4. CMV $4. MB.

PETITE PIGLET 1972
2" long embossed clear glass with gold cap. Holds 1/4 oz. perfume in Field Flowers, Bird of Paradise, Elusive & Charisma. OSP $5. CMV $7. BO, $9. MB.

SNAIL PERFUME 1968-69
1/4 oz. gold cap, clear glass. Came in Charisma, Brocade, Regence, Unforgettable, Rapture & Occur!. OSP $6.25. CMV $13.50 MB, $7. BO.

PERFUME PETITE MOUSE 1970
Frosted glass with gold head and tail, holds 1/4 oz. perfume in Elusive, Charisma, Brocade, Regence. OSP $7.50. Unforgettable, Rapture & Occur!. OSP $6.25. CMV $17.50 MB, $12. BO.

HUGGABLE HOP-A-LONG 1982
1 oz. green glass frog. Plastic hat. Comes with 20 stick on decals. Choice of Sweet Honesty for girls or Light Musk for guys. SSP $5. CMV $5. MB.

SONG OF CHRISTMAS 1980
.75 oz. frosted glass. Red cap. Choice of Moonwind, Sweet Honesty or Bird of Paradise. SSP $2.22. CMV $3. MB.

CHRISTMAS SOLDIER 1980
.75 oz. clear glass, gold cap. Choice of Sportif, Sweet Honesty, Charisma or Moonwind. SSP $2. CMV $3. MB.

OWL MINIATURE 1980-81
.6 oz. clear glass, gold owl cap. Choice of Tasha, Ariane, Candid or Timeless. SSP $1.95. CMV $2. MB.

COLOGNE GO ROUND 1980
.5 oz. clear glass, gold cap. Choice of Roses Roses, Honeysuckle, Hawaiian White Ginger, Field Flowers. SSP $1.75. CMV $2. MB.

SEAHORSE MINIATURE 1980-81
.5 oz. clear glass, gold cap. Choice of Sweet Honesty, Charisma, Occur! or Moonwind. SSP $3. CMV $3. MB.

COLOGNE RONDELLE 1980
5 oz. clear glass, gold cap. Choice of Moonwind, Charisma, Topaze, Occur!, Sweet Honesty, Zany Sportif or Country Breeze. In special Christmas box. SSP $1.40. CMV $1. MB.

SCENTIMENTAL DOLL ADORABLE
ABIGAIL 1979-80
4.5 oz. clear glass painted beige. Beige plastic top. Comes in Regence or Sweet Honesty cologne. SSP $10. **CMV $8. BO, $10. MB.**
MRS. QUACKLESS 1979-80
2 oz. clear glass painted off white. Off white plastic top with white lace and green bonnet. Comes in Delicate Daisies Cologne. SSP $6. **CMV $4. BO, $6. MB.**
SWEET TOOTH TERRIER 1979-80
1 oz. white glass and white plastic top. Comes in Topaze or Cotillion Cologne. SSP $4. **CMV $4. BO, $5. MB.**

WEDDING FLOWER MAIDEN 1979-80
(Left) 1.75 oz. white painted over clear glass. Holds Unforgettable or Sweet Honesty cologne. SSP $6. **CMV $6. BO, $7. MB.**
GARDEN GIRL 1978-79
4 oz. pink painted over clear glass. Holds Charisma or Sweet Honesty cologne. SSP $5. **CMV $6. BO, $8. MB.**
ANGEL SONG DECANTER 1978-79
1 oz. frosted glass base with off white plastic top. Holds Here's My Heart or Charisma cologne. SSP $3. **CMV $4. BO, $6. MB.**

ON THE AVENUE 1978-79
2 oz. blue painted over clear glass. Pink plastic top with lavender hat. White detachable umbrella. Holds Topaze or Unforgettable cologne. SSP $8. **CMV $8. BO, $10. MB.**
PROUD GROOM 1978-80
2 oz. white painted over clear glass. Holds Sweet Honesty or Unforgettable Cologne. SSP $7. **CMV $7. BO, $9. MB.**

FASHION FIGURINE 1971-72
(Left) 4 oz. white plastic top & white painted bottom, over clear glass. 6" high. Came in Field Flowers, Elusive, Bird of Paradise, Brocade. SSP $4. **CMV $10. BO, $12. MB.**
VICTORIAN FASHION FIGURINE 1973-74
(Center) 4 oz. light green (some call it blue or aqua) painted over clear glass base with green plastic top. Came in Charisma, Field Flowers, Bird of Paradise Cologne. SSP $4. **CMV $30. BO, $33. MB.**
ELIZABETHAN FASHION FIGURINE 1972
(Right) 4 oz. pink painted glass bottom over clear glass with pink plastic top. 6" high. Came in Moonwind, Charisma, Field Flowers & Bird of Paradise Cologne. SSP $5. **CMV $16. BO, $20. MB.** Also came pink painted over white milk glass. Remove cap to see difference. **CMV $15.**

TUG-A-BRELLA 1979-80
2.5 oz. clear glass painted yellow, yellow plastic top. Black plastic umbrella on wire. Holds Moonwind or Cotillion Cologne. SSP $10. **CMV $9. BO, $11. MB.**
GOOD FAIRY 1978-79
3 oz. clear glass painted blue. Blue plastic top. Plastic wand. Blue and pink fabric purse and wings. Holds Delicate Daisies cologne. SSP $6. **CMV $6. BO, $8. MB.**

GARDEN GIRL 1975
4 oz. sprayed frosted glass with yellow plastic top. Holds Sweet Honesty, Somewhere, Cotillion ot To A Wild Rose. OSP $3.50. **CMV $9. BO, $11. MB.**
FLOWER MAIDEN 1973-74
4 oz. yellow skirt painted over clear glass with white plastic top. Came in Unforgettable, Somewhere, Topaze, Cotillion. SSP $5. **CMV $9. MB, $7. BO.**
DEAR FRIENDS 1974
4 oz. pink painted with light pink plastic top. Came in Field Flowers, Bird of Paradise or Roses Roses Cologne. SSP $4. **CMV $10. BO, $13. MB.**

ANGEL SONG WITH MANDOLIN 1979-80
(Left) 1 oz. frosted over clear glass. White plastic top. Holds Moonwind or Unforgettable cologne. SSP $3. **CMV $4. MB.**
SKATER'S WALTZ 1979-80
(Center) 4 oz. blue flock base over clear glass. Light blue plastic top. Holds Charisma or Cotillion cologne. SSP $8. **CMV $9. MB.**
LITTLE JACK HORNER 1979-80
(Right) 1.5 oz. white glass painted white frosted. Came in Topaze or Roses Roses cologne. SSP $6. **CMV $7. MB.**

SONG OF SPRING 1977
(Left) 1 oz. frosted glass with frosted plastic bird bath top. Blue plastic bird attachment. Came in Sweet Honesty or Topaze. OSP $6. **CMV $6. MB.**
FELINA FLUFFLES 1977-78
(Right) 2 oz. blue paint over clear glass, white plastic top, blue ribbon on head. Pink cheeks. Came in Pink & Pretty Cologne. OSP $6. **CMV $5. BO, $6. MB.**

FLY-A-BALLOON 1975-77
3 oz. glass sprayed blue with light blue top & red plastic balloon. Holds Moonwind or Bird of Paradise cologne. OSP $7. **CMV $7. BO, $8. MB.**

SKIP-A-ROPE 1977
4 oz. yellow sprayed glass with yellow plastic top and white plastic rope. Holds Sweet Honesty, Bird of Paradise or Roses Roses cologne. OSP $7. **CMV $7. MB, $5. BO.**

BETSY ROSS 1976
4 oz. white painted over clear glass. Came in Sonnet or Topaze Cologne. Sold 2 campaigns only. SSP $7. **CMV $7. BO.** Also came white painted over white milk glass. Remove cap to see color of bottle. **CMV $20. MB.** The regular issue Betsy Ross bottle was one of the all time biggest sellers in Avon history.

MAGIC PUMPKIN COACH 1976-77
1 oz. clear glass, gold cap. Comes in Bird of Paradise or Occur! Cologne. OSP $5. **CMV $4. BO, $6. MB.**

PRETTY GIRL PINK 1974-75
(Left) 6 oz. glass sprayed pink base with light pink top. Holds Unforgettable, Topaze, Occur! or Somewhere cologne. OSP $4. **CMV $7. BO, $9. MB.**

LITTLE GIRL BLUE 1972-73
(Center) 3 oz. blue painted glass with blue plastic cap. Came in Brocade, Unforgettable, Somewhere or Cotillion. SSP $4. **CMV $7. BO, $9. MB.**

LITTLE KATE 1973-74
(Right) 3 oz. pastel orange painted glass with orange plastic hat over cap. Came in Bird of Paradise, Charisma, Unforgettable. SSP $4. **CMV $8. BO, $10. MB.**

MY PET FIGURINE 1973
(Left) Green & brown, white kitten, ceramic figurine. 1973 embossed in ceramic & printed on box. OSP $10. **CMV $40.**

JENNIFER FIGURINE 1973
(Right) Pastel turquoise dress & hat figurine. 1973 embossed in ceramic & printed on box. Some came with flowers in center of hat & some with flowers on the right side of hat. OSP $10. **CMV $45.** Both issued from Springdale, Ohio branch only.

18th CENTURY CLASSIC FIGURINE YOUNG BOY 1974-75
(Left) 4 oz. white sprayed glass with white plastic head. Choice of Sonnet or Moonwind cologne or foaming bath oil. OSP $5. **CMV $7. BO., $9. MB.**

18th CENTURY CLASSIC FIGURINE YOUNG GIRL 1974-75
(Right) 4 oz. white sprayed glass with white plastic head. Choice of Sonnet or Moonwind cologne or foaming bath oil. OSP $5. **CMV $7. BO, $9. MB.**

LITTLE MISS MUFFET 1978-80
(Left) 2 oz. white painted over milk glass. Came in Sweet Honesty or Topaze. OSP $7. **CMV $7. MB, $6. BO.**

CHURCH MOUSE BRIDE 1978-79
Plastic top with separate white veil. Came in Delicate Daisies cologne. Base is white dull paint over milk glass. OSP $6. **CMV $6. BO, $7. MB.**

AMERICAN BELLE 1976-78
(Left) 4 oz. yellow dull paint over clear glass, yellow cap. Came in Cotillion or Sonnet cologne. SSP $5. **CMV $8. MB, $6. BO.**

LITTLE BO PEEP DECANTER 1976-78
(Right) 2 oz. white dull paint over white milk glass base, white plastic top & can. Came in Sweet Honesty or Unforgettable cologne. SSP $5. **CMV $8. MB, $7. BO.**

CATCH-A-FISH 1976-78
3 oz. dark tan, painted over clear glass, light tan plastic top, yellow hat & brown plastic removable pole. Came in Field Flowers or Sonnet cologne. OSP $9.50. **CMV $8. BO, $10. MB.**

ROLL-A-HOOP 1977-78
3.75 oz. dull pink painted over clear glass base. Light pink plastic top, white plastic hoop. Came in Field Flowers or Cotillion cologne. OSP $10. **CMV $8. BO, $10. MB.**

VICTORIAN LADY 1972-73
5 oz. white milk glass, white plastic cap. Came in Bird of Paradise, Unforgettable, Occur!, Charisma Foaming Bath Oil. SSP $4. **CMV $6. BO, $8. MB.**

WISHFUL THOUGHTS 1982-83
5 1/2" high porcelain figurine. Blue & white. SSP $15. **CMV $15. MB.**

LIBRARY LAMP 1976--77
(Left) 4 oz. gold plated base over clear glass, gold cap. Came in Topaze & Charisma cologne. OSP $9. **CMV $8. BO, $10. MB.**

BRIDAL MOMENTS 1976-79
(Right) 5 oz. white paint over clear glass. White plastic top. Came in Sweet Honesty or Unforgettable cologne. OSP $9. **CMV $10. MB, $8. BO.**

SCOTTISH LASS 1975
(Left) 4 oz. blue with red, green & blue plaid skirt, blue plastic top. Holds Sweet Honesty, Bird of Paradise, Rosos Roses or Cotillion cologne. OSP $5. **CMV $8. BO, $10. MB.**

SPANISH SENORITA 1975-76
(Center) 4 oz. red base with white designs and pink plastic top. Holds Moonwind, To A Wild Rose or Topaze cologne. OSP $5. **CMV $10. BO, $12. MB.**

ROARING TWENTIES FASHION FIGURINE 1972-74
(Right) 3 oz. purple painted over clear glass with plastic purple top. Came in Unforgettale, Topaze, Somewhere, Cotillion. SSP $4. **CMV $8. BO, $10. MB.**

CLASSIC DECANTER 1969-70
(Left) 8 oz. white glass bottle with gold cap. 11" high, filled with Skin-So-Soft bath oil. SSP $5. **CMV $10. MB, $7. BO.**

SEA MAIDEN SKIN-SO-SOFT 1971-72
(Right) 6 oz. gold cap, clear glass, 10" high. SSP $5. **CMV $10. MB, $7. BO.**

DUTCH MAID 1977-79
(Left) 4 oz. blue painted base over clear glass, flower design & blue plastic top. Came in Sonnet or Moonwind cologne. OSP $7. **CMV $9. MB, $7. BO.**

MARY MARY 1977-79
(Center) 2 oz. frosted white over milk glass & white plastic top. Came in Sweet Honesty or Topaze. OSP $7. **CMV $9. MB, $7. BO.**

SKATERS WALTZ - RED 1977-78
(Right) 4 oz. red flock on clear glass & pink plastic tip. Came in Moonwind or Charisma cologne. OSP $8.50. **CMV $9. BO, $11. MB.**

PRECIOUS PRISCILLA 1982-83
(Left) 3 oz. pale pink paint over clear glass. Plastic head top. Holds Sweet Honesty or Moonwind. SSP $10. **CMV $10. MB.**

AMERICAN HEIRLOOM PORCELAIN HEAD DOLL 1981
(Right) 11" high fabric doll with porcelain head. Blue ribbon around waist. SSP $16.50. **CMV $16.50. MB.**

FIRST PRAYER 1981-82
(Left) 1.5 oz. light bisque yellow painted bottom over clear glass. Light yellow top. Choice of Charisma, Occur!, Topaze cologne. 4" high. SSP $7. **CMV $7. MB.**

PRIMA BALLERINA 1981
(Center) Pink frosted glass over clear glass, 1 oz. Choice of Zany or Sweet Honesty. Bottle & box label dated 1981. SSP $7. **CMV $7. MB.**

NOSTALGIC GLOW 1981-82
(Right) 1 oz. clear glass lamp bottom, blue plastic shade top. Choice of Moonwind, Wild Jasmine or Topaze. SSP $6. **CMV $6. MB.**

DUTCH GIRL FIGURINE 1973-74
(Left) 3 oz. blue painted with light blue plastic top. Came in Unforgettable, Topaze or Somewhere. SSP $5. **CMV $8. BO, $11. MB.**

GAY NINETIES 1974
(Center) 3 oz. orange sprayed bottle with white top and orange hat. Holds Unforgettable, Topaze or Somewhere. OSP $4. **CMV $10. BO, $13. MB.**

SWEET DREAMS 1974
(Right) 3 oz. sprayed white bottom with blue top. Holds Pink & Pretty or Sweet Honesty cologne. OSP $4. **CMV $13. BO, $15. MB.**

PIERROT COLOGNE 1982-83
(Left) 1.75 oz. bottle. Black & white. Choice of Charisma or Occur! SSP $10. **CMV $10. MB.**

PIERRETTE COLOGNE 1982-83
(Right) Same as Pierrot. SSP $10. **CMV $10. MB.**

LOVING TREATS BUTTERMINTS 1982
Flowered tin box filled with buttermint candy. Tin dated 1982. Comes in lavender box. SSP $10 **CMV $4. MB. empty.**

BEST FRIENDS PORCELAIN FIGURINE 1981
(Left) 6" high boy figurine. Dated 1981. SSP $19.50. **CMV $19.50. MB.** 1 made in Taiwan and 1 in Japan.

MOTHER'S LOVE PORCELAIN FIGURINE 1981
(Center) 5 1/2" high girl figurine holding a baby. Bottom tan painted label is dated 1981. Made in Taiwan sticker is tan color. SSP $19.50. **CMV $19.50. MB.**

MOTHER'S LOVE FIGURINE ADVANCED 1981
(Right) Factory sample. About 75 were given by Avon Products Inc. to Avon collectors at the 10th Annual National Association of Avon Collectors Convention in Long Beach, California. These factory samples do not have Avon label on bottom & is 1/4" higher. Made in Taiwan, label is green. Rare. Came in plain box. **CMV $100. mint.**

FOSTORIA CRYSTAL BUD VASE 1980
(Left) 6" high clear glass. Dated 1980 on bottom. Comes with white scented carnation. SSP $13. **CMV $13. MB.**

CRYSTAL SNOWFLAKE CHRISTMAS BELL 1980
(Center) 3.75 oz. clear glass. Bottom label dated 1980. Choice of Charisma, Topaze, Occur! or Cotillion cologne. SSP $8. **CMV $8. MB.**

MARCHING PROUD 1980-81
(Right) 8 1/2" high, 2 oz. blue base paint over clear glass. White top, red hat, cloth flag. Choice of Sweet Honesty or Topaze cologne. SSP $12. **CMV $12. MB.**

MOTHER'S LOVE PORCELAIN FIGURINE TEST PRODUCTS 1981
24 were given to Avon collectors at the 10th Annual National Association of Avon Collectors Convention on the Queen Mary Ship June 1981. It is not in the regular issue box & figurine is not marked on bottom. Came with letter from Avon as very rare. **CMV $150 with letter & plain box.**

LITTLE DREAM GIRL 1980-81
(Left) 1.25 oz. aqua paint over clear glass. Cream color top. Choice of Sweet Honesty or Occur! cologne. SSP $5. **CMV $5. MB.**

BUNDLE OF LOVE 1980-81
(Center) .75 oz. light blue paint over clear glass. Sits on red plastic sled. Choice of Hello Sunshine cologne or Sure Winner Bracing Lotion. SSP $5. **CMV $5. MB.**

FLOWER MOUSE 1980-81
(Right) .75 oz. dull red paint over clear glass and white & yellow mouse cap. Choice of Cotillion or Zany cologne. SSP $4. **CMV $4. MB.**

HOLIDAY TREATS CAN 1981
(Left) Green metal can made in England for Avon Christmas 1981. Full of Candy. SSP $9. **CMV $4. MB. Empty.**

SWEET SCENTIMENTS VALENTINE CANDY 1981
(Right) Metal pink & tan can full of candy. Bottom stamped "Avon Valentine's Day 1981" SSP $8. **CMV $4. MB empty.**

SPRING DYNASTY VASE 1982-83
7" high glass vase with fragranced outer coating in blue, pink or green. SSP $11 **CMV $6. MB each color.**

NATIVITY HOLY FAMILY FIGURINE SET 1981
Box holds 3 piece white porcelain bisque nativity scene. Each dated 1981. SSP $38.50 **CMV $38.50. set MB.**

DAPPER SNOWMAN 1978-79
(Left) 1 oz. white milk glass with black painted spots and black hat cap. Holds Moonwind or Sweet Honesty cologne. Brown, blue and red neck scarf. SSP $3. **CMV $4. MB.**
JOLLY SANTA 1978-79
(Right) 1 oz. clear glass, white painted beard. Red cap. Came in Here's My Heart or Topaze cologne. SSP $1.50 **CMV $3**

SHARING THE CHRISTMAS SPIRIT FIGURINE 1981
First in a series of Christmas figurines from Avon. Dated 1981. 6" high. SSP $45. **CMV $45. MB.**

BEARING GIFTS LIP BALM 1981-82
Small fuzzy bear, head turns, holds red & green lip balm in red box. SSP $5. **CMV $5. MB.**

CHRISTMAS SPARKLERS 1968-69
4 oz. bubble bath. Came in gold, green, blue and red with gold caps. 2 sides of bottle are indented. OSP $2.50 **CMV $12. MB, $8. BO. Mint.**
CHRISTMAS SPARKLER PURPLE 1968
4 oz. painted over clear glass, gold cap. OSP $2.50 **CMV $25 Mint. Sold only in West Coast Area.**

HOLIDAY PLATTER 1981
11" clear glass, holly & berry decal. Plate does not say Avon. SSP $15 **CMV $15 MB.**
HOLIDAY COMPOTE 1981
4" high clear glass, holly decoration. Avon on bottom. SSP $12. **CMV $12. MB.**
HOLIDAY CANDLESTICKS 1981
3" high clear glass, holly decoration. Avon on bottom. SSP $10 set. **CMV $10. MB.**

CHRISTMAS TREE HOSTESS SET 1979
9" high ceramic green tree. Comes with Mountain Pine fragrance wax chips and rag Doll & Teddy Bear ceramic salt & pepper shakers. This was a very short issue at X-mas. 1979. SSP $25. **CMV $25. MB.**

HEARTHSIDE 1976-77
(Left) .6 oz. bronze plated over clear glass. Came in Sweet Honesty or Occur!. SSP $3.50 **CMV $5. MB, $4. BO.**
GOLDEN ANGEL 1976-77
(Right) 1 oz. gold plated over clear glass. White angel head cap. Came in Sweet Honesty or Occur!. SSP $3. **CMV $4. BO, $5. MB**

CHRISTMAS TREES 1968-70
4 oz. bubble bath. Came in red, green gold silver painted over clear glass. OSP $2.50 **CMV $12. MB. $8. BO mint.**

HEAVENLY ANGEL 1974-75
(Left) 2 oz. clear glass with white top. Holds Occur!, Unforgettable, Somewhere, Here's My Heart, or Sweet Honesty cologne. OSP $4. **CMV $7. MB. $5. BO.**
GOLDEN ANGEL BATH OIL 1968-69
(Right) 4 oz. gold bottle, gold paper wings. Gold & white cap. OSP $3.50 **CMV $12. MB. $7. BO mint.**

SPRING BOQUET VASE 1981
6" glass vase with special plastic coated scented outside. Comes in red, green or amber. SSP $9. each **CMV $6. each MB.**

YULE TREE 1974-79
(Left) 3 oz. green with plastic with green plastic top and gold star. Came in Sonnet, Moonwind or Field Flowers cologne. OSP $4. **CMV $3. BO, $4. MB.**

TOUCH OF CHRISTMAS 1975
(Center) 1 oz. green glass with red cap. Holds Unforgettable or Imperial Garden. OSP $2.50 **CMV $3. MB, $2. BO.** Reissued 1979 in Zany & Here's My Heart. Same CMV.

CRYSTAL TREE COLOGNE 1975
(Right) 3 oz. clear glass with gold plastic star cap. Holds Moonwind or Sonnet. OSP $6. **CMV $6. BO, $8. MB.**

HEAVENLY MUSIC 1978-80
(Left) 1 oz. clear glass, gold cap. Holds Charisma or Topaze cologne. SSP $3. **CMV $3. MB.**

LITTLE BURRO 1978-79
(Center) 1 oz. light gray glass. Straw hat with red flower. Holds Sweet Honesty or Charisma cologne. SSP $3. **CMV $3. BO, $4. MB.**

HONEY BEE 1978-80
(Right) 1.25 oz. amber coated over clear glass. Gold bee on lid. Holds Honeysuckle or Moonwind cologne. SSP $4. **CMV $4. MB.**

SNIFFY "SKUNK" 1978-80
1.25 oz. black glass, white trim. Holds Sweet Honesty or Topaze cologne. SSP $5. **CMV $5. MB.**

"CALCULATOR" IT ALL ADDS UP 1979-80
4 oz. black glass. Holds Deep Woods After Shave or Sweet Honesty Body Splash. SSP $6. **CMV $8. MB.**

CHRISTMAS COLOGNE 1969-70
3 oz. each. Unforgettable is silver & pink, Occur! is gold & blue, Somewhere is silver & green, Topaze is bronze and yellow. OSP $3.50 **CMV $8. BO, $11. MB.**

CHRISTMAS ORNAMENTS 1967
Round 4 oz. bubble bath. Came in gold, silver, red, green. Silver caps. OSP $1.75. **CMV $12. MB, $9. BO mint.**

KANGAROO TWO 1978-79
8" red calico stuffed Kangaroo with Avon tag. Green neck ribbon. Came with .75 oz. frosted glass kangaroo bottle with gold head. Holds Topaze or Sweet Honesty cologne. SSP $10. **CMV $10. both MB, BO $4., Stuffed toy $5.**

FESTIVE FACETS DECANTER 1979-80
1 oz. with gold caps. Comes in Charisma "red glass", Sweet Honesty "green glass", and Here's My Heart in "blue glass". SSP $1.50 each. **CMV $3. BO, $4. MB.**

PRETTY PIGLET 1979-80
(Left) .75 oz. clear glass. Holds Roses Roses, pink cap; Honeysuckle, yellow cap; Hawaiian White Ginger, blue-green cap. Fabric flower around neck. SSP $3. **CMV $3. MB.**

MONKEY SHINES 1979-80
(Inside Left) 1 oz. clear glass painted light gray, brown eyes and ears. Red cap and neck strap. Holds Sonnet or Moonwind cologne. SSP $6. **CMV $5. BO, $6. MB.**

BON BON 1979-80
(Inside Right) .75 oz. dark amber glass. Pink and green top came with Sweet Honesty cologne or Cotillion with yellow and green top. SSP $4. **CMV $4. MB.**

GENTLE FOAL 1979-80
(Right) 1.5 oz. dark amber glass and plastic head. Comes in Charisma or Sun Blossoms cologne. SSP $5. **CMV $5. MB.**

FAIRYTALE FROG 1976
1 oz. clear glass with gold frog cap. Choice of Sweet Honesty or Sonnet Cologne. OSP $3. **CMV $5. MB, $3. BO.**

LUCKY PENNY LIP GLOSS 1976-80
2" diameter copper colored. Contains 2 colors lip gloss. OSP $3. **CMV $2. MB, $1. no box.** Reissued in 1980 with R on bottom.

GOLDEN NOTES (CANARY) 1979-80
1.75 oz. clear glass coated light yellow, Yellow head. Came in Charisma or Woonwind cologne. SSP $3. **CMV $4. MB.**

CHURCH MOUSE GROOM 1979-80
.75 oz. white glass, white plastic top. Holds Delicate Daisies cologne. SSP $6. **CMV $6. MB.**

FUZZY BUNNY 1979-80
1 oz. clear glass coated with white flock. Pink ears, orange carrot. Holds Sweet Honesty or Honeysuckle cologne. SSP $6. **CMV $6. MB.**

WOMEN'S DECANTERS, CERAMICS & FIGURINES

MERRY MOUSE 1979-80
(Left) .75 oz. white milk glass bottle & head. Stick on holly leaf. Choice of Zany or Cotillion cologne. SSP $5. **CMV $6. MB.**

PRECIOUS CHICKADEE 1979-80
(Center) 1 oz. white glass. Red & white cap. Came in Here's My Heart or Sun Blossoms cologne. SSP $4. **CMV $5. MB.**

SNUG CUB 1979-80
(Right) 1 oz. milk glass. Green cap. Pink & green paint. Comes in Occur! or Sweet Honesty cologne. SSP $3. **CMV $5. MB.**

ROCKING HORSE TREE ORNAMENT 1979-80
.75 oz. clear glass rocker shapes bottle with gold plastic rocking horse top. Bottom of horse says 1979. Holds Sweet Honesty or Moonwind cologne. SSP $5. **CMV $6. MB.**

LOVE SONG 1973-75
6 oz. frosted glass with gold cap. Holds Skin-So-Soft bath oil. OSP $6. **CMV $6. MB, $4. BO.**

BATH TREASURE SNAIL 1973-76
6 oz. clear glass with gold head. Holds Skin-So-Soft. OSP $6. **CMV $9. MB, $7. BO.**

BABY HIPPO 1977-80
1 oz. frosted glass with silver head. Came in Sweet Honesty or Topaze cologne. OSP $5. **CMV $6. MB, $5. BO.**

LITTLE LAMB 1977-78
.75 oz. white milk glass, white head. Came in Sweet Honesty or Topaze cologne. OSP $5. **CMV $5. BO, $6. MB.**

PERFUME CONCENTRE 1974-76
1 oz. clear glass with gold cap. Came in Imperial Garden, Moonwind, Sonnet, Charisma or Bird of Paradise. SSP $4. **CMV $4. MB, $2. BO.**

UNICORN 1974-75
2 oz. clear glass with gold cap. Came in Field Flowers, Charisma, Bired of Paradise or Brocade. SSP $4. **CMV $7. MB, $5. BO.**

ENCHANTED FROG CREAM SACHET 1973-76
(Left) 1.25 oz. cream colored milk glass with cream colored plastic lid. Came in Sonnet, Moonwind or Occur!. OSP $3. **CMV $5. MB, $4. BO.**

HANDY FROG 1975-76
(Right) 8 oz. white milk glass with red cap. OSP $6. **CMV $8. MB, $6. BO.**

SNOW BUNNY 1975-76
3 oz. clear glass with gold cap. Holds Moonwind, Charisma, Bird of Paradise or Sweet Honesty cologne. OSP $4. **CMV $6. MB, $4. BO.**

LA BELLE TELEPHONE 1974-76
1 oz. clear glass with gold top. Holds Moonwind, Sonnet or Charisma perfume concentre. OSP $7. **CMV $9. MB, $7. BO.**

TEDDY BEAR 1976-78
.75 oz. frosted glass, gold cap. Came in Sweet Honesty or Topaze. SSP $3. **CMV $5 MB, $4. BO.**

PRECIOUS DOE 1976-78
1/2 oz. frosted glass bottle. Came in Field Flowers or Sweet Honesty. SSP $3. **CMV $5 MB, $4. BO.**

HIGH-BUTTONED SHOE 1975-76
2 oz. clear glass with gold cap. holds Occur! or Unforgettable cologne. OSP $3. **CMV $5. MB, $4. BO.**

GRACEFUL GIRAFFE 1976
1.5 oz. clear glass with plastic top. Holds Topaze or To A Wild Rose cologne. OSP $4. **CMV $6. MB, $5. BO.**

GOOD LUCK ELEPHANT 1975-76
1.5 oz. frosted glass, gold cap. holds Sonnet, Imperial Garden or Patchwork cologne. OSP $3. **CMV $5. MB, $4. BO.**

SWISS MOUSE 1974-75
3 oz. frosted glass, gold cap. Holds Roses Roses, Field Flowers or Bird of Paradise cologne. OSP $4. **CMV $7. MB, $5. BO.**

HUGGABLE HIPPO 1980
1.75 oz. white glass. Red hat. Holds Zany cologne or Light Musk After Shave. Comes with card of stick on decals. SSP $4. **CMV $5. MB.**

GREEN-BLUE-BROWN EYED SUSAN COMPACT 1980
3 different color centers with yellow flower rim. SSP $5. **CMV $2. each MB.**

COUNTRY KITCHEN 1973-75
6 oz. white milk glass with red plastic head. Holds moisturized hand lotion. SSP $5. **CMV $8. MB, $6. BO.**

BATH URN 1971-73
5 oz. white glass & cap with gold top plate. Foaming bath oil in Elusive & Charisma or bath foam in Lemon Velvet & Silk & Honey. 6" high. SSP $4. **CMV $7. MB, $5. BO.**

KOFFEE KLATCH 1971-74
5 oz. yellow paint over clear glass pot with gold top. Foaming Bath Oil in Field Flowers, Honeysuckle or Lilac. Also Lemon Velvet Bath Foam. SSP $5. **CMV $8. MB, $6. BO.**

BATH SEASONS 1967
3 oz. foaming oil. Each is white glass & top with orange design in Honeysuckle, green in Lily of the Valley. Lavender in Lilac, yellow in Jasmine. Matching ribbons on each. OSP $2.50 each. **CMV $7. BO each, $10. MB.**

ORIENTAL EGG - CHINESE PHEASANT 1975
Upside down label mistake made at factory. Upside down bottle only. **CMV $18.**

VENETIAN PITCHER COLOGNE MIST 1973-75
3 oz. blue plastic coated bottle with silver plastic top. Came in Imperial Garden, Patchwork, Sonnet or Moonwind. SSP $6. **CMV $5. MB, $3. BO.**

COMPOTE DECANTER 1972-75
5 oz. white milk glass bottle, gold cap. Came in Moonwind, Field Flowers, Elusive or Brocade. SSP $5. **CMV $7. MB, $5. BO.**

VICTORIAN MANOR 1972-73
(Left) 5 oz. white painted over clear glass with pink plastic roof. Holds Roses Roses, Bird of Paradise, Unforgettable, Cotillion. SSP $5. **CMV $9. MB, $8. BO.**

HOBNAIL DECANTER 1972-74
(Center) 5 oz. white opal glass. Came in Moonwind, Elusive, Roses Roses Bath Foam, Lemon Velvet Bath Foam. SSP $6. **CMV $6. MB, $4. BO.**

HOBNAIL BUD VASE 1973-74
(Right) 4 oz. white milk glass with red & yellow roses. Holds Charisma, Topaze, Roses Roses cologne. SSP $6. **CMV $6. MB, $4. BO.** Also came 4.75 oz. size.

ROYAL COACH 1972-73
5 oz. white milk glass, gold cap. Holds Moonwind, Bird of Paradise, Charisma or Field Flowers foaming bath oil. OSP $5. **CMV $8. MB, $6. BO.**

SITTING PRETTY 1971-73
4 oz. white milk glass with gold cat cap. Came in Topaze, Rapture, Cotillion, Somewhere or persian Wood. OSP $5. **CMV $9. MB, $7. BO.**

FRAGRANCE HOURS 1971-73
6 oz. ivory glass grandfathers clock, gold cap. Bird of Paradise, Field Flowers, Charisma or Elusive. SSP $5. **CMV $8. MB, $6. BO.**

EIFFEL TOWER 1970
3 oz., 9" high clear glass with gold cap. Came in Occur!, Rapture, Somewhere, Topaze, Cotillion or Unforgettable. SSP $4. **CMV $9. MB, $6. BO.**

BUTTERCUP CANDLESTICK 1974
(Left) 6 oz. white milk glass, yellow & white flowers. Holds Moonwind, Sonnet or Imperial Garden cologne. OSP $7. First issue has yellow band around neck. **CMV $9. MB.** Later issue was plain with no band on neck and yellow or brown decals. **CMV $7. MB, $2. less no box.**

BUTTERCUP FLOWER HOLDER 1974
(Center) 5 oz. milk glass with plastic white top. Holds Moonwind, Imperial Garden or Sonnet. OSP $5. **CMV $5. MB, $3. BO.**

BUTTERCUP SALT SHAKER 1974
(Right) 1.5 oz. white milk glass with yellow & white flowers, yellow plastic cap. Came in Moonwind, Sonnet or Imperial Garden. OSP $2.50. **CMV $3. MB, $2. BO.**

DUTCH TREAT DEMI-CUPS 1971
3 oz. white glass filled with Cream Lotion in Honeysuckle, yellow cap; Blue lotus, blue cap; Hawaiian White Ginger, pink cap. OSP $3.50. **CMV $8. MB, $6. BO.** Also each came with white caps.

SALT SHAKERS 1968-70
3 oz. pink ribbon, pink flowers. Yellow ribbon & flowers in Hawaiian Ginger White, Honeysuckle & Lilac bath oil. OSP $2.50. **CMV $8. MB each, $6. BO.**

SWEET SHOPPE PIN CUSHION 1972-74
(Left) 1 oz. white milk glass bottom with white plastic back with hot pink pin cushion seat. Came in Sonnet, Moonwind, Field Flowers, Roses Roses, Bird of Paradise or Charisma. SSP $4. **CMV $7. MB, $5. BO.**

FRAGRANCE TOUCH 1969-70
(Right) 3 oz. white milk glass. Cologne came in Elusive, Charisma, Brocade or Regence. OSP $5. **CMV $6. MB, $4. BO.**

BLUE DEMI-CUP 1968-70
(Left) 3 oz. white glass, blue cap & design, some came with gold top with blue lid. Came in Brocade, Topaze or Unforgettable. OSP $3.50. **CMV $8. MB, $6. BO.**

DEMI-CUP 1969-70
(Center Two) 3 oz. white milk glass. Charisma has red cap and design. Regence has green cap and design. OSP $3.50. **CMV $8. MB, $6. BO.**

TO A WILD ROSE DEMI-CUP 1969
(Right) 3 oz. white glass, red rose, pink cap. 6 1/2" high. Contains Foaming Bath Oil. OSP $3.50. **CMV $9. MB, $7. BO.**

VICTORIANA SOAP DISH 1978
Blue marbleized glass - white soap. May 1978 on bottom. SSP $5. **CMV $7., $4. no box, $2. dish only.**

VICTORIANA PITCHER & BOWL 1978
Blue marbleized glass bowl and 6 oz. pitcher. Holds bubble bath. May 1978 on bottom. SSP $9. **CMV $9. MB, $6. no box.**

ENCHANTED HOURS 1972-73
(Left) 5 oz. blue glass bottle with gold cap. Came in Roses Roses, Charisma, Unforgettable or Somewhere cologne. SSP $5. **CMV $8. MB, $6. BO.**

BEAUTIFUL AWAKENING 1973-74
(Right) 3 oz. gold painted over clear glass front paper clock face, gold cap. Came in Elusive, Roses Roses or Topaze. SSP $5. **CMV $6. BO, $7. MB.**

LEISURE HOURS 1970-72
5 oz. white milk glass bottle contains foaming bath oil in 6 fragrances. Gold cap. OSP $4. **CMV $6., $8. MB.**

LEISURE HOURS MINIATURE 1974
1.5 oz. white milk glass bottle, gold cap. Holds Field Flowers, Bird of Paradise or Charisma cologne. OSP $3. **CMV $5., $6. MB.**

ORIENTAL EGG CHINESE PHEASANT 1975
(Left) 1 oz. white opal glass, black plastic base. Came in Imperial Garden, Charisma and Bird of Paradise cologne. OSP $6.50. **CMV $14. MB, $11. BO.**

ORIENTAL EGG PEACH ORCHARD 1974-75
(Right) 1 oz. white opal glass with green marbleized plastic base. Came in Imperial Garden, Sonnet or Moonwind or Patchwork perfume concentre. SSP $5. **CMV $14. MB, $11. BO.**

ORIENTAL EGG DELICATE BLOSSOMS 1975-76
(Center) 1 oz. light blue opal glass with blue-green plastic base. Came in Patchwork, Sonnet & Charisma cologne. OSP $7.50. **CMV $14. MB, $11. BO.**

LOVABLE SEAL 1976-77
1 oz. frosted glass, gold cap. Came in Cotillion or Here's My Heart. OSP $4. **CMV $4. MB, $2. BO.**

LOVE BIRD 1978
1 1/2 oz. milk glass bottle with gold cap. Came in Charisma or Moonwind cologne. SSP $4. **CMV $4. MB, $2. BO.**

HEARTSCENT CREAM SACHET 1976-77
.66 oz. white glass bottom with white plastic top. Gold dove design. Came in Charisma, Occur! or Roses Roses. OSP $3. **CMV $4. MB, $3. BO.**

FOSTORIA COMPOTE 1975-76
12 Skin-So-Soft capsules. Clear glass with glass top. OSP $8. **CMV $6. MB, $5. BO**

GRECIAN PITCHER 1972-76
6 1/2" high, 5 oz. white glass bottle & white stopper holds Skin-So-Soft. SSP $5. **CMV $7. MB, $5. BO.**

CORNUCOPIA 1971-76
6 oz. white glass, gold cap. 5 1/2" high. SSP $5. **CMV $7. MB, $5. BO.**

BUTTERFLY FANTASY PORCELAIN TREASURE EGG 1974-80
5 1/2" long white porcelain multi-colored butterfly decals. Sold empty. 1974 stamped on bottom. Sold 1974-75 then reissued 1978. The 1978 issue was a 1974 "R" for reissue on bottom and the big butterfly on top is much lighter than the 1974 issue. OSP $12. **CMV $25. MB for 1974 issue. CMV $15. MB for 1974 "R" issue.** 1979-80 issue has "R" 1979 on bottom, **CMV $15. MB.** Also came with bottom label upside down or backwards, **Add $6. CMV.**

VICTORIANA PITCHER & BOWL 1971-72
6 oz. turquoise glass pitcher with Skin-So-Soft bath oil & turquoise glass bowl with Avon bottom. Some bowls have double Avon stamp on bottom. OSP $7.50. **CMV $11. MB, $9. no box, $12. with double stamp on bottom.**

VICTORIANA PITCHER & BOWL 1972-73
Same as above only came in Moonwind, Field Flowers Foaming Bath Oil. SSP $7. **CMV $8. no box, $11. MB.**

VICTORIANA POWDER SACHET 1972-74
1.5 oz. turquoise glass jar & lid. Came in Moonwind, Field Flowers. SSP $5. **CMV $6. BO, $8. MB.**

VICTORIANA DISH & SOAP 1972-73
Turquoise glass dish with white soap. SSP $4. **CMV $8. MB, dish only $3.**

SECRETAIRE 1972-75
7" high, pink paint over clear glass, gold cap. Holds 5 oz. of Foaming Bath Oil in Moonwind, Charisma, Brocade, Lilac & Lemon Velvet. OSP $6. **CMV $10. MB, $7. BO.**

ARMOIRE 1972-75
7" high, 5 oz. white glass bottle with gold cap. Choice of Field Flowers, Bird of Paradise, Elusive or Charisma bath oil. 1975 came in Field Flowers, Charisma & Bird of Paradise only. SSP $4. **CMV $8. MB, $6. BO.**

FRENCH TELEPHONE 1971
6 oz. white milk glass base with gold cap & trim. Holds Foaming Bath Oil. Center of receiver holds 1/4 oz. of perfume in frosted glass. Came in Moonwind. OSP $22. Bird of Paradise, Elusive or Charisma. OSP $20. **CMV $30. MB, $25. BO.**

CHRISTMAS BELLS 1979-80
1 oz. red glass. Silver cap. Holds Topaze or Sweet Honesty cologne. SSP $3. **CMV $3. MB.**

RED CARDINAL 1979-80
2 oz. clear glass painted red. Red cap. Holds Bird of Paradise or Charisma cologne. SSP $5. **CMV $6. MB.**

SILVER SWIRLS SALT SHAKER 1977-79
3 oz. silver plated over clear glass. Silver top. Came in Sweet Honesty or Topaze cologne. SSP $4. **CMV $4. MB, $2. BO.**

ISLAND PARAKEET 1977-78
1.5 oz. blue glass base & blue & yellow plastic top. Approx. 4 1/2" high. Came in Moonwind or Charisma Cologne. OSP $6. **CMV $6. MB, $4. BO.**

WOMEN'S DECANTERS, CERAMICS & FIGURINES

REGAL PEACOCK 1973-74
4 oz. blue glass with gold cap. Came in Patchwork, Sonnet or Moonwind. SSP $6. **CMV $10. MB, $7. BO.**

PRECIOUS HEARTS 1980
(Left) Heart embossed clear glass, 5 oz. gold tone cap. Comes in Here's My Heart, Unforgettable, Moonwind, Topaze or Sweet Honesty. SSP $1.29. **CMV $1. MB.**
FLUFFY CHICK 1980
(Center) 1 oz. clear glass yellow flock coated. Holds Hello Sunshine cologne. SSP $6. **CMV $4. MB.**
FLUTTERING FANCY 1980
(Right) 1 oz. clear glass with pink butterfly on yellow frosted plastic cap. Holds Sweet Honesty or Charisma cologne. SSP $5. **CMV $5. MB.**

SNOW OWL POWDER SACHET II 1979-80
(Left) 1.25 oz. frosted glass. Holds Moonwind or Timeless powder sachet. Blue Rhinestone eyes. Label in black lettering. SSP $7. **CMV $7. MB.**
CUTE COOKIE 1979-80
(Center) 1 oz. dark amber glass. Pink cap & point. Holds Hello Sunshine cologne. SSP $2.75. **CMV $2.75 MB.**
CHARMING CHIPMUNK 1979-80
(Right) 5 oz. clear glass painted frosted peach color. Holds Field Flowers or Sweet Honesty. SSP $4. **CMV $4. MB.**

FLAMINGO 1971-72
5 oz. clear bird shaped bottle with gold cap. 10" tall. Came in Bird of Paradise, Elusive, Charisma, Brocade. SSP $4.50. **CMV $7. MB, $4. BO.**
SWAN LAKE 1972-76
8" high, 3 oz. white glass bottle with white cap. Came in Bird of Paradise, Charisma & Elusive. Moonwind SSP $5. **CMV $8. MB, $6. BO.**
BATH URN (CRUET) 1963-64
8 oz. white glass top & bottle. Perfume bath oil in Somewhere, Topaze, Cotillion. OSP $3.75 each. Here's My Heart, Persian Wood, To A Wild Rose. OSP $3.50 each. **CMV $12. MB, $6. bottle with label.**

COUNTRY STORE COFFEE MILL 1972-76
5 oz. ivory milk glass, white plastic cap & plastic handles on side with gold rim. Came in Sonnet, Moonwind, Bird of Paradise, Charisma cologne. SSP $6. **CMV $10. MB, $7. BO.** Came in 2 different size boxes.
LITTLE DUTCH KETTLE 1972-73
5 oz. orange painted clear glass with gold cap. Came in Cotillion, Honeysuckle Foaming Bath Oil or Lemon Velvet Bath Foam. SSP $5. **CMV $7. MB, $5. BO.**

SILVER DOVE ORNAMENT 1976
1/2 oz. bottle with gold or silver cap. Came in silver metal bird holder marked Christmas '76 on both sides & Avon on inside. Came in Bird of Paradise or Occur! cologne. SSP $4. **CMV $6. MB, $4. no box.**

SONG BIRD 1971-72
1.5 oz. clear glass with gold base cap. Came in Unforgettable, Topaze, Occur!, Here's My Heart & Cotillion. OSP $3. **CMV $6. MB, $4. BO.**
BIRD OF HAPPINESS 1975-76
1.5 oz. light blue glass, gold cap. Holds Charisma, Topaze, Occur!, or Unforgettable cologne. OSP $3. **CMV $5. MB, $4. BO.**

DR. HOOT 1977-79
(Left) 4 oz. white milk glass owl with blue plastic cap and white, gold or green tassel. Came in Sweet Honesty or Wild Country. OSP $7.50. **CMV $7. MB, $5. BO.**
DR. HOOT 1975-76
4 oz. opal white glass, black cap, gold tassel. Holds Wild Country After Shave or Sweet Honesty cologne. OSP $5. **CMV $8. MB, $6. BO.**
PRECIOUS OWL 1972-74
(Center) 1 1/2 oz. white bottle with gold eyes. Came in Moonwind, Field Flowers, Charisma, Roses Roses. OSP $3. **CMV $5. MB, $3. BO.**
SNOW OWL 1976-77
(Right) 1.25 oz. frosted glass base and frosted plastic head with blue eyes. Came in Moonwind or Sonnet. Label in blue lettering. SSP $4. **CMV $5. MB, $4. BO.**

ROYAL SWAN 1971-72
1 oz. white glass, gold crown cap. Came in Elusive, Charisma, Bird of Paradise, Topaze, Unforgettable, Cotillion. SSP $3. **CMV $7. MB, $5. BO.**
ROYAL SWAN 1974
1 oz. blue glass with gold crown cap. Came in Unforgettable, Topaze, Cotillion, Here's My Heart. SSP $2.50. **CMV $6. BO, $8. MB.**

CRYSTAL FACETS 1973-75
3 oz. clear glass. Choice of Roses Roses or Field Flowers. OSP $4. **CMV $4. MB, $3. BO.**

OWL FANCY 1974-76
4 oz. clear glass. Came in Raining Violets or Roses Roses. SSP $4. **CMV $4. MB, $3. BO.**

SNOW BIRD 1973-74
1.5 oz. white milk glass, white plastic cap. Came in Patchwork, Moonwind, Sonnet Cream Sachet. OSP $2.50. **CMV $4. MB, $3. BO.**

ROBIN RED-BREAST 1974-75
2 oz. red frosted glass with silver plastic top. Holds Charisma, Roses Roses, Bird of Paradise. OSP $4. **CMV $4. MB, $3. BO.**

FLIGHT TO BEAUTY 1975
5 oz. glass jar with white frosted top. Holds Rich Moisture or Vita-Moist Cream or SSS Skin Softener. OSP $5. **CMV $4. MB, $3. BO.**

PARTRIDGE 1973-75
5 oz. white milk glass with white plastic lid. Came in Unforgettable, Topaze, Occur!, Somewhere. OSP $5. **CMV $5. MB, $4. BO.**

CRYSTALSONG BELL 1975-76
4 oz. red glass with frosted bow and handle. Holds Timeless or Sonnet. OSP $6. **CMV $6. BO, $8. MB.**

CHRISTMAS BELLS 1974-75
1 oz. red painted glass with gold cap. Came in Topaze, Occur!, Cotillion To A Wild Rose or Sweet Honesty. OSP $2.25. **CMV $4. BO, $5. MB.**

FRAGRANCE BELL 1968-69
(Left) 1 oz. gold handle. Bell actually rings. Came in Charisma, Brocade, Regence, Unforgettable, Rapture, Occur!, Somewhere, Topaze, Cotillion, Here's My Heart, To A Wild Rose, Wishing. OSP $3.50. **CMV bell with tag $15., $20. MB.**

FRAGRANCE BELL 1965-66
(Center) 4 oz. clear glass, plastic handle, neck tag. Came in Rapture, Occur!, Somewhere, Topaze, Cotillion, Here's My Heart, To A Wild Rose, Wishing. OSP $3.50. **CMV bell with tag $15., $20. MB.**

HOBNAIL BELL 1973-74
(Right) 2 oz. white milk glass with gold handle & gold bell underneath. Holds Unforgettable, Topaze, Here's My Heart, To A Wild Rose or Sweet Honesty. SSP $4. **CMV $6. MB, $5. BO.**

JOYOUS BELL 1978
Light blue frosted over clear glass. Silver cap. Came in Charisma or Topaze cologne. In blue & white box. SSP $3. **CMV $5. MB.**

SUNNY SHINE UP 1978-79
White plastic base with yellow screw on egg lid. SSP $3. **CMV $1. MB.**

ROSEPOINT BELL 1978
(Left) 4 oz. clear glass, clear plastic top. Came in Charisma or Roses Roses cologne. OSP $8.50. **CMV $8. MB, $6. BO.**

HOSPITALITY BELL 1976-77
(Right) Silver top, 3.75 oz. blue glass bottom. Came in Moonwind or Roses Roses cologne. Avon 1976 stamped in bottom. OSP $8. **CMV $8. MB, $6. BO.**

GARDEN FRESH DECANTER 1979-80
10 oz. clear glass. Yellow & gold pump & cap. Green box. SSP $7. **CMV $5. MB.**

HEAVENLY CHERUB HOSTESS BELL 1979-80
3.75 oz. clear glass painted frosted tan. Gold plastic handle. 1979 embossed on bottom. Comes in Topaze or Bird of Paradise cologne. SSP $7. **CMV $7. MB.**

KITTEN PETITE 1973-74
1.5 oz. amber glass ball with white plastic cat for cap. Came in Sonnet or Moonwind. SSP $3. **CMV $4. BO, $5. MB.**

MING CAT 1971
6 oz. white glass & head, blue trim & neck ribbon. Came in Moonwind, Bird of Paradise, Elusive, Charisma. SSP $6. **CMV $10. MB, $8. BO.**

KITTEN LITTLE 1972-76
3 1/2" high, white glass bottle holds 1 1/2 oz. cologne in Occur!, Topaze, Unforgettable, Somewhere, Cotillion. SSP $2. **CMV $3. BO, $4. MB.**

MOONLIGHT GLOW ANNUAL BELL 1981-82
3 oz. glass bell, frosted top. Choice of Moonwind or Topaze. SSP $9. **CMV $9. MB.**

SITTING PRETTY 1976-77
1.5 oz. white milk glass base, white plastic top. Came in Charisma or Topaze. Pink ribbons painted on each corner. OSP $6. **CMV $8. MB, $6. BO.**

ROYAL ELEPHANT 1977-79
1/2 oz. white milk glass with gold snap on top. Came in Charisma or Topaze. OSP $6. **CMV $6. MB, $5. BO.**

CURIOUS KITTY 1979-80
2.5 oz. clear glass, yellow cat cap. Came in Sweet Honesty or Here's My Heart cologne. SSP $6. **CMV $6. MB, $4. BO.**

PEEK A MOUSE CHRISTMAS STOCKING 1978-79
1.25 oz. green glass with gold mouse cap. Holds Sweet Honesty or Unforgettable cologne. Came with red velvet stocking with gold trim. SSP $5. **CMV $6. MB, $3. BO.**

ROYAL SIAMESE CAT 1978-79
Light gray paint over clear glass. 4.5 oz. gray plastic head has blue glass jewel eyes. Came in Cotillion or Moonwind cologne. SSP $7. **CMV $7. MB, $6. BO.**

EMERALD BELL 1978-79
3.75 oz. light green glass. Gold and green plastic cap. Bottom has "Avon 1978" embossed. Came in Sweet Honesty or Roses Roses cologne. SSP $6. **CMV $6. MB, $4. BO.**

KITTEN LITTLE 1975-76
1.5 oz. black glass with black head. Holds Sweet Honesty, Bird of Paradise or Roses Roses. OSP $4. **CMV $6. MB, $4. BO.**

TABATHA 1975-76
3 oz. black glass and plastic. Holds Imperial Garden, Bird of Paradise or Cotillion cologne. OSP $6. **CMV $7. MB, $5. BO.**

MANSION LAMP 1975-76
6 oz. blue glass with white plastic top. Holds Bird of Paradise or Moonwind cologne. OSP $8. **CMV $10. MB, $8. BO.**

EMPIRE GREEN BUD VASE 1975
3 oz. green glass with silver base. Holds moonwind, Sonnet or Imperial Garden cologne. OSP $6. **CMV $5. MB, $3. BO.**

BUTTERFLY GARDEN BUD VASE 1975-76
6 oz. black glazed glass with gold stopper. Holds Roses Roses, Bird of Paradise or Topaze cologne. OSP $6. **CMV $6. MB, $4. BO.**

SEAGREEN BUD VASE 1972-73
5 oz. 9" high green glass bottle holds foaming bath oil in Field Flowers, Honeysuckle or Bird of Paradise. SSP $4. **CMV $4. MB, $2. BO.**

LADY SPANIEL 1974-76
1.5 oz. opal glass with plastic head. Holds Patchwork, Sonnet or Moonwind cologne. OSP $3. **CMV $5. MB, $4. BO.**

KITTEN'S HIDEAWAY 1974-76
1 oz. amber basket, white plastic kitten cap. Came in Field Flowers, Bird of Paradise or Charisma Cream Sachet. OSP $4. **CMV $6. MB, $4. BO.**

BLUE EYES 1975-76
1.5 oz. opal glass with blue rhinestone eyes. Available in Topaze or Sweet Honesty cologne. OSP $4. **CMV $5. BO, $7. MB.**

SEA TREASURE 1971-72
5 oz. clear glass coated iridescent sea shell shaped bottle, gold cap. Came in Field Flowers, Charisma, Honeysuckle, Lilac. 7" long. SSP $5. **CMV $10. MB, $7. BO.**

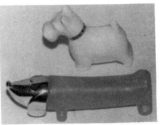

PRINCESS OF YORKSHIRE 1976-78
(Left) 1 oz. off white over milk glass. Came in Sweet Honesty or Topaze cologne. SSP $4. **CMV $5. MB, $4. BO.**

ROYAL PEKINESE 1974-75
(Center) 1.5 oz. white glass & white plastic head. Came in Unforgettable, Somewhere, Topaze. OSP $5. **CMV $7. MB, $5. BO.**

FUZZY BEAR 1977-79
(Right) Tan flock over clear glass base & head. Came in Sweet Honesty or Occur! OSP $6.50. **CMV $6.50 MB, $4. BO.**

TIFFANY LAMP 1972-74
5 oz. brown glass base with pink shade, pink and orange flowers, green leaves on lavender background. Came in Sonnet, Moonwind, Field Flowers, Roses Roses. SSP $7. **CMV $12. MB, $9. BO.** Also came in pink and yellow flowers on shade, also all white flowers. **CMV $13. MB.**

HEARTH LAMP 1973-76
8 oz. black glass with gold handle, has daisies around neck with yellow & white shade. Holds Roses Roses, Bird of Paradise or Elusive. SSP $8. **CMV $12. MB, $9. BO.**

CHIMNEY LAMP 1973-74
2 oz. clear glass bottom with white plastic shade with pink flowers. Holds Patchwork Sonnet or Moonwind. SSP $4. **CMV $6. MB, $5. BO.**

QUEEN OF SCOTS 1973-76
1 oz. white milk glass, white plastic head. Came in Sweet Honesty, Unforgettable, Somewhere, Cotillion, Here's My Heart. SSP $3. **CMV $6. MB, $4. BO.**

DACHSUND 1973-74
1.5 oz. frosted glass, gold cap. Came in Unforgettable, Somewhere, Topaze, Cotillion. SSP $3. **CMV $7. MB, $5. BO.**

SEA SPIRIT 1973-76
5 oz. light green glass with green plastic tail over cap. Holds Elusive, Topaze or Cotillion. OSP $5. **CMV $7. MB, $5. BO.**

SONG OF THE SEA 1974-75
80 bath pearls, aqua colored glass with plastic head. Holds Moonwind, Sonnet or Imperial Garden. OSP $7. **CMV $8. MB, $6. BO.**

EUROPEAN DOLPHIN
(Right) Bath oil, 165 cc size, frosted glass, gold tail cap. Foreign Dolphin smaller than U.S. size. **CMV $25.**

DOLPHIN 1968-69
(Left) 8 oz. frosted glass with gold tail cap. Sold in U.S.A. SSP $4. **CMV $9. MB, $5. BO.**

DOLPHIN FROM MEXICO
(Center) About same size as American Dolphin, only bottle is clear glass, with gold tail. Also came in frosted glass. **CMV $20. each.**

FLORAL BUD VASE 1973-75
5 oz. white milk glass. Holds Roses Roses, Lemon Velvet Bath Foam, Field Flowers or Honeysuckle Foaming Bath Oil. SSP $5. **CMV $6. MB, $5. Bo.**

SUZETTE 1973-76
5 oz. cream colored milk glass with cream colored plastic head & a pink-lavender bow around neck. Holds Field Flowers, Bird of Paradise or Cotillion Foaming Bath Oil. SSP $5. **CMV $9. MB, $6. BO.**

BUTTERFLY 1972-73
1 1/2 oz. 3 1/2" high, gold cap with 2 prongs. Holds cologne in Occur!, Topaze, Unforgettable, Somewhere & Here's My Heart. SSP $3. **CMV $7. MB, $5. BO.** Reissued in 1976 in Field Flowers & Sweet Honesty. **Same CMV.**

DOLPHIN MINIATURE 1973-74
1.5 oz. clear glass, gold tail. Holds Charisma, Bird of Paradise or Field Flowers cologne. OSP $3. **CMV $5. MB, $3. BO.**

CRYSTAL POINT SALT SHAKER 1976-77
1.5 oz. blue glass. Holds Sonnet or Cotillion cologne. OSP $3. **CMV $4. MB, $2. BO.**

PARISIAN GARDEN 1974-75
.33 oz. white milk glass with gold cap. Came in Sonnet, moonwind or Charisma perfume. OSP $5. **CMV $5. MB, $4. BO.**

EVENING GLOW 1974-75
.33 oz. white milk glass with green flowers, white and gold plastic cap. Came in Moonwind, Sonnet or Charisma. OSP $6. **CMV $6. BO, $7. MB.**

FRAGRANCE SPLENDOR 1971-74
4 1/2" high clear glass bottle with gold cap & frosted plastic handle. Holds perfume oil in Bird of Paradise, Elusive, Occur!, Charisma or Unforgettable. OSP $5. **CMV $6. MB, $4. BO.**

BON BON "BLACK" 1973
1 oz. black milk glass with black plastic cap. Holds Field Flowers, Bird of Paradise, Roses Roses or Elusive. OSP $2. **CMV $7. MB, $5. BO.**

BON BON "WHITE" 1972-73
1 oz. white milk glass with white cap. Holds Unforgettable, Topaze, Occur!, Cotillion or Here's My Heart cologne. OSP $2. **CMV $7. MB, $5. BO.**

SEA HORSE 1970-72
Clear glass 6 oz. container holds Skin-So-Soft, gold cap. SSP $5. **CMV $9. MB, $7. BO.**

SEA HORSE MINIATURE COLOGNE 1973-76
1.5 oz. clear glass, gold cap. Came in Unforgettable, Here's My Heart, Cotillion. SSP $3. **CMV $6. MB, $5. BO.**

MING BLUE LAMP 1974-76
5 oz. blue glass lamp, white plastic shade with gold tip. Holds Charisma, Bird of Paradise or Field FLowers Foaming Bath Oil. OSP $6. **CMV $8. MB, $6. BO.**

CHARMLIGHT 1975-76
.88 oz. cream sachet in white shade and 2 oz. cologne in pink base. Holds Imperial Garden, Sonnet or Moonwind. OSP $7. **CMV $8. MB, $6. BO.**

AVONSHIRE DECANTER 1979
6 oz. clear glass painted blue and white. Holds Charisma or Somehwere cologne. R on bottom for Reissue and dated May, 1979. SSP $9. **CMV $9. MB.**

AVONSHIRE BATH OIL DECANTER
6 oz. clear glass painted blue and white. Holds Skin-So-Soft. R on bottom for reissue and dated May, 1979. SSP $10. **CMV $8. MB.**

AVONSHIRE HOSTESS SOAPS
Blue box holds 3 white bars. SSP $4. **CMV $6. MB.**

COUNTRY CHARM 1976-77
(Left) 4.8 oz. white milk glass, yellow stove window. Green & white plastic top. Came in Field Flowers or Sonnet. SSP $7. **CMV $8. BO, $10. MB.**

HURRICANE LAMP 1973-74
(Right) 6 oz. white milk glass bottom with clear glass shade, gold cap. Holds Roses Roses, Field Flowers, Bird of Paradise or Charisma cologne. SSP $8. **CMV $13. MB, $10. BO.**

SKIN-SO-SOFT DECANTER 1966
(Left) 10 oz. bottle with glass & cork stopper. 10" high. OSP $5. **CMV $8. BO, $12. MB.**

SKIN-SO-SOFT DECANTER 1967
(Right) 8 oz. bottle with glass & cork stopper. 11" high. OSP $5. **CMV $8. BO, $12. MB.**

PARLOR LAMP 1971-72
2 sections. Gold cap over 3 oz. cologne top section in light amber iridescent glass. Yellow frosted glass bottom with talc 6 1/2" high. Holds Bird of Paradise, Elusive, Charisma, Regence or Moonwind. OSP $7. **CMV $14. MB, $10. BO.**

COURTING LAMP 1970-71
5 oz. blue glass base with white milk glass shade & blue velvet ribbon. Holds Elusive, Brocade, Charisma, Hana Gasa or Regence. OSP $6. **CMV $14. MB, $10. BO.**

FLOWER FANCY 1979-80
1.25 oz. clear glass, gold flower cap. Holds Field Flowers or Roses Roses. SSP $4. **CMV $4. MB.**

SPRING SONG 1979-80
1.5 oz. clear glass. Comes with plastic frosted flower stopper. Came in Lily of the Valley or Sweet Honesty cologne. SSP $6. **CMV $6. MB.**

SKIN-SO-SOFT DECANTER 1965-66
10. oz. bottle with gold painted glass stopper. 1st issue came with solid painted gold around center & later issue not solid band as pictured. OSP $5. **CMV solid band $13. MB, $9. BO mint. Not solid band $12. MB, $8. BO mint.**

CREAMERY DECANTER 1973-75
8 oz. yellow painted over clear glass with brown basket of blue & orange flowers. Holds Roses Roses, Field Flowers, Bird of Paradise hand & body cream lotion. OSP $5. **CMV $10. MB, $7. BO.**

LIQUID MILK BATH 1975-76
6 oz. frosted glass bottle with gold cap. Holds Imperial Garden, Sonnet or Moonwind. OSP $5. **CMV $5. MB, $3. BO.**

SKIN-SO-SOFT DECANTER 1964
(Left) 6 oz. gold crown top, came with gold neck tag. OSP $3.50. **CMV $12. MB, $6. BO with tag, mint.**

SKIN-SO-SOFT DECANTER 1962-63
(Right) 5 3/4 oz. gold neck string with white label, pink & white box. OSP $3.50. **CMV $12. MB, BO $5. mint with tag.**

COUNTRY STYLE COFFEE POT 1979-80
Came in special color of box. 10 oz. clear glass painted red or green, blue or yellow. Holds moisturized hand lotion. Comes with matching hand pump. SSP $8. **CMV $8. MB.**

OOPS COLOGNE DECANTER 1981
(Left) White glass, brown spots. Ice Cream bottle with tan plastic cone top. 1.5 oz. Sweet Honesty or Country Breeze. SSP $6. **CMV $6. MB.**

BIG SPENDER 1981-82
(Center) 1 oz. green glass, silver cap. Light Musk for men or Sweet Honesty cologne. SSP $4. **CMV $4. MB.**

ULTRA CRYSTAL COLOGNE 1981-82
(Right) Gray box holds 2 oz. clear glass & glass cap. Choice of Tasha, Foxfire, Timeless, Ariane. SSP $10. **CMV $3. MB.** See Soap Dish section & Candle section for other Ultra Crystal Collections.

HUDSON MANOR COLLECTION 1978-79
SALTCELLAR CANDLE & SPOON
Silver plated. Comes with glass lined candle. Bottom says HMC Avon Silver Plate on both pieces. Silver and white box. SSP $19. **CMV $19. MB.**

SILVER PLATED DISH AND SATIN SACHET
6" silver plated dish with red satin sachet pillow. Bottom of dish says Avon Silver Plate HMC, Italy. SSP $19. **CMV $15. MB.**

SILVER PLATED HOSTESS BELL
5 1/2" high silver plated bell. Avon Silver Plate HMC on bottom. SSP $19. **CMV $19. MB.**

SILVER PLATED BUD VASE AND SCENTED ROSE
8" high silver plated bud vase. Came with long stemmed fabric rose and 2 Roses Roses pellets. SSP $19. **CMV $15. MB.**

BATH SEASONS 1969
(Left) 3 oz. bath oil. Came in Charisma & Brocade. Black milk glass with silver cap & base. OSP $4.50. **CMV $6. MB, $4. BO.**

EMOLLIENT FRESHENER FOR AFTER BATH 1972-74
(Center) 6 oz. clear glass with gold cap, holds Sonnet, Charisma, Imperial Garden or Moonwind pearlescent liquid. SSP $4. **CMV $3. MB, $1. BO.**

AMBER CRUET 1973-75
(Right) 6 oz. light amber ribbed glass. Holds Field Flowers, Bird of Paradise or Charisma foaming bath oil. SSP $5. **CMV $5. MB, $3. BO.** 1975 Came only in Field Flowers & Bird of Paradise.

LADY SKATER TALC 1979-80
3.75 oz. gold top can. Red cap. Choice of Ariane or Sweet Honesty talc. SSP $4. **CMV $2. mint, no box issued.**

GENTLEMAN SKATER TALC 1979-80
3.75 oz. gold top can. Blue cap. Choice of Clint or Trazarra talc. SSP $4. **CMV $2. mint. No box issued.**

COUNTRY CREAMERY "MILK CAN" 1978-79
10 oz. white painted over clear glass. Holds moisturized hand lotion. SSP $6. **CMV $6. MB.**

ICE CREAM LIP POMADE 1974-76
.13 oz. white plastic bottom with light pink, dark pink, or red top for Cherry, Strawberry or Tutti-Frutti flavors. OSP $2. **CMV $3. BO, $4. MB.**

ICE CREAM CONE LIP POMADE 1974-76
Yellow cone with different color tops for Cherry, Strawberry, Tutti-Frutti, Mint, Chocolate. OSP $2. **CMV $3. BO, $4. MB.**

COLOGNE ELEGANTE 1973-74
3 oz. clear glass, gold cap with atomizer, also white plastic cap. Holds Imperial Garden, Patchwork, Sonnet or Moonwind. SSP $6. **CMV $4. MB, $2. BO.**

COURTING ROSE 1974
1.5 oz. red glass rose with gold cap & stem. Came in Moonwind, Sonnet or Imperial Garden. SSP $5. Later issue painted red over clear glass. **CMV $7. MB each.**

SWEET TREAT COLOGNE 1974-76
White & brown painted glass with red cap. Came in Pink & Pretty cologne. SSP $2.50. **CMV $4. MB.**

COURTING ROSE 1977
(Right) 1.5 oz. amber coated over clear glass rose bottle with gold top. Came in Roses Roses or Moonwind cologne. SSP $5. **CMV $6. MB, $5. BO.**

PYRAMID OF FRAGRANCE 1969
Top is 1/8 oz. perfume, gold cap. Center is 2 oz. cologne. Bottom is 2-3 oz. cream sachet in black glass. 6" high, came in Charisma, Brocade or Regence. OSP $12.50. **CMV $12.50, $20. MB.**

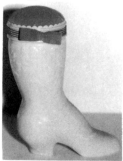

FASHION BOOT PIN CUSHION 1972-76
5 1/2" tall, blue milk glass with lavender bow & velvet cushion that fits over cap. Holds 4 oz. cologne. Roses Roses or Charisma. Regular price $6. Sonnet or Moonwind SSP $6. **CMV $7. MB, $6. BO.**

PICTURE FRAME COLOGNE 1970-71
4 oz. gold paint on clear glass. Gold cap & gold plastic frame to hold bottle. Came in Elusive, Charisma, Brocade, Regence. SSP $8. **CMV $10. mint, $15. MB.**

ALADDIN'S LAMP 1971-73
7 1/2" long, 6 oz. green glass bottle with gold cap. Holds foaming bath oil in Charisma, Bird of Paradise, Elusive, Occur! or Unforgettable. SSP $7. **CMV $10. MB, $7. BO.**

VENETIAN BLUE 1974-76
Frosted turquoise glass with turquoise plastic lid & gold tip. Holds 75 bath pearls. Came in Moonwind, Sonnet or Imperial Garden. SSP $6. **CMV $6. MB, $4. BO.**

DOVECOTE 1974-76
4 oz. clear glass with gold roof & 2 white doves. Holds Field Flowers, Bird of Paradise, Charisma or Roses Roses cologne. SSP $3. **CMV $4. MB, $2. BO.**

ROYAL APPLE COLOGNE 1972-73
(Left) 3 oz. frosted red glass with gold cap. Came in 4 fragrances. SSP $4. **CMV $7. MB, $5. BO.**

GARNET BUD VASE 1973-76
(Right) 3 oz. garnet colored translucent glass bottle & stopper. Came in Occur!, Somewhere, Topaze or To A Wild Rose cologne. SSP $5. **CMV $5. MB, $3. BO.**

ROYAL VASE 1970
(Left) 3 oz. blue cologne bottle in Elusive, Charisma, Brocade or Regence. OSP $5. **CMV $5. MB, $3. BO.**

RUBY BUD VASE 1970-71
(Right) 3 oz. red box holds ruby glass vase filled with Unforgettable, Rapture, Occur!, Somewhere, Topaze or Cotillion. OSP $5. **CMV $5. MB, $3. BO.**

LOVELY TOUCH DECANTER 1971
(Left) 12 oz. clear glass, gold cap with dispenser cap. Holds Vita Moist or Rich Moisture body lotion. SSP $4. **CMV $3. MB, $2. BO.**

LOVELY TOUCH DECANTER 1972-73
(Inside Left) 12 oz. clear glass with dispenser cap. Holds Vita Moist or Rich Moisture body lotion. SSP $4. **CMV $3. MB, $2. BO.**

CLASSIC BEAUTY 1972-76
(Inside Right) 10 oz. clear glass. Holds Bird of Paradise or Field Flowers hand & body cream. SSP $5. **CMV $3. MB, $2. BO.**

PINEAPPLE 1973-74
(Right) 10 oz. clear glass with green plastic leaves, dispenser top. Holds Moisturized Hand Lotion. SSP $5. **CMV $4. MB, $3. BO.**

GRAPE BUD VASE 1973
(Left) 6 oz. grape frosted glass holds Skin-So-Soft. SSP $5. **CMV $5. MB, $3. BO.**

NILE BLUE BATH URN 1972-74
(Right) 6 oz. deep blue glass with gold trim. SSP $6. **CMV $5. MB, $4. BO.**

NILE GREEN BATH URN 1975
(Right) Same as above only green glass. **CMV $5. MB, $4. BO.**

BELL JAR 1973-75
(Left) 5 oz. clear glass with bouquet of pink & white flowers. Had gold cap & base with pink ribbon. Holds Field Flowers, Bird of Paradise, Charisma or Brocade cologne. SSP $7. **CMV $7. BO, $9. MB.** 1976 sold only in Field Flowers, Bird of Paradise & Charisma. **Same CMV.**

CRUET COLOGNE 1973-74
(Right) 8 oz. clear glass with glass stopper & flat dish. Holds Imperial Garden, Patchwork, Sonnet or Moonwind cologne. SSP $13. **CMV $10. BO & dish, $13. MB.**

CRYSTALIQUE COLOGNE 1975
(Left) 4 oz. clear glass with glass stopper. Holds Moonwind, Sonnet or Imperial Garden. OSP $5. **CMV $5. MB, $3. BO.**

BREATH FRESH APOTHECARY DECANTER 1974
(Center) 8 oz. clear glass with gold cap. Holds Breath Fresh Mouthwash. SSP $3. **CMV $3. MB, $2. BO.**

COUNTRY PUMP 1975
(Right) 10 oz. clear glass with plastic top. Holds Rich Moisture or Vita Moist body lotion. OSP $5. **CMV $4. MB, $3. BO.**

PERSIAN PITCHER 1974-76
(Left) 6 oz. blue glass. Holds Bird of Paradise, Charisma or Elusive foaming bath oil. OSP $5. **CMV $3. MB, $2. BO.**

COLOGNE ELEGANTE 1971-72
(Center) 4 oz. gold sprayed over clear glass & red rose on gold cap. 12" high. Came in Bird of Paradise, Hana Gasa, Elusive or Charisma. OSP $8.50. Moonwind OSP $10. **CMV $10. MB, $7. BO.**

EMERALD BUD VASE 1971
(Right) 3 oz. green glass & glass top, 9" high. Came in Topaze, Occur!, Unforgettable, Here's My Heart or To A Wild Rose. OSP $5. **CMV $4. MB, $3. BO.**

APOTHECARY 1973-74
(Left) 8 oz. Spicy After Shave in light brown glass with gold cap.

APOTHECARY 1973-76
(Center) 8 oz. Lemon Velvet Moisturized Friction Lotion in light yellow glass with gold cap. Also came in light green or blue-green glass.

APOTHECARY 1973
(Right) 8 oz. Breath Fresh in dark green with gold cap.
SSP $3. each. **CMV $6. MB each, $4. BO each.**

SAPPHIRE SWIRL 1973-74
(Left) 5 oz. blue glass with gold cap. Holds Charisma or Bird of Paradise perfumed skin softener. SSP $4. **CMV $1. MB.**

PERIOD PIECE 1972-73
(Right) 5 oz. frosted glass. Came in Moonwind, Bird of Paradise, Charisma or Elusive. 1976 came with Charisma & Bird of Paradise. SSP $6. **CMV $7. MB, $5. BO.**

PETTI FLEUR COLOGNE 1969-70
(Left) 1 oz. gold cap. Shaped like flower. Came in Elusive, Brocade, Charisma or Regence. OSP $2.50. **CMV $7. MB, $5. BO.**

PURSE PETITE COLOGNE 1971
(Right) 1 1/2 oz. embossed bottle with gold trim and cap & chain. Elusive, Charisma, Bird of Paradise, Field Flowers or Hana Gasa. OSP $4. **CMV $8. MB, $6. BO.**

COUNTRY CHARM BUTTER CHURN 1973-74
(Left) 1.5 oz. clear glass, gold bands & cap. Came in Field Flowers, Elusive, Occur! or Somewhere cologne. SSP $3. **CMV $6. MB, $4. BO.**

GOLDEN THIMBLE 1972-74
(Right) 2 oz. clear glass with gold cap. Came in Bird of Paradise, Brocade, Charisma or Elusive cologne. SSP $2. **CMV $5. MB, $3. BO.**

COUNTRY JUG 1976-78
(Left) 10 oz. gray painted over clear glass. Blue & gray plastic pump. Came with almond scented hand lotion. OSP $8. **CMV $5. MB, $4. BO.**

SEA FANTASY BUD VASE 1978-79
(Right) 6 oz. bottle. Gold & white fish & seaweed design on both sides. Holds Skin-So-Soft bath oil, bubble bath & Smooth As Silk. SSP $7. **CMV $4. MB, $3. BO.**

DEW KISS DECANTER 1974-75
(Left) 4 oz. clear glass with pink lid. OSP $3. **CMV $2. MB, $1. BO.**

SEA LEGEND DECANTER 1975-76
(Right) 6 oz. clear glass with white cap. Holds Moonwind or Sonnet foaming bath oil or Roses Roses creamy bath foam. OSP $5. **CMV $4., $3. BO.**

GOLDEN FLAMINGO 1975
(Left) 6 oz. clear glass with gold flamingo on front. Holds Bird of Paradise, Charisma or Field Flowers foaming bath oil. OSP $6. **CMV $4. MB, $2. BO.**

ATHENA BATH URN 1975-76
(Right) 6 oz. clear glass. Holds Field Flowers, Bird of Paradise foaming bath oil or Roses Roses cream bath foam. OSP $6. **CMV $4. MB, $2. BO.**

COUNTRY STYLE COFFEE POT 1975-76
(Left) 10 oz. yellow speckled paint over clear glass. Came with yellow & white pump top. Came with moisturized hand lotion. OSP $6. **CMV $7. MB, $6. BO.**

GOLDEN HARVEST 1977-80
(Right) 10 oz. ear of corn shaped clear & green glass bottle. Gold & plastic pump top. Came with Avon almond scented hand lotion. OSP $8.50. **CMV $6. MB, $5. BO.**

KEEPSAKE CREAM SACHET 1971-73
(Left) 6 1/2" high, gold lid on marbleized glass jar with flower in colors. Came in Moonwind. OSP $5. Bird of Paradise, Field Flowers, Elusive, Charisma. SSP $3. **CMV $4. - $6. MB.**

KEEPSAKE CREAM SACHET 1970-73
(Right) 5 1/2" high gold metal tree lid on .66 oz. frosted glass jar. Came in Bird of Paradise, Elusive, Charisma, Brocade or Regence. SSP $3.50. **CMV $5. - $7. MB.**

BAROQUE CREAM SACHET 1974
(Left) 2 oz. white milk glass with gold top & bottom. Came in Imperial Garden, Sonnet or Moonwind. SSP $5. **CMV $7. MB, $5. BO.**

COUNTRY STORE MINERAL SPRING BATH CRYSTALS 1973-75
(Right) 12 oz. clear glass with gold cap. Holds green Mineral Springs Bath Crystals. SSP $5.50. **CMV $5. MB, $3. BO.**

PORCELAIN FLORAL BOUQUET 1980
(Left) 4" high porcelain. Dated 1980 on bottom. SSP $18. **CMV $18. MB.**

ULTRA MIST ATOMIZER 1980-81
(Right) 1.5 oz. clear swirl glass bottle with gold top & atomizer bulb. Choice of Ariane, Timeless, Tasha or Candid. SSP $11. **CMV $2. MB.**

CRYSTALINE BOWL & FLOWERS 1982
Pink box holds 5" long glass bowl with plastic insert to hold artificial flowers. Comes with fragrance tablet. SSP $18. **CMV $18. MB.**

FOAMING BATH OIL DECANTER 1975
6 oz. clear glass with gold cap. Came in Cotillion, Field Flowers, Bird of Paradise, Charisma, Sonnet, Imperial Garden, Moonwind & Timeless. SSP $2.88. This sold C26 - 1975 only. Very short issue. **CMV $8. MB.** This is the same bottle as the 1972-74 Emollient Freshener for After Bath. Only label & box are changed.

TREE MOUSE 1977-79
(Left) .66 oz. clear glass & clear plastic top. Gold mouse. Came in Sweet Honesty or Charisma. OSP $6. **CMV $4. MB, $2. BO.**
SILVER PEAR 1977
(Center) .66 oz. silver plated over clear glass. Silver top. Came in Sweet Honesty or Charisma. SSP $4. **CMV $3. BO, $4. MB.**
ENCHANTED APPLE 1976-78
(Right) .66 oz. gold plated over clear glass. Gold top. Came in Charisma or Sonnet. OSP $5.50. **CMV $3. BO, $4. MB.**

FLAVOR FRESH APOTHECARY 1977-80
6 oz. clear glass bottle & stopper. Holds mouthwash. OSP $4.50. **CMV $2.50 MB, $1. BO.**

HONEY BEAR BABY 1974-76
4 oz. yellow painted glass with blue plastic bear on lid. SSP $4. **CMV $4. MB, $3. BO.**

PEAR LUMIERE 1975-76
(Left) 2 oz. clear glass & plastic with gold leaf. Holds Roses Roses, Charisma or Bird of Paradise cologne. OSP $5. **CMV $5. MB, $4. BO.**
SONG OF LOVE 1975-76
(Right) 2 oz. clear glass, clear plastic top with white bird. Holds Bird of Paradise, Charisma or Sweet Honesty. 1976 issued with blue base, blue top in Moonwind & Here's My Heart. OSP $4. **CMV $3. MB, $2. BO.**

LOOKING GLASS 1970-72
6 1/2" high, clear glass mirror. Frame holds 1 1/2 oz. cologne in Bird of Paradise, Elusive, Charisma, Brocade, Regence, Unforgettable, Rapture, Occur!, Somewhere, Topaze, Cotillion, Here's My Heart or To A Wild Rose. With gold handle cap. OSP $3.50. **CMV $10. BO, $13. MB.**

WINTER GARDEN 1975-76
(Left) 6 oz. clear glass with gold cap. Holds Here's My Heart, Topaze or Occur! cologne. OSP $5. **CMV $5. MB, $3. BO.**
REGENCY DECANTER 1974-75
(Right) 6 oz. clear glass filled with Skin-So-Soft bath oil. OSP $5. **CMV $5. MB, $3. BO.**

VICTORIAN SEWING BASKET 1974-76
(Left) 5 oz. white milk glass basket with lavender plastic, gold cord holds pink flower. Came in Roses Roses, Bird of Paradise or Charisma perfumed Skin-So-Soft. OSP $4. **CMV $6. MB, $4. BO.**
VANITY JAR 1975-76
(Right) 5 oz. clear glass with silver lid. Choice of Rich Moisture Cream or SSS skin conditioner. OSP $4. **CMV $1. MB.**

CASTLEFORD COLLECTION EMOLLIENT BATH PEARLS 1974-76
(Left) Holds 60 bath pearls. Clear glass. Came in Imperial Garden, Sonnet or Moonwind. OSP $8. **CMV $9. MB, $6. BO.**

CASTLEFORD COLLECTION COLOGNE GELEE 1975-76
(Right) 4 oz. glass holds Raining Violets, Roses Roses or Apple Blossoms cologne gelee. OSP $8. **CMV $8. MB, $6. BO.**

HUMPTY DUMPTY BANK 1982
Box holds ceramic bank made in Korea for Avon. Dated 1982. Sold empty. 5" high. SSP $12. **CMV $12. MB.**

CRYSTAL CLEAR HOSTESS DECANTER 1980-81
Clear glass jar & glass lid, Avon stainless spoon. Comes in 5.5 oz. Strawberry Bubble Bath Gelee. SSP $11. **CMV $6. MB.**

TEATIME POWDER SACHET 1974-75
1.25 oz. frosted white with gold cap. Holds Moonwind, Sonnet or Roses Roses. OSP $4. **CMV $7. MB, $5. BO.**

NATURE'S BEST WOODEN DISPLAY SPOON HOLDER 1981-82
Made of wood, 3 1/2" x 7". Does not say Avon. Comes in Avon box. SSP $7. **CMV $7. MB.**

NATURE'S BEST COLLECTOR'S SPOONS 1981-82
4 different stainless spoons with Avon on them. 5" long in flannel pouch. porcelain inlaid with fruit - strawberry, orange, plum, raspberry. SSP $10. each. **CMV $10. each MB.**

SCENTIMENTS COLOGNE 1978-79
(Left) 2 oz. clear glass. Came with pink card on front to write your own message. Came in Sweet Honesty or Here's My Heart cologne. SSP $4.99. **CMV $4. MB, $2. BO.**

GOLDEN BAMBOO VASE 1978-79
(Right) 1 oz. yellow painted over clear glass, black cap, base. Came in Moonwind or Sweet Honesty cologne. SSP $3. **CMV $4., $3. BO.**

VICTORIAN WASHSTAND 1973-74
(Left) 4 oz. buff painted with gray plastic simulated marble top with blue pitcher & bowl for cap. Came in Field Flowers, Bird of Paradise or Charisma foaming bath oil. SSP $5. **CMV $8. MB, $6. BO.**

REMEMBER WHEN SCHOOL DESK 1972-74
(Right) 4 oz. black glass with light brown plastic seat front & desk top, red apple for cap. Came in Rapture, Here's My Heart, Cotillion or Somewhere cologne. SSP $5. **CMV $8. MB, $6. BO.**

TAPESTRY COLLECTION BELL 1981
5" high white porcelain bell. Dated 1981. Dove on top of bell. SSP $15. **CMV $10. MB.**

TAPESTRY COLLECTION PICTURE FRAME 1981
(Right) 5" high white porcelain picture frame. Dated 1981. SSP $13. **CMV $8. MB.**

FUNBURGER LIP GLOSS 1977-78
(Left) Came in Frostlight Rose & Frostlight Coral lip gloss. Brown plastic. OSP $4.50. **CMV $2.50 - $4.50 MB.**

CHRISTMAS SURPRISE 1976
(Center) 1 oz. green glass boot. Came in Sweet Honesty, Moonwind, Charisma or Topaze cologne. Red cap or silver cap. SSP 99c. **CMV $2. MB, $1. BO.**

ORIENTAL PEONY VASE 1977
(Right) 1.5 oz. red paint over clear glass with gold design. Came in Sweet Honesty or Moonwind. OSP $6. **CMV $5. BO, $7. MB.**

AMERICAN HEIRLOOM SHIPS DECANTER 1981-82
(Left) 6 oz. clear glass, glass top. Choice of Wild Country After Shave or Sweet Honesty Body Splash. SSP $9. **CMV $9. MB.**

SOFT SWIRLS BATH DECANTER 1981-82
(Right) 8 oz. clear glass, frosted cap. Choice of Smooth As Silk bath oil or Skin-So-Soft. SSP $10. **CMV $10. MB.**

BUTTERFLY FANTASY PORCELAIN TREASURE FAN 1980-81
Fan shaped porcelain box. Dated 1980 on botom. SSP $13. **CMV $13. MB. Add $5. for backward printed bottom label.**

CHRISTMAS REMEMBRANCE CERAMIC WREATH 1980
White ceramic, gold tassel. Dated 1980. 3" across. 1st in series. SSP $8. **CMV $8. MB.**

SWEET REMEMBRANCE 1982
(Left) 3 1/4" porcelain box. Valentines Day 1982 on bottom. "A Token of Love" on inside with a gold foil wrapped chocolate. Short issue. SSP $15. **CMV $15. MB.**

CHRISTMAS REMEMBRANCE DOVE 1981
(Right) Second in a series of tree ornaments from Avon. White ceramic dove, gold cord. SSP $8. **CMV $8. MB.**

AMERICAN HEIRLOOM PORCELAIN BOWL 1981
6" across 4" high, white bowl. "Independence Day 1981" on bottom. Comes with black plastic base stand. SSP $20. **CMV $20. MB.**

AMERICAN FASHION THIMBLES 1982-86
Hand painted porcelain ladies from 1890s to 1940s design. 8 different. DP $6. each. **CMV $10. each MB, 1938 CMV $15. MB.**

AMERICAN FASHION THIMBLE DISPLAY RACK 1983
12 1/2" long mahogany rack with 8 pegs. Can hang on wall or sit on shelf. SSP $13. **CMV $13. MB.**

ANNIVERSARY KEEPSAKE - MEN 1981-82
Replica of California Perfume Co. "Early Day Avon". Bay Rum After Shave. 3 oz. clear glass with glass top in plastic cork. SSP $7. **CMV $7. MB.**

ANNIVERSARY KEEPSAKE - WOMEN 1981-82
3 oz. clear glass CPC replica of 1908 design. Holds White Lilac cologne. Dated 1981. SSP $7. **CMV $7. MB.** Both came to Avon managers as a Demo empty and marked Not For Sale. **CMV $10. each.**

CALIFORNIA PERFUME CO. ANNIVERSARY KEEPSAKE COLOGNE 1975
(Left) Issued in honor of 89th Anniversary. 1.7 oz. bottle, pink ribbon & gold cap. Came in Charisma or Sweet Honesty cologne. Sold in 2 campaigns only. **CMV $5., $7. MB.** 1st issue Avon Presidents Club Reps received this bottle with 4A design under bottom label. Regular issue had Avon on bottom. **CMV for 4A deisgn & "M" for Managers.** Given to Managers only. **CMV $15. MB.**

CPC ANNIVERSARY KEEPSAKE COLOGNE 1976
(Right) 1.7 oz. clear glass bottle, gold cap. Bottle is embossed on back side (Avon 90th Anniversary Keepsake). Came in Moonwind or Cotillion cologne. Sold 2 campaigns only. OSP $6. **CMV $7. MB, $5. BO.**

DINGO BOOT 1978-79
6 oz. camel tan plastic bottle and cap. Choice of Sweet Honesty Body Splash or Wild Country After Shave. SSP $4. **CMV $2. MB.**

VINTAGE YEAR "CHAMPAIGN YEAR" 1978-79
2 oz. green glass, gold cap. 1979 embossed in bottom. Came in Sweet Honesty or Wild Country cologne. Green and gold box. SSP $4. **CMV $4. MB, $2. BO.**

ANNIVERSARY KEEPSAKE C.P.C. 1978-79
1.5 oz. clear glass. Old style C.P.C. label and design. Pink neck ribbon. Came in Trailing Arbutus, Sweet Honesty or Somewhere cologne. SSP $5. **CMV $5. MB, $3. BO.**

ANNIVERSARY KEEPSAKE EAU DE TOILETTE 1979
Large 8 oz. clear glass bottle, CPC embossed on back side. Avon 1979 on bottom. Gold cap. Pink and green box. Came in Trailing Arbutus cologne. Pink neck ribbon. SSP $10. **CMV $10. MB.**

ANNIVERSARY KEEPSAKE C.P.C. FLACON 1979
.75 oz. clear glass. Silver cap has 1979 on top. Came with Sweet Honesty or Trailing Arbutus cologne. SSP $5. **CMV $6. MB.**

COUNTRY TALC SHAKER 1977-79
3 oz. gray and blue speckled metal can shaker top. Came in Sweet Honesty or Charisma perfumed talc. SSP $5. **CMV $3. MB, $2. BO.**

CALIFORNIA PERFUME CO. ANNIVERSARY KEEPSAKE 1977-78
3.75. oz. blue can sold to public with Avon 1977 on the bottom. SSP $3. **CMV $2. MB, $1. BO.** Was also given to Avon Reps during 91st Anniversary with "Anniversary Celebration Avon 1977" on the bottom. **CMV $4. MB.** Came in Roses Roses or Trailing Arbutus Talc.

LIP TOPPING LIP GLOSS 1982-83
Tin box holds choice of Chocolate Fudge or
Butterscotch. SSP $1.50. each. **CMV $1.
each.**

CAPE COD 1876 COLLECTION
(all are ruby red glass)

SILVER FAWN 1978-79
.5 oz. silver coated over clear glass. Choice of
Sweet Honesty or Charisma cologne. SSP $2.
CMV $3. BO, $4. MB.

1876 HOSTESS BELL 1979-80
6 1/2" high "Christmas 1979" on bottom. SSP
$10. **CMV $12. MB.** Also came clear glass
coated red.
CAPE COD DESSERT PLATES 1980
Box of 2 red glass plates marked Avon. SSP
$11. **CMV $12. MB.**
CAPE COD CRUET 1975-80
5 oz. red glass. Holds Skin-So-Soft. SSP $8.
CMV $8. MB.
**CAPE COD CANDLESTICK COLOGNE
1975-80**
5 oz. red glass. Came in Charisma, patchwork
or Bird of Paradise. SSP $8. **CMV $9. MB.**
CAPE COD WINE GOBLET 1976-80
Red glass candle. SSP $5. **CMV $7.** Also
issued to Reps with Presidents Celebration
1976 embossed on bottom. **CMV $8.**

DESSERT BOWL & GUEST SOAPS 1978-80
SSP $9. **CMV $10. MB.**
SALT SHAKER 1978-80
May 1978 on bottom. SSP $4. **CMV $5. MB.**
Latter issue not dated on bottom.
CAPE COD WATER GOBLET 1976-80
Red glass candle. SSP $9. **CMV $9. MB.**
CAPE COD WINE DECANTER 1977-80
16 oz. red glass holds bubble bath. SSP $14.
CMV $15. MB.
CAPE COD DINNER PLATE 1982-83
Full size ruby red glass dinner plate. SSP $14.
CMV $14. MB.

LAVENDER & LACE 1970-72
Lavender & white box holds 1.7 oz. white glass
botle of Lavender cologne with lavender
ribbon. A lavender & white lace handkerchief
came with it. OSP $4.50. **CMV $8. set, BO
$3. MB.**

CAPE COD SUGAR BOWL 1980-83
3 1/2" high red glass. Comes with 3 sachet
tablets. SSP $10. **CMV $10. MB.**
CAPE COD CREAMER CANDLE 1981-84
4" high ruby red glass. holds candle, also
came 1983 without candle. SSP $9. **CMV
$10. MB.**
CAPE COD DESSERT SERVER 1981-84
8" long, ruby red plastic handle. Stainless
blade made by Regent Sheffield for Avon.
SSP $10. **CMV $10. MB.**
1876 CAPE COD PEDESTAL MUGS 1982-84
Box holds 2 ruby red glass mugs 5" high. SSP
$16. set. **CMV $16. MB set.**
**1876 CAPE COD COVERED BUTTER DISH
1983-84**
7" long red glass. SSP $15. **CMV $15.**
CAPE COD CANDLE HOLDERS 1983-84
3 3/4" wide, 2 in a box. SSP $15. **CMV $15.
MB.**

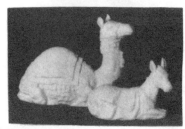

**NATIVITY CAMEL & DONKEY FIGURINES
1984**
Goes in Nativity set. White porcelain. DP $10.
each. **CMV $15. each MB.**

MOTHERS DAY FIGURINE "LITTLE THINGS" 1983-84
(Left) 3 3/4" high hand painted porcelain boy figurine. SSP $18. **CMV $18. MB.**
MOTHERS DAY FIGURINE "CHERISHED MOMENTS" 1983-84
(Right) 4" high hand painted porcelain girl figurine. SSP $18. **CMV $18. MB.**

KEEPING THE CHRISTMAS TRADITION 1982
Hand painted porcelain figurine dated 1982. 2nd in Christmas Memories Series. SSP $49.50. **CMV $49.50 MB.**

MRS. CLAUS SUGAR BOWL & CREAMER 1983-84
Red, white and green ceramic sugar bowl & creamer. SSP $13. each. **CMV $13. MB each.**

NATIVITY "THREE WISE MEN" 1982
(Left to Right) All are white bisque porcelain. The Magi Kaspar, The Magi Melchior, The Magi Balthasar. SSP $19.50 each. **CMV $19.50. each MB.**

MELVIN P. MERRYMOUSE ORNAMENT 1982
Small plastic mouse Santa. Back of mirror says Avon Christmas, 1982. SSP $10. **CMV $10. MB.**
McCONNELLS CORNER TOWN SHOPPERS 1982
(Right) 3" high ceramic figurine. Bottom says Christmas, 1982. SSP $10. **CMV $10. MB.**

MELVIN P. MERRYMOUSE KEEPSAKE ORNAMENT 1983
2 3/4" high Santa mouse on sleigh. Dated 1983. Plastic, 2nd in a series. SSP $10. **CMV $6. MB.**

HEART STRINGS DECANTER 1983
.5 oz. red glass with gold cap. Choice of three fragrances. SSP $3. **CMV $3. MB.**
AUTUMN SCURRY "SQUIRREL" 1982-83
.5 oz. clear glass squirrel, gold cap. Choice of Moonwind, Topaze or Charisma cologne. SSP $2.25. **CMV $2. MB.**
BABY BASSETT DECANTER 1978-79
1.25 oz. amber glass and matching plastic head. Holds Topaze or Sweet Honesty Cologne. SSP $3. **CMV $2. BO, $3. MB.**

CHRISTMAS PORCELAIN FIGURINE 1983
5 1/2" high hand painted porcelain figurine. Called "Enjoying the Night Before Christmas." Dated Christmas 1983. SSP $52.50. **CMV $45. MB.**

NATIVITY COLLECTION 1983
All are white porcelain.
SHEPHERD - 6 1/2" high. SSP $22.50. **CMV $22.50 MB.**
SHEEP - 4" long. SSP $13.50. **CMV $13.50.**
SHEPHERD BOY - 4 3/4" high. SSP $19.50. **CMV $19.50 MB.**

McCONNELLS CORNER GENERAL STORE 1982
5 1/2" ceramic box, roof lifts off. Dated "Christmas 1982". SSP $24. **CMV $24. MB.**

EMERALD ACCENT COLLECTION DECANTER 1982-83
10" high, clear glass, green glass stopper. SSP $15. **CMV $15. MB.**
CORDIAL GLASSES
Set of two clear glasses with green glass stems, 4 1/2" high. SSP $13. **CMV $13. MB set.**
SERVING TRAY
11 1/2" long green glass tray. SSP $15. **CMV $15. MB.**

VICTORIAN COLLECTOR DOLL 1983-84
8" high 19th century doll with porcelain head, arms and legs. Comes with metal stand. Fancy box. SSP $24.50. **CMV $25. MB.**

MOM'S PRIDE AND JOY PICTURE FRAME 1983
6 1/2" x 2" clear glass MOM frame. SSP $10. **CMV $10. MB.**

CHRISTMAS REMEMBRANCE ANGEL 1982
White ceramic angel, gold tassel. Comes in white felt bag. SSP $9. **CMV $9. MB.**

MEMORIES PORCELAIN MUSIC BOX 1983-84
White 4 1/4" long porcelain box with music box in lid. SSP $27.50. **CMV $27.50 MB.**
IMAGE OF LOVE PAPERWEIGHT 1983
4" wide clear glass heart, red felt bottom. SSP $10. **CMV $10. MB.**

AMERICAN HEIRLOOM PORCELAIN BOWL 1983-84
6" across, 4" high porcelain bowl. Plastic stand. Flower design on bowl. SSP $17.50. **CMV $17.50 MB.**

STYLISH LADY DECANTER 1982-83
8 oz. white glass pig with white and pink pump top. Choice of Country Orchard Liquid Cleanser or Moisturizer Hand Lotion. SSP $9. **CMV $9. MB.**

CHRISTMAS THIMBLE 1982
(Left) White porcelain, dated 1982.
CHRISTMAS THIMBLE 1981
(Right) Issued in 1982, but dated 1981. SSP $9. each. **CMV $9. each MB.**

SWEET DREAMS 1979-80
1.25 oz. blue frosted over clear glass. White plastic boys head cap. Holds Zany or Somewhere cologne. SSP $5. **CMV $5. MB.**

PIERRE DECANTER 1984
8 oz. white glass pig. Cloth apron on front.
Holds Care Deeply Hand Lotion. SSP $10.
CMV $10. MB.

SNOWFLAKE ORNAMENT 1983
(Left) White porcelain snowflake dated 1983.
2 1/2" wide on gold tassel. SSP $8. **CMV $8.
MB.**

**CAPTURED MOMENTS FRAME ORNAMENT
1983**
(Right) Green and red plastic wreath. Slide a
picture in center. 4" across. SSP $4. **CMV $4.
MB.**

FRED ASTAIRE FIGURINE 1984
6 3/4" high porcelain. 3rd in series. DP $18.
CMV $25. MB.

GINGER ROGERS FIGURINE 1984
4th in series. 6" high porcelain. DP $18. **CMV
$25. MB.**

**IMAGES OF HOLLYWOOD 1983-84 -
SCARLETT O'HARA**
1st in a series porcelain figurine, 4 1/2" high.
Vivian Leigh as Scarlett O'Hara. DP $18.
CMV $25. MB.

RHETT BUTLER FIGURINE 1984-85
Clark Gable figurine, 5 3/4" high. DP $18.
CMV $30. MB.

**BUNNY MATES SALT & PEPPER SHAKERS
1983**
Bunny box holds two small ceramic white rabbit
shakers. SSP $12. **CMV $12. MB.**

**CLAUS & COMPANY SANTA'S HELPERS
SALT & PEPPER SHAKERS 1983**
Red box holds two small green and red
ceramic boy and girl salt & pepper shakers. 2
1/2" high. SSP $10. **CMV $10. MB.**

SUMMER FUN FIGURINE 1986
(Right) 3 1/2" wide porcelain figurine by Jessie
Wilcox Smith. DP $21. **CMV $27. MB.**

GIVING THANKS FIGURINE 1986
(Left) 3 1/4" wide porcelain figurine by Jessie
Wilcox Smith. DP $21. **CMV $27. MB.**

CHRISTMAS BELL 1985
(Right) Wood handle, porcelain bell dated
Xmas 1985. DP $9. **CMV $15. MB.**

AVON COUNTRY PORCELAIN BELL 1985
(Center) 3 1/4" high porcelain bell. DP $6.
CMV $10. MB.

GOOD LUCK BELL 1983
(Left) 4 1/2" high porcelain elf on flower bell.
DP $9. **CMV $15. MB.**

FRAGRANCE KEEPSAKE 1983
.5 oz. fan shaped clear glass, with rose red
cap. Choice of Somewhere, Here's My Heart,
Regence, Rapture, Persian Wood, Brocade,
Cotillion. SSP $2. **CMV $2. MB.**

GINGERBREAD COTTAGE 1983-84
.5 oz. dark amber glass, pink cap. Choice of
Sweet Honesty or Charisma cologne. 2" high.
SSP $3. **CMV $3. MB.**

WRITE TOUCH MOUSE 1982-83
(Left) 1 oz. green glass and white plastic
mouse with stick on decals. Choice of Sweet
Honesty or Charisma cologne. SSP$6. **CMV
$6. MB.**

FRAGRANCE NOTABLES 1982
(Center) .5 oz. clear glass with ribbon design.
Red cap and box. Choice of Wild Jasmine,
Occur!, Moonwind, Charisma, Topaze or Sweet
Honesty cologne. SSP $1.50. **CMV $1. MB.**

CRYSTALLIQUE TREE 1982
(Right) .5 oz. clear glass tree bottle with
bronze color cap. Choice of Foxfire, Timeless
or Odyssey cologne. SSP $3. **CMV $3. MB.**

WE WISH YOU A MERRY CHRISTMAS FIGURINE 1986
(Left) 3 1/2" wide porcelain figurine with music box base. DP $12. **CMV $18. MB.**
A WINTER SNOW FIGURINE
(Right) Porcelain figurine by Jessie Wilcox Smith. DP $20. **CMV $27. MB.**

PORCELAIN CAT FIGURINES 1984
Choice of 4 porcelain cat figurines. Siamese Tabby, Calico, Persian. DP $2. each. **CMV $4. each MB.**

JUDY GARLAND FIGURINE 1985
5 1/2" high porcelain. DP $20. **CMV $30. MB.**
CHRISTMAS FIGURINE 1984
6 3/8" high porcelain. Dated Christmas 1984. DP $30. **CMV $40. MB.**

CARDINAL FIGURINE 1985
Red porcelain bird.
BLUEBIRD FIGURINE 1986
Blue, orange & white porcelain bird. DP $24. on both birds. **CMV $32. each MB.**

JOAN WALSH ANGLUND FIGURINE COLLECTION 1986-87
(Top) 3 1/2" high porcelain figurines is "School Days" & "My ABCs". 1986 "Magic Slippers" & "Home Run" is 3 3/4" high. DP $8.50. **CMV $12 MB each.**
JESSIE WILCOX SMITH FIGURINES 1986
(Bottom) 3 1/2" wide porcelain figurines choice of "Be My Valentine", "Springtime", & "Helping Mom". DP $21. each. **CMV $28. MB each.**

BUNNY BUD VASE 1986
3 1/2" high porcelain. Comes empty. DP $6. **CMV $9. MB.**
BUNNY LUV CERAMIC BOX 1982
Ceramic top & bottom. Rabbit on lid. Sold empty. DP $8. **CMV $12. MB.**

PURRFECT CAT 1987
1.5 oz. cologne. Black glass. DP $3.25. **CMV $5 MB.**
COUNTRY CHICKEN 1987
9.5 oz. white ceramic bottle with pump. Holds hand loiton. DP $7.25. **CMV $7.25 MB.**

JOY TO THE WORLD MUSICAL FIGURINE 1985
(Left to Right) Small porcelain figurine, music base. DP $14. **CMV $20. MB.**
EASTER CHARM FIGURINE 1985
4" high porcelain. Dated Easter 1985. DP $9. **CMV $15. MB.**
MOTHERS TOUCH FIGURINE 1984
Shiny glaze porcelain. Mother's Day figurine. DP $25. **CMV $35. MB.**

YOU'RE THE BERRIES CANDY JAR 1984
Clear glass 5" high fruit jar with berry cloth lid cover. Holds hard candy. DP $4. **CMV $6. MB.**
COUNTRY CHARM LOTION PUMP 1985
10 oz. jug bottle with pump. DP $5. **CMV $5. MB.**

BIRTHDAY BELL 1986
5 3/4" high clear lead crystal bells. Choice of 12 different flowers on bells. DP $9. **CMV $12. MB.**
BUNNY BELL 1984
3" high ceramic rabbit bell. DP $6. **CMV $8. MB.**

FOUR SEASONS EGG SERIES 1984
4 different porcelain eggs - wood base. Winter, Spring, Summer, Autumn. DP. $9. each. **CMV $14. MB.**

POINSETTIA SEASONS IN BLOOM 1986
(Right) Red porcelain flower. DP $21. **CMV $28. MB.**

MAGNOLIA SEASONS IN BLOOM 1986
(Left) Yellow, white and green porcelain flower. Both have Avon label. DP $21. **CMV $28. MB.**

TREASURED MOMENTS BELL 1984
Fostoria glass bell. 5" high. DP $8. **CMV $11. MB.**

CHRISTMAS THIMBLE 1983
(Right) Small white porcelain thimble with decal. 1983 Christmas in gold. SSP $9. **CMV $9. MB.**

STATUE OF LIBERTY CENTENNIAL BOWL 1985
6" porcelain white bowl. Wood base. DP $15. **CMV $20. MB.**

EUROPEAN TRADITION CUP & SAUCER'S COLLECTION
FRANCE 1985
2 1/4" cup & 4 1/2" saucer. Pink & white porcelain.
GERMANY 1985
Yellow & white porcelain.
NETHERLANDS 1984
Blue & white porcelain.
FLORENCE 1984
Blue & white porcelain.
DP $15. each. **CMV $15. each MB.**

BEAR COOKIE JAR 1985
Brown ceramic cookie jar. DP $18. **CMV $25. MB.**

BABY BEAR BANK 1986
Ceramic blue & tan bank with small green & white bear blanket. Comes with iron on letters. DP $7. **CMV $7. MB**

CHRISTMAS THIMBLE 1984
Porcelain - Dated Christmas 1984. DP $5. **CMV $7. MB.**

CHRISTMAS LIGHTS MUG 1985
White mug cup. DP $3. **CMV $6. MB.**

SWEET SENTIMENTS MUG 1986
White ceramic mug, heart handles. DP $3. **CMV $6. MB.**

HEARTS FROM THE HEART 1987
Heart shaped lead crystal dish & 8 pink heart shaped bath pearls. DP $5.50. **CMV $8. MB**

STATUE OF LIBERTY BRASS STAMP 1985
1886-1986 on wood base. DP $10. **CMV $10. MB.**

HOSPITALITY SPOON SERIES 1985
Wood rack with 4 spoons - Italian Grapes, German Maiden, Scottish Thistle, American Pineapple. DP $6. each piece. **CMV $30. set MB with rack.**

CHRISTMAS TREE MUG 1985
(Right) 4" high porcelain cup. DP $5. **CMV $6. MB.**

SANTA'S STORY MUG 1984
(Left) 3 5/8" high porcelain. DP $3. **CMV $6. MB.**

LOVE MUG JELLY BEANS 1983-84
3 1/2" high ceramic mug filled with 8 oz. of jelly beans. Some mugs came with Heart on bottom and no date or lettering and some came with heart on bottom and dated 1983 in red or black letters. DP $6. **CMV $7. MB.**

HAPPINESS MUG 1984
Ceramic mug cup with jelly beans. DP $6. **CMV $7. MB.**

COUNTRY VILLAGE CANISTER SET 1985
White pottery canisters by Plaltzgraff. Marked Avon on bottom. DP $39. set. **CMV $50. set MB.**

FOREVER YOURS MUG 1987
White ceramic heart shaped mug. DP $3.85. **CMV $6. MB.**

MOM MUG 1987
White ceramic mug. Comes with silk yellow rose. DP $4.25. **CMV $7. MB**

MR. CLAUS MUG 1984
MRS. CLAUS MUG 1984
Both white porcelain, each came with 4 packets of cocoa. DP $6. each. **CMV $8. each MB.**

CAPE COD SERVING PLATTER 1986
(Not Shown) Red glass, 10 3/4" x 13 1/2". DP $17.50. **CMV $24 MB.**
CAPE COD SERVING BOWL 1986
8 3/4" red glass bowl. DP $14. **CMV $19. MB.**

CAPE COD COLLECTION 1984-88
All red glass.
CONDIMENT DISH 1985
SSP $9. **CMV $12. MB.**
HURRICANE CANDLE HOLDER 1985
DP $9. **CMV $12. MB.**
COLLECTION FLOWER VASE 1985
8" tall. DP $9. **CMV $12. MB.**
WATER PITCHER 1984
8 1/4'" high. DP $15. **CMV $20. MB.**

HUMMINGBIRD CRYSTAL BELL 1985
Each piece is clear glass & etched frosted design. DP $9. **CMV $12. MB.**
HUMMINGBIRD CHAMPAIGN GLASSES 1985
9" high box of 2 glasses. DP $21. **CMV $26. MB.**
HUMMINGBIRD CRYSTAL VASE 1986
7 1/2" high vase. DP $22.50. **CMV $27 MB.**
HUMMINGBIRD CRYSTAL CAKE PLATE 1985
12" glass cake plate on 3" glass stand. DP $22.50. **CMV $25 MB.**
HUMMINGBIRD CRYSTAL TREE ORNAMENT 1986
3 1/2" high glass. DP $6. **CMV $8. MB.**

HOLY FAMILY NATIVITY FIGURINES 1986
Porcelain figurines 2 1/2" to 3 3/4" high. Mary, Joseph & Baby Jesus in manger. DP $12. **CMV $17. set MB.**
THE MAGI NATIVITY FIGURINES 1986
Porcelain figurines. Melchior, Balthasar & Kaspar. DP $6. each. **CMV $9. each.**

DONKEY & CAMEL NATIVITY FIGURINES 1986
(Left) Heavenly Blessings Nativity collection. Both pastel porcelain. 3 1/2" long. DP $6. ea. **CMV $8. ea. MB.**

NATIVITY ANGEL & STABLE 1985
White porcelain angel & plastic stable. DP $20. set. **CMV $23. set MB.**

FOSTORIA ORNAMENTS 1985
Christmas village, Christmas tree or Angel ornament. DP $5. **CMV $7. each.**

BABY'S FIRST CHRISTMAS ORNAMENT 1986
(Above) 4" high white porcelain by Joan Walsh Anglund. **CMV $7. MB**

MERRY CHRISTMAS ORNAMENT CARD 1985
Xmas card holds 3" porcelain ornament. DP $5. **CMV $7. MB.**

NATIVITY ORNAMENT COLLECTION 1985
All white porcelain. The Shepherd, The Holy Family, The Three Magi. DP $5. each. **CMV $8. MB each.**

CAPE COD TWO TIER SERVER 1987
9 3/4" high red glass server. Brass handle. SSP $30. **CMV $30. MB.**

CHRISTMAS BELL 1986
White porcelain bell 5" high dated 1986. Gold trim. DP $11. **CMV $15. MB.**

SNOW ANGEL TREE TOPPER DOLL 1986
10 1/2" high. Head & hands are porcelain. Blue lace dress. DP $7. **CMV $12. MB.**

CAPE COD NAPKIN RINGS 1989
1 1/2" red glass napkin rings. Set of 4. SSP $20. **CMV $20. MB Set.**

CAPE COD FOOTED GLASS SET 1988
Set of 2 red glass 3 3/4" glasses. SSP $15. **CMV $15. MB Set.**

ANGEL NATIVITY FIGURINES 1986
3" porcelain angel. DP $6. **CMV $8. MB.**

CHRISTMAS TREE POMANDER 1986
9" high green ceramic tree. Comes with wax chips. DP $12. **CMV $17. MB.**

CAPE COD CANDY DISH 1987
6 " wide 3 1/2" high, red glass dish. SSP $12. **CMV $12. MB.**

CAPE COD FOOTED SAUCE BOAT 1988
8" long red glass. SSP. $25. **CMV $25. MB.**

CAPE COD HEART BOX 1989
4" wide red glass heart box. SSP $13. **CMV $13. MB.**

CAPE COD CUP & SAUCER 1990
Red glass cup 3 1/2" high and saucer 5 3/4" wide. SSP $18. **CMV $18. MB.**

CAPE COD CHRISTMAS ORNAMENT 1990
3 1/4" wide red glass with plaid bow. Back says "Christmas 1990". SSP $10. CMV $10. MB.

CAPE COD TALL BEVERAGE GLASS SET 1990
Set of 2 red glasses 5 1/2" tall. SSP. $17. CMV $17 Set. MB.

HUMMINGBIRD CRYSTAL CANDLE HOLDERS 1987
Set of 2 – 4 1/4" wide, 2 5/8" high. SSP $20. CMV $20. MB.

HUMMINGBIRD CRYSTAL DESSERT PLATES. 1988
Set of 2 7 1/2" wide, lead crystal plates. SSP $25. CMV $25. Set MB.

HUMMINGBIRD CRYSTAL COVERED DISH 1989
Lead Crystal 5" wide dish. SSP $30.00 CMV $30 MB

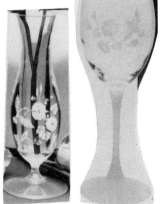

HUMMINGBIRD CRYSTAL BUD VASE 1990
9 1/2" high clear glass. SSP $15. CMV $25. MB.

HUMMINGBIRD CRYSTAL GOBLETS 1987
Set of 2 lead crystal goblets. SSP $25. CMV $25. MB.

HUMMINGBIRD ORNAMENT 1986
3 1/2" lead crystal ornament has "1986" on it. SSP $10. CMV $10.

ROARING TWENTIES DOLL 1989
8" high porcelain doll, black dress. Feather Boa on metal stand. SSP. $30. CMV $30. MB.

FAIRY PRINCESS PORCELAIN DOLL 1989
8 1/2" high, blue dress on metal stand. SSP $30. CMV $30. MB.

VICTORIAN FASHION OF AMERICAN TIMES PORCELAIN DOLL 1987
8 3/4" high on metal stand. SSP $25. CMV $25. MB.

SOUTHERN BELL PORCELAIN DOLL 1988
8 1/4" high, pink and blue dress, on metal stand. SSP. $30. **CMV $30. MB.**

LUPITA MEXICAN INTERNATIONAL DOLL 1990
8 " tall doll with porcelain head, feet and hands. On metal stand. SSP $35. **CMV $35. MB.**

LITTLE DRUMMER BOY 1988
Hand painted porcelain 3 1/4" high figurine. SSP $10. **CMV $10. MB.**

COLLEEN FROM IRELAND DOLL 1990
1st in series porcelain doll 8" high on metal stand. SSP $35. **CMV $35. MB.**

MASSAKO INTERNATIONAL DOLL 1990
9 " high Japanese doll on metal stand. Has porcelain head, hands and feet. SSP $35. **CMV $35. MB.**

NATIVITY INNKEEPER & STAND 1988
4 1/2" high white porcelain. SSP $24. **CMV $24. MB.**
WOOD STAND
11" wide. SSP $20. **CMV $20. MB.**

NIGERIAN ADAMA PORCELAIN DOLL 1990
8 1/2" high doll. Porcelain head, hands and feet. 4th in series, on metal stand. SSP $35. **CMV $35. MB.**

NATIVITY COLLECTION - STANDING ANGEL & COW FIGURINE 1987
White bisque porcelain Angel 6" high. Cow 5 1/2" long.
ANGEL SSP $25. **CMV $25. MB.**
COW SSP $18. **CMV $18. MB.**

'O HOLY NIGHT THREE KINGS SET 1989
Hand painted bisque porcelain. Melchior & Balthasar each 3 1/2" high. Kaspar is 2 5/8" high. SSP $15 ea. **CMV $15 each MB.**

O HOLY NIGHT NATIVITY SET – CAMEL, SHEPERD BOY & LAMB 1990
Both are bisque porcelain and dated on bottom. SSP $13 ea. **CMV $13 ea. MB.**

FLORAL BOUQUET CRYSTAL BELL 1989
6" high lead crystal bell. SSP $23. **CMV $23. MB.**

HEAVENLY BLESSINGS NATIVITY FIGURINES 1987
Choice of Boy Angel 2 1/2" high. Sheperd Boy 3 1/4" high & Sheep 2 3/4" high. SSP $10. **CMV $10. MB. each.**

NATIVITY COLLECTION 1990 – POOR MAN - WOMAN WITH WATER JAR
White porcelain man is 3 1/2" high and woman is 6 3/4" high. SSP $25. ea. **CMV $25. each MB.**

CHERUB NATIVITY PORCELAIN FIGURINE 1989
White porcelain, 3" high. SSP $20. **CMV $20. MB.**

HEART SONG CRYSTAL BELL 1988
4 3/4" high clear glass bell. Red heart top dated 1988. SSP $13. **CMV $13. MB.**

CHRISTMAS ORNAMENT 1987
Clear lead crystal dated 1987. Gold Tassel. SSP $10. **CMV $10. MB.**

'O HOLY NIGHT NATIVITY COLLECTION 1989
Made of porcelain. Background - "CRECHE" 5 1/4" high. SSP $15. **CMV $15. MB.**
Baby Jesus 1 5/8" long, Mary 2 3/4" high, Joseph 3 1/2" high. SSP $25 set of 3 **CMV $25 set MB.**

SPARKLING ANGEL ORNAMENT 1990
Silver plate angel with gold 1990 star. 3 1/4" high. SSP $10. **CMV $10. MB.**

HARVEST BOUNTY CRYSTAL BELL 1988
6 1/2" lead crystal bell. Hand painted porcelain handle. SSP $20. **CMV $15. MB.**

JOAN WALSH ANGLUND FIGURINES 1987
Choice of Christmas Wishes, Boy or The Night Before, Girl. Hand painted porcelain. 4" high. SSP $15 ea. **CMV $15 ea. MB.**

CHRISTMAS BELL 1987
4 3/4" high porcelain bell. SSP $15. **CMV $15. MB.**

CRYSTAL BUTTERFLY BELL 1990
Lead crystal bell 6 1/2" high butterfly decals. SSP $15. **CMV $15. MB.**

BEARY CUTE BEAR BANK 1990
6" high ceramic bank. SSP $15. **CMV $15. MB.**

GIVING THANKS BELL 1990
4 1/2" high porcelain pumpkin bell. SSP $15. **CMV $15. MB.**

MOTHERS LOVE PORCELAIN BELL 1988
3" high porcelain bell. SSP $10. **CMV $10. MB.**

FOREST FRIENDS MINI FIGURINES 1987
Choice of Story Time, Sleigh Ride, or All Tucked In. 2" high by 2 1/4" wide ea. SSP $5. **CMV $5. ea.**

IRIS FLOWER FIGURINE 1987
8" long porcelain Iris. Marked Avon. SSP $35. **CMV $35. MB.**

UNDER THE MISTLETOE CHRISTMAS BELL 1989
Porcelain bell 5 1/2" high. SSP $20. **CMV $20. MB.**

CHRISTMAS BELL 1990 "WAITING FOR SANTA"
5 1/2" high porcelain bell. SSP. $20. **CMV $20. MB.**

PEACE ROSE FIGURINE 1987
7" long porcelain yellow rose. Marked Avon.
SSP $35. **CMV $35. MB.**

MOTHER'S LOVE BUNNY FIGURINE 1990
Hand painted porcelain. Baby 1 1/4" high,
Mother 2 1/2" high. SSP $10 set. **CMV $10.
set MB.**

ANGEL'S MELODY DECANTER 1987
8" high angel. Holds 3 oz. of cologne. SSP
$10. **CMV $10. MB.**

**HUMMINGBIRD PORCELAIN FIGURINE
1989**
7 1/2" high hand painted porcelain. SSP $60.
CMV $60. MB.

HOLIDAY HUGS BEAR FIGURINE SET 1990
Papa Bear and Mama Bear with baby. Both 2
5/8" high and dated on bottom. SSP $10 set.
CMV $10. MB.

COUNTRY GOOSE DECANTER 1988
4 3/4" high holds 1.75 oz. cologne. Ceramic
goose head. Wicker hat, cotton dress. SSP
$8. **CMV $8. MB.**

FOREST FRIENDS FIGURINES 1988
2" high hand painted. Choice of Easter Fun,
Sunday Best and Springtime Stroll. SSP $5.
ea. **CMV $5. ea. MB.**

GOD BLESS MY DOLLY FIGURINE 1990
3" high porcelain in choice of Black or White
girl. SSP $15. **CMV $15. MB. each.**

PANDA SWEETHEART FIGURINE 1990
Boy and girl hand painted porcelain. 2 1/2"
high. SSP $10. set. **CMV $10. set MB.**

MEADOW BLOSSOMS DECANTED 1987
1.75 oz. Frosted glass bottle, porcelain flower
top. Holds cologne. SSP $8. **CMV $8.**

PRETTY CAT DECANTER 1988
1.5 oz. white glass 4" high. Holds cologne.
SSP $6. **CMV $6. MB.**

BREAKFAST 'N BED MUG AND NAPKIN 1989
Bears on mug and a 13" square cotton napkin. SSP $10. **CMV $10. MB.**

BEAR MUGS SET 1987
Big Dipper 3 1/2" high. Little Dipper 3" high. SSP $10 set. **CMV $10 set or $5 ea.**

SNUG CUB DECANTER 1987
1 oz. white glass, red cap. Holds cologne. SSP $4. **CMV $4. MB.**

SECRET SURPRISE MUG 1989
Ceramic mug with 11 piece bear puzzle. SSP $8. **CMV $8. MB.**

SEA SHELL DECANTER 1990
2 oz. sea shell. Holds S.S.S. bath oil. SSP $7. **CMV $7. MB.**

MUGS ESPECIALLY FOR YOU 1987
Choice of Mom, Dad, Special Friend or Teacher. SSP $7. **CMV $7 ea. MB.**

WILD REST CERAMIC MUG 1988
Ceramic hat mug 6 1/4" long. SSP $10. **CMV $10. MB.**

AMERICAN FAVORITES PORCELAIN SPOONS 1989
Porcelain spoons on wood rack. Daffodil, Daylily, Rose, Pansy. SSP $10 ea. **CMV $10 ea. MB, Rack $5. MB.**

CHRISTMAS CHEER MUG 1987
White mug cup came with choice of clip on Reindeer or Polar Bear. SSP $10. **CMV $10. MB.**

HOLIDAY TRIO MUSICAL MUG 1990
4" high ceramic mug with Jingle Bells music box on base. SSP $9. **CMV $9. MB.**

GIFT OF LOVE CRYSTAL BOX 1988
1 1/4" high, 2 3/4" wide glass box. SSP $10.
CMV $10. MB.

AUTUMN'S COLOR PORCELAIN EGG 1987
3" high egg on wood base. SSP $15. **CMV $15. MB.**

HONEY BEAR MUG'S 1988
2 different mugs. "Special Friend" or "Sweetheart". SSP $7. **CMV $7. MB. ea.**

SOME BUNNY SPECIAL MUG 1990
4" high ceramic mug with rabbits on side. SSP $9. **CMV $9. MB.**

CRYSTAL CONFECTIONS JAR 1988
Lead crystal glass jar 5 3/4" high. SSP $15.
CMV $15. MB.

SUMMER'S ROSES PORCELAIN EGG 1988
3" high porcelain egg. 1" wood base. SSP $15. **CMV $15. MB.**

SIPS & SIGNS ASTROLOGY MUGS 1989
12 different zodiac mugs with cartoons on each. SSP $6 ea. **CMV $6. ea. MB.**

FORGET ME NOT PORCELAIN BOX 1989
Heart shaped box and matching pin. SSP $10. **CMV $6. MB.**

WINTER'S TREASURE PORCELAIN EGG 1987
3" high egg. 1" wood base. SSP $15. **CMV $15. MB.**

SPRING BRILLIANCE EGG 1988
3" porcelain egg on wood base. SSP $15. **CMV $15. MB.**

McCONNELLS CORNER TOWN TREE 1982
6" high ceramic tree, green and white. Dated "Christmas 1982". SSP $12. **CMV $12. MB.**

PERFUME JEWEL GLACE 1965-66
Gold & white box contains gold locket. Came as pin or on a chain with solid perfume in Unforgettable, Rapture, Occur!, Somewhere, Topaze, Cotillion, Here's My Heart, To A Wild Rose and Wishing. OSP $5.50. **CMV $17. each MB, $12. locket only.**

PERFUME GLACE NECKLACE 1966-67
Silver with black stone & gold with brown stone. Came in Unforgettable, Rapture, Somewhere, Cotillion, Topaze, To A Wild Rose, Here's My Heart, Wishing. OSP $8. **CMV $17. each MB, $12 locket only.**

GOLDEN CHARMER LOCKET 1968-70
(Left) Gold locket holds perfume glace in Somewhere, Topaze, Cotillion, Here's My Heart, To A Wild Rose, Unforgettable, Rapture, Occur!, Brocade, & Regence. OSP $9.50 **CMV $14. MB, $9 locket only.**

PILLBOX PERFUME GLACE 1967
(Top Right) Black & gold with red rose on top. Came in Occur!, Rapture, Unforgettable, Somewhere, Topaze, Cotillion, Here's My Heart, To A Wild Rose. OSP $4.50 **CMV $15. MB, pill box only $10 mint.**

DAISY PIN PERFUME GLACE 1969
(Bottom Right) White & gold pin Charisma, Brocade, Regence, Rapture, Occur!, Unforgettable, Somewhere, Topaze, Cotillion. OSP $6. **CMV $7., $10. MB.**

MEMORY BOOK PERFUME GLACE 1971-75
1 1/2" long gold book. Choice of Moonwind, Elusive, Brocade, Regence or Bird of Paradise perfume glace. OSP $7. **CMV $9. MB, $6. no box.**

BABY GRAND PIANO PERFUME GLACE 1971-72
2" wide gold piano. Came in same fragrances as Memory Book. OSP $10. **CMV $14. MB, $10. piano only.**

OWL PIN PERFUME GLACE 1968-69
(Left) Gold metal pin with green eyes. Green & gold box. Came in Unforgettable, Brocade, Regence, Rapture, Occur!, Cotillion, Here's My Heart, To A Wild Rose. OSP $6. **CMV Owl only $9. $12 MB.**

FLOWER BASKET PERFUME GLACE 1970-71
(Right) 1 1/2" x 1 1/4" gold tone. Choice of Bird of Paradise, Elusive, Charisma, Brocade, or Regence. OSP $7. **CMV $10. MB, $6 pin only.**

PERFUME GLACE NECKLACE 1966-67
Special issue gold round box. Came with either silver with black stone or gold necklace with brown stone. **CMV $20. as shown.**

RING OF PEARLS GLACE 1969-70
Perfume glace ring is gold with white pearls. Comes in Charisma, Regence & Bracade. OSP $7.50 **CMV $10, MB $7. ring only.**

MANDOLIN PERFUME GLACE 1971-72
2 1/2" long gold mandolin Choice of Moonwind, Elusive, Charisma, Brocade, Regence, or Bird of Paradise perfume glace. OSP $9. **CMV $14. MB, $8 no box.**

TORTOISE PERFUME GLACE 1971-75
2 1/2" long gold turtle with turquoise back. Came in same fragrances as Mandolin. OSP $9. **CMV $10 MB, $7. turtle only.**

CAMEO RING & PIN 1970
Both are perfume glace. Comes in Elusive, Charisma, Brocade, Regence, & Bird of Paradise. OSP $10. each. **CMV $9. each, $15 each MB.**

GOLDEN LEAF PIN 1969-70
Blue box contains gold leaf pin with pearl at stem. Perfume glace comes in Elusive, Charisma, Brocade, Regence, Unforgettable, Rapture, Occur!, Topaze, Somewhere, & Cotillion. Same pin also issued with out glace. OSP $6.50 **CMV $11 MB. $7. Pin only.**

DAYTIME-NIGHTTIME DOLL 1985
Reversible cloth doll. 8" high. Blue on one side. DP $4. **CMV $4.**

BABY BEAR FLOATING DECANTER 1987
6oz. yellow & blue plastic. Holds shampoo. SSP $6.00 **CMV $4.00**

SNOOPY'S SKI TEAM 1974-75
7 oz. white plastic bottle, red skis, yellow "Woodstock". Holds bubble bath. OSP $5. **CMV $5. MB.**

WOODSTOCK BRUSH & COMB 1975-78
Yellow plastic brush, green comb. OSP $4. **CMV $1. BO, $2. MB.**

PERCIVAL PENGUIN & SOAP 1986
7" stuffed penguin & penguin wrapped bar of soap. DP $4. **CMV $4.**

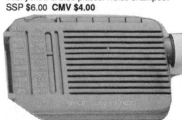

SUN SOUNDS TANNING LOTION DE-CANTER 1987
6oz. blue plastic. SSP $6.00 **CMV $4.00**

LULLABY BUNNY 1987
8 1/2" yellow plush movable rabbit with music box. DP $9.50. **CMV $14. MB.**

HORATIO HARE 1987
7" high stuffed toy rabbit. Blue, pink, white & yellow. DP $4. **CMV $7. MB.**

SPACE MISSION DECANTER 1988
10 3/4" long space ship in blue & yellow plastic. Holds liquid soap & shampoo. SSP $7.00 **CMV $4.00 MB**

SNOOPY MUG 1969-72
5 oz. white glass, 5 inches high. Came 2 ways, red or blue top. Blue top is more rare. Also came with oval or round decal. OSP $3.50. **CMV $7. red top MB, $9. blue top MB, $2. less no box.**

HOLIDAY SLEIGH & TEDDY BEAR 1986
Red wicker sleigh 12" long brown bear & red cap & neck scarf. DP $11. **CMV $11. MB.**

CUDDLE BUNNY 1987
Light brown wicker basket with white stuffed rabbit. Pink & lavender ribbon. DP $6.75. **CMV $6.75 MB.**

LIP POP COLA'S 1973-74
.13 oz. plastic tube with plastic top. Came in Cherry (light red case), Cola (brown case), Strawberry (pink case) lip pomade. Strawberry & Cherry also came solid red plastic (**rare CMV $7.**) others OSP $1.50. **CMV $3. BO, $4. MB.**

PERRY THE PENGUIN 1966-67
Black and white penguin soap dish and white plastic soap dish. OSP $6., penguin $4., vest soap $5. **Set $12. MB.**

SNOOPY SOAP DISH 1968-76
White bar of Avon soap sets in black and white plastic soap dish. OSP $6. **CMV $6. MB, Snoopy only $2.**

CHILDREN'S TOYS & COLLECTIBLES

Children's toys and collectibles continue to be popular with many collectors. Almost all children's toys are plastic which are about the only plastic items in the book truly collectible. All children's items must be in new mint condition. If they are not, I suggest you do not buy them.
Be sure to read <u>What's Hot and What's Not</u> in the introduction section of this book.

SNOOPY COME HOME SOAP DISH AND SOAP 1973-74
6" long, brown raft with white sail, has 3 oz. brown soap. SSP $3. **CMV $6. MB.**

CHARLIE BROWN 1968-72
4 oz. red, white and black plastic bottle of Non Tear Shampoo. OSP $2.50. **CMV $5. MB, $3. BO.**
LUCY 1970-72
4 oz. red, white and black plastic bottle holds bubble bath. OSP $2.50. **CMV $5. MB, $3. BO.**

LUCY MUG 1969-70
5 oz. white glass, yellow top and label. White cap, Non Tear Shampoo. OSP $3.50. **CMV $8.**
CHARLIE BROWN MUG 1969-70
5 oz. white glass, blue top and label. White cap, bubble bath. OSP $3.50. **CMV $8.**

SNOOPY & DOG HOUSE 1969-72
8 oz. white plastic dog and red plastic 3" high dog house, holds Non Tear Shampoo. OSP $3. **CMV $3., $5. MB.**
LINUS 1968-74
Red, white and green plastic 4 oz. tube of Gel Bubble Bath with red, white and black plastic Linus, plastic holder. OSP $3.50. **CMV $5. MB, $3. Linus & tube only.**

SNOOPY COMB & BRUSH SET 1971-75
5 1/2" long black and brush and white comb. OSP $3.50. **CMV $5. MB.**

SNOOPY THE FLYING ACE 1969
4 oz. 6" high white plastic with blue hat, yellow glasses, holds bubble bath. OSP $3. **CMV $2., $5. MB.**
JUMPIN' JIMMINY 1969-73
8 oz. 6" high, green, red and yellow pull toy with yellow cap. Holds bubble bath. OSP $3.50. **CMV 45. MB, $3. BO.**

SIX SHOOTER 1962-63
6 oz. gray plastic and white gun with No Tears Shampoo. OSP $1.98. **CMV $18. BO mint, $24. MB.**

BO BO THE ELEPHANT 1973-74
6 oz. pink plastic with squeeze head. Filled with baby shampoo. SSP $3. **CMV $3. BO, $5. MB.**
SNOOPY'S SNOW FLYER 1973
10 oz. red, white and black. Holds bubble bath. SSP $4. **CMV $5. MB, $3. BO.**

CLEAN AS A WHISTLE 1960-61
8 oz. red & white plastic bottle, real whistle cap. Came in bubble bath. OSP $1.79. **CMV $15. MB, $10. BO.**
E.T. FLOWERS FIGURINE 1984
2 1/2" high hand painted porcelain. SSP $8. **CMV $5. MB.**

CHARLIE BROWN COMB & BRUSH 1972
4 1/2" long, red, black and white with white comb. SSP $3. **CMV $5. MB.**

GRID KID BRUSH & COMB 1973-74
4 1/2" long, red, black and white with white comb. SSP $3. **CMV $5. MB.**

LITTLE RED RIDING HOOD 1968
4 oz. yellow plastic bottle, red cap. Holds bubble bath. OSP $1.50. **CMV $2. BO, $6. with glasses MB.**

WOLF 1968
4 oz. yellow and blue plastic bottle, green cap, holds Non Tear Shampoo. OSP $1.50. **CMV $2. BO, $6. MB with white fang teeth.**

BUBBLE BUNNY 1964-65
Pink and white rabbit puppet with 6 oz. tube of bubble bath gel. OSP $1.98. **CMV $5. puppet only, $11. MB.**

SNOOPY'S BUBBLE TUB 1971-72
5" long, 12 oz. blue and white plastic tub, bottle holds bubble bath. OSP $2. **CMV $3. BO, $5. MB.**

PEANUTS PALS SHAMPOO 1971-72
6 oz. plastic, white, red, and black bottle with yellow cap. 6" high. OSP $3.50. **CMV $5. MB, $3. BO.**

MR. MANY MOODS 1965-66
6 oz. white plastic bottle with blue and yellow hat, red nose and mouth, black eyes. Holds shampoo. OSP $1.98. **CMV $8., $10. MB.**

MR. PRESTO CHANGO 1968
6 oz. yellow plastic bottle with red hat, black eyes and pink lips. Holds No Tear Shampoo. OSP $2.25. **CMV $6., $8. MB.**

BUGLE 1965
6 oz. blue plastic bugle with yellow cap. Holds Tot 'N Tyke Shampoo. OSP $1.79. **CMV $10. BO, $15. MB.**

FIFE 1965
6 oz. yellow plastic bottle with red cap. Came in hand lotion or hair trainer. OSP $1.49. **CMV $10. BO, $15. MB.**

THREE LITTLE PIGS 1967-68
3 oz. each, 4 1/2" high. Blue pigs, yellow hat holds bubble bath, yellow pig, green hat holds baby shampoo, and pink pig with pink hat holds baby lotion. OSP $1.35. **CMV $6. each, $9. MB.**

GOOD HABIT RABBIT 1967
3 oz., 4 1/2" high. White plastic rabbit, green hat and orange carrot. Came in Tot 'N Tyke Shampoo. OSP $1.50. **CMV $8., $12. MB.**

THREE BEARS 1966-67
4 3/4" high each. 3 oz. each. White plastic bottles with blue caps. OSP $1.25 each. Papa Bear holds baby oil. **CMV $10. BO, $14. MB.** Mama Bear holds baby lotion, Baby Bear holds shampoo. **CMV $8. BO, $12. MB each.**

A WINNER 1960-62
4 oz. maroon plastic boxing gloves with white caps. Tied togehter with white plastic cord. Hand Guard and Hair Guard. OSP $1.98. **CMV $20. MB, $7. each bottle.**

SPACE AGE 1968-69
4 oz. silver and yellow plastic rocket holds liquid hair trainer. OSP $1.50. **CMV $3., $5. MB.**

BO BO THE ELEPHANT 1970
5 oz. light or dark pink plastic bottle of Non Tear Shampoo. OSP $2.50. **CMV $3. BO, $5. MB.**

RED STREAK BOAT 1972-73
5 oz. red plastic boat, white cap. Holds bubble bath. OSP $2. **CMV $5. MB, $3. BO.**

SPINNING TOP 1966-67
4 oz. red and white top holds bubble bath, yellow top spinner. OSP $1.75. **CMV $10. MB, $6. BO.**

LITTLE CHAMP 1967-68
1/2 oz. each with white caps. Blue boxing glove holds Non Tear Shampoo, yellow glove holds Hair Trainer. OSP $2.50. **CMV $17. MB. Each glove $5.**

WHISTLE TOTS 1966-67
6 3/4" high, 4 oz. white plastic bottle with whistle cap. Red cap fireman holds Tot 'N Tyke Shampoo. Blue cap policeman holds Hair Trainer and green clown holds bubble bath. OSP $1.50 each. **CMV $7. BO mint, $10. MB.**

SCHOOL DAYS 1966-67
8 oz. red and white plastic ruler holds Non Tear Shampoo. Yellow cap. OSP $1.98. **CMV $7., $10. MB.**

MILK BATH 1968-69
6 oz. pink plastic milk can holds powdered bubble bath. OSP $4. **CMV $3. BO, $5. MB.**

CUCKOO CLOCK 1965-66
10 oz. red, white and blue plastic clock holds bubble bath. OSP $2.50. **CMV $8., $10. MB.**

WRIST WASH BUBBLE BATH 1969-70
2 oz. orange plastic clock with blue cap. OSP $3. **CMV $6. MB, $4. BO.**

RING 'EM UP CLEAN 1970-72
8 oz. orange plastic bottle with red or white cap holds Non Tear Shampoo. OSP $2.50. **CMV $3., $5. MB.**

SAFE SAM 1965
8 oz. red and black plastic safe holds bubble bath. OSP $1.98. **CMV $8., $11. MB.**

GLOBE BANK 1966-67
10 oz. blue plastic globe holds bubble bath. Black base. Bank has 5 different colored sets of stick on countries. North America came in orange, blue, tan, pink or yellow. OSP $2.50. **CMV $16. MB, $10. BO.**

MAD HATTER 1970
6 oz. bronze plastic with pink hat and clock. Came in bubble bath. OSP $3. **CMV $4. BO, $6. MB.**

CONCERTINA 1970-72
8 oz. blue and yellow plastic squeeze bottle. Holds bubble bath. Musical cap with pink strap. OSP $2.50. **CMV $8. MB, $6. BO.**

CONCERTINA 1962-65
8 oz. red and yellow plastic squeeze bottle with musical cap. Holds bubble bath. OSP $1.98. **CMV $12., $15. MB.**

MR. LION 1967
4 oz. white plastic bottle with red bubble pipe over white cap. Holds bubble bath. OSP $1.50. **CMV $6. BO, $8. MB.**

TIN MAN 1967
4 oz. white plastic bottle with blue bubble pipe over white cap. Holds Non Tear Shampoo. OSP $1.50. **CMV $6. BO, $8. MB.**

STRAW MAN 1967
4 oz. white plastic bottle with yellow bubble pipe over white cap. Holds hand lotion. OSP $1.50. **CMV $6. BO, $8. MB.**

BIRD HOUSE 1969
7" high orange plastic bottom with tan roof. Holds 8 oz. of Powdered Bubble Bath. OSP $3.75. **CMV $7. BO, $9. MB.**

SANTA'S HELPER 1967-68
Red and white sponge with 6 oz. tube of Gel Bubble Bath. OSP $2.50. **CMV $8. MB.**

AVONVILLE SLUGGER 1961-62
6 oz. tan plastic bat holds shampoo. OSP $1.49. **CMV $12. BO, $17. MB.**

SURE WINNER SLUGGER DECANTER 1973
6 oz. yellow plastic bat. Holds Sure Winner Bracing Lotion or Liquid Hair Trainer or Avon Spicy After Shave. SSP $2. **CMV $4. mint, no box issued.**

TOPSY TURVEY CLOWN 1965 ONLY
10 oz. red, white and yellow plastic clown. Blue hat, black feet. Holds bubble bath. OSP $2.50. **CMV $16. MB, $12. BO mint.**

ONE TWO LACE MY SHOE 1968-69
8 oz. bubble bath. Pink plastic shoe with orange tie on and yellow cap. Green or yellow roof. OSP $2.98. **CMV $6. BO, $9. MB.**

TIC TOC TURTLE 1968-69
8 oz. 5 1/2" high. Green turtle, yellow clock face with pink hands. Bubble bath. OSP $2.50. **CMV $6. BO, $9. MB.**

LAND HO 1961-62
(Left) 8 oz. blue & white plastic telescope holds Hair Trainer. OSP $1.49. **CMV $17. MB, $12. BO mint.**

NAUGHTY-LESS 1961-62
(Right) 8 oz. red & white submarine with whtie & blue cap. Holds bubble bath. OSP $1.79. **CMV $15. BO mint, $20. MB.**

FIRST MATE SHAMPOO 1963-64
8 oz. blue and white plastic sailor with white hat. OSP $1.98. **CMV $15. MB, $11. BO.**

CAPTAIN'S BUBBLE BATH 1963-64
8 oz. white, yellow and black plastic bottle with blue hat. OSP $1.98. **CMV $15. MB, $11. BO.**

AQUA CAR 1964-65
(Left) 8 oz. red & white plastic bottle of bubble bath. OSP $1.98. **CMV $10., $15. MB.**

S.S. SUDS 1970-71
(Right) 8 oz. blue & white plastic boat holds No Tear Shampoo. OSP $3. **CMV $5., $7. MB.**

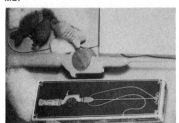

TUB CATCH 1968-69
2 ft. long yellow rod & reel holds 6 oz. bubble bath. Pink, green & blue plastic fish. OSP $3.50. **CMV $9. MB.**

SMILEY THE WHALE 1967-68
(Left) 9" blue plastic whale holds 9 oz. bubble bath. OSP $1.98. **CMV $6. BO, $9. MB.**
WHITEY THE WHALE 1959-62
(Right) 8 oz. white plastic whale holds bubble bath. OSP $1.79. **CMV $15. MB, $10. BO.**

EASTER DEC A DOO 1968-69
(Left) 8 oz. pink & yellow plastic egg holds bubble bath. Came with stick on decorations. OSP $2.50. **CMV $6. MB, $4. BO.**
HUMPTY DUMPTY 1963-65
(Right) 8 oz. plastic bottle of bubble bath. Blue bottom, white top, black belt. OSP $1.98. **CMV $9. MB, $6. BO.**

LITTLE MISSY ROLLING PIN 1966-67
12" long, 8 oz. pink plastic center with orange ends. Holds Non Tear Shampoo. OSP $2.25. **CMV $9. BO mint, $13. MB.**

SANTA'S CHIMNEY 1964-65
Red & white box holds 5 oz. of powdered bubble bath. Top of box makes a puzzle game. OSP $1.98. **CMV $20. MB.**

LIL FOLKS TIME 1961-64
(Left) 8 oz. yellow & white plastic clock with yellow cap & red time hands, holds bubble bath. OSP $1.75. **CMV $8. BO, $11. MB.**
TIC TOC TIGER 1967-69
(Right) 8 oz. orange & white plastic clock with yellow cap & hands, holds bubble bath. OSP $1.75. **CMV $6. BO, $8. MB.**

BIRD FEEDER 1967-68
11" high, black and white plastic center with red base and yellow top. Holds 7 1/2 oz. powdered bubble bath. OSP $3.50. **CMV $8. BO, $12. MB.**

PACKY THE ELEPHANT 1964-65
3 oz. each. OSP $1.10 each. Each has white hat. Blue holds baby oil, yellow holds baby shampoo, baby lotion in red. **CMV red & blue $10. BO each, $15. MB, Yellow $15. BO, $20. MB.**

TOOFIE TWOSOME 1963-64
This is the 1st issue of the Toofie series. 3 1/2 oz. green & blue tube & green cap. Choice of red, yellow, blue or green toothbrush. OSP $1.25. **CMV $8. MB, BO $3.**

TOOFIE TOOTHPASTE 1967-68
3 1/2 oz. white tube with racoon & pink cap & toothbrush, pink & white box. OSP $1.25 **CMV $6. MB, $2. BO.**

MARY NON TEAR SHAMPOO 1968-69
(Left) 3 oz. pink plastic bottle. OSP $1.35.
CMV $6. BO, $8. MB.
LITTLE LAMB BABY LOTION 1968-69
(Center) 3 oz. white plastic lamb with blue cap.
OSP $1.35. **CMV $5. BO, $7. MB.**
LITTLE RED SCHOOLHOUSE 1968-69
(Right) 3 oz. red plastic school with yellow cap.
Contains bubble bath. OSP $1.35. **CMV $6.
BO, $8. MB.**

LITTLE HELPER IRON 1962-64
(Left) 8 oz. blue plastic iron with white handle.
Holds bubble bath. OSP $2. **CMV $13. mint,
$17. MB.**
WATERING CAN 1962-64
(Right) 8 oz. yellow plastic bottle holds bubble
bath. Blue cap. OSP $2. **CMV $13. mint,
$17. MB.**

TOOFIE TOOTHPASTE 1969-70
3 1/2 oz. blue & green tube with pink cap &
toothbrush in blue & green box. OSP $1.35.
CMV $5. MB, $2. BO.

CHIEF SCRUBBEM 1969-70
(Left) 4 oz. red & yellow plastic Indian holds
liquid soap. OSP $2.50. **CMV $6. MB, $4.
BO.**
SCRUB MUG 1968-69
(Right) 6 oz. blue plastic mug with blue brush
lid. Holds liquid soap. OSP $2.50. **CMV $6.
MB, $4. BO.**

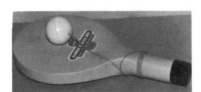

LIL TOM TURTLES 1961-63
3 oz. plastic turtles. OSP $1.10 each. Each
has white hat. Yellow holds baby shampoo,,
blue has baby oil & baby lotion in red. **CMV
$10. each, $15. MB.**

PADDLE 'N' BALL SET 1966-67
6 oz. tan plastic paddle with red cap. Holds
shampoo. Rubber ball hooked to paddle. 8"
long by 4 1/2" wide. OSP $1.75. **CMV $12.,
$15. MB.**

TOY SOLDIERS 1964
4 oz. each. Red, white & blue plastic bottles,
black caps. Came in Hair Trainer, shampoo,
hand lotion, bubble bath. OSP $1.25 each.
CMV $10. each BO, $12. MB.

MICKEY MOUSE 1969-71
(Left) 4 1/2 oz. red pants, black & white palstic
Mickey with yellow feet. Holds bubble bath.
OSP $3.50. **CMV $5. BO, $7. MB.**
PLUTO 1970-71
(Right) 4 oz. yellow & black plastic dog with
red collar. Holds Non Tear shampoo. OSP
$3.50. **CMV $5. BO, $7. MB.**

JET PLANE 1965 ONLY
3 oz. red, white & blue plastic tube with white
plastic wings came in gel bubble bath,
children's gel shampoo or Hair Tainer. OSP
$1.50. **CMV $10. mint, $15. MB.**

TOPSY TURVEY 1970-72
(Left) 4 oz. green plastic bottle with white cap
holds bubble bath. OSP $2. **CMV $3. MB, $1.
BO.**
BALL & CUP 1972-73
(Right) 4 oz. blue bottom with green cup &
ball. Holds shampoo. OSP $2. **CMV $4. MB,
$2. BO.**

TUB TALK TELEPHONE 1969
(Blue) 6 oz. blue plastic telephone with yellow cap & holder. Holds No Tear Shampoo. OSP $2.25 **CMV $7., $9. MB.**

VERY OWN TELEPHONE 1964-65
(Red) 6 oz. red plastic telephone & base. Holds Baby Shampoo. OSP $1.98 **CMV $9. BO, $13. MB.**

TUB TALK TELEPHONE 1967-68
(Yellow) 6 oz. yellow telephone with red cap & holder. Holds Tot 'N' Tyke shampoo. OSP $1.75 **CMV $8. BO, $11. MB.**

FRILLY DUCK 1960-62
(Left) 3 oz. yellow plastic duck with blue cap. Came in baby oil, baby lotion & Tot 'N' Tyke shampoo. OSP 98c. **CMV $10., $13. MB.**

PIG IN A POKE 1960-62
(Right) 8 oz. pink plastic pig holds bubble bath. Came in pink bag. OSP $1.79. **CMV $9. BO, $14. BO with bag, $18. MB.**

BUNNY FLUFF PUFF 1979-80
(Left) 3.5 oz. yellow plastic with fluff tail & pink eyes & ears. Holds children's talc. SSP $6. **CMV $3.50 MB.**

RED STREAK CAR 1979-80
(Right) 7 oz. red plastic with blue & silver stick on decals. Holds bubble bath for children. SSP $4. **CMV $3. MB.**

TOOTHBRUSH DUO (CHILDREN'S) 1979
(Left) Red & pink box holds 1 red & 1 white toothbrush for kids. SSP 89c. **CMV .50¢ MB.**

PINK PANTHER TOOTHBRUSH HOLDER 1979
(Right) Pink plastic holder. Yellow & red toothbrushes. Blue & pink box. SSP $5. **CMV $3. MB.**

BARNEY BEAVER TOOTHBRUSHES & HOLDER 1973
(Left) 4" high, brown plastic with white & blue. Has pink & blue toothbrushes. Comes with a sticker to put on wall. SSP $2.50. **CMV $4. MB.**

'I LOVE TOOFIE' TOOTHBRUSHES & HOLDER 1973
(Right) 5" high, white & pink, holds red & blue toothbrushes. Comes with sticker to put on wall. SSP $2. **CMV $4. MB.**

BABY SHOE PIN CUSHION 1973-74
(Left) 7 oz. whie plastic with pink pin cushion & blue bow. Filled with baby lotion. SSP $4. **CMV $4. BO, $5. MB.**

SUNNY BUNNY BABY POMANDER 1973-76
(Center) Wax figurine with nursery fresh fragrance. SSP $5. **CMV $5. BO, $6. MB.**

SAFETY PIN DECANTER 1973-74
(Right) 8 oz. yellow plastic filled with baby lotion. SSP $3. **CMV $4. BO, $5. MB.**

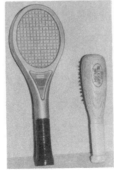

TENNIS ANYONE? 1975-76
(Left) 5 oz. gray & black plastic. Holds Sweet Honesty after bath freshener or Avon Spicy after shave. OSP $3. **CMV $2.50.**

SLUGGER BRUSH 1974-75
(Right) 7" long brown & black plastic. OSP $3.50. **CMV $3.**

ON THE RUN "JOGGING SHOE" 1978-79
(Left) 6 oz. blue plastic with white stripes. Holds Wild Country after shave or Sweet Honesty body splash. SSP $4. **CMV $4. MB.**

CONAIR "HAIR DRYER" 1978-79
(Right) 6 oz. off-white plastic. Blue letters and cap. Holds Naturally Gentle shampoo. SSP $5. **CMV $4. MB.**

ACCUSING ALLIGATOR 1978-79
(Left) 6 oz. green, yellow & tan plastic. Holds bubble bath. SSP $5. **CMV $3.50 MB.**

SUPERMAN BUBBLE BATH 1978-79
(Right) 8 oz. blue, red & gray plastic. Holds bubble bath. Box came with 2 red and yellow plastic cut out capes. SSP $6. **CMV $5. MB.**

HANG TEN SKATEBOARD DECANTER 1978-79
(Left) 5.5 oz. yellow plastic with top stick on decal. Holds bubble bath for children. SSP $5. **CMV $2.50 MB.**

KARROT TAN DECANTER 1978-79
(Center) 4 oz. orange plastic with green leaf top. Holds Bronze Glory tanning lotion. SSP $5. **CMV $4. BO, no box issued.**

HEAVY HITTER DECANTER 1978-79
(Right) 4 oz. dark blue plastic. White letters. holds non tear shampoo. SSP $5. **CMV $3. MB.**

SPACE PATROLLER DECANTER 1979-80
(Left) 8 oz. gray plastic, black cap & stick on decals. SSP $5. **CMV $3.**

SPIDERMAN TOOTHBRUSH & HOLDER 1979-80
(Right) Red & blue plastic. Yellow & green Avon toothbrushes. SSP $5. **CMV $2.50 MB.**

TOOFIE THE TIGER 1966-67
(Left) 3 1/2 oz. green & orange tube, green cap, toothbrush. OSP $1.35. **CMV $6. MB, $3. BO mint.**

TOOFIE ON GUARD 1968-69
(Right) 3 1/2 oz. red, white, & blue tube, blue cap. Avon toothbrush. OSP $1.25. **CMV $2. BO mint, $5. MB.**

MY PUPPY 1986
Brown stuffed pup 11" high. DP $12. **CMV $12.**

SPOTTY TO THE RESCUE TOOTHBRUSH HOLDER 1976-77
Red, white & black plastic toothbrush holder holds 2 Avon toothbrushes. SSP $2.49. **CMV $2. MB.**

BATMOBILE 1978-79
(Left) 6 oz. blue & silver plastic with stick on decals. Came in bubble bath for children. SSP $5. **CMV $5. MB.**

LIP POP POMADE "PEPSI" 1978-79
(Right) Dark amber plastic. Gray cap. Looks like Pepsi Cola bottle. SSP $3. **CMV $3. MB.**

SWEET PICKLES FUN BOOK & RECORD 1978-79
Book & record issued by Avon Products. Came in an envelope. There are 4 different ones. SSP $2. **CMV $3. complete mint.**

GRID KID LIQUID HAIR TRAINER 1974-75
(Left) 8 oz. red, black & white plastic. OSP $2. **CMV $2. BO, $3. MB.**

ARCH E. BEAR BRUSH & COMB 1975-76
(Right) Red, white & blue brush with white comb. OSP $3. **CMV $2., $3. MB.**

JACKKNIFE COMB & BRUSH 1974-76
(Left) Blue & silver plastic comb. Cub Scout gold label on top. OSP $5. **CMV $3. MB.**

ICE CREAM COMB 1977-78
(Center) Orange plastic comb with pink & brown ice cream & red cherry on top. OSP $3. **CMV $2. MB.**

REGGIE RACCOON HAIRBRUSH & COMB 1977
(Right) 6 1/4" long. Brown, white, pink & black brush & white comb. SSP $4. **CMV $2. MB.**

GIRAFFABATH BATH BRUSH 1977-79
(Left) Orange & beige plastic. Blue eyes. OSP $6. **CMV $3.50 MB.**

BATMAN STYLING BRUSH 1977-78
(Center) Blue, gray & black plastic brush. OSP $6. **CMV $5. MB.**

SUPERMAN STYLING BRUSH 1977
(Right) Red & blue plastic brush. OSP $6. **CMV $5. MB.**

WALLY WALRUS TOOTHBRUSH HOLDER & TOOTHBRUSH 1977-78
Adhesive back holder sticks to wall. Came with 2 child sized Avon toothbrushes in red & white. Plastic holder is blue & red with white hat & trim. SSP $2. **CMV $2. MB.**

HOT DOG! BRUSH & COMB 1975-76
(Left) Yellow & red plastic comb. OSP $3.
CMV $2., $3. MB.

SUNANA BRONZE GLORY TANNING LOTION 1974-76
(Right) 6 oz. yellow plastic banana. OSP $2.75. **CMV $3. BO, no box issued.**

TED E. BEAR TOOTHBRUSH HOLDER 1974-75
Box holds tan, pink & white plastic holder & pink & white Avon toothbrushes. OSP $2.75.
CMV $3. MB.

TOOFIE THE CLOWN 1978
Orange, yellow & white plastic toothbrush holder. Blue & pink toothbrushes. SSP $3.
CMV $2. MB.

PRECIOUS LAMB BABY LOTION 1975-76
6 oz. white plastic lamb with blue bow. Holds baby lotion. SSP $3. **CMV $4. MB.**

SCRUBBO THE ELEPHANT BATH BRUSH 1975
White plastic, pink ears & cheeks. SSP $2.29.
CMV $2. MB. 1976 issue was all pink plastic.
Each is 8" long. SSP $2. **CMV $2. MB.**

SCHOOL DAYS RULER COMB 1976-79
Box holds yellow plastic 6" ruler comb. OSP $3. **CMV $2. MB.**

TOOFIE TOOTHPASTE 1971-73
(Left) 3 1/2 oz. yellow & orange tube & box.
OSP 89c. **CMV $2., $3. MB.**

TOOFIE TOOTHBRUSH DUO 1973-74
(Right) Pak of 2, green worm & yellow bird.
SSP $2. **CMV $2. MB.**

ELLA ELEPHANT SCENTED STUFFED ANIMAL 1979-80
Pink box holds pink scented elephant with turquoise ears & pink ribbon. Has Avon tag.
Made in Taiwan. SSP $8. **CMV $6. MB.**

LOVING LION DECANTER 1978-79
(Left) 8 oz. plastic purple, yellow, pink & orange. Holds Non Tear Shampoo. SSP $5.
CMV $3.50 MB.

THREE RING CIRCUS CHILDREN'S TALC 1978-79
(Center) 5 oz., 2 sections of center turn around. SSP $2.49. **CMV $2. MB.**

OCTOPUS TOOTHBRUSH HOLDER 1978-79
(Right) Purple & orange plastic toothbrush holder. Comes with orange & white Avon toothbrushes. SSP $4. **CMV $2.50 MB.**

MOST VALUABLE GORILLA 1979-80
(Left) 4 oz. orange & blue plastic stick on front & back decals in any letter. Holds bubble bath for children. **CMV $3.50 MB.**

WILLIE WEATHERMAN 1979-80
(Center) 6 oz. tan plastic, pink cap. Blue umbrella changes color with the weather.
Holds Non Tear Shampoo. SSP $5. **CMV $3. MB.**

IMP THE CHIMP BATH BRUSH 1980
(Right) Brown plastic, yellow, black & pink trim.
10" long. SSP $7. **CMV $4. MB.**

TOOFIE TIGER TOOTHBRUSHES & HOLDER 1976
(Left) Yellow, black, white & pink. Has 1 pink & 1 white toothbrush. OSP $2.50. **CMV 42. MB.**

TOOFIE TOOTHBRUSH DUO 1971-73
(Center) One yellow giraffe, 1 pink rabbit brush. OSP $1. **CMV $2. MB.**

TORTOISE 'N' HARE TOOTHBRUSH DUO 1975-76
(Right) Green tortoise & yellow hare. OSP $1.80 **CMV $1. MB.**

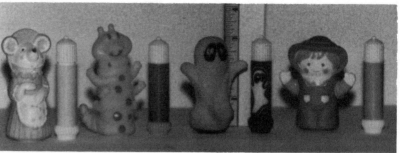

BRONTOSAURUS BUBBLE BATH 1975-76
(Left) 10 oz. blue gray plastic. OSP $3.50.
CMV $2. BO, $3. MB.
LOVABLE LEO 1974-76
(Right) 10 oz. yellow plastic, pink cap.
Children's shampoo. OSP $3. **CMV $2. BO,
$3. MB.**

SURE WINNER CATCHER'S MITT 1974-75
(Left) 6 oz. brown plastic with brown cap.
Holds Avon liquid hair trainer. OSP $2. **CMV
$3.**
**WINKIE BLINK CLOCK BUBBLE BATH
1975-76**
(Right) 8 oz. yellow with blue clock hands &
blue cap. OSP $4. **CMV $3. BO, $4. MB.**

TURN A WORD BUBBLE BATH 1972-74
8 oz. pink plastic bottle with white cap & green
lettered sides. OSP $3.50. **CMV $3.**
**CLANCY THE CLOWN SOAP HOLDER &
SOAP 1973-74**
Orange, pink and white clown holds green and
white, pink and orange 3 oz. soap. SSP $3.50.
CMV $6. MB.

MILLICENT MOUSE DEMI STICK 1977-78
(Left) Came with Pink & Pretty fragrance demi
stick. Colors are pink & white. OSP $3.75.
CMV $3.50 MB.
GLOW WORM 1977-79
(Inside Left) Came with Care Deeply lip balm.
White rubber top with purple spots. Demi stick
is blue & green. OSP $3.50. **CMV $3.50 MB.**
GILROY THE GHOST 1977-78
(Inside Right) Came with Care Deeply lip
balm. White & black rubber top with black,
green & white demi stick. OSP $3.50. **CMV
$3.50 MB.**
HUCK L. BERRY 1977-78
(Right) Came with Care Deeply lip balm. Blue,
yellow & white rubber top with yellow & white
demi stick. OSP $3.75. **CMV $3.50 MB.**

**COUNTRY KITCHEN SPICE ANGEL DOLL
1982-83**
Box holds spice fragrance doll 7 1/2" high. DP
$8. **CMV $8. MB.**

JACK IN A BOX GLACE 1976
(Left) White plastic with pink & green trim. SSP
$2. **CMV $3.50 MB.**
CHICK A PEEK GLACE 1977
(Right) Yellow plastic back & chick with purple
egg. SSP $2. **CMV $3.50 MB.**

**KISS 'N' MAKEUP LIP GLOSS COMPACT
1977-79**
(Top) Came with Frostlight Peach & Frostlight
Pink lip gloss. Red plastic container. OSP $4.
CMV $1.
LOVE LOCKET GLACE 1972
(Bottom) **CMV $6. MB, $4. BO.**

TOOFIE TRAIN 1974-75
Red plastic train, yellow plastic cup. Red &
blue toofie toothbrushes & yellow with red cap
Toofie toothpaste. OSP $5. **CMV $5., $7. MB.**

RAPID RABBIT PIN PAL 1974-75
(Left) White plastic with pink & green. Feet swing. Filled with perfumed glace. SSP $2.
CMV $2., $3. MB.
MYRTLE TURTLE PIN PAL 1974
(Right) Green plastic with pink & green. Filled with perfumed glace. SSP $2. **CMV $2., $3. MB.**

CHILDREN'S FUN JEWELRY
LUV-A-DUCKY 1973
(Top Left) Yellow & orange. SSP $2. **CMV $3.50, $5. MB.**
PANDY BEAR PIN 1973
(Bottom Left) Black & white. SSP $1.50.
CMV $3.50, $5. MB.
FLY-A-KITE 1973
(Center) Red, white and blue. SSP $2. **CMV $3.50, $5. MB.**

FUZZY BUG 1973-74
(Top Right) Blue with green fur. SSP $2.
CMV $3.50, $5. MB.
PERKEY PARROT 1973
(Bottom Right) Red & green. SSP $1.50.
CMV $3.50, $5. MB.

ON THE FARM BANK 1985
(Center) Stick on stickers & packets of bubble bath inside. DP $3. **CMV $3.**
CHRISTMAS TOYLAND CANDY 1984
(Left) 8 1/4" high tin can full of candy. DP $4.
CMV $2. can only.
PLUSH LAMB BANK 1984
(Right) 8" long, 6" high. Fabric covered plastic bank. DP $8. **CMV $8. MB.**

ROTO-BOAT FLOATING SOAP DISH & SOAP 1973-75
9" long blue & white boat with red rudder holds 3 oz. blue soap. SSP $3. **CMV $5.** Reissued with "R" on bottom.

BOBBIN' ROBIN PIN 1975-76
(Top Left) White cage, red bird (bird movable).
OSP $2. **CMV $3. MB.**
MINUTE MOUSE PIN 1974-75
(Bottom Left) White with blue clock, orange hands & numbers. OSP $2. **CMV $3. MB.**
PEDAL PUSHER PIN 1975-76
(Top Center) Blue elephant with green jacket & pink bike. OSP $1.89. **CMV $3. MB.**

LICKETY STICK MOUSE PIN 1974-76
(Bottom Center) White plastic with green hat & pink striped stick. OSP $2. **CMV $3. MB.**
MAGIC RABBIT PIN 1975-76
(Top Right) White & pink rabbit with gray hat.
OSP $2. **CMV $3. MB.**
COTTON TAIL GLACE 1976-78
(Bottom Right) Yellow & pink with white tail.
OSP $2. **CMV $3. MB.**

BUMBLEY BEE PINS 1973-74
Yellow with black stripes. One with big stripes & 1 narrow stripes. OSP $2. **CMV $4., $6. MB.**

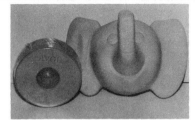

GREAT CATCH, CHARLIE BROWN, SOAP HOLDER & SOAP 1975-76
(Left) Red, white, black & brown plastic. OSP $4. **CMV $6. MB.**

QUACK & DOODLE FLOATING SOAP DISH & SOAP 1974-75
(Right) Yellow rubber with yellow soap. OSP $3.50. **CMV $5. MB.**

RING AROUND ROSIE 1966-67
Pink rubber elephant sticks on wall with blue bar of Avon soap. OSP $2.25. **CMV $15. MB, soap only $6., elephant only $4.**

CLEAN SHOT 1970-72
Orange net holds orange basketball sponge & 1 bar of Clean Shot soap. OSP $4.50. **CMV $6. MB. set.**

CHILDREN'S PERFUME GLACE PIN PALS
Add $1. each MB.

FUNNY BUNNY 1973-74
(Top Left) Pink & white. SSP $2. **CMV $4.**

CALICO CAT 1973
(Top Center) Red with white dots. Also came red & no dots. SSP $2. **CMV $4.**

CALICO CAT 1974-75
(Repeat Top Center) Blue with white dots. Also came blue with no dots on bottom half. OSP $2. **CMV $3. each.**

BLOUSE MOUSE 1972
(Top Right) Green & pink. Also came green with white trim. SSP $2. **CMV $4.**

BLUE MOO 1974
(Middle Left) Blue & pink. SSP $2. **CMV $3.**

SNIFFY PIN PAL 1972-75
(Middle Center) Black, white & pink. SSP $2. **CMV $3.**

ELPHIE THE ELEPHANT 1973
(Middle Right) Yellow & pink. SSP $2. **CMV $4.**

GINGERBREAD PIN PAL 1973
(Bottom Center) Brown & pink. Also came brown & white. SSP $2. **CMV $5. pink, $6. white.**

PUPPY LOVE PIN PAL GLACE 1975
(Top Left) Beige dog with black ears & pink pillow. OSP $2. **CMV $4. MB.**

WEE WILLY WINTER PIN PAL GLACE 1974-75
(Top Center) White snowman with pink hat, scarf & mittens. OSP $1.88. **CMV $4. MB.**

SUNNY FRESH ORANGE GLACE NECK-LACE 1974-75
(Top Right) Orange & yellow with green cord. OSP $3. **CMV $4. MB.**

PETER PATCHES PIN PAL GLACE 1975-76
(Bottom Left) Yellow with red & blue trim. OSP $2. **CMV $4. MB.**

CHICKEN LITTLE PIN PAL GLACE 1975
(Bottom Inside Left) Yellow chicken with pink flower & green leaf. OSP $2.49. **CMV $4.**

WILLIE THE WORM PIN PAL GLACE 1974-75
(Bottom Inside Right) Red apple, green worm. OSP $2. **CMV $4. MB.**

ROCK-A-ROO PIN PAL GLACE 1975-77
(Bottom Right) Pink with dark pink rocking pouch. OSP $2. **CMV $3. MB.**

WASH AWEIGH SOAP & DISH 1966-67
Green plastic boat dish & yellow anchor soap
on a rope. OSP $1.98. **CMV boat $6., anchor
soap $9., set $18. MB.**

ORIENTAL FAN PERFUME GLACE 1982-83
(Left) Red plastic fan, black tassel, choice of
Timeless or Candid. Red & black box. SSP
$4. **CMV $2. MB.**
STRAWBERRY CONE LIP GLOSS 1982-83
(Right) Yellow & pink plastic, yellow &
lavender box. SSP $4. **CMV $2. MB.**

**REGGIE RACOON HAIR BRUSH AND COMB
1973**
6 1/2" long, tan and black with tan comb. SSP
$3. **CMV $4. MB.**

REGINALD G. RACOON III 1970-71
Black, brown and white rubber soap dish and 3
oz. pink vest soap. OSP $3.50. **CMV racoon
only $2., $6. set MB.**
RANDY PANDY SOAP DISH 1972-74
Black, white & pink rubber soap dish & 3 oz.
white soap. OSP $3.50. **CMV panda only
$2., set $6. MB.**

FREDDIE THE FROG 1969-70
(Left) Green rubber frog soap dish & green
vest soap. Pink lips & pink band around hat.
OSP $1.75. **CMV frog only $2., with soap
$6. MB.**
FREDDIE THE FROG 1965-66
(Right) Green rubber frog with yellow hat &
eyes, pink lips, green soap. OSP $3. **CMV
frog only $5., with soap $10. MB.**

GAYLORD GATER 1967-69
10" long green and yellow rubber soap dish
with yellow soap. OSP $2.25. **CMV gater
only $2., $7. set MB.**
**TOPSY TURTLE FLOATING SOAP DISH &
SOAP 1973-74**
7" long green rubber soap dish with 3 oz. pink
soap. SSP $2. **CMV $3. MB.** Reissued 1979.
Some came light green body and dark green
head. Also came matching body and head.

**BARNEY BEAVER SOAP DISH & SOAP
1971-72**
10 1/2" long, brown soap dish and brown vest
soap. OSP $3.50. **CMV $6. MB, Beaver only
$2.**

FIRST DOWN 1965-67
Large box holds real junior size football & 6 oz.
brown football soap on a rope. Rope comes
out side of soap. OSP $3.95 Avon soap & ball.
CMV soap $9. MB, ball $15., set MB $27.50 .

**PADDLEWOG FROG FLOATING SOAP DISH
& SOAP 1975-76**
Green plastic with pink propeller and yellow
soap. OSP $4. **CMV $3. MB.**

**SOAP BOAT, FLOATING SOAP DISH AND
SOAP 1973-74**
7 1/2" long blue and red boat with white sail
and white soap. SSP $2. **CMV $5. MB.**

PINK PEARL SCRUB AWAY NAIL BRUSH AND SOAP 1977-78
3 oz. soap, pink brush shaped like pink pearl eraser. OSP $4. **CMV $4. MB.**

FREDDY THE FROG MUG 1970
5 oz. white glass with red or orange top and white cap. holds bubble bath. OSP $3.50. **CMV $5., $7. MB.**

GAYLORD GATOR MUG 1970-72
5 oz. white glass mug with yellow top and white cap. Holds Non Tear Shampoo. OSP $3.50. **CMV $5., $7. MB.**

TERRIBLE TUBBLES FLOATING SOAP DISH AND SOAP 1977-78
(Left) Blue plastic dish with 3 oz. soap. SSP $4. **CMV $5. MB.**

RANDY PANDY SOAP DISH AND SOAP 1976-77
(Right) Black, light blue and red rubber soap dish and 3 oz. blue and white soap. SSP $4. **CMV (Panda only) $1., Set $5. MB.**

MOON FLIGHT GAME 1970-72
4 oz. white Space Capsule holds Non Tear Shampoo. Comes with black game sheet. OSP $4. **CMV $5. MB, $1.50 BO.**

MR. ROBOTTLE 1971-72
8" high plastic bottle with blue body and red legs and arms. Silver and yellow cap. Holds bubble bath. Came with white plastic wrench to put together. OSP $3.50. **CMV $4. BO, $6. MB.**

KANGA WINKS 1971-72
7" high yellow and orange plastic bottle with pink hat, holds 8 oz. of bubble bath. Box also holds black and white plastic target and package of 16 plastic chips for tiddlywinks. OSP $4. **CMV $4. complete set, $1. Kangaroo only, $6. set MB.**

CHOO-CHOO TRAIN 1971-72
Soap coach is 4" long plastic soap dish with yellow bar of soap. OSP $150 **CMV $6. MB with soap, $1. soap coach only.** Caboose is pink plastic bottle, 3" long with Non Tear Shampoo. OSP $2. **CMV $4. MB** Puffer Chugger is $" long green plastic bottle with yellow cap and nose. Holds bubble bath. OSP $2. **CMV $4. MB**

SPLASH DOWN BUBBLE BATH 1970-71
8 oz. white plastic bottle with red cap and yellow base ring. Came with 3 plastic toss rings. OSP $4. **CMV $3. BO, $5. MB.**

HICKORY DICKORY CLOCK 1971-72
5 1/2" high, 8 oz. yellow plastic cheese clock with orange face and pink hands, purple mouse cap. Contains Non Tear Shampoo. OSP $4.50. **CMV $4. BO, $6. MB.**

POP-A-DUCK GAME 1978
6 oz. blue plastic with red-orange cap. Came with 3 green balls. Pink, orange and yellow ducks and red-orange ball holder. Bottle holds bubble bath for children. SSP $4. **CMV $4. MB.**

ROCKABYE PONY DECANTER 1975-76
6 oz. yellow plastic, holds Clearly Gentle Baby Lotion. OSP $4. **CMV $3. BO, $4. MB.**

JACK-IN-THE-BOX 1975-76
4 oz. yellow and pink plastic, holds baby cream. OSP $4. **CMV $3. BO, $4. MB.**

POP A DUCK 1971-72
6 oz. blue plastic bottle holds bubble bath. 3 plastic ducks and ball. OSP $3.50. **CMV $5. complete set MB.**

LOOP-A-MOOSE GAME AND SOAP 1972-75
7" high brown plastic moose, yellow antlers. has green, pink and yellow rings to toss. Comes with 3 oz. yellow soap. SSP $3. **CMV $3., $4. MB.**

EASTER DEC-A-DOO FOR CHILDREN 1978
(Left) 8 oz. plastic yellow base, pink top. Came with stick on decals. This is different from 68-69 issue. Old one does not say for children on label. Holds bubble bath. SSP $3.99. **CMV $3. MB, $2. BO.**

DUSTER D. DUCKLING FLUFF PUFF 1978-82
3.5 oz. yellow plastic and fluff top. Holds Delicate Daisies or Sweet Pickles perfumed talc. SSP $4.44. **CMV $3. MB, $2. BO.**

MAZE GAME 1971-72
6 oz. green plastic bottle, white cap. holds Non Tear Shampoo. OSP $2.50. **CMV $5. MB, $3. BO.**

HUGGY BEAR 1971-72
8 oz. brown plastic bottle with lace-up vest, holds bubble bath. OSP $3.50. **CMV $5. MB, $3. BO.**

SCHROEDER 1970-72
6 oz. red, white, black and yellow plastic bottle holds bubble bath. in piano shaped box. OSP $3.50. **CMV $4., $9. MB in piano box.**

LINUS 1970-72
4 oz. red, white and black plastic bottle holds Non Tear Shampoo. OSP $3. **CMV $6. MB, $3. BO.**

TYRANNOSAURUS REX 1976-78
4 oz. green plastic bottle, green rubber head. holds bubble bath for children. SSP $3. **CMV $2. BO, $3. MB.**

TUB SUB 1978-79
6 oz. yellow plastic, 10" long. Holds bubble bath for children. SSP $4. **CMV $2. BO, $3. MB.**

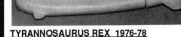

LITTLE WIGGLY GAME & BUBBLE BATH 1973
8 oz. green with pink legs, red and yellow hoops. Holds bubble bath. SSP $3.50. **CMV $3.50 MB.**

CUSTOM CAR 1976-78
7 oz. blue plastic bottle with red tire cap. Filled with bubble bath for children. OSP $5. **CMV $2. BO, $3. MB.**

TRICERATOPS 1977-78
8 1/2 oz. green plastic bottle. Came with bubble bath for children. OSP $5.50. **CMV $2. BO, $3. MB.**

LITTLE RAG DOLL 1982-83
4" high doll, red dress, yellow hair, green hair ribbons, black shoes. Comes with Demi Stick in moonwind or Sweet Honesty. SSP $7. **CMV $7. MB.**

ARISTOCAT 1971-72
4 oz. gray cat with pink collar holds Non Tear Shampoo. OSP $3. **CMV $4. BO, $5. MB.**

CLUCK A DOO 1971
8 oz. yellow bottle, pink hat. Came with stick on decals. holds bubble bath. OSP $3. **CMV $5. MB, $3. BO.**

COMBSICLE 1979-80
Popsicle box holds brown and beige Avon comb. SSP $2. **CMV $1. MB.**

CHOCOLATE CHIPLICK COMPACT 1979-80
Tan and brown plastic, holds lip gloss. SSP $3.50. **CMV $2. MB.**

POWDER DRILL 1979-80
5 oz. yellow plastic with silver plastic drill cap. Holds Wild Country or Electric Pre Shave. SSP $6. **CMV $4. MB.**

CLEAN-'EM-UP-PUMP 1981-82
8 oz. yellow plastic with white and yellow pump dispenser. Comes with card of stick on decals. Come in Liquid Cleanser. SSP $5. **CMV $3. MB.**

SUNBONNET SUE DEMI STICK 1975-77
.19 oz. red and white plastic. Pink & Pretty fragrance. OSP $2.50. **CMV $3. MB, $2. BO.**

NUTSHELL COLOR MAGIC LIPSTICK 1974-75
Peanut shaped case came in Pink Sorcery (blue lipstick) or Peach Sorcery (green lipstick). OSP $2. **CMV $3. MB, $2. BO.**

SCHOOL DAYS PENCIL LIP POMADE 1975-76
.13 oz. red, white and yellow plastic. Choice of strawberry, cherry or tutti-frutti. OSP $2.50. **CMV $3. MB, $2. BO.**

SWEET LIPS LIP GLOSS COOKIE 1975-76
Brown plastic with 2 shades of lip gloss. OSP $3. **CMV $3. MB, $2. BO.**

TUGGABLE TEDDY TOOTHBRUSH HOLDER 1980-81
Tan and blue plastic. Pink and green Avon toothbrushes. Orange ring on gold cord. SSP $5. **CMV $5. MB.**

SMILEY SNAIL TOOTHBRUSH HOLDER 1980-81
Yellow and green plastic. Orange and blue Avon toothbrushes. SSP $6. **CMV $6. MB.**

TED E. BEAR BABY LOTION DISPENSER 1981-82
10 oz. plastic in choice of pink or blue bear. Comes with matching pump dispenser. SSP $7. **CMV $2. MB.**

SPONGIE THE CLOWN 1981
6 oz. plastic bottle with green cap and comes with orange sponge for top. SSP $5. **CMV $1. MB.**

BED OF NAILS COMB 1978-79
5 1/2" comb, tan, white and red. SSP $2.49. **CMV $1. MB.**

WONDER WOMAN MIRROR 1978-79
7 1/2" long plastic mirror. SSP $6. **CMV $2. MB.**

SWEET PICKLES ZANY ZEBRA HAIR BRUSH 1978-79
White, black, pink and green plastic. SSP $5. **CMV $1. MB.**

TASTI MINT LIP GLOSS COMPACT 1978-79
Green and silver plastic. SSP $3. **CMV $2. MB.**

PLAYFUL PUPS LIGHT SWITCH COVER 1982
(Left & center) 3 1/2" x 4 1/2" plastic dog light switch covers. Both came with blue and yellow dot stick-on fragrance bows. Golden pup, and white and gray pup. SSP $4.50. **CMV $1. each MB.**

PLAY PUPS WALL HOOK 1982
(Right) Plastic wall hook, Avon back. SSP $3. **CMV $1. MB.**

AUTOGRAPH HOUND STUFFED ANIMAL & DIPLOMA LIP BALM 1980-81
8 1/2" high tan cotton. Blue plastic cap. White tassel, red satin ribbon on neck. Comes with Care Deeply lip balm Diploma. SSP $10. **CMV $7. MB.**

E.T. & ELLIOTT DECAL SOAP 1983
3 oz. blue bar with decal of E.T. on face. Back of bar says "I'll be right there". SSP $3. **CMV $3. MB.**

E.T. BATH DECANTER 1983-84
7 oz. blue plastic with tan plastic head. Holds Bubble Bath. SSP $9. **CMV $4. MB.**

E.T. MUG 1983-84
4 1/2" high white porcelain mug with E.T. for the handle. SSP $20. **CMV $15. MB.**

WABBIT CAR 1983
5 oz. blue plastic car & white rabbit cap. Choice of Children's Bubble Bath or Non-Tear Shampoo. Comes with sheet of stick on decals to decorate. SSP $6. **CMV $4. MB.**

BUBBA LEE BUNNY 1982-83
6 oz. white plastic rabbit, yellow cap. Choice of Bubble Bath or Non-Tear Shampoo. SSP $5.50. **CMV $3. MB.**

E.T. & GERTIE DECAL SOAP 1984
3 oz. pink bar. SSP $4. **CMV $3. MB.**

I.M. CLEAN II "ROBOT" 1980-81
Blue plastic robot with pump dispenser. Comes with card of stick-on decals. holds 8 oz. of Liquid Cleanser. SSP $7. **CMV $4. MB.**

TUB TUG 1980-81
5 oz. plastic. Comes in yellow and green cap with Non Tear Shampoo, red and lavender cap with bubble bath, and blue and red cap with Liquid Cleanser. SSP $3. each. **CMV $1. each. No boxes.**

ORANGATAN 1976
6 oz. orange shaped and colored plastic bottle. Holds suntan lotion. OSP $4. **CMV $2., no box issued.**

TWEETHOUSE PAPER CUP TOOTHBRUSH HOLDER 1982-83
(Left) White plastic cup holder with stick on decals & 2 child toothbrushes. SSP $7.50. **CMV $4. MB.**

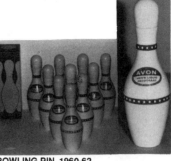

BOWLING PIN 1960-62
4 oz. white plastic trimmed in red. Came in Vigorate, Liquid Deodorant, Hand Guard, Hair Trainer, After Shaving Lotion, After Shower for Men, Liquid Hair Lotion, Shampoo, Cream Hair Lotion & Electric Pre-Shave. OSP $1.19. **CMV 10 different $10. each BO, $15. MB, Vigorate $15. BO, $20. MB.**

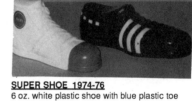

SUPER SHOE 1974-76
6 oz. white plastic shoe with blue plastic toe section cap. holds Sure Winner Liquid Hair Trainer or Sure Winner Bracing Lotion. OSP $3. **CMV $3. MB, $2. BO.**

JUST FOR KICKS 1974-75
7 oz. black & white plastic shoe with black plastic cap. Holds Avon Spicy or Avon Sure Winner Bracing Lotion. OSP $4. **CMV $4. MB, $3. BO.**

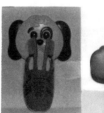

PLAY PUPS TOOTHBRUSH HOLDER 1981-82
Blue and orange shoe, brown ears, holds green and pink Avon toothbrushes. Dated 1981 on back. SSP $6. **CMV $3. MB.**

CLEAN FLIGHT DECANTER 1982
6 oz. plastic sea plane shaped. Choice of Non Tear Shampoo in yellow plastic with blue cap or Liquid CLeanser in orange with yellow cap. SSP $3. **CMV $1. No box issued.**

SCOOTER SEAL PUPPET 1983
13" long white puppet. Blue sweater & knit hat. SSP $18. **CMV $10.**

ROBOT BANK 1985
Blue, yellow & orange plastic bank. DP $6. **CMV $3. MB.**

BABY ELEPHANT PUMP 1985
8 oz. blue plastic, holds baby lotion. **CMV $2. MB.**

MUPPET BABIES - MISS PIGGY & KERMIT
4 oz. each plastic, rubber finger puppet tops. Non Tear Shampoo & Bubble Bath. **CMV $1. each MB.**

ALLSTAR LEAGUE "BASEBALL BAT" 1987
9 1/2"long tan plastic bottle. Holds shampoo. DP $2.75. **CMV $2.75 MB.**

TOOL KIT SCREWDRIVER 1986
6 3/4" yellow plastic. Holds 3.5 oz. Bubble bath. DP $2.25. **CMV $2.25 MB.**

TOOL KIT WRENCH 1986
6 1/2" green plastic. Holds 3.5 oz. Non Tear Shampoo. DP $2.20. **CMV $2.20 MB.**

E.T. ZIPPER PULL 1984
2" plastic. **CMV $1.**

BABY'S KEEPSAKE BEAR 1982
5" high white stuffed bear. Red hat, green ribbon dated 1982. SSP $7. **CMV $7. MB.**

FUN IN SPACE SOAPS 1986
Box holds yellow & blue soaps. DP $2. **CMV $2. MB.**

SUDSVILLE TRUCK & SOAP 1986
Box holds yellow, blue & red plastic dump truck & bar of yellow Sudsville soap. DP $4.50. **CMV $4.50 MB.**

SOMERSAULTS PAL DOLLS 1985
(Top) 6" to 10" stuffed toys. Miss Pear, Fergus, Charlie Barley, Zappy & Zippy. All have Avon Tags. DP $10. **CMV $10. each.**

SOMERSAULTS STUFFED TOYS 1986
(Bottom) Each about 10" long. Tabina Banana, One Two Sweetpeas, Herby Derby Cucumber & Tallulah Tomato. DP $8. each. **CMV $8. each.**

BY THE JUG 1974-75
All 3 - 10 oz. beige plastic. Strawberry Bath Foam, Astringent, Balsam Shampoo. Brown caps look like corks. SSP $3. each. No boxes issued. **CMV $1. each.**

CHICK N. MUG 1987
White ceramic mug & small stuffed yellow chick. Neither says Avon. Only on box. DP $5.50. **CMV $5.50 MB.**

TEDDY BEAR HUG MUG 1986
White ceramic mugs, Avon on bottom. 3 different mugs with small brown stuffed bears. DP $6. **CMV $6. MB.**

SOMERSAULTS PRODUCTS 1985-86
TABINA & HERBY DERBY
2 oz. plastic cologne green & yellow & yellow & pink. DP $2. **CMV $2. each.**

MINI DOLLS
Mini plastic - Zippy, Herby Derby, Charley Barley, Miss Pear & Tallulah. DP $2. each. **CMV $2. each MB.**

SOMERSAULTS MINI PALS WITH MUGS 1986
9 different plastic mugs & stuffed mini top. Tabina, One Two, Tallulah, Herby Derby, Miss Pear, Fergus, Zippy, Charlie Barley, Zappy. DP $4.50 each. **CMV $4.50 each MB.**

BEARIFF THE SHERIFF BEAR. 1986
9" tall brown stuffed bear & brown cowboy hat. Star says Beariff. Blue bandana. DP $8. **CMV $8 MB.**

PUFF THE MAGIC DRAGON 1986
9" tall turquoise & yellow stuffed dragon with 2 oz. dragon talc to put inside. DP $8.50. **CMV $8.50 MB.**

LITTLE BLOSSOM DOLL 1986
11" tall doll.

DAISY DREAMER DOLL 1986
11" high doll.

SCAMPER LILY DOLL 1986
10 1/2" high doll. DP $5.50 each. **CMV $5.50 each.**

SUMMER BRIDE FIGURINE 1986
(Left) 6" high white porcelain. DP $18. **CMV $25. MB.**

RAPUNZEL FAIRY TALE DOLL 1986
(Center) 8" tall doll with porcelain head, feet & hands. Lavender dress, gold trim. Blonde hair. DP $19.50. **CMV $25. MB.**

EARLY AMERICAN DOLL 1987
(Right) 18 1/2" doll with porcelain head, feet & hands. Burgandy top, green skirt, white apron. DP $13. **CMV $18. MB.**

BALLERINA KITTEN & GOLDEN SLIPPER NECKLACE 1986
(Right) 6" white stuffed kitten with pink clothes. Gold tone slipper necklace. DP $6. **CMV $6. MB.**

SPECIAL LOVE SACHET
(Left) Fabric sachet dolls-choice of boy or girl. DP $3. **CMV $2. each MB.**

PLUSH PUPPY 1985
Brown & white stuffed dog with red scarf & red & black shirt. Removable coat. DP $7. **CMV $7. MB.**

HUGGIE BEAR 1985
Tan colored stuffed bear. Red bow tie, came with record or tape. DP $11. **CMV $11.**

KIRBY BEAR 1984
Light brown stuffed bear with red night shirt & hat. Came with iron on personal letters. **CMV $10.**

HERBERT THE HEDGE HOG PUPPET 1984
Small hairy plush puppet. DP $9. **CMV $9.**

LITTLE RED RIDING HOOD DOLL 1985
(Left) 8 1/4" high, porcelain face, hands & feet. Red cape on metal stand. DP $18. **CMV $25. MB.**

CINDERELLA FAIRY TALE DOLL 1984
(Center) 9 1/4" high, porcelain head, hands & feet. Blue dress. Blonde hair. On Stand. DP $18. **CMV $25. MB.**

VICTORIAN COLLECTOR DOLL 1984
(Right) 8" high, porcelain face, hands & legs. DP $16. **CMV $22. MB.**

CARMICHAEL COLLECTIBLES 1985
Calendar-**CMV $1**
Plastic Clip-**CMV .50¢ each.**
Book of Nursey Rhymes-**CMV $1 MB.**
Stuffed Toy-Large-**CMV $15.**
Stuffed Toy Mini-**CMV $2. MB.**

CRAYOLA LIP GLOSS SET 1980-81
Crayola box holds 3 plastic crayon shaped Avon lip gloss in chocolate, grape and strawberry. SSP $5. **CMV $2. MB.**

MARIA MAKEOVER BATH DECANTER 1982
6 oz. plastic face bottle and sheet of stick-on decals. Choice of Non Tear Shampoo or Children's Liquid Cleanser. SSP $5. **CMV $2. MB.**

PLATES

TENDERNESS PLATE 1974-75
9 1/4" Ironstone plate. Blue & white with gold edge. Made in Spain for Avon by Pontesa. The plate sold to public with word "Pontesa" on the back side in blue letters. This was also awarded to Avon Reps. Plate was also sold with no inscription on back. No. 1 (Regular issue)-all blue lettering on back of plate, No. 2 (Reps Award)- all blue lettering including Pontesa logo. No. 3 (Reps Award)- all blue lettering on back of plate except the Pontesa logo which is red. **CMV $20 MB. regular issue, $25 Rep plate MB.**

BETSY ROSS PLATE 1973-77
White with colored scene, gold trim and lettering. 9" plate. SSP $13. **CMV $20. MB.**

CARDINAL NORTH AMERICAN SONG BIRD PLATE 1974-76
10" ceramic plate. Gold & green letters on back. SSP $13. **CMV $20. MB.**

FREEDOM PLATE 1974-77
9" ceramic plate, blue trim with gold edge. Blue printing on back. Made by Wedgewood, England for Avon. SSP $13. **CMV $20. MB.**

GENTLE MOMENTS PLATE 1975-77
8 3/4 ceramic plate. Green letters on back. Made by Wedgewood, England. SSP $15 **CMV $20. MB.**

CHRISTMAS PLATE - 15 YEAR 1978
Same plate as 15 year anniversary plate inscribed on back. We have no info on this or where it came from. Write Bud Hastin if you know what this plate is for. **CMV $50.**

MOTHERS DAY PLATE "CHERISHED MOMENTS" 1981
5" porcelain plate dated 1981, with stand. SSP $10 **CMV $10 MB.**

MOTHER'S DAY PLATE 1982
5" size plate. Little Things Mean A Lot inscribed on face. Comes in yellow box & plastic plate stand. SSP $10 **CMV $10 MB,** Same plate given to presidents Club Reps. Label on back reads "January 1982 Presidents Club Luncheon". **CMV $15 MB.**

CHILDRENS PERSONAL TOUCH PLATE 1982-83
7 5/8 ceramic plate. SSP $12 **CMV $12 MB.**

CHRISTMAS ON THE FARM 1973 CHRISTMAS PLATE
White with colored scene, turquoise border, gold edge and lettering. 9" plate SSP $13 **CMV $55 MB.**

CHRISTMAS PLATE TEST 1976
8 3/4 test plate. Does not say Avon. Christmas 1976 on front 6 times in gold. Was never sold by Avon. Came from factory. Has blue border. **CMV $75.**

90

PINK ROSES CUP & SAUCER 1974-76
(Left) White china with pink flowers & green leaves with gold trim. Made by Stoke-on Trent, England. OSP $10 **CMV $12 MB. Also came with double printed letters on bottom. CMV $20 MB.**
BLUE BLOSSOMS CUP & SAUCER 1974-75
(Right) White china with blue & pink flowers and 22K gold rim. Made in England. OSP $10 **CMV $12. MB.**

CHRISTMAS "BETSY ROSS" PLATE 1973
Factory mistake 1973 Christmas plate has inscription on back for Betsy Ross plate. Very Rare. **CMV $100.**

COUNTRY CHURCH 1974 CHRISTMAS PLATE
9" ceramic plate. Second in a series of Christmas plates by Avon. Made by Wedgewood, England. Blue writing on back. Blue & white front, gold edge. SSP $13. **CMV $35 MB.** Rare issue came without Christmas 1974 on front of plate. **CMV $75 MB.**

SKATERS ON THE POND 1975 CHRIST-MAS PLATE
8 3/4 ceramic green & white plate. Green letters on the back. Made by Wedgewood, England for Avon. This plate was not sold till 1976 Christmas selling season. SSP $17. **CMV $20. MB. Some have 1976 on back Add $10.**

BRINGING HOME THE TREE 1976 CHRISTMAS PLATE
9" blue ceremic plate, gold edge. Blue printing on back. Made by Wedgewood, England for Avon. SSP $16. **CMV $20. MB. Some have 1975 on back Add $10.**

"CAROLLERS IN THE SNOW" 1977 CHRISTMAS PLATE
8 3/4 ceramic blue & white plate, gold edge. Blue letters on back. Made by Wedgewood, England for Avon. SSP $17. **CMV $20. MB.**

"TRIMMING THE TREE" 1978 CHRIST-MAS PLATE
(6th edition) 8 5/8 ceramic plate. Turquoise rim with gold edge trim. Made for Avon by Enoch Wedgewood in England. SSP $20. **CMV $20. MB.**

DASHING THROUGH THE SNOW 1979 CHRISTMAS PLATE
8 3/4 blue and white ceramic plate with gold trim. Christmas 1979 on front. Back of plate says Made for Avon Products by Enoch Wedgewood in England. SSP. $20. **CMV $20 MB.**

CHRISTMAS PLATE 1983
"Enjoying the night before Christmas". 9" porcelain plate. SSP $23.50 **CMV $20 MB.**

SHARING THE CHRISTMAS SPIRIT 1981 CHRISTMAS PLATE
9" porcelain plate has 2 lids carrying Christmas tree, Christmas 1981 on front. SSP $21.50 **CMV $20 MB.** Rare issue came with no Christmas 1981 on front. **CMV $75.**

PLATES

BAKED WITH LOVE PLATE 1982-83
9" porcelain plate dated 1982 SSP $18 **CMV $20 MB.**

CUPIDS MESSAGE PORCELAIN DISH 1984
White heart shaped dish with Angel Love in red letters. red box. SSP $10 **CMV $10 MB.**

BOUQUET OF LOVE PLATE 1987
7" white porcelain Bisque plate. DP $8.25 **CMV $10 MB.**
CHRISTMAS PLATE 1986
8" white bisque porcelain. "A Childs Christmas" DP $12. **CMV $15 MB.**

ABIGAIL ADAMS PLATE 1985
9" porcelain plate. Wood stand. DP $15. **CMV $20. MB.**
CHORUS LINE PLATE 1986
8" porcelain plate. Wood music box stand. DP $12. **CMV $20. MB.**

SWEET DREAMS KEEPSAKE PLATE 1983
7 5/8" porcelain plate. SSP $15 **CMV $15 MB.**

SINGIN IN THE RAIN PLATE 1986
8" porcelain plate. Both came with or without wood base music box. DP $12. **CMV $18 MB. Add $5 for music box base.**
EASTER PARADE PLATE 1986
8" porcelain plate came with wood base music stand, plays Easter Parade. DP $12. **CMV $18. MB. Add $5. for music box base.**

CLASSIC WEDDING PLATE 1986
9" bisque porcelain plate with 2 boxes on face. Gold trim. DP $12 **CMV $15 MB.**
FOUR SEASONS CALENDAR PLATE 1987
9" porcelain plate. DP $11 **CMV $15 MB.**

CHRISTMAS PLATE "KEEPING THE CHRISTMAS TRADITION" 1982
9" ceramic plate, back says Christmas Memories, 1982. Comes in green & gold box. SSP $23.50 **CMV $23.50 MB.**

CHRISTMAS PLATE 1985
"A Childs Christmas" 7 3/4 white bisque porcelain. DP $8. **CMV $10. MB.**
CHRISTMAS PLATE 1984
9" porcelain decal plate. Last in this series. DP $15. **CMV $20. MB.**

MOMENTS OF VICTORY SPORTS PLATES 1985
Set of 4 different 7" porcelain plates Football, Basketball, Hockey, or Baseball. SSP $8. **CMV $8. each MB.**

AMERICAN PORTRAITS PLATE COLLECTIONS 1985
Set of six 4 1/2" porcelain plates. Choice of The East, The West, The Rockies, The Southwest, The Midwest, The South. DP $6. **CMV $8. each MB.**

MOTHER'S DAY PLATE 1987
"A Mother In Love" 5" porcelain plate. DP $5.25 **CMV $7 MB.**

SCHOOL IS A NEW BEGINNING PLATE 1986
5" porcelain plate. DP $6. **CMV $8. MB.**

MOTHERS DAY PLATE 1989
Titles Loving is Caring, 5" plate with stand. SSP $10.00 **CMV $10.00 MB**

MOTHER'S DAY SPECIAL MEMORIES PLATES 1985
5" porcelain plate, choice of white or black body and child. DP $7. **CMV $9. each MB.**

12 DAYS OF CHRISTMAS COLLECTIONS 1985
All white porcelain.
CANDLE HOLDERS
DP $9. Pair. **CMV $11 Pair.**
DESSERT PLATES
Set of 4 DP $16 **CMV $20 Set.**
MUGS
Set of 4 DP $13 **CMV $16 Set.**

MOTHER'S DAY PLATE 1990
"A Message from the Heart" 5" porcelain plate, with stand. SSP $10.00 **CMV $10.00 MB**

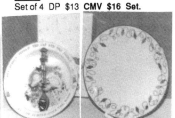

BABY KEEPSAKE SPOON & BOWL SET 1984
6 1/4 porcelain bowl & 5" spoon. DP $12 **CMV $14 MB.**

CHRISTMAS LIGHTS DESSERT PLATE 1985
7" white ceramic plate with X-mas light design. DP $4. **CMV $7 MB.**

MINIATURE CHRISTMAS PLATES 1989
1st issued in 1989 are the 1978, 1979, 1980 Christmas plates in 3" sige. SSP $8.00ea. **CMV $8.00 ea. MB**

MOTHER'S DAY PLATES 1983-84
5" ceramic plates. Both dated on back. DP $7. **CMV $9. each MB.**

MOTHER'S DAY PLATE 1986
5" porcelain plate called "A New Tooth" Comes in White or Black body & child. DP $6. **CMV $8. MB.**

MOTHERS DAY PLATE 1988
"A mother's work is never done". 5" wide. Choice of black or white child. SSP $10.00ea. **CMV $10.00 ea. MB**

CHRISTMAS PLATE 1990 "Bringing Christmas Home"
8" porcelain plate. Christmas 1990 on front. SSP $20.00 **CMV $20.00 MB**

NOTES

CHRISTMAS PLATE 1989
"Together for Christmas" bears on plate. 8" wide. SSP $20.00 **CMV $20.00 MB**

COUNTRY CHRISTMAS PLATE 1980
9" ceramic 1980 Christmas plate. SSP $22.00 **CMV $20.00 MB**

CHRISTMAS PLATE 1988
"Home for the Holidays" 8" porcelain plate. SSP $20.00 **CMV $20.00 MB**

CHRISTMAS PLATE 1987
Magic that Santa Brings. 8" plate. SSP $20.00 **CMV $20.00 MB**

CHRISTMAS PLATE 1986 - "A Childs Christmas"
8" porcelain plate with snowman and 2 kids. SSP $20.00 **CMV $20.00 MB**

CANDLES

Whats hot & whats not? Candles are very popular in Avon Collecting. Most popular are all glass figurine type candles. They are selling faster & at better prices then the non figurine type glass candles. All wax Figurine candles are popular but are hard to keep clean & in mint condition. Tin containers with candles are popular but not as much as glass figurines candles. The Tall or short wax taper type candles are hard to display & will not be as popular as the figurine candles and few people collect them. We will no longer picture wax taper candles. Keep these thoughts in mind when buying & collecting candles. Candle refills & wax chips are no longer considered collectable. There is no resale interest to most collectors in these items.

COLLECTORS

All containers are priced empty.

CO means ....Container Only
BO means ....Bottle Only (empty)
CMV means ....Current Market Value
SSP means ....Special Selling Price
OSP means ....Original Selling Price
MB means ....Mint and Boxed
DP means ....Avon Rep Cost

DANISH MODERN CANDLE 1970
(Left) Stainless steel candleholder with red candle. OSP $8. **CMV $10 with candle. MB.**
FLAMING TULIP FRAGRANCE CANDLE 1973
(Right) Red candle in Floral Medley fragrance. Gold holder. OSP $7. **CMV $7 CO, $10. MB.**

JOYOUS MESSAGE CANDLES 1985
3 elf candles 1 1/2 high. DP. $2. **CMV $3 MB.**

FLORAL FRAGRANCE CANDLE 1971-75
(Left) Metal gold leaf stand & pink or yellow flower candle. OSP $8.50 **CMV $10, $12 MB.**
WATER LILY FRAGRANCE CANDLE 1972-73
(Right) Green lily pad base with white plastic petals with yellow center candle. OSP $5. **CMV $8 CO, $10 MB.**

REVOLUTIONARY SOLDIER SMOKERS CANDLE 1979-80
Clear, or dark amber glass, clear harder to find, 2 different. Red & gold box. SSP $4. **CMV $6 MB.**
FOSTORIA CRYSTAL POOL FLOATING CANDLE 1979-80
6" clear crystal dish, green & white flower candle. SSP $12 **CMV $13.**

OVALIQUE PERFUME CANDLEHOLDER 1974-75
(Left) 4" high, clear gloss, choice of Sonnet, Moonwind, Patchwork, Roses Roses, Charisma, Bird of Paradise, Bayberry, Frankincense & Myrrh or Wassail. OSP $8. **CMV $10 MB.**
FACETS OF LIGHT FRAGRANCE CANDLETTE 1975-76
(Center) 4" high, clear glass. Came with Bayberry candle but any refill candlette will fit. OSP $5. **CMV $8. MB.**
GOLDEN PINE CONE FRAGRANCE CANDLETTE 1974-75
(Right) Gold toned glass. Choice of Bayberry only. OSP $5. **CMV $8 MB.**

CRYSTALLITE COLOGNE CANDLE 1970-71
(Left) Clear glass bottle with gold cap holds 4 oz. cologne in Unforgettable, Rapture, Occur!, Somewhere, Topaze, & Cotillion. OSP $5.50 **CMV $8. MB.**
CANDLESTICK COLOGNE 1972-75
(Right) 5 oz. silver painted over clear glass with silver cap. Came in Moonwind, Field Flowers, Bird of Paradise, Roses Roses. SSP $6. **CMV $10 MB. $8. BO. 1975 came only in Imperial Garden, Moonwind, or Sonnett.**

WASHINGTON GOBLET FOSTORIA CANDLEHOLDER 1975-77
Blue glass by Fostoria. Came with Frankincense & Myrrh or Floral Medley candle. OSP $10 **CMV $14 MB.**
MARTHA WASHINGTON GOBLET 1976-77
Blue glass Fostoria candleholder. OSP $12.50 **CMV $14. MB.**

TURTLE CANDLE 1972
(Left) White glass turtle candle with green glass shell top. OSP $5. **CMV $12 MB.**
MUSHROOM CANDLE 1972
(Right) White glass candle with pink glass mushroom top. OSP $5. **CMV $11 MB.**

COLOGNE & CANDLELIGHT 1975-76

(Left) 2 oz. clear glass with gold cap and clear plastic collar. Hold Imperial Gardens, Roses Roses, or Charisma. OSP $3. **CMV $6. BO, $5. MB.**

CANDLESTICK COLOGNE 1970-71

(Right) 4 oz. red glass bottle, gold cap. Holds Elusive, Charisma, Brocade, Regence, Bird of Paradise. OSP $6. **CMV $8 MB. $6. BO.** Also came in smoked red glass. Appears much darker than red glass issue. It looks smokey red. **CMV $15 MB.**

REGENCY CANDLESTICK COLOGNE 1973-74

(Left) 4 oz. clear glass. Came in Bird of Paradise, Charisma, Elusive, or Roses Roses. SSP $7. **CMV $10. MB, $8 BO.**

OPALIQUE CANDLESTICK COLOGNE 1976-77

(Right) 5 oz. swirl glass & cap. Came in Charisma or Sweet Honesty. SSP $8. **CMV $10. MB, $8. BO.**

CANDLESTICK COLOGNE 1966

3 oz. silver coated over clear glass. Silver cap. Came in Occur!, Rapture, Unforgettable. OSP $3.75 **CMV $15. mint, $25 MB.**

FLORAL MEDLEY PERFUMED CANDLES 1971-72

Box holds yellow & purple frosted glass candleholders. OSP $5.50 **CMV $10 MB.**

CRYSTAL GLOW PERFUMED CANDLE-HOLDER 1972-73

(Left) Clear glass. Came in Moonwind, Bird of Paradise, Elusive, Charisma, Brocade, Regence, Wassail, Bayberry, Frankincense, Myrrh, Roses Roses. SSP $8. **CMV $10, $12 MB.**

FOSTORIA PERFUMED CANDLEHOLDER 1973

(Right) Clear glass. Came with Patchwork, Sonnet, Moonwind, Roses Roses, Charisma, Bird of Paradise, Bayberry, Wassail, Frankincense, & Myrrh candles. SSP $6. **CMV $8, $10 MB.**

CHESAPEAKE COLLECTION JIGGER CANDLE 1981

Amber glass dog head candle, candle in bottom. SSP $10 **CMV $12 MB.**

FOSTORIA CANDLELIGHT BASKET CANDLEHOLDER 1975

(Left) Clear glass, gold handle. Choice of Sonnet, Moonwind, Patchwork, Charisma, Roses Roses, Bird of Paradise, Wassail, Frankincense, & Myrrh or Bayberry candle refill. OSP $9 **CMV $12 MB, $10 CO.**

FOSTORIA SALT CELLAR CANDLE 1969-70 & 1981

(Right) Clear glass with small silver spoon. OSP $6 **CMV $10 MB, $7 candle only.** Reissued in 1981 with "R" on bottom of foot for reissue. SSP $10 **CMV $10 MB.**

TULIP CLEARFIRE TRANSPARENT CANDLE 1980-82

(Left) Clear glass. 4" high. SSP $6 **CMV $6. MB.**

SPARKLING SWIRL CLEARFIRE CANDLE 1980-82

(Center) Clear glass 5 1/8" high. SSP $11 **CMV $11. MB.**

SHERBERT DESSERT CANDLE 1980-82

(Right) 5" high clear glass. Comes with red, yellow or pink candle. SSP $8 **CMV $8 MB.**

HEARTS & FLOWERS FRAGRANCE CANDLE 1973-74

(Left) White milk glass with red green & pink design. Came in Floral Medley fragrance. SSP $4 **CMV $10 MB, $8 CO.**

POTPOURRI FRAGRANCE CANDLE 1972-73

(Right) White milk glass, came with Potpourri candle. SSP $4 **CMV $8 CO, $10. MB.**

HEART & DIAMOND FOSTORIA LOVING CUP PERFUMED CANDLEHOLDER 1978
(Left) Approx. 7" high claer Fostoria glass. Came with floral Medley perfumed candle. Embossed with "Avon 1978" on it's base. Refillable. OSP $15 **CMV $15. MB. glass only $10.**

MOUNT VERNON SAUCE PITCHER 1977-79
(Right) Approx. 5 1/2" high. Blue Fostoria glass. Came with Floral Medley perfumed candle. Refillable. Avon on bottom. OSP $15.50 **CMV $16 MB. pitcher only $12.**

SUNNY BUNNY CERAMIC CANDLE-HOLDER 1981-82
5 1/2" high ceramic candleholder Dated 1981 . $15 **CMV $15 MB.**

HEART & DIAMOND CANDLESTICK 1978-79
7" high heart embossed Fostoria clear glass candle. Avon 1979 on bottom. COmes with long red candle for one end or turn it over and insert the small glass candleholder on other end. Comes in red box. SSP $13. **CMV $13 MB.**

CHINA TEA POT CANDLE 1972-73
White china with blue flower design or without decal. Thousands came from factory, not sold by Avon, with or without decals, some decals were on front, some on back. The factory rejects **CMV $9 each.** Came from Avon with Roses Roses, Moonwind, Bird of Paradise, Elusive, Charisma, Brocade, Regence, Wassail, Bayberry, Frankincense & Myrrh candles. SSP $10 **CMV $15 MB, $10 CO.**

WHITE MILK GLASS CANDLE 1964-66
(Left) OSP $3.50 **CMV $10, $15 MB.**

AMBER GLASS CANDLE 1965-66
(Center) Amber Paint over clear glass. OSP $4 **CMV $20 MB, $15 candle only.**

RED GLASS CANDLE 1965-66
(Right) Red paint over clear glass OSP $4 **CMV $13, $18 MB,** Dark red 1968 glass candle, not painted **CMV $50.**

KITCHEN CROCK FRAGRANCE CAN-DLETTE 1974-75
(Left) Yellow crock with red, yellow & blue flowers with cork cap. Came in Meadow Morn fragrance. SSP $4 **CMV $7 CO, $8 MB.**

WASSAIL BOWL CANDLE 1969-70
(Right) Silver paint over red glass with silver spoon. OSP $8. **CMV $15 CO, $18 MB.**

REGENCE CANDLE 1967
(Left) Gold paint over clear glass with green paper band. Lid makes base for bottom. OSP $6. **CMV $25. MB, $20 CO MINT**

REGENCE CANDLE 1968-69
(Right) Green glass candleholder with gold handle & base. OSP $10 **CMV $20 candle only, $25 MB.**

CHRISTMAS CHARMER CANDLESTICK 1981
Small white, red & green girl, plastic candle holder. Remove top sleeve to fit small bottle of cologne with red cap. Choice of Zany or Charisma. .33 oz. cologne, red box. SSP $6. **CMV $6. set MB.**

FROSTED GLASS CANDLE 1967
(Left) Gold band around edge. lid makes stand for base. OSP $5 **CMV $20 MB, $15 CO.**

WHITE & GOLD CANDLE 1966-67
(Right) White glass top & bottom with gold band. Top makes stand for base. OSP $5. **CMV $15, $20 MB.**

CRYSTAL CANDLEIER 1969-70
(Left) 7" high, clear glass with blue crystals inside, gold handle on glass lid. OSP $7. **CMV $15 MB, $12 CO.**

GOLD & WHITE CANDLE 1969-70
(Right) Painted gold & white over clear glass, lid makes stand for base. OSP $8 **CMV $15, $20 MB.**

FIRST CHRISTMAS CANDLE 1967
All gold, red inside 1967 had label on bottom and no Avon. OSP $5. **CMV $10 CO, $15 MB.** 1972 Reissued-Avon on Bottom, no label. **CMV $15 MB, $10 CO.**
FIRST CHRISTMAS CANDLE FOREIGN
(Right) All silver with red inside. **CMV $20.**

SCENTIMENTS CANDLES 1982-83
2" high metal can candles, 2 different designs. Lid says "May Love Always Fill Your Heart" or "The Beauty of Friendship is Everlasting." SSP $7. each. **CMV $7. MB each.**

ULTRA CRYSTAL CANDLE 1981-82
(Left) 2 1/2" high clear glass. Gray box. SSP $10. **CMV $10. MB.**
ULTRA SHIMMER CANDLE 1981-82
(Right) 2 1/2" high clear glass octagonal shaped. Gold box. SSP $9. **CMV $9. MB.**

NESTING DOVE CANDLE 1970
White base glass & lid with dove on top. OSP $7.50 **CMV $15 MB.**
HOBNAIL PATIO CANDLE 1973
(Right) White milk base clear glass top. Came with Sonnet, Moonwind, Roses Roses, Bird of Paradise, Charisma, Wassail, Bayberry, and Frankincense & Myrrh candles. SSP $8. **CMV $12 MB, $10 CO.**

GAMESMAN CANDLE GIFT SET 1981-82
Green & red box holds small metal green can with candle & set of green playing cards with deer in 2 corners. Made by Arco Playing Card Co., Chicago. Cards do not say Avon. SSP $10. **CMV $10. MB complete set.**

HOT CHOCO-LITE CANDLE 1981-82
(Left) Beige or white color wax cup with brown chocolate smelling candle. SSP $7. **CMV $7. MB.**
PITKIN HAT CANDLE 1981-82
(Right) Blue swirled glass hat holds candle. Comes in green box. SSP $8. **CMV $8. MB.**

GOLDEN APPLE CANDLE 1968-69
Shiny gold over clear glass. OSP $6. **CMV $18 mint, $25 MB.**
SILVER APPLE CANDLE 1968
Factory test sample same as gold apple only in shiny silver over clear glass. Was not filled. **CMV $90 on silver top & bottom, Silver bottom with gold top CMV $55 mint.**

PERSONALLY YOURS FRAGRANCE CANDLE 1980-82
(Left) Clear glass with refillable candle. Comes with sheet of stick on gold letters. SSP $12. **CMV $12. MB.**
STAR BRIGHT FRAGRANCE CANDLE 1980-81
(Right) Icy clear glass holds refillable candle. SSP $7. **CMV $8. MB.**

BRIGHT CHIPMUNK CANDLETTE 1978-79
Clear glass candleholder. Refillable. SSP $6. **CMV $8. MB.**
FRESH AROMA SMOKERS CANDLE 1978-79
Non refillable brown wax like pipe with black plastic and chrome top. Bottom cardboard label. SSP $7. **CMV $8. MB.**

FLORAL LIGHT CANDLE REFILL 1980-81
(Left) Comes in lavender, green or yellow. Flower shaped. SSP $4. **CMV $4. MB.**

FLORAL LIGHT FRAGRANCE CANDLE 1980-81
(Right) Clear glass flower shaped base holds flower shaped refill candle. SSP $7. **CMV $7. MB.**

SNUG 'N COZY "CAT" FRAGRANCE CANDLE 1980-82
Clear glass cat candleholder. SSP $10. **CMV $10. MB.**

GLISTENING TREE CLEARFIRE CANDLE 1981-82
4 1/2" high clear ribbed glass tree shaped candle. SSP $10. **CMV $10. MB.**

LOVE LIGHT CLEARFIRE CANDLE 1982
Clear ribbed glass heart shape candle. SSP $10. **CMV $10. MB.**

SHIMMERING PEACOCK CANDLE 1979-80
(Left) Box holds clear glass peacock. SSP $10. **CMV $10. MB.**

BUNNY PATCH CANDLE 1988
6" tall wax rabbit candle. SSP $5. **CMV $5. MB.**

CATNIP FRAGRANCE CANDLE 1975-76
4" high yellow plastic. Floral Medley fragrance. OSP $3. **CMV $7. MB.**

DYNAMITE FRAGRANCE CANDLETTE 1975-76
Red & white. OSP $4. **CMV $8. MB.**

CHRISTMAS TEDDY CANDLE 1988
3" high bear candle. SSP. $5. **CMV $5. MB**

NATURAL HOME SCENTS TOWNHOUSE CANDLE 1988
4 3/4" high ceramic candle town house. SP $18. **CMV $18. MB.**

NORTH POLE PALS CANDLES 1988
Reindeer, Penguin & Polar Bear candles also used as tree ornaments. SSP $4 ea. **CMV $4 ea. MB.**

PLUM PUDDING CANDLE 1978-79
(Left) 4" high brown, green & white candle. Bottom label. SSP $6. **CMV $6. MB.**

WINTER LIGHTS CANDLETTE 1978-79
(Right) Clear glass square candleholder. Holds glass candlette. Avon on bottom of both. SSP $8. **CMV $10. MB.**

GEM GLOW CANDLE 1981-82
(Left) Clear glass multi-faceted. Comes with green, amber or red filled candle. SSP $10.
CMV $10. MB.

CAPE COD CREAMER CANDLE 1981-84
(Right) 4" high ruby red glass. Holds candle. See Cape Cod in Women's Decanters for other Cape Cod candles. SSP $9. **CMV $10.**

MRS. SNOWLIGHT CANDLE 1979-81
(Left) White, red & green wax candle. SSP $7. **CMV $7. MB.**

WINTER WONDERLAND CENTERPIECE CANDLE 1979-80
(Right) White wax base, green wax trees, red & white wax house. Center holds glass candlette. SSP $15. **CMV $15. MB.**

ENCHANTED MUSHROOM FRAGRANCE CANDLE 1975
(Left) White wax shell / yellow cover. Meadow Morn fragrance. OSP $4. **CMV $6. MB, $4. CO.**

SLEIGH LIGHT FRAGRANCE CANDLE 1975-76
(Right) 4" high, red & green. Bayberry scented. OSP $5. **CMV $7. MB, $5. CO.**

HOLIDAY CANDLE DISH & WREATH 1980
Clear glass candleholder, red candle and holly wreath. SSP $9. **CMV $9. MB.**

BLACK-EYED SUSAN FRAGRANCE CANDLE 1975-76
Yellow with brown center. Wild Flowers fragrance. OSP $5. **CMV $8. MB, $6. CO.**

GRAPEFRUIT FRAGRANCE CANDLE 1974-76
Yellow with red center. Has grapefruit fragrance. OSP $3. **CMV $7. MB, $5. CO.**

CRYSTALGLOW CLEARFIRE CANDLE 1980
(Left) Clear glass. Avon on bottom under candle. SSP $10. **CMV $10. MB.**

BUNNY BRIGHT CERAMIC CANDLE 1980
(Right) White ceramic with pink & green trim. "1980 Avon" on bottom. SSP $12. **CMV $12. MB.**

CAROLLING TRIO CANDLES 1981-82
Comes in separate boxes. Melodic Mouse candle, Howling Hound candle, Crooning Cat candle. SSP $5. each. **CMV $5. each MB.**

HARVEST TIME FRAGRANCE CANDLE 1980-81
Tan wax candle, 6" high. SSP $10. **CMV $8. MB.**

GINGERBREAD HOUSE FRAGRANCE CANDLE 1977-79
Brown & white candle. Came in Frankincense & Myrrh fragrance. OSP $8.50. **CMV $9. MB, $5. no box.**

GLOW OF CHRISTMAS CANDLE 1980
White wax with red center refillable candle. SSP $10. **CMV $10. MB.**

MR. SNOWLIGHT CANDLE 1981
5 1/2" high white wax, green trim. SSP $7.
CMV $7.

LOTUS BLOSSOM PERFUMED CANDLE-HOLDER 1974-75
(Left) Black glass with green & white design. Available with candle fragrance: Bayberry, Frankincense & Myrrh, Wassail, Sonnet, Moonwind, Roses Roses, Bird of Paradise or Charisma. OSP $8. **CMV $15, $18. MB.**
DYNASTY PERFUMED CANDLE 1971-72
(Right) 6" high, white glass jar & lid. OSP $7.50. **CMV $15, $18. MB.**

AMERICAN HEIRLOOM CANDLESTICK & CANDLE 1982-84
Pewter metal candlestick & 6" red candle. SSP $11. **CMV $11. MB.**

TERRA COTTA BIRD CANDLETTE 1976-77
Reddish brown clay bird candleholder. Avon on bottom. OSP $8. **CMV $8. MB, $3. bird only.**

GARDEN BOUNTY CANDLE 1979-80
(Left) Beige & pink cart, red candle. SSP $8. **CMV $8. MB.**
COUNTRY SPICE CANDLE 1979-80
(Center) Light blue green glass jar & lid. Wire bale. Comes with candle inside. SSP $8. **CMV $9. MB.**
FLOWER FROST COLLECTION WATER GOBLET CANDLETTE 1979-80
(Right) Frosted glass goblet holds glass candle insert. SSP $10. **CMV $11. MB.**

TOCCARA SPECIAL EDITION CANDLE 1982-83
(Left) Clear cut glass Fostoria candle. Blue box. SSP $13. **CMV $13. MB.**
HARVEST GLOW CANDLE 1982-83
(Right) Clear glass pumpkin shaped candle and lid. SSP $13. **CMV $13. MB.**

DOVE IN FLIGHT CANDLETTE 1977-78
Clear glass dove candleholder. Came in Meadow Morn fragrance candlette. Refillable. SSP $6. **CMV $10. MB.**
BUNNY CERAMIC PLANTER CANDLE-HOLDER 1977-79
3 different rabbits. One made in Brazil and recesses on bottom; one flat bottom made in U.S. and lighter in weight; 1978 issue same flat bottom only different type letters on bottom. Came with Floral Medley or Roses Roses perfumed candle. SSP $11. **CMV $12. MB each, rabbit only $10. each.**

BUNNY CERAMIC PLANTER CANDLE 1979-80
Made of ceramic in Brazil for Avon. Green, pink & yellow flowers. Brown eyes, pink inner ears. Comes with Floral Medley or Spiced Garden candle. SSP $15. **CMV $15. MB.**
TENDER BLOSSOM CANDLE 1977-80
Light pink wax base with dark pink inner candle. SSP $7. **CMV $7. MB.**

SNUGGLY MOUSE CANDLEHOLDER 1983
Ceramic mouse holder base 4 1/4" wide. Comes with 6" red candle. SSP $13. **CMV $13 MB.**

CANDLES

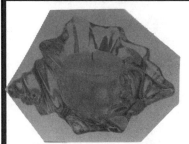

CORAL GLOW CANDLE 1983-84
Clear glass Conch shell design candle. SSP
$12. **CMV $12. MB.**

SPARKLING TURTLE CANDLETTE 1978-79
4 1/2" long clear glass turtle. SSP $7. **CMV
$9. MB, $7. CO.**

HOLIDAY FLOATING CANDLES 1983
Box of 2 candles in choice of Red Poinsettia
flowers or green & red wreath, 2 1/2" wide.
SSP $5. each set. **CMV $5. set MB.**

COUNTRY JAM CANDLES 1985
2" high clear glass. Cloth covers over lid.
Comes in Mint, Black Raspberry, Strawberry
and Orange. DP $4. **CMV $4. each MB.**

**FIREPLACE FRIENDS CANDLE HOLDER
1988**
3 1/2" high fire place has candle holder on
back side. SSP $10. **CMV $10. MB**

FESTIVAL OF COLORS CANDLES 1985
(Right) 2" high tin cans in Green Apple-stripes,
Raspberry-polka dots, or Lemon-confetti. DP
$4. each. **CMV $6. MB each.**
SOFT ROSE FLOATING CANDLES 1985
(Left) Box holds white, pink & red flower
candle. DP $4. **CMV $6. MB.**

**YEAR TO YEAR BIRTHDAY CANDLE
1983-84**
4 1/2" ceramic clown candle holder with yellow
candle, 1-2-3-4 on sides. SSP $10. **CMV $10.
MB.**

COUNTRY EGG CANDLE'S 1989
Choice of plastic eggs in blue-rabbits, pink-
sheep. SSP $5. **CMV $3. ea.**

SPICE CUPBOARD CANDLE 1982
(Left) 1 1/2" high clear glass refillable candle.
SSP $5. **CMV $5. MB.**
**RAIN OR SHINE GREETING CANDLE
1983**
(Right) 2" high candle with mouse decal on
side. SSP $5. **CMV $5. MB.**

**HO HO GLOW "SANTA" CANDLE 1982-
83**
5" ceramic red, white & black Santa candle.
SSP $16. **CMV $16. MB.**

CHRISTMAS FUN CANDLE GIFT SET 1985
Green horse, white doll, red soldier candles.
DP $3. **CMV $4. set MB.**

GLISTENING GLOW CANDLE 1986
Clear glass candle. DP $6. **CMV $8. MB.**
GINGERBREAD HOUSE CANDLE 1986
Ceramic house holds glass cup candle. DP.
$13.50. **CMV $16.**

THREE WEE TEDDY CANDLES 1987
3-11/2" high bear candles on 1 wick. Cut
separate. SSP $4. **CMV $4 set or $1 ea. Mint**

**SHIMMERING GLASS CONVERTIBLE
CANDLEHOLDER 1985**
2 3/4" high clear glass. Holds big candle on 1
side, flip it over to holds taper candle. DP $5.
CMV $7. MB.

PERSONAL CREATION CANDLE 1985
GLISTENING CREATING CANDLE 1985
(Right & Center) Both glass candles the same.
Different boxes & candle mix. DP $4. **CMV
$6. each MB.**
AUTUMN IMPRESSIONS CANDLE 1984
(Left) 2 1/4" high clear glass. DP $3. **CMV
$4. MB.**

**GLITTER & GLOW HOLIDAY CANDLE'S
1989**
Red or gold metallic candles. SSP $5. **CMV
$5. MB.**

**SPARKLING JEWEL STACKABLE
CANDLES 1984**
Green or blue glass. DP $5. **CMV $7. MB
each.**

MOTHERS DAY CANDLE 1986
4" high wax candle. Decal on front says "A
Mother's Gift is Love 1986". DP $2. **CMV $3.
MB.**
**TRINKET BOX "SEA SHELL" CANDLE
1987**
Small ceramic 3 1/2" pearlized sea shell. DP
$4.75. **CMV $7. MB.**

**SUMMER LIGHTS INDOOR-OUTDOOR
CANDLE 1984**
(Left) 2 1/4" high green glass. DP $4. **CMV
$5. MB.**
CLEARFIRE TULIP CUP CANDLE 1986
(Right) Clear glass. 4" high. DP $6. **CMV $8.
MB.**

SOFT MUSK CANDLE 1985
Small tin can candle, lid. DP $4. **CMV $5.
MB.**

NATURAL HOME FRAGRANCE CANDLE HOLDER 1986
(Left) 3 3/4" high ceramic top & bottom dish. Not marked Avon. Currier & Ives Scene. Comes with small candle. DP $9. **CMV $11. MB.**

SPRING HOSTESS CANDLE HOLDERS 1987
(Right) 2 white ceramic candle holders 2 3/4" high. Not marked Avon. DP $6.75. **CMV $7 MB.**

NATURE'S FRIEND CANDLE HOLDER 1988
Hand painted ceramic squirrel holds scented candle. SSP $12. **CMV $12. MB.**

FRAGRANCE CANDLE 1985
Tin can. DP $4. **CMV $5. MB.**

SSS CANDLE 1989
3" high can holds candle. SSP $2. **CMV $2. MB**

HURRICANE LAMP CANDLE 1986
8" high glass dome sits on wood base. Does not come with candle. Is not marked Avon. DP $11. **CMV $11. MB.**

ANNIVERSARY TAPER CANDLE HOLDER 1985
Small porcelain doves & flowers. DP $9. **CMV $11. MB.**

PORCELAIN ANGELS CANDLE HOLDER 1985
5" high white porcelain. Empty DP $11. **CMV $13. MB.**

SKIN-SO-SOFT CANDLE 1990
3 1/2" High tin can holds refillable candle. SSP $5. **CMV $5. MB**

DOVE CANDLE HOLDERS 1986
2 white bisque porcelain candle holders. DP $7.25. **CMV $9 MB.**

BUNNY TAPER CANDLE HOLDERS 1987
2 small ceramic rabbit candle holders. DP $8.25. **CMV $10 MB.**

AVON COUNTRY FRESH CANDLE 1985
Chicken egg candle with blue or red base. DP $2. **CMV $3. MB.**

JOLLY SANTA CANDLE 1986
5 1/2" high Santa candle. DP $3. **CMV $5. MB.**

NOTES

GLOWING MESSAGE CANDLE 1984
1" high each. Flower - Star - Apple. DP $2.50.
CMV $3.50 MB each.

EXCHANGING GIFTS CANDLE 1987
Mr. & Mrs. Santa candle. SSP $4. **CMV $4.
MB.**

PEARLS & LACE CANDLE 1987
1 1/2" high candle in pink lace design, tin can &
white lid. DP $3.50. **CMV $5.**
SUPERSTAR FOOTBALL CANDLE 1986
3" wide green tin can holds candle. DP $3.
CMV $5. MB.

CRYSTAL CANDLE _____ 1987
Clear pressed cut crystal glass. Pear shaped or
Apple shapped. SSP $8 ea. **CMV $8 ea. MB**

EGG CANDLES MARBELIZED 1987
2 1/4" high wax egg candles in Blue, Pink or
Green. DP $2.25. **CMV $3.50 MB.**
JACK 0-LANTERN TRIO CANDLES
1 1/4" high orange candles. Box of 3. DP
$2.50. **CMV $3.50 MB.**

WARNING

KEEP ALL SOAPS
OUT OF SUNLITE
AS THEY FADE
QUICKLY.
ALL SOAPS MUST BE
MINT & BOXED FOR
FULL VALUE.
DAMAGED SOAPS
HAVE NO VALUE.

CHILDREN'S SOAPS

"OLD 99" SOAP 1958
Yellow train engine soap. OSP 69c. **CMV $65. MB.**

CIRCUS WAGON SOAP SET 1957-58
Pink, yellow, black & white circus wagon box contains 1 blue elephant, 1 pink monkey, 1 yellow lion soaps. OSP $1.25. **CMV $75. MB.**

POOL PADDLERS SOAP 1959
Pond display box holds green frog, yellow fish & blue turtle soap. OSP $1.39. **CMV $45. MB.**

BO PEEP SOAP 1953-54
Blue & green box holds 3 white sheep soaps. OSP $1. **CMV $75. MB.**

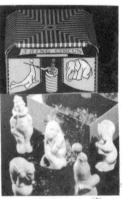

CIRCUS SOAP SET 1939-41
5 ring circus on box holds 5 figural soaps. This set is Avon's first figurals. Soaps are clown, elephant, monkey, seal & horse. OSP $1.19. **CMV $325. MB.** Very rare.

BEST FRIEND SOAP 1956
Blue & white box holds blue dog soap. OSP 59c. **CMV $60. MB.**

FIRE ENGINE SOAP 1957
Red box contains red fire truck soap. OSP 59c. **CMV $70. MB.**

FORWARD PASS 1958
7 1/2 oz. brown football soap on a white rope on side of soap. OSP $1. **CMV $45. MB.**

KIDDIE KENNEL SOAP 1955
Blue & yellow box holds blue, yellow & pink dog soaps. OSP $1.49. **CMV $150. MB.**

AWAY IN THE MANGER SOAP SET 1955
Box holds 4 bars of pink, blue, white & yellow soap. 2 different scenes as shown. Remove panel on bottom picture to show inner panel as shown on top picture. OSP $1.49. **CMV $80. each set, MB.**

SANTA'S HELPER SOAP 1956
(Left) Box holds 3 green, yellow & red Santa & 2 helpers soaps. OSP $1.19. **CMV $120. MB.**
SANTA'S HELPER SOAP 1955
(Right) Box holds green, red & yellow soap. Red Santa soap much larger than 1956 set. OP $1.49. **CMV $110. MB.**

HIGH SCORE 1959
Green net box holds brown basketball soap on a rope. OSP $1.19. **CMV $15. soap only mint, $30. MB.**

CASEY JONES JR. 1956-57
Red, white & blue box holds red engine soap, yellow passenger car & red carboose. OSP $1.19. **CMV $65. MB.**

THREE LITTLE BEARS SOAP SET 1954
3 brown bear soaps. OSP $1.19. **CMV $80. MB.**

FRILLY DUCK SOAP 1960
Box contains yellow & blue soap 5 3/4 oz. OSP 89c. **CMV $30. MB.**

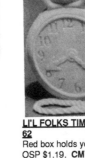

LI'L FOLKS TIME SOAP ON A ROPE 1961-62
Red box holds yellow clock soap on a rope. OSP $1.19. **CMV $35. MB.**

A HIT! SOAP ON A ROPE 1961-62
Box holds white baseball soap on a rope. OSP $1.19. **CMV $30. MB.**

AVONLITE SOAP ON A ROPE 1960-61
Green bowling ball shaped soap in green box. Brochure says "Bowl 'em Over", soap says "Avon Lite". OSP $1.19. **CMV $35. MB, soap only $20. mint.**

SHERIFF'S BADGE SOAP 1962-63
Box holds yellow soap on a rope with embossed sheriff's badge. OSP $1.19. **CMV $35. MB.**

HANSEL & GRETAL SOAP 1965
Blue & pink soap in a box. OSP $1.35. CMV
$35. MB.

"WATCH THE BIRDIE" SOAP 1962-64
White molded camera soap on a rope. OSP
$1.19. **CMV $40. MB.**

LIFE PRESERVER SOAP 1963-64
White life preserver soap on a rope. OSP
$1.19. **CMV $35. MB.**

LIL TOM TURTLE SOAP 1962-63
Box holds green turtle soap with white hat.
OSP 98c. **CMV $35. MB.**

LITTLE SHAVER SOAP 1966-67
(Left) Yellow shaver soap on a rope. OSP
$1.35. **CMV $25. MB.**
TEXAS SHERIFF SOAP 1958
(Right) Box holds 2 blue pistol soaps & silver
sheriff's badge. Box comes with band around
outside of box as shown at top. OSP $1.19.
CMV $65. MB.

PACKY THE ELEPHANT SOAP 1964-65
Green box holds pink elephant with white hat.
OSP 98c. **CMV $30. MB.**

GINGERBREAD SOAP TWINS 1965
Pink, white & brown box holds 2 blue plastic
gingerbread cookie cutters with 2 yellow bars
of gingerbread soap. OSP $1.50. **CMV $30.**

SPEEDY THE SNAIL 1966
Green snail soap on a rope. OSP $1.35. CMV
$30.

GOLDILOCKS SOAP 1966-67
5 oz. yellow soap. OSP $1. **CMV $25. MB.**

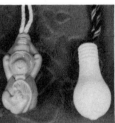

MR. MONKEY SOAP ON A ROPE 1965
(Left) Brown monkey soap. OSP $1.35. **CMV
$25. MB.**
LIGHT BULB SOAP ON A ROPE 1967
(Right) Yellow soap on black, orange & yellow
rope. OSP $1.50. **CMV $25. MB.**

SUNNY THE SUNFISH SOAP 1966
Yellow fish soap on a rope. OSP $1.19. **CMV $25. MB.**

SEA BISCUIT - THE SEA HORSE SOAP ON A ROPE 1964-66
Box holds green soap on a rope. Sea Horse. OSP $1.25. **CMV $25. MB.**

CHICK-A-DEE SOAP 1966-67
Yellow soap on a rope. OSP $1.35. **CMV $20. MB.**

YO YO SOAP SET 1966-67
Pink & red wood Yo Yo & pink soap. OSP $1.50. **CMV $25. MB, Yo Yo only $6.**

BUNNY'S DREAM SOAP ON A ROPE 1967
Box holds orange carrot soap on a green rope. OSP $1.25. **CMV $20. MB.**

EASTER QUACKER SOAP ON A ROPE 1968
Yellow soap. OSP $1.35. **CMV $18. MB.**

RUFF, TUFF & MUFF SOAP SET 1968-69
Blue, pink & yellow dog soaps. OSP $1.25. **CMV $12. MB.**

TUB RACERS SOAP 1969
Green box holds red, yellow & green racer soap. OSP $1.75. **CMV $15. MB.**

MIGHTY MITT SOAP ON A ROPE 1969-72
Brown soap. OSP $2. **CMV $15. MB.**

YANKEE DOODLE SHOWER SOAP 1969-70
White drum shaped soap on a rope. OSP $2. **CMV $15. MB.**

MODELING SOAP 1969-70
Pink 6 oz. soap in blue & pink box. OSP $2. **CMV $7. MB.**

CHILDREN'S SOAPS

MIITTENS KITTENS SOAP 1969-70
Pink, green & yellow soap. Blue box. OSP $2.
CMV $12. MB.

M.C.P. SOAP 1977-79
Tan color Male Chauvinist Pig soap. Came in Deep Woods scent. OSP $5. **CMV $8. MB.**
BUTTON BUTTON GUEST SOAPS 1977-79
Cardboard spool container holds 5 blue button shaped soaps. OSP $6. **CMV $8. MB.**

FIRST DOWN SOAP 1970-71
Box holds brown 5 oz. football soap on a rope. This soap is different from older one. Rope is on end of football. OSP $1.50. **CMV $10. MB.**

TWEETSTERS SOAPS 1971
Yellow box holds 3 pink bird soaps. OSP $2.
CMV $12. MB.

TUBBY TIGERS SOAP SET 1974-75
3 orange soaps in orange & green box. OSP $2. **CMV $6. MB.**

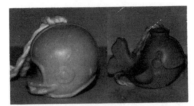

FOOTBALL HELMET SOAP ON A ROPE 1974-75
(Left) Yellow soap, white cord. OSP $2. **CMV $7. MB.**
WILBUR THE WHALE SOAP ON A ROPE. 1974-75
(Right) 5 oz. blue soap with white rope. SSP $2. **CMV $7. MB.**

PERCY PELICAN SOAP ON A ROPE 1972-73
5 oz. yellow soap on white rope. SSP $1.50. **CMV $10. MB.**
PETUNIA PIGLET SOAP ON A ROPE 1973-74
5 oz. pink soap on white rope. SSP $2. **CMV $10. MB.**

SCRUB TUG SOAP 1971
4" long plastic boat scrub brush holds 2 oz. yellow boat soap. OSP $2.50. **CMV brush & soap $8. MB, brush only $1.**
PIG IN A TUB SOAP 1973-75
3" long yellow scrub brush holds 2 oz. pink pig soap. SSP $2.20. **CMV $6. MB.** Reissued 1979.

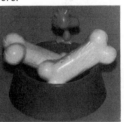

SNOOPY'S PAL SOAP DISH & SOAPS 1973-74
4 1/2" diameter red plastic dish says "Snoopy" on front with yellow bird. Comes with two 2 oz. white bone shaped soaps. SSP $3. **CMV $10. MB.**

HOOTY & TOOTY TUGBOAT SOAPS 1973-75
2 oz. yellow & orange tugboat shaped soaps. SSP $2. **CMV $8. MB.**

PEEP A BOO SOAP ON A ROPE 1970
Yellow chick soap on pink or white rope. OSP $1.35. **CMV $12. MB.**
EASTER BONNET SOAP ON A ROPE 1970
Yellow soap. OSP $1.35. **CMV $12. MB.**

SURE WINNER SOAPS 1973-75
(Left) 3 snowmobile soaps in blue, red & yellow. SSP $2. **CMV $7. MB.**
SURE WINNER SHOWER SOAP 1972-73
White with blue cord. SSP $2. **CMV $8. MB.**

FURRY, PURRY & SCURRY SOAPS 1978-79
Red box with white dots holds 3 kitten shaped soaps in yellow, blue & green. SSP $3. **CMV $6. MB.**

TREE TOTS SOAP 1970-72
Red & green box holds 3 squirrel soaps. OSP $1.75. **CMV $10. MB.**

BLUE MOO SOAP ON A ROPE 1972
(Left) 5 oz. blue cow soap on a rope. OSP $1.75. **CMV $10. MB.**
HONEY LAMB SOAP ON A ROPE 1971-72
(Center) 5" high yellow soap on blue rope. OSP $1.19. **CMV $10. MB.**
AL E. GATOR SOAP ON A ROPE 1971-72
5" high green soap on white rope. OSP $2. **CMV $10. MB.**

TUBBO THE HIPPO SOAP DISH & SOAP 1978-80
(Left) Blue box holds light green plastic hippo soap dish & 3 oz. pink embossed wrapped bar of hippo soap. SSP $5. **CMV $6. MB, soap dish only $1, soap only wrapped $1.50.**
ALKA SELTZER SOAPS 1978-79
Blue, white & red box holds 2 white embossed bars. SSP $4. **CMV $7. MB.**

ARISTOCAT KITTENS SOAP 1971
Box holds white, brown & blue kitten soaps. OSP $2. **CMV $10. MB.**

HOOPER THE HOUND SOAP HOLDER & SOAP 1974
White & black plastic head with pink, green & yellow hoops. Has yellow soap. SSP $4. **CMV $8. MB.**

SAFE COMBINATION BANK SOAPS 1978-79
Black & gold tin bank comes with 2 yellow bars of soap embossed "Avon, 99.9 mint". Bottom of bank says "Made in England, exclusively for Avon". SSP $8. **CMV $10. MB.**

TUB RACERS 1970-72
Three speed boat soaps in red, blue & yellow. OSP $2. **CMV $10. MB.**

HYDROJET SCRUB BRUSH & SOAP 1972-73
Red plastic jet with yellow soap. SSP $2. **CMV $8. MB.**

HAPPY HIPPOS NAIL BRUSH & SOAP 1973-74
3" Long pink nail brush with yellow soap. SSP $2. **CMV $8. MB.**

PEANUTS GANG SOAP 1970-72
Red Lucy, yellow Charlie, white Snoopy soaps. OSP $2. **CMV $12. MB.**

THREE MICE SOAPS 1971-72
Box holds green, white & pink mice soaps.
OSP $2. **CMV $10. MB.**

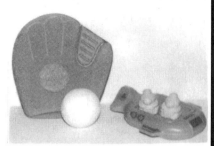

ALL STAR BASE BALL MITT & SOAP 1987
7" orange sponge mitt & white baseball soap.
No box. DP $3.25 **CMV $5. MB.**
SEA SUB & CREW SOAPS 1987
Orange plastic boat holds 2 small sea creature
soaps. D P $4. **CMV $6. MB.**

SCRIBBLE DEE DOO PENCIL SOAPS 1980-81
(Top) 3 pencil shaped yellow soaps. SSP
$4.50 **CMV $7. MB.**
ORCHARD FRESH GUEST SOAPS 1980-81
(Bottom) Choice of orange, lemon or peach
shaped soaps. 6 bars in each box. SSP $5.
CMV $7. each kind.

DARLING DUCKLINGS SOAP 1983
Box holds 3 yellow duck soaps. SSP $4.
CMV $5. MB.

EGGOSAURS SOAPS 1986
Yellow & blue shells hold soaps. Comes with
20 pg. mini book. DP $3. **CMV $5. MB.**

GOOD HABIT RABBIT SCRUB BRUSH & SOAP 1975
(Left) Pink plastic with white bristles. OSP
$2.50 **CMV $8. MB.**
GAYLORD GATOR SCRUB BRUSH & SOAP 1974-75
(Right) Green plastic with white bristles. OSP
$2.50 **CMV $8. MB.**

BUBBLE BLAZER SOAP 1982-83
(Left) Box holds 4 oz. yellow space gun bar.
SSP $3. **CMV $5. MB.**
PARTY LINE SOAP ON A ROPE 1982-83
(Right) Box holds 5 oz. yellow telephone bar
on white rope. SSP $4. **CMV $5. MB.**
TRAIN SOAP 1982-83
(Bottom) 5 3/4" long blue train soap breaks
into 3 cars. Must be all together or of no value.
SSP $3.50 **CMV $5. MB.**

STORY BOOK SOAPS 1984
Book shaped soaps. Pinnochio, Hansel &
Gretel or Cinderella. DP $1. **CMV $3. MB. ea.**

GRIDIRON SCRUB BRUSH & SOAP 1976-77
Brown plastic with yellow soap. OSP $4.
CMV $8. MB.

BATH TUB BUGGIES SOAP SET 1986
Box holds blue, red or yellow truck soaps.
OSP $2.50 **CMV $3.50 MB.**

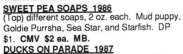

BONNIE & BENNY BUFFLE & SOAP 1990
Plastic water squirters and 3oz. bar of Soap for each. SSP $4.00 **CMV $4.00 MB each set.**

SWEET PEA SOAPS 1986
(Top) different soaps, 2 oz. each. Mud puppy, Goldie Purrsha, Sea Star, and Starfish. DP $1. **CMV $2 ea. MB.**

DUCKS ON PARADE 1987
Box holds 3 small yellow duck soaps. DP $1.50 **CMV $3. MB.**

SOUNDS OF CHRISTMAS SOAPS 1986
3 different small bars. Drum, Horn or Harp soap. DP .75c **CMV $1.50 ea. MB.**

MICKEY & MINNIE HOLLYWOOD SOAP 1989
Micky, blue & Minnie, yellow. Box of 2. SSP $2.50 **CMV $2.50 MB**

SNOOPY & WOODSTOCK SOAP 1990
White Snoopy & yellow Woodstock soap. SSP $2.00 **CMV $2.00 MB**

CHRISTMAS FRIENDS ORNAMENT SOAPS 1988
Red Santa, Blue Penquin, Green Elf soaps. SSP $1.50 **CMV $1.50 ea. MB**

ANIMAL SOAPS 1985
Choice of Elephant, Hippo or Lion. DP $1. **CMV $2. MB.**

EASTER FUN BATH CUBES 1985
Box holds 6 Easter cubes. SSP $2.50 **CMV $3. MB.**

SOMERSAULTS SOAP & MINI BOOKS 1985
Each box has different colored soaps. DP $2. **CMV $3. MB.**

SAY CHEESE SOAP SET 1990
3oz. pink mouse bar snaps apart. SSP $2.00 **CMV $2.00 MB**

PUMPKIN PALS SOAP SET 1989
Orange Box holds 3 black cat soaps. SSP $3.00 **CMV $3.00 MB**

BILLY ROCKET & SKY BLAZERS CO-LOGNE GIFT SET 1987
Box holds soap & 2oz. cologne. SSP $4.00 **CMV $4.00 MB**

SOAP PETS 1987
Ruffy the puppy in blue, Squeaky the mouse in lavender, Fluffy the kitten in orange. SSP $1.50each **CMV $1.50 each MB**

MICKEY & FRIENDS SOAP 1990
5 different soaps. Mickey, Pluto, Minnie, Gofy, Donald. 1oz. ea. SSP $1.30ea. **CMV $1.30 ea. MB**

CHILDRENS SOAPS

NOTES

UR2B CLEAN ROBOT SOAP 1988
Orange & lavender robot soaps. SSP $1.50ea.
CMV $1.50 ea. MB

GARFIELD SOAP 1990
Orange cat soap. SSP $2.50 **CMV $2.50 MB**

FISH N' FUN FINGER PAINT SOAP 1989
Red, yellow & blue fish soap in matching
plastic boxes. SSP $6.00 **CMV $6.00 Set MB**

TINY TEDDY BEAR SOAPS 1988
3 yellow bear soaps. SSP $2.00 **CMV $2.00
MB**

BABY BUNNY SOAPS 1989
3 green bunny soaps. SSP $2.50 **CMV $2.50
MB**

NEW KITTY TRIO SOAPS 1987
3-kitten soaps 1oz. ea. SSP $2.00 **CMV $2.00
MB**

BUMBEE BABEE TOY & SOAP 1987
Bumble Bee wind up tub toy & matching soap.
SSP $5.00 **CMV $5.00 MB**

BATH FLOWERS SOAP & SPONGE 1965-66
Pink and white floral box contains 1 bar To A
Wild Rose soap pink, green and white sponge.
OSP $2.50 **CMV $12. MB.**

MINNIE THE MOO SOAP & SPONGE 1965-66
White foam cow with yellow ears and black eyes.
Soap is in green wrapper. OSP $1.75 **CMV $8
soap and sponge only mint., $14. MB.**

MISTERJAW BATH MITT & SOAP 1978
Blue sponge mitt 9" long with fish design bar of
soap. SSP $5. **CMV $7. MB.**

**CHARLIE BROWN BATH MITT & SOAP
1969-71**
Red and white sponge with white bar of Snoopy
embossed soap. OSP $3. **CMV $10. MB.**

**CEDRIC SEA SERPENT SPONGE AND
SOAP 1973**
(Left) 9 1/2" long, green and pink sponge,
white soap. OSP $2.50 **CMV $10. MB.**
**CEDRIC SEA SERPENT SPONGE AND
SOAP 1974-75**
(Right) 9 1/2" long, purple and pink sponge.
OSP $3. **CMV $10. MB.**

**POLLY PARROT PUPPET SPONGE & SOAP
1969-70**
Green and orange sponge with bar of soap.
OSP $3. **CMV $12. MB, Soap and sponge
only $6.**

SPONGAROO SOAP & SPONGE 1966-67
Brown kangaroo sponge is 15" x 5 3/4". White
kangaroo soap. OSP $2.25. **CMV $15.,
soap only $7. mint.**

SPIDERMAN SPONGE & SOAP 1980
Blue and red sponge. Red wrapped soap.
SSP $4. **CMV $6. MB.**

**YAKETY YAK TAXI SOAP AND SPONGE
1978-79**
Box holds yellow taxi and bar of wrapped
Sweet Pickles soap. SSP $4. **CMV $7. MB.**

CLARENCE THE SEA SERPENT 1968-69
Orange and yellow sponge with bar of serpent
soap in blue and yellow wrapper. OSP $2.25
CMV $12. MB.

OSCAR OCTUPUS & SOAP 1980-81
Yellow and orange with blue and green trim
sponge. Green, red and purple rings, 1 bar of
Oscar Octupus soap. SSP $6. **CMV $7. MB.**

SOAPS WITH SPONGES

BABY KERMIT & MISS PIGGY SPONGE & SOAP 1986
3 1/2" high sponge with soap inside, doubles in side when wet. Kermit in green & Piggy in red. DP $2. **CMV $3. MB.**

LITTLE PRO SOAP 1966
White baseball soap and brown sponge. OSP $2.25 **CMV $14. MB, $8 soap and sponge only.**

NEST EGG SOAP & SPONGE 1967-68
Box holds yellow nest sponge and pink soap. OSP $2.25 **CMV $12. MB.**

BATH BLOSSOMS 1969
Pink and yellow sponge with pink soap. OSP $3.50 **CMV $10 MB, $4. soap and sponge only.**

GOOD HABIT RABBIT BATH MITT & SOAP 1974
White and pink foam mitt with yellow carrot soap. SSP $2.50 **CMV $7 MB.**

MONKEY SHINES 1969
Brown and pink sponge and bar of soap. OSP $3. **CMV $9 MB, Soap and sponge only $5.**

BATH BLOSSOM SPONGE AND SOAP 1979-80
(Left) Box holds yellow, green and blue sponge and yellow soap. SSP $6. **CMV $6 MB.**
SWEET PICKLES WORRIED WALRUS SOAP AND SPONGE 1979-80
(Center) Purple, green and brown sponge. Comes with wrapped bar of Sweet Pickles childrens bath soap. SSP $5. **CMV $5. MB.**
FEARLESS FISH SPONGE AND SOAP 1979-80
(Right) Green fish sponge and Sweet Pickles wrapped soap with fish on a scooter. SSP $4. **CMV $4 MB.**

PINK PANTHER SPONGE MITT AND SOAP 1977-80
Pink mitt, yellow eyes. Blue, green and pink wrapped soap. OSP $6. **CMV $8. MB.**

LITTLE LEAGUER SOAP AND SPONGE 1972
Tan sponge mitt and white baseball soap. Sponge is different from Little Pro soap and sponge in 1966. **CMV $10 MB, $6 soap and sponge only mint.**

HUBIE THE HIPPO SOAP & SPONGE 1970-71
Turquoise and red sponge with Hippo wrapped soap. OSP $4. **CMV $10 MB.**

SOAPY THE WHALE BATH MITT AND SOAP 1973-74
8 1/2" long blue and red sponge mitt with blue soap. SSP $3. **CMV $7 MB.**

NOTES

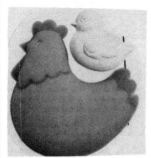

CHEERY CHIRPERS KITCHEN SOAP & SPONGE 1990
Yellow chicken sponge, white chick soap. SSP $4.00 **CMV $4.00 MB**

BATH TIME BASKETBALL & SOAP SET 1989
Orange sponge basketball & purple slam dunk soap. SSP $7.00 **CMV $7.00 MB**

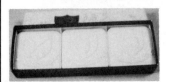

MOST VALUABLE SOAP SET 1963-64
Yellow box holds 3 yellow bars. OSP $1.35
CMV $30. MB.

SHAVING SOAP 1949-57
Two bars in green & red box. OSP 59c. **CMV
$32.50 MB.**

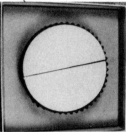

LONESOME PINE SOAP 1966-67
Green & gold box holds woodgrained soap cut
in half. OSP $2. **CMV $25. MB.**

CPC SHAVING SOAP 1908
White bar embossed. Came in yellow box.
OSP 20c. **CMV $60 MB.**

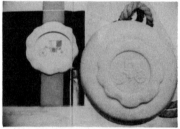

CARRIAGE SHOWER SOAP 1960-62
Red, white and black box contains 6 oz. cake
embossed Stage Coach soap on red or white
rope. OSP $1.35 **CMV $35.**

BATH SOAP FOR MEN 1966-67
Two white soaps with red buttons, silver &
white box. OSP $2.50 **CMV $25 MB.**

SHAVING SOAP 1930-36
White bar. OSP 25c. **CMV $35. MB.**
STYPTIC PENCIL 1930
OSP 10c. **CMV $10. MB.**

OATMEAL SOAP 1961-63
Two brown bars, 2 different boxes. "A spicy
fragrance." OSP $1.35 **CMV $30. MB,
deluxe box $35. MB.**

SHAMPOO SHOWER SOAP FOR MEN
1972-73
5 oz. bar on red & black rope. Also came with
white rope. Red & black box. OSP $2.50
CMV $8. MB.

SHAVING SOAP 1936-49
Two bars in maroon box, white soap. OSP
31c. **CMV $42.50 MB.**

OATMEAL SOAP FOR MEN SPICY 1963-64
Embossed stage coach on brown bar of soap.
OSP 39c. **CMV $10 in wrapping.**

MODEL 'A' 1928 SOAP SET 1975
Two 3 oz. white bars of soap with dark & light
blue wrapper & box. OSP $3. **CMV $6. MB.**

GOLF BALL SOAPS 1975
Three white soaps in yellow & green box. Spicy scented OSP $2. **CMV $7 MB.**

BARBER SHOP DUET MUSTACHE COMB & SOAP SET 1978-79
Box holds white bar man's face soap & small brown plastic mustache comb. SSP $4. **CMV $6. MB set.**

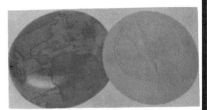

ANCIENT MARINER BOX & SOAP 1982-83
Tin box with bar compass design soap. SSP $6. **CMV $6. MB.**

ON DUTY 24 SOAP 1977-84
Deodorant soap. OSP 3 for $1. **CMV .50¢ each. 3 different labels.**
MUSK FOR MEN 1983-84
Shower soap on rope. SSP $3. **CMV $3. MB.**

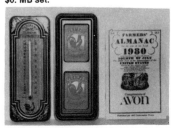

FARMERS ALMANAC THERMOMETER & SOAPS 1979-80
Box holds tin top with plastic bottom with 2 bars of Farmers Almanac soap. Comes with copy of Avon 1980 Farmers Almanac. SSP $9. **CMV $12 MB complete, CMV Farmers Almanac only $1.**

THATS MY DAD DECAL SOAPS 1983
(Left) Choice of 3 different decal soaps. "We love you dad" or "You taught me all the important things Dad" or "You're always there when I need you Dad" SSP $2. **CMV $3 each bar MB.**
GRANDFATHERS & GRANDMOTHERS ARE SPECIAL SOAPS 1983
(Right) Metal can holds choice of black or white grandfather or black or white grandmother. SSP $6. **CMV $6. MB.**

ROYAL HEARTS SOAP 1978-79
(Left) King & Queen box holds 2 white bars with king & queen of hearts soaps. SSP $5. **CMV $7. MB.**
SUITABLY GIFTED SOAP 1978-79
(Right) Blue box holds blue bar that is shaped like a shirt and tie. SSP $5. **CMV $7. MB.**

LUCKY SHOEHORSE SOAP DISH & SOAP 1979-80
(Left) Brown box holds amber glass horseshoe soapdish & soap. SSP $8. **CMV $10. MB.**
PERPETUAL CALENDAR CONTAINER & SOAP 1979-80
(Right) Yellow box holds Avon tin can calendar & white bar of soap. Bottom of can says Made in England for Avon. SSP $8. **CMV $8. MB.**

BUFFALO NICKEL 1913 SOAP DISH & SOAP 1978-79
5" nickel plated Buffalo Nickel metal soap dish & light gray or off white color soap. SSP $8. **CMV $10 MB.**

WEEKEND SOAP ON A ROPE 1979-80
Tan soap on green rope. **CMV $3.**

HUDDLES SOAP ON A ROPE & CARDS 1984
Box holds brown football marked Huddles & deck of NFL football team playing cards. DP $4. **CMV $5. MB.**
DAD SOAP ON A ROPE 1985
Yellow bar. DP $3. **CMV $4. MB.**

NOTES

AURES SOAP ON A ROPE 1986 AMERICAN CLASSIC SOAP ON A ROPE 1987
Both boxed single bar on rope. DP $2.75
CMV $4. MB.

WILDERNESS BOX SOAP 1988
Wood box 3 1/4" wide with deer lid & soap.
SSP $9.00 CMV $9.00 MB

MEN'S SOAPS 1984
Cool soap, Cordovan, Wild Country, Musk for Men. CMV $1. Each.
DADS LUCKY DEAL DECAL SOAP & CARDS 1984
Bar of dog soap & deck of cards. DP $4.
CMV $6. MB.

GENTLEMEN'S QUARTER GIFT SET 1989
Box holds black suede soap & sponge. SSP $7.00 CMV $7.00 MB

SPORTING DUCK SOAP 1990
3oz. brown duck bar. SSP $2.00 CMV $2.00 MB

LEMONOL TOILET SOAP 1931-36
Yellow soap wrapped in blue and silver paper. Came in box of 3. OSP 50c. **CMV $45. MB. Box of 12 bars $1.75 CMV $65. MB.**

LEMONOL SOAP 1958-66
Yellow and green box holds 3 yellow bars with flat edges. Box comes lift off, (older) and flip up as shown. OSP $1.19 **CMV $30. MB.**

LEMONOL SOAP 1921-33
Box of 12 cakes. OSP $1.50 **CMV $100 MB.**

FACIAL SOAP 1945-55
Box holds 2 bars. OSP 89c. **CMV $25. MB.**

LEMONOL SOAP 1966-67
Blue and yellow box holds six 2 1/2" yellow bars. OSP $2.25 **CMV $30. MB.**

LEMONOL TOILET SOAP 1923-31
Box of 3 bars. OSP 45c. **CMV $80 MB.**

FACIAL SOAP 1955-61
Turquoise box holds 2 bars. OSP 89c. **CMV $20. MB.**

HOSTESS BOUQUET SOAP 1959-61
Pink and yellow box holds bars OSP $1.39 **CMV $25. MB.**

LEMONOL SOAP 1941-58
Yellow and green lemon box holds 3 flat bars with round edges and flat on bottom. OSP $1. **CMV $35 MB.**

WHIPPED CREAM SOAP 1968
Green, blue, pink and yellow soap. OSP $3. **CMV $15. MB.**

GIFT BOWS SOAP 1962-64
Box holds 6 bow tie soaps. OSP $2.25. **CMV $30. MB.**

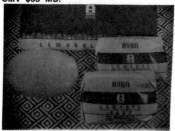

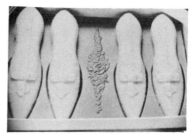

LEMONOL TOILET SOAP 1936-41
Three yellow bars in turquoise and white box and wrapping. OSP 51c. **CMV $40. MB.** Box of 12 bars OSP $1.79 **CMV $60 MB. Add $3 per bar for CPC label mint.**

HOSTESS SOAP SAMPLER 1964-65
Floral box holds 12 cakes of soap. OSP $2.50 **CMV $30. MB.**

LADY SLIPPERS SOAP 1965-66
4 shoe soaps in box. OSP $2.25 **CMV $35. MB.**

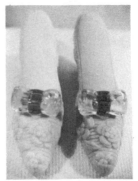

CHERUB SOAP SET 1966-67
Blue box holds 2 pink angel
soaps. $2. **CMV $30. MB.**

PINE CONE GIFT SOAPS 1970-73
Box contains blue, yellow and green pine
scented soaps. OSP $3. **CMV $10. MB.**

SOAP TREASURE 1963
Gold and white box holds 5 bars of perfumed
soap in choice of Lilac, Lily of the Valley,
Floral, Lemonol, Cotillion, Here's My Heart,
Rose Geranium, To A Wild Rose, Royal
Jasmine, Persian Wood, Somewhere, Royal
PIne, and Topaze Set. Came with 2 different
kinds of soap as shown. OSP $1.95. **CMV
$25. MB each set.**

PARTRIDGE & PEAR SOAPS 1968-70
Two green pears and white partridge. OSP
$3. **CMV $12. MB.**

SLIPPER SOAP & PERFUME 1970-71
1/8 oz. bow tie perfume sits in light pink slipper
soap in Cotillion, and dark pink soap in
Charisma. OSP $5. **CMV $15. MB. soap
and perfume only mint.**

BAY BERRY SOAP 1967
Blue and gold box holds 3 wrapped bars in
plastic holder. OSP $3. **CMV $25. Soap
only $5. each.**

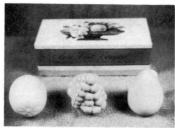

FRUIT BOUQUET SOAP 1969
Orange, lavender, and green soap. OSP $3.
CMV $12. MB.

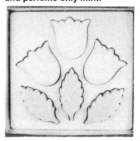

SPRING TULIPS SOAP 1970-73
Blue and pink box holds 6 green white and pink
soaps. OSP $3.50 **CMV $20. MB.**

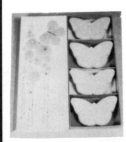

BUTTERFLY SOAP 1966-67
4 bars in box. OSP $2. **CMV $30. MB.**

DECORATOR SOAPS 1969
Pink box holds 3 egg shaped soaps in green,
pink and blue. OSP $3. **CMV $12 MB.**

CUP CAKE SOAP 1972-73
Green, pink and orange soap. 2 oz. each. SP
$2.50 **CMV $10. MB.**

GRADE AVON HOSTESS SOAPS 1971-72
Plastic carton holds 2 blue and 2 pink egg shaped soaps. OSP $4.50 **CMV $8. MB.**

HIDDEN TREASURE SOAP 1972-75
Two 3 oz. turquoise soaps with pearl colored and shaped 1/8 oz. bottle of perfume. Came in Bird of Paradise only. SSP $5. **CMV $12. MB.**

LACERY HOSTESS BATH SOAP 1972-73
Cream colored with foil center design. Box gold and pink. SSP $3. **CMV $6. MB.**

HOSTESS BOUQUET GUEST SOAP 1972-73
3 pink bars shaped like flower bouquet tied with green ribbon. Came in pink and blue boquet box. OSP $3.50 **CMV $10. MB.**

FRAGRANCE & FRILLS SOAP 1972-75
4 lavendar soaps in lavender plastic box. In center a 1/8 oz. bottle of Dazzling perfume in Field Flowers or Bird of Paradise. SSP $6. **CMV $15. MB.**

MELON BALL GUEST SOAP 1973
1 oz. honey dew and cantaloupe colored balls inside cantaloupe shaped plastic container. SSP $4. **CMV $8 MB.**

SOAP SAVERS 1973
9 oz. total of green soaps in spearmint fragrance. SSP $3. **CMV $10. MB.**

SOAP FOR ALL SEASONS 1973
1.5 oz. each, 4 soaps, yellow, green, blue and orange. SSP $3. **CMV $8 MB.**

RECIPE TREASURES 1974-75
5 orange scented soaps in yellow and orange decorative metal file box. OSP $5. **CMV $10. MB.**

COUNTRY KITCHEN SOAPDISH AND SOAP 1974-75
Red plastic scooped dish contains 5 green apple fragranced soaps. OSP $6. **CMV $10. MB.**

1876 WINTERSCAPES HOSTESS SOAPS 1976
Two Currier and Ives scenes soaps. Came in Special Occasion fragrance. OSP $5.50 **CMV $10. MB.**

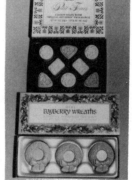

PETIT FOURS GUEST SOAPS 1975-76
Eight 1 oz. soaps, 3 pink hearts, 2 yellow squares. 3 rounds. OSP $4. **CMV $10. MB.**

BAYBERRY WREATHS GIFT SOAPS 1975
3 Bayberry scented in Christmas box. OSP $3. **CMV $8. MB.**

ANGEL LACE SOAPS 1975-76
3 blue soaps in blue and white box. OSP $3.
CMV $10. MB.
TOUCH OF LOVE SOAPS 1975
3 white soaps in lavender box. Spring
lavender fragrance. OSP $4. CMV $8. MB.

PICK A BERRY STRAWBERRY SOAPS &
CONTAINER 1975-76
4 1/2" high red plastic with 6 strawberry
scented soaps. OSP $6. CMV $10. MB.

LITTLE CHOIR BOYS HOSTESS SOAPS
1976
Box holds 3 pink soaps. Came in light or dark
pink. SSP $2.88 CMV $8. MB.

TAPESTRY HOSTESS SOAPS 1981
Box holds 2 decorator bars. SSP $4. CMV
$6. MB.

TIDINGS OF LOVE SOAPS 1976
3 pink soaps in pink and white box. OSP $3.
CMV $8. MB.
PARTRIDGE 'N PEAR HOSTESS SOAP
1974-75
3 yellow soaps in festive Christmas box. OSP
$3. CMV $10. MB.

GOLDEN BEAUTIES HOSTESS SOAP 1974-
76
2 oz. each, 3 cakes yellow soap. SSP $2.
CMV $8. MB.

MERRY ELFKINS GUEST SOAPS 1977
Box holds 3 green soaps. OSP $5.50 CMV
$7. MB.

BLUE TRANQUILITY REFRESHING SOAP
1978-80
5 oz. blue embossed bar on white rope. Blue
box. SSP $3. CMV $4. MB.

BOUQUET OF PANSIES SOAP 1976-77
Blue box holds 2 flower decorated special occasion
white soaps. OSP $5.50 CMV $8. MB.

TENDER BLOSSOMS GUEST TOWELS &
SOAPS 1977-78
Came with 12 paper hand towels and 3 special
occasion fragranced soaps. OSP $6.50.
CMV $7. MB.

WINTER FROLICS HOSTESS SOAPS 1977-
78
Came with 2 Festive Fragrance scented soaps
with long lasting decals. 3 oz. each. OSP
$5.50 CMV $8. MB.

PERFUMED SOAP CHRISTMAS WRAP
1979-80
Single fragrance bar in red. Tempo or Ariane,
bronze Candid, Blue Emprise or Unspoken.
SSP $1. CMV $1.50 MB.

ANGEL FISH HOSTESS SOAPS 1978
Box holds 3 blue fish soaps. SSP $3.66 **CMV $6. MB.**

TREASURE BASKET GUEST SOAPS 1978-79
Silver basket holds 2 yellow and 2 pink tulip soaps. SSP $9. **CMV $10. MB.**

COUNTRY GARDEN SOAPS 1978-80
Box holds 2 Avon bar flower soaps with 2 different flower decals. SSP $4. **CMV $5. MB.**

CHRISTMAS CAROLLERS SOAPS 1978-79
Box holds 2 turquoise color carollers. SSP $3. **CMV $5. MB.**

SUMMER BUTTERFLIES HOSTESS SOAPS 1977-78
Two scented soaps with long lasting decals. 3 oz. each. OSP $5.50 **CMV $7. MB.**

BALLET PICTURE SOAPS 1978-80
White plastic box and lid holds 2 blue picture decal bars of soap. SSP $6. **CMV $8. MB.**

A TOKEN OF LOVE HOSTESS SOAPS 1978
All three pieces are special occasion fragranced soaps. Light pink outside dark pink inside soap. OSP $6. **CMV $8. MB.**

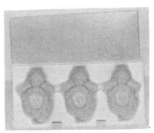

LITTLE ANGELS HOSTESS SOAPS 1980-81
Blue box holds 3 blue angel soaps. SSP $4. **CMV $6. MB.**

COMPLEXION BAR 1966-70
4 oz. bar. OSP $1.25 **CMV $4. MB.**

BUBBLY BEAR SOAP-IN-SOAP 1980-81
Blue box holds small ribbon box of blue soap with small white bear soap inside. SSP $6. **CMV $7. MB.**

CALIFORNIA PERFUME CO. 1980 ANNIVERSARY SOAPS 1980-81
1980 CPC box holds two Violet bars. SSP $4. **CMV $6. MB.**

CLEAR SKIN SOAP 1960-63
Brown bar in gray and white box. OSP 49c. **CMV $4.**

CLEAR SKIN SOAP 1964-69
Brown bar in gray and white wrapper. OSP 59c. **CMV $3.**

PERFUMED SOAPS & PERFUMED DEODORANT SOAPS 1961-64
1 bar of each in Lemonol, Persian Wood, Somewhere, Facial, Floral, Royal Pink, Royal Jasmine, Here's My Heart, Cotillion, To A Wild Rose, Topaze and Rose Geranium. OSP 39c. **CMV $4. each mint.**

FEELIN' FRESH SOAP 1978-83
Regular issue bar on left. **CMV .50¢.**
Introductory trial size bar on right, short issue. **CMV $2.**

PERFUMED DEODORANT SOAP 1963-67
OSP 39c. **CMV $4. mint.**

PERFUMED SOAP HOLIDAY WRAPPING 1977
Came in Charisma and Touch of Roses in red poinsettia wrap. Sonnet and Field Flowers in green and Moonwind and Bird of Paradise in blue. SSP $1.25. **CMV $2. each.**

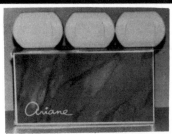

ARIANE PERFUMED SOAPS 1978
Red box holds 3 white soaps. SSP $5. **CMV $7. MB.**

SCENTED SOAPS 1971-73
3 oz. bars in matching soap and wrapping. Mint, Pine Tar, Almond, Camomile, Papaya, Avacado. OSP 75c. **CMV $4. MB.**

FRESH AS NATURE SOAP 1982-83
3 different bars in Aloe Vera, Wheat Germ and Glycerine, Witch Hazel and Lyme. SSP $2. **CMV $1.50 each MB.**

SOFT MUSK SOAP 1982-84
Single 3 oz. bar. SSP $1.50. **CMV $1. mint.**

CANDID PERFUMED SOAPS 1977-78
Open end box, 3 cakes each. 3 oz. white bars. OSP $7. **CMV $5. MB.**

FIVE GUEST SOAPS 1983
Flower design box holds 5 small bars in Timeless, Candid, Ariane, Tasha, Foxfire, Odyssey or Soft Musk. SSP $4. **CMV $5. MB.**

CREAM SOAPS 1981-83
1 pink, yellow or blue wrapped bar. SSP .50¢. **CMV .50¢.**
HEARTS & LACE SPECIAL OCCASION SOAP 1981
Pink flower wrapped bar. SSP .75¢. **CMV .75¢ mint.**

EMPRISE PERFUMED SOAPS 1977-78
Open end box holds 3 beige color bars. OSP $7. **CMV $5. MB.**

FLORAL BOXED SOAPS 1983
(Left) Box has different flower design for each fragrance. 4 flowered bars. Choice of Wild Jasmine "gold", Hawaiian White Ginger "white", Honeysuckle "yellow" or Roses Roses "pink". SSP $4. **CMV $4. MB.**
FLORAL GUEST SOAP 1983
(Right) Single 1 oz. bar in box. Different color soap for each fragrance. Choice of Roses Roses, Wild Jasmine, Hawaiian White Ginger. SSP 75c. **CMV .75¢ MB.**

CHRISTMAS WISHES DECAL SOAPS 1983
3 different boxed bars. Choice of Happiness in pink, Togetherness in green & Sharing in tan color soap. SSP $1.50. each. **CMV $1.50. each MB.**

A MOTHER'S JOY SOAP SET 1983
Blue box holds 2 white mother & child soaps. SSP $4. **CMV $4. MB.**

COUNTRY CHRISTMAS DECAL SOAPS 1982
Box holds 2 bars. SSP $4. **CMV $5. MB.**

RICH MOISTURE BATH BAR SOAP 1972-82
Single 5 oz. bar, turquoise & white wrapper. SSP $1. **CMV $1. mint.**

TIMELESS SOAP 1975-78
3 cakes amber soap in amber, gold & yellow box. OSP $4. **CMV $7.**
TIMELESS PERFUMED SOAP 1976-78
3 oz. bar. OSP $1.25. **CMV $1.**

SWEET HONESTY PERFUMED SOAPS 1978
Boxed 3 cakes, 3 oz. each. OSP $6.50. **CMV $7. MB.**
SWEET HONESTY SOAP 1982-83
Single bar. **CMV .75¢.**
SEA GARDEN PERFUMED BATH SOAP 1970-73
6 oz. blue bar with blue box. OSP $2. **CMV $4. MB.**

TIS THE SEASON SOAPS 1985
Small bars of Mistletoe, Poinsettia or Holly. DP $1. **CMV $1. each MB.**
SPRING GARDEN GLYCERINE SOAPS 1985
White, pink or yellow bars. **CMV $1. each MB.**
FIVE GUEST SOAPS 1984
Flowered box has 5 small bars in choice of 7 fragrances. DP $3. **CMV $3. MB.**

FLORAL BATH CUBES 1984
Box of 6 wrapped cubes. DP $2. **CMV $3. MB.**
LIGHT ACCENT SOAP 1984
Single bar, choice of Tea Garden, Willow, Amber Mist. **CMV $1. each.**
VALENTINE SOAP SET 1986
Pink box holds 3 pink heart soaps. DP $3. **CMV $4. MB.**

LETTER PERFECT GUEST SOAP 1984
Single bar with choice of pesonal letter on soap. DP $1. **CMV $1. MB.**
ULTRA GUEST SOAPS 1984
Silver box holds choice of 5 small bars in 7 fragrances. DP $3. **CMV $3. MB.**
WATER LILY BATH CUBES 1985
Blue box holds 6 soap cubes. DP $3. **CMV $3. MB.**

SKIN-SO-SOFT SOAP 1965-74
3 oz. bar. OSP 49c. **CMV $1. mint.**
WINTER GLOW SOAP 1981
Green & white. **CMV $1.**
SOFT MUSK SOAP 1983-84
Single bar. **CMV $1.**
5 GUEST SOAPS
CMV $4. MB.

GARDEN FRESH SOAPS 1985
Box holds 3 peach shaped soaps or box of 6 strawberry soaps. DP $3. each. **CMV $4. each MB.**

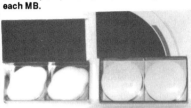

IMARI LUXURY PERFUMED SOAPS 1986
Maroon & gold box holds 2 bars. DP $4.50. **CMV $4.50 MB.**

FIFTH AVENUE SCULPTURED SOAPS 1986
Black, white & purple box holds 2 lavender bars. DP $4.50. **CMV $4.50 MB.**

PEACEFUL TIDINGS SOAP & BATH CUBE SET 1985
Blue box has soap bar & 2 bath cubes. DP $3. **CMV $3. MB.**

COLONIAL ACCENT SOAP & SACHET 1985
Box holds decorator bar soap & 3 packets of sachet. DP $4. **CMV $4. MB.**

FERAUD SOAP 1985-87
5 oz. bar. Silver, black wrapper. **CMV $1.**

SOFT MUSK SOAP 1982-85
TOCCARA SOAP 1981-85
CLEAR SKIN SOAP 1984-86
PEARLS & LACE SOAP 1984-87
All single bars. **CMV .50¢ each.**

ENCHANTED LAND SOAP SET 1984
(Right) Box holds 2 white bars with fairy decals. DP $2.50. **CMV $3. MB.**

CALIFORNIA PERFUME CO. SOAP 1984
(Left) Small bars, choice of Violet, Apple Blossom or Lilac. DP $1. **CMV $1. each MB.**

TRANQUIL MOMENTS SOAP 1986
SILK TAFFETA SOAP 19866
Single bars each. DP $1.25. **CMV $1.25 each.**

HOLIDAY FRIENDS SOAP 1987
Choice of Santa - red soap, Teddy - green or Mr. Snowman in white. SSP $1.00ea. **CMV $1.00 ea. MB**

JOLLY REINDEER SOAP 1987
Box holds 5" long soap that can break apart. Must be in 1 piece to be mint. SSP $2.00 **CMV $2.00 MB**

GIFTS OF THE SEA SOAP SET 1988
Box holds 4 pink shell soaps. SSP $2.50 **CMV $2.50 MB**

CHRISTMAS BERRIES SOAP SET 1988
Holly box holds 2 holly decal bars. SSP $4.00 **CMV $4.00 MB**

FRIENDSHIP GARDEN SOAPS 1988
Flower embossed bars in yellow, green & violet. SSP $1.00ea. **CMV $1.00ea. MB**

COUNTRY CHRISTMAS SOAPS 1988
Choice of green, pink or yellow bars. SSP .80¢ **CMV $1.00ea. MB**

NOTES

TENDER LOVE SOAP SET 1989
Box holds 2 white swan soaps. SSP $2.00
CMV $2.00 MB

CITRUS SCENTS SOAP SET 1989
Box holds 3 fruit slice bars. SSP $2.50 **CMV $2.50 MB**

SCENTIMENTAL SOAPS 1989
Box holds 3 pink heart bars. SSP $2.00 **CMV $2.00 MB**

GLISTENING HOLIDAY SOAPS 1990
1oz. bar in Angel, Dove or Bell. SSP $1.00 ea.
CMV $1.00 ea. MB

CHRISTMAS COUPLES MINI SOAP 1989
Choice of Snowman, Reindeer, & Santa Claus.
SSP $1.00 ea. **CMV $1.00 ea. MB**

GEM SOAPS 1990
Box holds 4 Gem-like bars. SSP $3.00 **CMV $3.00 MB**

PEACH ORCHARD SOAP SET 1989
3 bars peach soaps in box. SSP $3.00 **CMV $3.00 MB**

ASPIRIN SOAP 1990
4oz. white bar inscribed ASPIRIN. SSP $2.00
CMV $2.00 MB

Soaps must be mint for CMV.

COLLECTORS:
All Containers are Priced Empty

BO means .... Bottle only (empty)
CMV means ...... Current Market Value (mint)
SSP means .... Special Selling Price
OSP means .... Original Selling Price
MB means .... Mint and Boxed
DP means .... Avon Rep Cost

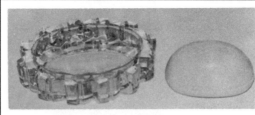

ULTRA CRYSTAL SOAP DISH & SOAP 1981-82
5" long clear glass soap dish and bar of cream color soap. SSP $10. **CMV $10. MB.**

MOUNT VERNON PLATE & SOAPS 1979-80
9" long blue glass plate. Has Mount Vernon, George and Martha Washington on front. Came with 2 white George and Martha bars of soap. SSP $11. **CMV $11. MB.**

AVON SOAP JAR 1965-66
Pink ribbon on clear glass jar and lid. Came with 12 cakes of soap. OSP $4.50. **CMV $25. MB, jar only with ribbon and no soap $6., jar and soap with ribbons mint $16.**

HOSTESS FANCY SOAP DISH & SOAP 1975-76
8" wide clear glass with 5 pink soaps. OSP $6. **CMV $10. MB.**

FLOWER FROST SHERBERT GLASS AND SOAPS 1979-80
Frosted glass holds 6 yellow Avon balls of soap. SSP $10. **CMV $11. MB.**

BIRD IN HAND SOAP DISH AND SOAPS 1978-80
5 1/2" long white glass hand soap dish with 3 small blue bird soaps. SSP $6. **CMV $8. MB.**

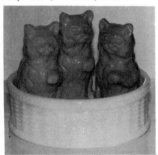

SITTIN' KITTENS SOAP DISH AND SOAPS 1973-75
White milk glass dish with 3 kitten soaps in gold colored, yellow and orange. SSP $4. **CMV $10. MB.**

DOLPHIN SOAP DISH AND HOSTESS SOAPS 1970-71
Silver and aqua plastic soap dish holds 4 blue soaps. OSP $8. **CMV $12. MB.**

BUTTERFLY FANTASY DISHES & SOAPS 1979-80
Two 4" porcelain with butterfly design. 1 pink butterfly soap. SSP $10. **CMV $12. MB.**

FLOWER FROST COLLECTION CRESCENT PLATE & GUEST SOAPS 1979-80
Frosted glass soap dish holds 3 yellow flower soap bars. SSP $13. **CMV $14. MB.**

NESTING HEN SOAP DISH & SOAP 1973
White milk glass hen with beige painted nest. Holds 4 yellow egg soap, 2 oz. each. SSP $7. **CMV $15. MB.**

BICENTENNIAL PLATE & SOAP 1975-76
Clear glass plate with blue soaps embossed with the face of George & Martha Washington on each. Some have Avon on bottom and some don't. OSP $7. **CMV $10. MB.**

WINGS OF BEAUTY SOAP DISH & SOAP 1975-76
White milk glass dish with 2 pink soaps. OSP $5. **CMV $10. MB.**

NUTTY SOAP DISH & SOAPS 1974-76
Plastic dish with 2 peanut scented soaps. OSP $4. **CMV $8. MB.**

BIRDS OF FLIGHT CERAMIC BOX & SOAP 1980-81
Embossed ducks on lid and sides. Bar of duck soap inside. Made in Brazil. SSP $23. **CMV $23. MB.**

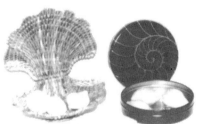

GIFTS OF THE SEA SOAPS & BASKET 1987
6 1/2" wide wicker basket holds 4 pink sea shell soaps. DP $4.25. **CMV $6. MB.**

SEA TREASURE SOAPS 1986
Black & gold trim tin box holds 4 pink sea shell soaps. DP $4. **CMV $6. MB.**

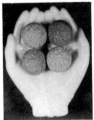

TOUCH OF BEAUTY 1969-70
White milk glass hand holds 4 small bars of pink soap. OSP $5. **CMV $15. MB.**

COUNTRY PEACHES SOAP JAR & SOAPS 1977-79
Replica of a 19th century mason jar. Holds 6 yellow peach seed soaps. Blue glass jar with wire bail. Avon on bottom. OSP $8.50. **CMV $8. MB., Jar only $3.**

FOSTORIA EGG SOAP DISH & SOAP 1977
Blue soap came in Spring Lilacs fragrance. Egg dish about 4 1/2" long clear glass. Avon on bottom. OSP $15. **CMV $15. MB. Egg dish only $5.** 1st issue had "Mother's Day 1977" on bottom. **CMV $18. MB.**

LOVE NEST SOAPS 1978
Light green glass holds 3 yellow bird soaps in Special Occasion fragrance. SSP $5. **CMV $10. MB.**

"HEART AND DIAMOND" SOAP DISH & SOAP 1977
Fostoria clear glass soap dish. Came with red heart shaped Special Occasion fragranced soap. Avon on dish. OSP $9. **CMV $10. MB.**

SKIN-SO-SOFT DISH & SOAP 1965
Blue & white plastic soap dish with white bar of SSS soap. OSP $1.50. **CMV $10. MB, soap & dish $8., dish only $3.**

FOSTORIA HEART VASE & SOAPS 1985
(Right) 5" high heart shape vase with 5 pink heart soaps. DP $6. **CMV $8. MB.**

CITRUS FRESH SOAPS 1984
(Left) Glass jar holds 5 lemon soaps. DP $7. **CMV $9. MB.**

HOLIDAY CACHEPOT SOAPS 1985
(Right) Metal can holds 5 red apple soaps. DP $5. **CMV $7. MB.**

WATER LILY SOAP DISH & SOAPS 1985
(Left) Blue glass dish. 3 white flower soaps. DP $6. **CMV $8. MB.**

BUTTER DISH & HOSTESS SOAPS 1973-74
Clear glass with 2 yellow 3 oz. butter soaps. SSP $7. **CMV $12. MB.**

NATURE BOUNTIFUL CERAMIC PLATE & SOAPS 1976-78
Wedgewood ceramic plate made in England, edged in 22K gold. Two soaps decorated with pears decals. Avon stamped on plate. OSP $25. **CMV $20. MB. Plate only $10.**

DECORATOR SOAP DISH & SOAPS 1971-73
7" long frosted glass dish on gold stand. Came with 2 pink soaps. OSP $7. **CMV $12. MB.**

FLOWER BASKET SOAP DISH & SOAP 1972-74
Clear glass dish with gold handle. Came with 5 cakes of soap (2 yellow, 3 pink) 1 oz. each. Hostess Fragrance. SSP $5. **CMV $10. MB.** Also came with double stamp on bottom, add $4.

CRYSTALUCENT COVERED BUTTER DISH & SOAP 1975-76
7" long clear glass with 2 yellow soaps. OSP $10. **CMV $14. MB.**

SUNNY LEMON SOAP DISH & SOAP 1975-76
8 1/2" long clear glass with 3 lemon scented yellow soaps. OSP $4. **CMV $9. MB.**

GIFT OF THE SEA SOAP DISH & SOAPS 1972-73
Iridescent white glass dish looks like a shell. 6 cakes, 1 oz. each, pink soap. 2 each of 3 different shells. SSP $5. **CMV $10. MB.**

LOVE NEST SOAP DISH & SOAPS 1973-75
White dish with green plastic lining, holds 2 aqua and 1 blue bird soap. OSP $4. **CMV $8. MB.**

STRAWBERRY PORCELAIN PLATE & GUEST SOAPS 1978-79
7 1/2" plate made in Brazil for Avon. Comes with 6 red strawberry soaps SSP $13 **CMV $13 MB. $8 plate only.**

LOVEBIRDS SOAP DISH & SOAPS 1974
White milk glass dish with two 4 oz. pink soaps. SSP $6. **CMV $10. MB.**

BEAUTY BUDS SOAP DISH & SOAP 1974-76
6" long white milk glass with 4 yellow soaps. OSP $5. **CMV $10. MB.**

HOSTESS BLOSSOMS FLOWER ARRANGER SOAP DISH & SOAP 1975-76
4 1/2" high white milk glass, plastic top and light green soap. OSP $6. **CMV $10. MB.**

SHIMMERING SEA SOAP GIFT SET 1990
Sea shell glass bowl holds 3 pearlized sea shell soaps. SSP $10.00 **CMV $10.00 MB**

OWL SOAP DISH 1971-73
5 1/2" long white glass soap dish with 2 owl eyes in bottom of dish. Holds 2 yellow bars of owl soap. OSP $4.50. **CMV $12. MB.**

HEAVENLY SOAP SET 1970
White glass dish and 2 pink soaps. OSP $5. **CMV $14. MB.**

BLUE BIRD SOAP SET 1988
Wicker basket nest holds 2 blue bird soaps. SSP $4.00 **CMV $4.00 MB**

NOTES

HEARTS OF HEARTS BASKET SOAPS 1988
Red wicker basket holds 5 1oz. red heart
soaps. SSP $8.50 **CMV $8.50 MB**

MARBLEIZED EGG SOAP IN BASKET 1989
3 egg soaps in wicker basket. SSP $6.00
CMV $6.00 Mint

AWARDS & REPRESENTATIVES GIFTS

What's Hot & What's Not in Awards

Avon Representative Awards continue to be one of the hottest areas of Avon Collecting. California Perfume products are the single best investment followed closely by Avon Rep Awards in the Avon Collection.

What's Hot in Awards is all jewelry type awards that are marked Avon or the Avon symbols on them. Most all glass awards, figurines, clocks, watches, ceramic items such as cups, dishes, plates, etc. Metal trays, plates, boxes. Anything with sterling silver or real gold in it. Paper weights, lucite items, perfume bottles, pen & pencil sets, buttons. Sets in boxes, key chains, stuffed toys marked Avon, Order Book covers, radios, telephones & Avon umbrellas. All of the above must be marked Avon on the Award. If it's not marked Avon, don't buy it. These are the main items most award collectors are looking for & pay a fair price for.

What's Not Hot

Plaques - picture frames or pictures, trophies, cloth material items, clothes, bags, anything that is too big or hard to display. Paper items, purses, sets of silverware, display banners, guide books, portfolios. Only things that are very old "1940s" or older of this type award will bring a fair price. Most collectors do not want these items as they don't display well. T-shirts and jackets with Avon logos are popular items and an exception to collecting clothes. All of the above items should be bought with caution. I have a lot of this type of collectibles in this book but some may be removed in future issues due to low collector interest.

MANAGERS DIAMOND 4A PIN 1961
4A diamond pin with diamond crown guard. Given to managers reaching a special quota in 1961. **CMV $125.**

MANAGERS DIAMOND RING 1968
1/4 carat art carved 58 faceted diamond set in a gold 4A design mounting. Given to managers for achievement of sales goals for several quarters. **CMV $500. mint**

PRESIDENT'S CLUB RING "LADY'S" 1978
(Left) Gold plated sterling 4A ring with red simulated ruby. Stone comes in several different shades. Given to all female President'ts Club Reps. **CMV $25. MB.**
MANAGERS 4A RING 1978
(Right) Silver 4A ring with high grade ruby stone given to 4 managers in Atanta branch for best planning.
CMV price not etablished.

CPC I.D. PIN 1900
Brass I.D. pin given to early day Reps. to show they worked for the CPC company. This is the 1st I.D. pin ever given by the CPC. **CMV $125.00**

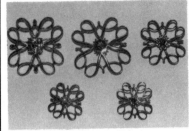

MANAGERS DIAMOND PIN 1961
Gold 4A pin same as Representatives except has an "M" made of 11 diamonds. **CMV $100. MB.**

DIAMOND 4A PIN 1961-76
Larger than other 4A pins; set with diamond. Given for selling $3,000. at customer price in an 18 campaign period. In 1974-76 you had to sell $4,500. in 13 campaigns. **CMV $35. MB.**

SAPPHIRE 4A PIN 1963-76
Set with a genuine sapphire. Awarded for reaching $2,000. in customer sales price in a 9 campaigne period. In 1974-76 you had to sell $,500. in 13 campaigns. **CMV $20. MB.**

PEARL 4A PIN 1963-70
10 kt. gold in a 4A design with a pearl in center. Awarded for reaching $1,000 in customer price sales in a 9 campaign period. 5/8" diameter. **CMV $15. MB**

RUBY 4A PIN 1973-76
10 kt. gold with ruby in center. Awarded for selling $2,500. in customer price sales in 6 month period to become eligible for President's Club Membership. **CMV $10.**

CIRCLE OF EXCELLENCE RING 1971
Same as pin only ring. **CMV $275. mint.**
CIRCLE OF EXCELLENCE PIN 1969
4A gold pin circled with pearls and diamonds in center. Managers only pin has a logo on back and can also be worn as a pendant. **CMV $200.**

JEWELED PIN - DIAMOND 1956-61
Same as pearl jeweled pin except has five diamonds instead of pearls. Came with black and gold star guard also containing five diamonds. This was the top award and was given after attaining the 4 diamond star guard. A minimum of $25,000 in sales were required for this award. **CMV $175. mint.**

CPC IDENTIFICATION PIN 1910-25
Given to all Representatives to identify them as official company Representatives. Says CPC 1886 on face. also came with blue enamel center. **CMV $90. mint**

CPC IDENTIFICATION HONOR PIN 1910-15
Given to Representatives for selling $250. in merchandise. **CMV $90. mint. Both pins are brass.**

CPC AVON I.D. PIN 1929-38
(Top) Given to all Reps to show they work for Avon and the CPC. Silver pin with blue enamel. "California Perfume Co., Inc., "Avon" on face of pin. This pin is larger in size than the 1938-45 I.D. pins. This pin came in two different ways. The A and V on Avon is close together on one and wide apart on the others. **CMV $45.**

I.D. HONOR AWARD PIN 1929-38
(Bottom) Gold tone with dark blue enamel. Given to Reps for $250. in sales. "CPC - AVON - HONOR" on face of pin. **CMV $55. mint.**

CITY MANAGERS I.D. PIN & PEARL GUARD 1945-61
Given to all City Managers. Pin has 5 pearls. Guard is set with 11 seed pearls. **CMV $75. mint.**

QUEENS AWARD PIN 1964
Gold colored metal 1 1/4" across. Given to each member of the winning team during the 78th Anniversary for top sales. **CMV $20.**

IDENTIFICATION PIN 1938-45
Silver with aqua enamel. Given to all Representatives for identification. "Avon Products, Inc., Avon" on face of pin. **CMV $30 mint.**

HONOR I.D. PIN "GOLD" 1938-45
Gold plated with aqua enamel Given for $250. in sales. "Avon Products, Inc., Avon Honor" on face of pin. **CMV $35. mint.**

JEWELED PIN PEARL - HIGHEST HONOR CASE 1945-61
10K gold with black enamel background. 5 oriental pearls are set in the A. Came in black highest award case above. Given for sales of $1000. **CMV $30. pin, $40 in case.**

IDENTIFICATION PIN 1945-51
Gold pin with black background. "A" has scroll design rather than jewels. Edges are plain, no writing. Given to Representatives for $1,000. in sales. **CMV $20.**

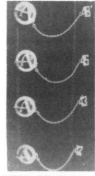

I.D. HONOR PIN & CASE "SILVER" 1938-45

(Left) Silver with aqua enamel. Given to all Representatives for identification. "Avon Products, Inc., Avon Honor on face of pin. **CMV $30.**

FIELD MANAGER'S I.D. PIN & GUARD 1945-61

(Right) Same design as the jeweled pin but has no printing. The "M" guard is smooth gold. **CMV $55.**

JEWEL PIN NUMERAL GUARDS 1945-56

Smooth gold numerals given for additional sales in multiples of $1,000. starting with No. 2. There was no No. 1. These are made to attach to the jewel pin. Highest numeral known is 115. The higher the number the more valuable. **CMV $8. on numbers 2 to 10, $12. on 11 to 20, $14. on 21 to 30, $18. on 31 to 40, $20. on 41 to 75, $25. each on 76 up.**

GOLDEN ACHIEVEMENT AWARD 1971-76

Bracelet & 1st charm awarded for $5,500. total sales in 6 month period. Each succeeding charm awarded for $5,500. within each subsequent 6 month period. First charm - 2 joined 4A design with green stone. Second charm - Avon Rose with red stone. Third charm - The First Lady with a genuine topaze. Fourth charm - The "World of Avon" set with a genuine aquamarine. Fifth charm - "The Doorknocker" with a genuine amethyst. Sixth charm - jeweled "A" with a genuine sapphire. Seventh charm - the "Key" with a genuine garnet. Eighth charm - Great Oak. (Above order of charms correct) **CMV $20. each charm. Charm No. 8 $30.**

50th ANNIVERSARY PIN 1936

Red circle with gold feather. Given to every representative who made a house to house sales trip of her area. **CMV $40. mint.**

HEART DIAMOND A PIN 1977

14k gold heart shape pin with 12 small diamonds. Can also be used as a pendant on chain. Came in gray felt box with white outer box. Only 1 given in each division for top Rep. Rare. **CMV $400. mint**

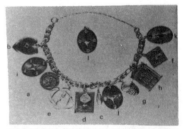

MANAGERS CHARM BRACELET 1963-65

One charm was given each quarter for 3 years making a total of 12 charms possible. These were won by attaining certain sales increases which increased with each quarter making the later charms very difficult to get. For this reason past the eighth quarter are very hard to find. The bracelet charms are 10 kt. gold. Only four bracelets were won with all 12 charms. A total of 6191 individual charms were given to 1445 managers. The last four charms are like the one pictured in center of bracelet. No. 9 has Rubys, No. 10 Sapphire, No. 11, Emerald & No. 12 Diamond. Each one had 4 stones. **CMV 1st 8 charms $45. each., plus bracelet No. 9 & 10 $60. each, No. 11, 12, $75. ea., CMV all 12 charms $800. mint.**

JEWELED PIN - HIGHEST HONOR - "PEARL" 1945-61

10K gold with black enamel background, 5 oriental pearls are set in the A. Given for sales of $1,000. **CMV $30.**

STAR GUARDS 1956-61

Raised star on round gold metal pin. Given for each $5,000. in sales in any 12 month period. Four guards could be won, each had an additional diamond. Made to wear with the jeweled pin. **CMV $15. one diamond. Add $10 for each additional diamond.**

CHARM BRACELET AWARD 1969

22 kt. gold finish, double-link bracelet with safety chain & 5 charms. Each charm given for progressively higher sales. **CMV $5. ea. charm, plus bracelet.**

A PIN AWARD 1976-78

Given to Reps. for selling $1,500. in Avon in a 13 campaign period. **Came in blue lined box, CMV $5. MB. Red lined box, CMV $4. MB**

CHARM BRACELET - SILVER 1959
Only 2 districts won in each branch. This was a test bracelet & very few were given for sales achievement. **CMV $200. mint with all 6 charms.**

GOLDEN CIRCLE CHARM BRACELET AWARD 1965
22 kt. gold finish double-link bracelet with safety chain and 5 gold charms. Each charm given for progressively higher sales. **CMV $7. each charm, plus bracelet $7. Came in an Avon box.**

CIRCLE OF EXCELLENCE CHARM BRACELET 1972-79
10K gold bracelet & gold charm with 3 diamonds & 4A design. Black & gold Avon box. Green inside. Given to managers only. **CMV $300. MB. Also came charm with 4 diamonds last charm. CMV $350. MB.**

PRESIDENT'S CLUB RING FOR MEN 1978
Gold plated sterling silver 4A ring with ruby stone. Given to male Avon Reps. for selling $6000 worth of Avon in 1 year period. Came in plain blue velvet ring box. **CMV $100. MB.**

ALBEE RING AWARD 1982
Gold plated sterling silver. Given to Reps for meeting sales goals. **CMV $15. MB.**

PRESIDENT'S CELEBRATION DIAMOND RING AWARD 1977
14K gold ring with 8 small diamond in center. Given to managers in Pasadena branch for largest increase in sales. Only 20 rings given in this branch. Does not say Avon. **CMV $100.**

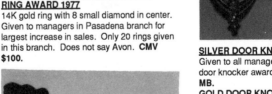

BUTTERFLY PIN AWARD 1981
Gold tone enameled stick pin given to Reps. Does not say Avon. **CMV $5.**

SMOKY QUARTZ RING - MANAGERS 1978
Smoky quartz stone, 14K gold mounting marked Avon. Given to managers in C26-78 for best activity event in Atlanta branch. **CMV $40.**

PRESIDENT'S CELEBRATION STAR AWARD 1977
Sterling silver star & chain with small diamond made by Tiffany. Was given to winning district manager in division. **CMV $35.**

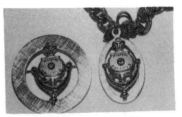

MANAGERS ACHIEVEMENT AWARD PIN & CHARM BRACELET 1974
1 given to top sales manager in each division. Brush sterling silver with blue sapphire in center of Avon Door Knocker. **CMV $70., $75. MB each.**

DIVISION MANAGERS ACHIEVEMENT CUFF LINKS AWARD 1974
Same as awards pin on left, only are cuff links. Given to male Division Managers. **CMV $85. set. Mint.**

SILVER DOOR KNOCKER PIN 1964
Given to all managers in conjunction with the door knocker award program. **CMV $25., $30 MB.**

GOLD DOOR KNOCKER PIN 1964-83
Came on green or white cards. **CMV $3 on card. CMV pin only $2. Also came in bue box with white sleeve. Same CMV.**

DON'T KNOCK ME DOORKNOCKER NECKLACE AWARD 1981
Gold tone door knocker with simulated diamond. Given to Reps. Comes in "Jo Anne Jewels" box. Made only for Avon. **CMV $15. MB.**

IDENTIFICATION PIN AUSTRALIA 1980
Gold toned door knocker pin. **CMV $10.**
AVON REPRESENTATIVE STICK PIN 1980
Blue & gold. (Says Avon Representative) **CMV $20.**

DOOR KNOCKER DIAMOND PIN 1981
Gold with small diamond. Given to managers. Came in Tan box. **CMV $40. MB.**

DOOR KNOCKER EARRINGS 1966
Gold tone earring. Avon Calling on them.
CMV $20 pr. MB.

HEART STICK PIN AWARD 1978
Sterling silver heart pin made by Tiffany & Co. with Avon products slip. Given to managers only, during President's Celebration. Does not say Avon. Must be in box with Tiffany & Co. Avon card. **CMV $15. MB.**

ACORN STICK PIN AWARD 1979
Sterling silver acorn pin from Tiffany & Co. given to managers. Came with small card with great oak & Tiffany card for Avon products. **CMV $15. MB.**

PRESIDENT'S CELEBRATION "A" PIN AWARD 1978
White box holds "A" sterling silver pin given to President's Club Reps. only. **CMV $7.50 MB.**

PRESIDENT'S CLUB PIN AWARD 1980-81
Gold tone pin given to President's Club Members only. Comes in Blue Avon box. Given in 1980 & 1981. **CMV $7.50 MB.**

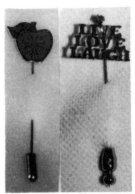

APPLE STICK PIN 1977
Red apple with 4A design 1977 & P.C. for President's Club on green Leaf. Pin is gold tone color. Given to winning team in each district for highest sales. **CMV $15.**
LIVE-LOVE-LAUGH DIAMOND PIN AWARD 1978
14K gold with 2 point diamond. Given to Avon managers for reaching appointment goal for August conference. **CMV $30. MB.**

EMPLOYEES GIFT KEY CHAIN 1971
Blue box with gray flannel bag holds gold horseshoe with Avon on one side and You're in Demand on back side of charm. **CMV $15. MB.**

AN OPEN LETTER TO ALL AVON REPS.

Do you want to increase the number of Avon collectors in the world? This would greatly increase your sales, too, you know! Try to find out your customer's various interests and those of her children and husband, too! For example:

Mrs. Smith loves animals - bring every animal decanter to her attention as they appear on the market. Sell her the first one and she'll likely buy more, or all, that come! Mr. Smith is a sports fan! Point out what a smart collection he could have on a neat shelf in his den. Young Johnny would love the majestic elephant, or that dinosaur decanter and teenager Sue really "digs" the "Fried Egg" or "Hamburger" compacts.

All these people have a good chance of ending up being a collector! So what does that really mean? Well it means that your collectibles will maintain their value and the market will grow steadily. Avon Reps. will have good steady sales. Collectors will have a wider and wider circle of ever growing and interested folk to swap and shop with.

Show your own collection to friends, help to stir the interest of others. Believe me, it will pay off in the end!!

Most important of all, don't forget to carry a copy of Hastin's Avon Collectors Guide Book to show your customers. "By showing this book to your customers, you can help create new collectors and you will profit 10 fold, as collectors will buy many more Avon products from you. Be sure to point out information on the Avon Times - Avon Club which they can enjoy right from their own living room. Tell them about the free advertising to thousands of members to buy, sell or trade Avons. Remember, if you help educate your customers on Avon Collecting you will profit greatly in larger future sales.

For more information on the Avon Times, write or send $17.00 for 1 full year subscription in U.S. or $20.00 U.S. Funds in Canada to: Avon Times, Box 9868, Kansas City, Missouri 64134. **Send a SASE when requesting information.**

PRESIDENT'S CELEBRATION MEN'S AWARD KEY CHAIN 1980
Sterling silver with oak tree on one side & inscribed on other. Given to men Reps. only for top sales. **CMV $100. MB.**

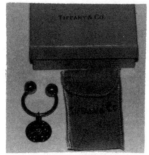

5 YEAR SERVICE AWARD KEY RING 1970'S
Sterling silver - 4A design on front comes in Blue felt Tiffany bag & box. **CMV $25.**

SALES ACHIEVEMENT KEY CHAIN 1976-77
Silver tone key chain. 4A emblem on front & back market "Avon Sales Achievement Award C/23/76, C/9/77." In special Sales Achievement Award Avon box. **CMV $11. MB.**

ANNIVERSARY CAMPAIGN KEY CHAIN 1968
(Left) Silver charm and key chain. **CMV $15**
CIRCLE OF EXCELLENCE KEY CHAIN 1972
(Right) Silver charm and chain with 4A design on one side and Mexico 1972. This was given by Mexico Avon branch to Circle of Excellence Award winning managers for the year 1971. Trip was made in 1972 for approximately 185 winning managers. **CMV $40. mint.**

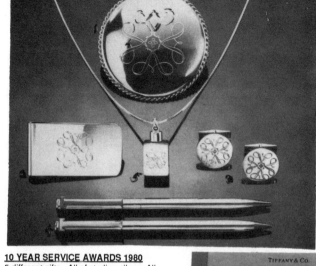

10 YEAR SERVICE AWARDS 1980
5 different gifts. All of sterling silver. All marked with 4A design. Each comes in Tiffany & Co. box. Given to Avon managers & all Avon Employees for 10 years service. They had their choice of Pen & Pencil set with T clips, 3 inch purse mirror, Cuff Links 7/8" diameter, & Small 1 1/4" high silver flask that opens, on sterling silver chain 23 1/2" long. **CMV each item or set $40 MB, Flask $60, Pen set $50 MB.**

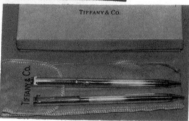

ANNIVERSARY CAMPAIGN HONOR AWARD KEY CHAIN 1968
White Avon box holds gold & silver double key ring. Made by Swank. **CMV $15 MB.**

4A KEY RING AWARD 1973-75
Gold lucite key ring in green or red lined box. **CMV $10. MB each.**

DISTINGUISHED MANAGEMENT AWARD 1967
Sterling silver key chain with raised 4A design set in brushed finish area. Given to top manager in each division. **CMV $35. MB, $27.50 chain only.**

BOCA OR BUST MANAGERS KEY CHAIN 1975
Silver 4A design, **CMV $15. MB.**

"KEY CHAIN" DISTRICT MANAGER SAFE DRIVER AWARD 1978

Large brass key chain has "4A" on one side & "Avon District Manager Safe Driver Award 1978" on other side. Came in white & green box. 4A on box lid. Came also with Avon card shown. **CMV $10. MB.**

KEY CHAIN "THANKS AMERICA" AWARD 1979

Team leader white box holds silver tone heart key chain "Thanks America for making us number one" Back side says "Avon loves team leaders." **CMV $10 MB.**

LUCKY 7 PIN 1964

Gold tone pin with simulated pearl in center. Given to each representative who sent in a certain size order. **CMV $10., $13. MB.**

GOOD LUCK BRACELET 1966

Gold double link bracelet with gold charm. Good luck four leaf clover on the front. Back is plain. Not marked Avon. **CMV $12., $15. MB.**

AWARD BRACELET 1953

1953 on back of sterling silver heart shaped charm. **CMV $40 MB**

AVON ATTENDANCE CHARM 1969-70

1969 AD on one round charm & 1970 Heart shape AD on the other. Both gold tone & chain. **CMV $17 ea.**

FIGURE 8 CHARM BRACELET 1951

Sterling silver bracelet with 2 skates attached. Given to representatives for interviewing 120 Avon customers during the figure 8 campaign 3-1951. Made only for Avon. **CMV $50.**

MANAGERS BRACELET 1956

Bracelet given to top selling city & district managers during President's campaign 1956. **CMV $100 MB.**

BELL BRACELET AWARD 1961

Silver bracelet & bell that rings. Avon not on bell. **CMV $30.**

BELL AWARDS 1964

Gold bell earrings. Christmas sales award. Gold bell charm bracelet. **CMV $20.** Christmas sales award. **CMV $30.**

DREAM CHARM MANAGERS NECKLACE 1979

Gold tone necklace & 3 charms of orchid, butterfly & sea shell. Given to Avon managers at 1979 Dream Conference. Does not say Avon on charms. Came in maroon satin bag with pink tie string. **CMV $25. mint in bag.**

TLC NECKLACE AWARD 1977

Given to Team Leaders. 14K gold. **CMV $25.**

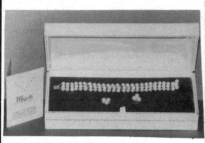

MANAGERS CHRISTMAS GIFT 1961
Pearl bracelet with small diamonds & matching earrings. Given to Avon managers at Chritmas 1961. Does not say Avon. Made by Majestic. **CMV $300. MB.**

MANAGERS GIFT DIAMOND LOOP 1977
Diamond Loop necklace given to managers in special gold bar type box, on introduction of Avons new 14K gold filled jewelry. **CMV $40. MB as pictured.**

SUNNY STAR AWARD NECKLACE 1975
Given to managers on introduction to Sunny Star necklace. This is the same one that sold only it has Aug. 1975 engraved on it. It can easily be duplicated so a price above the cost from Avon should not be paid. Brass star & chain. **CMV $10. MB.**

PRESIDENTS CELEBRATION AWARD 1974
14 kt. gold necklace with 3 point diamond. Given to 10 top representatives in each of the 81 winning districts for outstanding sales during this presidents celebration. **CMV $60. MB.**

SMILE PENDANT AWARD 1978
Red and gold pendant, given to all Avon Team Leaders. Back side says Avon, Team Leader, March 1978. **CMV $10.** MB. Also given to District Managers with D.M. on back. **CMV $15.** Both came in red box with Avon sleeve. Smile Pendant also given to Division managers at conference. Back says "N.Y. March, 78, Avon". Red box comes with plain white sleeve. **CMV $30. MB.**

PRESIDENT'S CELEBRATION DIAMOND HEART LOCKET AWARD 1969
Given to top 20 Reps. in each district during President's Celebration. Inscribed on back "President's Club 1979" **CMV $20. MB.** Same given to district managers only has DM Inscribed on back also. **CMV $30. MB.**

FIRST AVON LADY PENDANT AWARD 1975
Siver toned with scroll 'A' design around glass insert. On the presentation card it starts "Congratulations! We're happy to present you with this exclusive award. Designed especially for you. It's symbolic of the personal service upon which Avon was founded and which has guided us throughout the years" **CMV $15., $20. MB.**

HONOR AWARD CAMEO PERFUME GLACE NECKLACE 1966
Blue & white set trimmed in gold. **CMV $12., $17.50 MB.**

CHRISTMAS GIFT - REPS. 1979
Sterling silver goldtone chain with 10K gold charm with 2 small diamonds. Came in black felt box. Back is marked District managers 1979 **CMV $50.**, Team Leaders 1979 **CMV $35.**

VALENTINE HEART PENDANT AWARD 1978
14K gold heart. Does not say Avon. Only 2500 were given to Reps. at sales meetings. Must have C3-78 brochure with heart to prove it's from Avon. **CMV $25. with brochure.**

SILVER CIRCLE CELEBRATIONNECKLACE AWARD, ENGLAND 1982
Blue box holds clear crystal pendant on sterling silver chain. Marked Avon. Given to Silver Circle Reps **CMV $40. MB.**, Also shown with silver Circle Celebration Banquet Menu **CMV $5.**

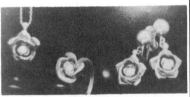

85th ANNIVERSARY AWARD JEWELRY 1971
22 Kt. gold plated sterling silver necklace, ring & earrings. Each shaped like a rose with diamond in center. Necklace was for representatives not in the presidents club, and the earrings for the presidents club members only. Two diamond rings were given in each district by a drawing. One was given to a presidents club member the other to a non-member. Ring also available in prize catalog for 2400 points. **CMV necklace $35., $40. MB. Ring $80., $85. MB. Earrings $35., $40. MB.**

EARRINGS - TEAM LEADER CHRISTMAS GIFT 1978
10K solid gold with small diamond chip. Given to team leaders at Christmas, 1978. Came in Avon box. **CMV $40. MB.**

ACORN NECKLACE AWARD 1980
Sterling Silver acorn Pendant & necklace. Comes with great oak card & Tiffany Box in velvet pouch. Given to managers only. **CMV $40. MB with card.**

TEAM LEADER TEDDY BEAR AWARD 1982
Sterling silver bear with movable arms & sterling silver chain. From Tiffany. Approx. 1/2 inch high. Marked T.L. on back of bear. **CMV $30. MB.**

"YOU'RE PRECIOUS TO US" PENDANT MANAGERS GIFT 1978
14K gold filled with real pearl & small diamond. Gold box says "You're Precious to Us" on lid. Given to Avon managers. Must be in box as described. Came with card signed by S.M. Kent. **CMV $50. MB.**

85th ANNIVERSARY PINS 1971
22 Kt. gold plated sterling silver pin with diamond. Small pin for representative not in president club, representatives only. Given for meeting sales goal in C-12-71. **CMV small pin $15., $20. MB. Large pin $20., $25. MB.**

HEART NO. 1 PENDANT AWARD 1979
14K gold heart with small diamond given to 1 top Rep. in each division. In Avon blue velvet box. **CMV $90. MB**

MOONWIND AWARD PIN 1971
Sterling silver pin given to Reps. for meeting sales goals. **CMV $22.50.**

"G" CLEF MANAGERS PIN 1968
Gold in color. Awarded to managers. **CMV $15. pin only, $20. MB.**

81st ANNIVERSARY PINS 1967
Sterling silver pins came in 12 different flowers. Representatives who met their personal prize goal for this anniversary campaign had their choice of one of these 12 flowers. Carnation, Violet, Daffodil, Daisy, Lily of the Valley, Rose, Lily, Gladiolus, Aster, Calendula. Chrysanthemum and Jonquil. **CMV Rose $15., $25. MB. Calendula $30., $40. MB. All others $20., $30. MB.**

AWARD PIN 1965
White plastic on blue background with silver or gold frame. **CMV $25. in box., $15. pin only.**

SALES ACHIEVEMENT AWARD 1969
Large gold Charisma design pin came in black Avon box. **CMV $20. MB.**

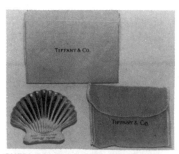

SHELL SALES LEADER AWARD 1979
Sterling silver shell comes in Tiffany felt bag & box. Given to managers. **CMV $125. MB.**

ANNIVERSARY AWARD ROSE PIN 1968
Victory luncheon July 9, 1968. Gold rose pin with ruby stone in Avon box. **CMV $27.50 MB only.**

SHELL JEWELRY 1968
(Left) Given for recommending someone as a representative. For each name representatives could choose either the pin or earrings. For 2 or more names you got the set. **CMV $12. Set.**

NEARNESS MANAGERS PIN 1955
(Right) Gold shell pin with pearl. **CMV $35.**

KEY PIN AWARD 1962
(Top) Gold key, surprise gift for activity. **CMV $10.**

AWARD EARRINGS 1961
(Bottom) Gold star design. Avon is not on them. **CMV $15. MB pair.**

AWARD PIN 1944 Only
Hand made sterling silver pin with roses & lilies, given to Reps. for selling $300. to $400. during Christmas campaign. **CMV $50, $60 MB.**

MANAGERS AWARD PIN 1943
Gold plated lapel pin with hand set stones, cost Avon $25. in 1943. Only 2 were given to the 2 top selling managers in U.S. during loyalty campaign, March 2-22, 1943. **CMV $125.**

BOW PIN AWARD 1944
Lapel pin is gold plate with center stone of synthetic aquamarine. Given to Reps. for selling over $300. in 1 campaign. **CMV $30, $45 MB.**

BOWKNOT AWARD PIN 1942
Gold pin with sequins shaped like bow. Given to representatives for selling $100. to $150. in one campaign. **CMV $40, $50 MB.**

5 YEAR SERVICE PIN 1970
For Avon plant employees, not Reps. Gold circle with 4A emblem & blue stone. **CMV $30. MB., $25. pin only.**

CLOVER TIME PIN 1951
Given to representatives for calling on 120 customers in one campaign. Made by Coro. Pin is outlined with imitation seed pearls & dotted with aquamarine stones for color. Does not say avon. Came with certificate from Avon in Coro box. **CMV $40. MB., $25. Pin only.**

VICTORY PIN AWARD 1942
Sterling silver wing pin with red, white and blue center. Given to Reps. during Acres of Diamonds campaign 1942 for getting new customers. **CMV $70., $80 MB.**

RED ROBIN PIN 1955
Sterling silver pins made by Cora Company. does not say Avon on it. Given in pairs for getting 12 new customers. **CMV $25., $30. MB.**

EIFFEL TOWER MANAGERS PIN 1979
Small gold tone tie tack type pin given to managers on Paris trip. Does not say Avon. In plain blue box. Pin is 1 1/8" high. **CMV $15.**

FLAG PIN AWARD 1979
Gold tone red, white and blue enamel lapel pin. Given to Circle of Excellence winners in Paris trip. Came in red velvet Avon ring box. **CMV $25. MB.**

MANAGERS PANELIST PIN 1976
Gold tone name pin. Marked "Nat. District Managers Panelist" **CMV $10.** Given each year.

25 YEAR SERVICE AWARD PIN 1970
1/10 yellow 10K gold 4A pin with 25 on it. Was for 25 years service. Was never issued. Very Rare. **CMV $100.**

TOP FIFTY PIN AWARD 1977
Gold tone pin has top 50 & 4A design with red backgound. Given to top 50 Reps. in division for sales. **CMV $16.**

TOP FIFTY PIN AWARD 1978
Same as 1977 pin only has red rose with green leaves. **CMV $12.50**

TELEPHONE TIE TAC AWARD 1981
Gold tone telephone Tie Tac. Given to Reps. **CMV $10.**

AVON PIN - DIVISION MANAGER v
Gold tone pin with red enamel filled heart shaped O given to division managers only. **CMV $15. MB, in red box.**

AVON PIN - REPS 1979
Gold tone pin same as above only does not have red heart. **CMV $5. MB, in white box.**

AVON PIN - DISTRICT MANAGERS 1979
Same gold tone pin as reps. above only DM inscribed on back. **CMV $15. MB, in white box.**

SHOOTING STAR PIN - MANAGERS 1980
Gold tone pin in brown box with outer sleeve. Given to managers. **CMV $15. MB.** Also came as tie tack for men. **CMV $25. MB.**

AVON'S BEST PIN AWARD 1982
Small brass pin says "Avon's Best, Morton Grove." With 4A design. Given to managers for Atlanta conference. **CMV $10.**

UNICORN PIN AWARD 1981
Brass unicorn lapel pin given to managers at August conference 1981. Back inscribed Conference 81. Avon box says For Display Only - not for resale, **CMV $15. MB.** Same pin given to Team Leaders, **CMV with TL on back $10.** Pin also sold to public only plain no marking on back, **No CMV.** Also came with SC on back, **CMV $20. MB.**

AVON NO. 1 PIN - HOLLAND 1979
Gold tone pin given to Zone Avon Managers in Holland. **CMV $50.**

ROYAL RIBBON TAC PIN AWARD 1980
Sterling silver with yellow, red, white, or blue enamel. Given to managers for recruiting new Reps. **CMV Yellow $5., Red $10., White $15., Blue $20., MB each.**

MONEY CLIP TEAM LEADER AWARD 1969
Green & white lined black & brass box holds 12K gold filled money clip with solid 10K gold emblem with 2 small diamonds on top. Awarded to male team leaders. Rare. "Team Leader 1979" on back. **CMV $75. MB.** Also given to male managers with D.M. on back. **CMV $75. MB.**

C OF E PIN 1980
Small pin says C of E 1980. **CMV $10.**
C OF E WINNERS PIN 1979
Blue Enamel on gold tone pin. **CMV $10.**
SELL A THON TIE TAC 1981
Red, white & blue tie tac pin. Given to all Reps. at sales meeting. **CMV $2.**
CABLE CAR STICK PIN 1980
Gold tone, sterling silver cable car stick pin given t o Avon managers on trip to San Francisco. Does not say Avon. **CMV $15.**

AVON STAR PIN
(left) **CMV $60.** If you have any information on what year or what this pin was given for, please write Bud Hastin and tell him.
SERVICE AWARD 1938
(Right) Bronze medallion hangs from aqua colored bar with Avon in gold. Given to representatives for outstanding improvement in sales. **CMV $50. mint.**

1500 PIN 1963
(Top) Given to reps. for $1,500. in sales in one campaign. **CMV $20.**
TEAM CAPTAIN PIN 1969-70
(Bottom) Torch pin says T C -69-70. **CMV $20.**

MEDALLION OF HONOR 1945
Made of solid gold, it is 7/8 inches long & 1 3/8 inches wide. Woman on the front is raised. Back side is engraved to person & date. Came with award scroll. Medal can be worn on a ribbon or brooch. This medal was given to women only in 1945 during World War II both military & civilian for service to their country above and beyond the call of duty. Very few medals were given out. **CMV medal $500., Scroll $50.**

MONEY CLIP 1963
(Left) 10K gold filled. Back says Pathways of Achievement 1963. 4A design on front and initials. **CMV $75. MB.**
MONEY CLIP 1969
(Center) Black and gold box holds 10K gold filled 4A design on front with initials. Back says Management Conference Atlanta, Georgia November 1969. **CMV $75 MB.**
MONEY CLIP 1960
(Right) 10K gold filled. Small 4A design on face and initials. Nothing on back. **CMV $75.**

AWARDS & REPRESENTATIVES GIFTS

KEY RING 5 YEAR SERVICE AWARD 1978
1/10 10K gold 4A symbol key ring given to Avon plant employees for 5 years service. Started in 1978. **CMV $17.50.**

STAR REPRESENATIVE GOLD MEDALLION 1931-37
10 kt. gold filled medal. Given to representatives for selling $1,000. worth of Avon in any 12 month period. **CMV $150., $165. MB.**

ANNIVERSARY PRINCESS BRACELET 1960
Awarded for increased sales. Bracelet with diamond. Bracelet with emerald, Bracelet with ruby or topaze. 14K gold. **CMV $260. each MB.**

SWEATER GUARD AWARD 1968
6" gold chain with 4A design clips on each end. Given as general managers honor award to each representative of the winning team in each district. **CMV $25., $30. MB**

SERVICE AWARD CHARM 1962
22 kt. gold finish slightly larger than a quarter, given to all representatives who sold 50 or more customers during campaign 6. **CMV $10.**

PRESIDENTS COURT CHARM 1969
22 kt. gold finish charm. Given to all representatives of the team in each district. **CMV $10.**

GOLD STAR REPRESENTATIVE MEDAL - CPC 1930-31
Highest honor given to Representatives that achieved the goal of $1000. in sales from January to January. If goal reached second year a second gold star is engraved, and so on. Made of gold. **CMV $275. MB.**

LOYAL SERVICE AWARD - 15 YEAR
Solid 10K gold. 4A emblem on front. Avon 15 years loyal service on back. Given to employees of Avon. Came on 10K gold wrist chain. **CMV $150.**

4A BLUE ENAMEL PIN 1978
Gold tone & blue enamel pin. Comes in Avon box. No information on what it's for. **CMV $12. MB.**

STAR REPRESENTATIVE GOLD MEDAL-LION 1937-45
10kt. gold filled medal, given to representatives for selling $1,000. worth of Avon in any 12 month period. **CMV $50., $60. in Black.** Highest Award box shown.

4A TIE CLIP SERVICE AWARD 1970's
Gold tone with 4A design. Given to Avon employees. **CMV $25.**

TOP SALES MEDALLION 1975
Gold colored metal medallion. Avon lady carrying case. Italy at bottom of foot. No Avon on it. Given to Avon Reps. for top sales and touring Springdale plant. 2 different designs. One star & one round. **CMV $17, $22.50 MB each.**

TIE TAC AWARD 1969
Small 1/10 10K gold tie tac given to Avon Male Executive with blue sapphire in center. Came in Avon Box. **CMV $50 MB.**

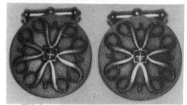

DEDICATED TO SERVICE AWARD 1962
1886-1962 4A deisgn - gold tone. **CMV $10.**

GREAT OAK NO. 1 MEDALLION AWARD 1980
Small medal - Avon Oak Tree on one side, Pasadena No. 1 - 1980 4A deisgn on other side. **CMV $12.**

CIRCLE OF EXCELLENCE PIN 1970'S
Brass - 4A design and C of E Managers only. **CMV $15.**

TOUR GUIDE JACKET GUARDS 1966
Silver color aluminum with 4A design. Used by Avon plant tour guides. **CMV $32.50.**

15 YEAR SERVICE CUFF LINKS
4A design on face and Avon 15 years Loyal Service on back with persons initials. Given to Avon male executives after 15 years service with Avon. Made of solid 10K gold. **CMV $300. pair mint.** Also came 30 year service. Same cuff links. **Same CMV.**

TOUR GUIDE JACKET GUARDS 1973
Gold metal with pressed flower in center of 4A. Used by Avon plant tour guides. **CMV $25.**

RETIREMENT PIN 1967
Gold disk with raised 4A design hanging from a golden bow. Given to retiring representatives with 10 years or more of service. **CMV $50.**

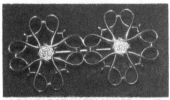

4A DOUBLE STICK PIN AWARD 1960'S - 1970'S
10K gold double 4A stick pin. We have no information on what it is. Please contact Bud Hastin if you know. Comes in Avon box. **CMV $75. MB.**

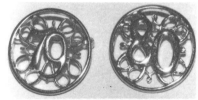

PRESIDENT'S CLUB LADY'S PINS 1979-80
Gold colored 4A pin - 79 in middle is 1st of an annual 4A year pin given to President's Club Reps. for meeting sales goal for that year. **CMV $5. each year.**

4A MENS CUFF LINKS 1966
Silver links with 4A design. Given to plant & office employees only. **CMV $35. pr.**

DISTINGUISHED MANAGEMENT AWARD EARRINGS 1965-68
4A design clip-on earrings. **CMV $35. pair MB.**

PRESIDENT'S CLUB MEN'S TIE TAC 1980-81
Small gold tone 4A - 81 on face. Given to male President's Club members. **CMV $15., $20. MB.**

PRESIDENT'S CLUB MEN'S PIN AWARD 1979-80
Gold tone 4A design & 79 on one & 80 on the other. Given to all male President's Club members. Smaller than lady's pin. **CMV $15, 20. MB.**

AVON HAWAIIAN HOLIDAY CHARM AWARD 1965
14K gold given to 7 avon managers in Hawaii in 1965. Each manager had their initials put on back. **CMV $150.**

CHARM "DAY TO REMEMBER" AWARD 1976
Small gold tone charm marked "A Day to Remember - C21-76" Came in blue Avon box. **CMV $15. MB.**

PRESIDENT'S CELEBRATION GREAT OAK MANAGER CHARM AWARD 1980
Sterling silver cut out great oak tree charm. Comes with oak tree card in Avon box. Given to top managers in each district. **CMV $100. MB.** 1 top manager in each division won a cut out silver oak charm with sapphire around edge. **CMV $150. MB.** 1 top manager in each branch won same charm only with Ruby's around edge. **CMV $200. MB.** The top manager in the U.S. won same cut out oak charm with a diamond. Very Rare. **CMV not established.**

DISTRICT MANAGERS CHARM BRACELET 1980
Sterling silver chain & heart shaped charm says "DM 1980". Came in Tiffany & Co. Box. Given to District Managers at September conference. **CMV $75.**

PRESIDENT'S CELEBRATION NECKLACE 1980
Gold tone charm with Great Oak on one side & The President's Celebration 1980 on other side. Given to top Reps. in each district. **CMV $10. MB.** Same charm in silver tone given to 10 top winning district Reps. **CMV $15. MB.**

SALES LEADERSHIP AWARD 1980
Gold tone & black face. Says "Outstanding Sales Leadership" 5th Qtr. 1979-80 Avon. Came with red neck velvet ribbon. **CMV $40.**

PRESIDENT'S CELEBRATION SALES ACHIEVEMENT MEDAL 1981
(Left) Dated Dec. 11, 1981 on back side. Only 1 given to each branch. Put on red, white and blue ribbon. **CMV $150.**

PRESIDENT'S CAMPAIGN KEY CHAIN 1976
(Right) Chrome & white with red letters. Given to President's Club Reps. **CMV $10.**

CIRCLE OF EXCELLENCE PIN 1987
Small pin C of E 1987 4A design. **CMV $10.**

ALBEE KEY CHAIN 1987
Blue & gold tone. For sponsorship of new Reps. **CMV $15.**

SPONSORSHIP PIN 1986
Gold tone pin for sponsorship. **CMV $10.**

90th ANNIVERSARY BICENTENNIAL PENDANT AWARD 1976
Brass coin & chain given to Reps. for selling $285. worth of Avon in 2 campaigns. Front & back view shown. **CMV $15. MB.**

INTERNATIONAL RUNNING CIRCUIT MEDALION & NECKLACE 1978-82
Silver tone medalion given to winners in each city in each age group for running in Avon races. Came in black & gold box. Rare. **CMV $125. MB.**

PRESIDENT'S CLUB ACHIEVEMENT PINS AWARD 1984-85-86
Brass pin with stones for sales increase. 4 steps, 1 stone, 2 stones, 3 stones, 4 stones. 1984 - Red Stones - 1985 - Pearl - 1986 - Blue Stones. **CMV $10. 1 stone., CMV $15. 2 stones., CMV $20. 3 stones., CMV $25. 4 stones.**

PERFECT ATTENDANCE PIN 1979-82
Gold tone pin given to Avon Branch employee for perfect attendance at work for a 1 year period. Marked with each year record. **CMV $25.**

PRESIDENT'S CLUB KEY RING AWARD 1984
Gray box says Avon Tribute 1984. Gold tone with Albee charm. **CMV $15.**

BLUE HEART AVON AWARD PIN 1986
Silver tone pin with blue heart stone. Given to Reps in Newark branch for 3 orders. **CMV $10. MB.**

ROYAL AVON PIN 1985
Blue, white & green enamel lapel pin. Given to Managers. **CMV $10.00**

AVON 86 ROSE PIN 1986
Gold tone Rose-Avon 86 lapel pin given to Avon Reps. **CMV $5.**

GOLD DIGGER PIN 1987
Small gold tone pick ax. Not marked Avon. Given for signing new avon Reps. **CMV $5.**

GOLD FEVER AWARD 1985
Small walnut plaque imprinted in wood says "Avon Gold Fever Additions Achievement Sept. 1985" with winners name on brass plaque. 1 oz. 999 fine pure gold "Avon 4A Pasadena" gold coin. Coin is loose but must be with plaque. **CMV $50. plus current value of 1 oz. of gold.**

I LOVE AVON PIN AWARD 1985
Gold tone - red heart. **CMV $5.**

LIBERTY PIN AWARD 1985
Avon on front. **CMV $5.**

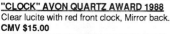

"CLOCK" AVON QUARTZ AWARD 1988
Clear lucite with red front clock, Mirror back. **CMV $15.00**

INDEX ALARM CLOCK & CALCULATOR AWARD 1990
Black case, red letters. **CMV $20.00**

AVON HOWARD MILLER CLOCK AWARD 1989
Maroone case, brass Avon front. **CMV $10.00**

AVON 5000 PIN 1985
(Left) Red, black & gold pin says Avon 5000. Given to Reps for top sales. **CMV $15.**

THOUSANDAIR CLUB 5000 PIN 1986
(Center) White & gold and red pin with "TC 1886-1986 $5,000.00" on face. **CMV $15.**

THOUSANDAIRE CLUB PIN 1986
(Right) White, gold & red pin 1886-1986. **CMV $10.**

4A STICK PIN AWARD 1980
1" 4A design in silver tone, gold outer trim. **CMV $10.**

AVON PIN AWARD 1987
Gold tone Avon pin. **CMV $15.**
PRESIDENT'S CLUB PIN AWARD 1987
Gold tone with hanging rose. **CMV $25.**
ALBEE AVON 100 PIN - ENGLAND 1986
Gold tone. Blue enamel. **CMV $65.**

SPONSORSHIP MEDALLION AWARD 1985
Gold tone pendant on white ribbon. **CMV $10.**
CIRCLE OF EXCELLENCE MEDALLION AWARD 1981
Gold tone 4A design, 1981 on back. Red ribbon. **CMV $10.**

HONOR SOCIETY PIN 1987
HS on gold tone pin.
Level 1 - Has a Ruby. **CMV $15.**
Level 2 - Has a Sapphire. **CMV $20.**
Level 3 - Has a Diamond. **CMV $25.**
PRESIDENT'S CLUB PIN 1987
Gold tone pin with "PC" on face.
Level 1 - Has a Pearl. **CMV $10.**
Level 2 - Has a Topaz. **CMV $15.**

PRESIDENT'S CLUB PIN "MENS" 1984
Brush gold tone stick pin or tie tac. Given to male Reps for meeting sales goals. 4A design on each. **1st goal 1 red ruby. CMV $35., 2 Rubys $50., 3 Rubys $75., 4 Rubys $100., All MB. In black velvet box. Maroon liner.**

GREAT OAK CUFF LINK AWARD 1983
Sterling Silver - not marked Avon. Plain black box. Given to male Div. Managers. **CMV $100.**
GREAT OAK COIN AWARD 1981
Sterling Silver coin says Kansas City #1 - 1981 with great oak tree. Given to Managers in Tiffany bag & box. **CMV $40.**

GROUP SALES LEADER I.D. PIN 1984
Gold tone stick pin comes in red velvet box. Pin says GSL - Avon. Comes with outer sleeve with Lang all over it. **CMV $15. MB.**

CHARM BRACELET AWARD 1980
Sterling silver charm & heart pendant. Both dated 1980 & "S.C." for Sales Coordinator & "TL" for Team Leader.
Comes in blue bag & blue Tiffany box, with white bow ribbon. **CMV "SC" $90. MB., CMV "TL" $40. MB.**

5 YEAR HEART KEY RING AWARD 1980s
In Tiffany box. Sterling silver. For 5 year Avon service. **CMV $15.**
OAK TREE ATLANTA BRANCH PENDANT 1976
(Right) Gray pewter on neck chain. **CMV $15.**

AVON SALES ACHIEVEMENT AWARD BRACELET 1975
Given for sales. Avon on one side and sales achievement on the other. Sterling. **CMV $15., $20. MB.**

GROUP SALES LEADER PIN AWARD 1983
Gold tone - 4A design. **CMV $8.**
MORTON GROVE 25 YEAR PIN 1981
Silver tone pin - not sterling. **CMV $8.**

#1 DIAMOND HEART PENDANT AWARD 1979
Given to top Manager for top sales. 7 diamond on gold heart & chain. **CMV $50.**
#1 PENDANT AWARD 1976
Given for top sales in Morton Grove Branch. Gold tone pendant. **CMV $15.**

HAPPY ANNIVERSARY NECKLACE 1964
For 38 years as a representative. October 1964. **CMV $35.**

TEAM LEADER PIN 1974
(Right) Gold raised letters & rim. Given to team leaders. **CMV $4., $6. MB.**
TEAM LEADER PIN 1975
(Left) Gold with indented letters. Given to team leaders. **CMV $4., $6. MB.**

SALES ACHIEVEMENT AWARD PENDANT 1977
1" gold pendant with 18" chain. Says 1977 Avon Sales Achievement Award & 4A design on other side. Came in white Avon box. Given to top 10% of sales Reps. in each division. **CMV $15. MB.** Same pendant slightly larger - came in blue box. **CMV $20. MB.**

SALES ACHIEVEMENT AWARD 1979
Solid bronze with Oak Tree on front with "District Manager Quarterly Sales Achievement Award - Avon" 4A symbol on back. Given to managers only. **CMV $50.**

RUNNING CIRCUIT AVON MEDAL 1980
2 1/4" medal has red, white and blue ribbon & medal says "Avon International Running Circuit." Given to people who ran in Avon Running Circuit. **CMV $25.**

FIELD OPERATIONS AWARD 1968
Solid brass, Avon 4A emblem on front. Field operations seminar on back. Given to managers in Pasadena branch in Better Way program. **CMV $55.**
GOLF LEAGUE CHARM 1960
1960 on back. Front has Avon League with 4A design & golfer. Solid brass. Given to Avon plant employees, Pasadena branch, for playing golf tournament. **CMV $40.**

PRESIDENT'S CLUB MEN'S POCKET WATCH AWARD 1981
Gold tone Swiss made 17 jewel watch. Avon on face of watch, metal face cover. Given to male President's Club members. **CMV $100 MB.**

PRESIDENT'S SALES CHALLENGE AWARD WATCH 1982
Black face, Avon Quartz & small diamond on 12 on face. Gold tone case. Black lizard strap. 1 top rep in each district won. Came in Avon gray felt case & outer sleeve. **CMV $100 MB & sleeve.**
Same watch only gold face watch & no diamond & black lizard look leather strap in tan felt Avon case & outer sleeve. 20 given in each district to Presidents Club reps only. **CMV $30 MB sleeve.**

CLOCK 20 YEAR AWARD 1978
(left) Small brass Tiffany & Co. Quartz clock. Top engraved "Avon 20 years & winners initials". Given to Avon managers for 20 years service. **CMV $75.**

CLOCK AUGUST CONFERENCE AWARD 1978
(right) Brass Relice 400 electronic clock. Given to managers for going to August Conference 1978, bottom engraved. **CMV $50.**

NEWARK FIRST AWARD CLOCK 1973
Alfry electric clock, black face, white painted over brass. Back side says "Newark First 1973" plus owners initials. Given to district supervisors. **CMV $40.**

HONOR SOCIETY CLOCK 1986
Small Lucite quartz clock given for selling $15,000 in Avon. **CMV $20.**

CUSTOMER SERVICE AWARD CLOCK 1980
(left) Brass Tiffany & Co. clock given to Avon managers. Engraved on top "Avon Customer Service Award Conference 1980". Comes in Tiffany box & felt bag. **CMV $75.**

MILLION DOLLAR INCREASE AWARD CLOCK 1981
(right) Gold tone round Seth Thomas alarm clock. Given to managers for 1 million dollar increase in sales. Engraved on back side "Our First Million $ Increase". **CMV $65.**

CLOCK - FIELD OPERATION SEMINAR 1970
(Left) Brass Relide 7 jewel clock. **CMV $50.**

CLOCK - SUMMER SHAPE UP AWARD 1970
(Right) Brass Linder clock - top inscribed "Summer Shape Up Award." **CMV $75.**

CIRCLE OF EXCELLENCE AWARD CLOCK 1982
Clear lucite digital clock with engraved name of winning Avon manager. Is not marked Avon. **CMV $50.**

PRESIDENTS CLUB CARD CASE AWARD 1982
Silver plated card case in Tiffany box & felt bag. Engraved on case "Presidents Club & 4A design". **CMV $20 MB.**

CIRCLE OF EXCELLENCE HOUR GLASS AWARD 1981
Tall brass hour glass C of E. 1981 on top. **CMV $50.**

40th AVON ANNIVERSARY CLOCK AWARD 1981
Hamilton Quartz clock, glass dome, Avon 40th name plate on base for 40 years of service. **CMV $100.**

SELLATHON CLOCK AWARD 1981
Mirrow Clock. **CMV $20.**

CLOCK SPEEDWAY DIVISION AWARD 1978
For outstanding sales. **CMV $35.**
SALES CLUB AWARD 1977
$100,000 sales increase plaque. Atlanta Branch. **CMV $15.**

MEN'S PRESIDENTS SALES CHALLENGE WATCH AWARD 1982
(Left) Gold tone case & face marked Avon. Black strap. Avon box. **CMV $100. MB.**
WINNING IS BEAUTIFUL WATCH AWARD
(Right) Ladies quartz watch. Avon on face & on box. **CMV $25. MB.**

PENDANT WATCH AWARD 1970
Gold tone watch on neck chain given to 6 Reps. in each district for top sales. Made by Sheffield. Also sold in stores. 9,000 watches given by Avon. **CMV $20.**

HEAT CLOCK AWARD 1981
(Left) Clear lucite - red face - Avon on front. **CMV $20.**
CLOCK PICTURE FRAME AWARD 1983
(Right) Clear lucite, purple & red clock face. Avon on front. **CMV $25.**

1974 PRESIDENT'S CLUB MEMBERS WATCH
Awarded to club members. Gold watch & hands with black strap. Box blue & white. **CMV $30. MB.**

CLOCK "WE'RE HOT" AWARD 1982
White plastic Isis quartz battery clock. **CMV $75.**
CLOCK "AVON" AWARD 1982
White plastic Isis electric clock. Face is red & marked Avon. **CMV $75.**

DIVISION MANAGERS AWARD CLOCK 1969
Sterling silver Seth Thomas electric clock. 4" square face, bottom says, "Divisional Managers Tribute 1969". **CMV $100 mint.**

PRESIDENT'S CLUB 1981 WATCH WOMEN'S 1980
(left) gold tone 17 jewel watch on chain. Back says "President's Club 81". **CMV $30. MB.**
PRESIDENT'S CLUB 1981 MEN'S WATCH 1980
(right) gold tone pocket watch on chain given to male President's Club Reps. Inscribed on back "President's Club 1981". **CMV $100 MB.** No face cover, **CMV $100 MB.**

25 YEAR WATCH BAUME & MERCIER AWARD
Gold case watch. Given for 25 year Avon service. Back inscribed "Avon - 25 years." **CMV $75. plus value of used watch.**

COLOR UP WATCH AWARD 1979
Le Jour Time Co. watch in gold tone case, white strap. Back side says "For the most colorful time of your life". Came in white box, sleeve & blue felt wrap. Given to Reps for customers served. **CMV $25 MB.**

Color never looked so good!

AVON MANAGERS ACHIEVEMENT CLOCK 1968
Box with 4A design & outer Avon sleeve. Clock set in top of brushed gold hour glass inscribed on bottom "1968 Avon Managers Achievement". **CMV $75 clock only.**, **$100 MB with outer sleeve.**

WATCH STICK PIN, MANAGERS 1979
(left) Gold tone 4A design on face. Given to managers. **CMV $75.**

FIELD SUPPORT PENDANT AWARD 1978
(right) 1/20 12K gold filled. Back is dated "1978 Field Support Manager". Given to managers. **CMV $30.**

NAT. DISTRICT MANAGER PANELIST PIN 1978
(bottom) Gold tone. Given to managers. **CMV $10.**

PRESIDENT'S CELEBRATION AWARD CLOCK 1976
Gold plastic & metal Westclock. 4 red roses on face. Was not made only for Avon. **CMV $12.**

TEAM LEADER WATCH 1977
Given to all Avon team leaders for Christmas 1977. 2 different. (left) for women, (right) for men. The cases are different and the difference in size of winding stem. Very few of the mens watches given. **CMV for womens $40 MB.**, **CMV for mens $100 MB.**

MANAGERS WATCH 1977
Avon watch same as team leader watch only face says Avon in place of Team Leader & 4A symbol that rotates instead of Avon. Came in male & female size watch as above. **CMV $75 MB.**

PRESIDENT'S CELEBRATION CLOCK AWARD 1974
Solid brass clock with "President's Celebration 1974" on face. Clock made by Relide, 15 jewels. Given to Avon managers. Came in plain box & pink felt bag. **CMV $75. mint.**

ANTIQUE CAR GLASSES 1971
Eight different glasses picturing Stanley Steamer, Silver Duesenberg, Gold Cadillac, Sterling Six, Electric Charger, Packard Roadster, Touring T & Straight Eight. Selling 10 Avon cars won a set of 4 glasses. Selling 15 Avon cars won a set of 8 glasses. **CMV set of 4 $12, set of 8 $27.50 MB.**

ANTIQUE CAR PITCHER 1971
Reps. won this by having one person they recommended a representative appointed. Also available in prize catalog for 1,400 points. 2 different pitchers. Rare one has silver Duesenberg & Stanley Steamer on it. **CMV $35, $40 MB.** Most of them have Straight Eight & Packard Roadster decal on it. **CMV $25, $30 MB.**

OUTSTANDING SALES MANAGEMENT CLOCK AWARD 1977
Relide 15 jewel Swiss solid brass clock. Inscribed on top "In Recognition of Outstanding Sales Management - Third Quarter 1977". Given to No. 1 Avon manager in each division. **CMV $100.**

LIBERTY CLOCK AWARD 1977
Given to managers for 1 million dollar sales increase. Gold tone clock by Bulova. Inside slide clock cover says "To a Million Dollar Baby (name of manager) Division $1,000,000 Sales Increase 1977". Came in Bulova Americana Collection. **CMV $75.**

HOURS FOR EXCELLENCE CLOCK AWARD 1977
Gold label on top of Bulova travel alarm. Does not say Avon. Given to Reps. **CMV $15 MB.**

PIN "WATCH US GROW" AWARD 1981
(left) Gren & white tie tac type pin . Says "Newark - Watch us Grow". Given to managers. **CMV $5.**

NEWARK NO. 1 1982 PENDANT AWARD 1982
(right) Gold tone 1/2" size pendant. Given to managers No. 1 in sales. Brown box. **CMV $15 MB.**

DIARY CLOCK 1968
Made by Seth Thomas. Gold, back opens & says "Avon Award", **CMV $40.**

KEY CHAIN SERVICE AWARD 10 YEARS 1970's
Gold tone key chain with blue stone in center of 4A design. Comes in Avon white & green lined box. Given to managers. **CMV $15 MB.**

ROSE ANNIVERSARY PITCHER AWARD 1980
9" tall clear glass with engraved rose. Given to Reps. for selling $800 in C14-15 1980. **CMV $25 MB.**

20 YEAR SERVICE AWARDS 1980's
Given for 20 years service. All are marked Avon or has 4A emblem on it. All from Tiffany. Choice of:
STERLING SILVER PICTURE FRAME
9" high x 7" wide. **CMV $100.**
QUARTZ POLISHED BRASS CLOCK
2 1/2" square. **CMV $75.**
CRYSTAL CANDLESTICKS - TALL
9 1/4" high, 4 1/8" wide baase. **CMV $75 set.**
CRYSTAL CANDLESTICKS - SHORT
4 1/2" high x 4 1/8" wide base. **CMV $75 set.**

HOP SKIP & JUMP MEDAL AWARD 1982
Gold tone medal with 4A design on one side & Hop, Skip & Jump Order Count Growth 1982 on back. Hangs on blue & yellow ribbon. **CMV $25.**

ROSE ANNIVERSARY GOBLETS AWARD 1980
6 1/2" high with engraved rose. Set of 4 for selling $400 in C14-15 1980. **CMV $15 set of 4.**

20 YEAR SERVICE AWARDS 1980's
Given for 20 years service. All are marked Avon or has 4A design. All come from Tiffany & Co. Choice of:
CRYSTAL PITCHER
5 3/4" high. **CMV $60.**
CRYSTAL VASE
7 1/2" wide. **CMV $60.**
CRYSTAL TULIP WINE GLASSES
Set of 6, 8" high. **CMV $75 set.**

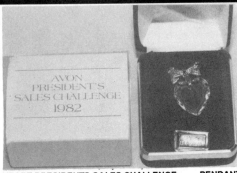

HEART PRESIDENTS SALES CHALLENGE AWARD 1982
Small clear crystal heart on gold tone ribbon pin. Maroon velvet Avon box & outer sleeve. **CMV $10 MB with sleeve.**

PENDANT - PRESIDENTS CELEBRATION 1980
Sterling silver chain & pendant with 25 blue sapphires around edge. Oak tree in center. Back says "The Presidents Celebration 1980 Avon". Given to 250 top managers in US, 1 per division. **CMV $150.**

ROSE STICK PIN AWARD 1981
Small Sterling silver rose. No markings in Tiffany & Co. turquoise box. Given to Avon reps for recruiting & sales goals. **CMV $20 MB.**

PRESIDENTS SALES COMPETITION JEWELRY AWARDS 1983
3 levels, all Sterling Silver made by Tiffany.
BRACELET
Given 10 to a district. **CMV $25 MB.**
PENDANT NECKLACE
Given 2 to a district. **CMV $35 MB.**
LAPEL PIN
Given to each rep in top sales group who met individual sales goals. **CMV $15 MB.**
Each comes in Tiffany box & Avon card.

CIRCLE OF EXCELLENCE TRINKET BOX 1982
Small leaded glass box with Rose embossed on lid. Comes with 4A brass coin. Back says "Roman Holiday C of E 1982". Only given to Pasadena Branch managers. **CMV $35 box & coin.**

20 YEAR SERVICE CLOCK AWARD 1980's
7" wide x 4 1/2" high Tiffany brass clock. Avon on top. Given for 30 years service at Avon. **CMV $75.**

30 YEAR SERVICE PEARL NECKLACE AWARD 1980's
17" long cultured pearl necklace with 14K gold Avon marked clasp. Given for 30 years service. Comes in blue holder from Tiffany. **CMV $75 mint.**

PRESIDENTS CLUB PIN AWARD 1981
Gold tone pin with 81 in center of 4A design cut out. **CMV $5 MB.**

DOOR KNOCKER TIE TAC AWARD 1970's
10K gold. Given to male executives at Avon. **CMV $60.**

TIE TAC MEN'S PRESIDENTS CLUB AWARD 1981-82
Gold tone 4A design Tie Tac given to men's Presidents Club. Comes in Avon box with 2 different backs as shown. CMV $20 MB.

FASHION HISTORY GLASSES AWARD 1980
Set of 6, 12 oz. glasses marked 1890's, 1920's, 1940's, 1950's, 1960's & 1970's. Given as set to Avon reps for signing up new Avon reps. CMV $20 set.

TEST DIVISION HEART PENDANT AWARD 1981
(left) Sterling silver & gold heart pendant & silver chain. Given to managers only in Tiffany & Co. box. CMV $150 MB.
ANNIE PENDANT MANAGERS 1982
(right) 14K gold filled pendant & chain. Back marked "I love you" & marked DM on side. Given to district managers. Came in gray Avon box with special card from Avon. CMV $60 MB.

ALBEE AWARDS GOLD & SILVER 1985
Gold tone Albee given 2 in each district. CMV $80.
SILVER TONE ALBEE
4 given in each district. Both have black bases & came in red felt bags. CMV $60.

ALBEE AWARDS - GOLD & SILVER 1986
Same as 1985 Albee's only base has "Avon 100 1886-1986" to match the gold tone or silver tone. CMV $80 gold, $60 silver MB.

15 YEAR SERVICE AWARDS 1980's
All are marked Avon or has 4A design. Each comes from Tiffany & design. Each comes from Tiffany & Co. Given for 15 years service at Avon. Choice of:
STERLING SILVER PERPETUAL CALENDAR
6" wide, 4 1/4" high. CMV $50.
CRYSTAL DECANTER WITH STERLING SILVER TAG
11" high. CMV $50.
STERLING SILVER SALT & PEPPER SET
2 1/4" high. CMV $50 set.
STERLING SILVER PIN BOX
3" diameter. CMV $50.

ALBEE AWARD - 1987 GOLD & SILVER
Gold tone Albee only 2 given in each district. Comes with "PC 1987 Sales Excellence" plaque across base on both gold & silver. CMV $80.
SILVER TONE ALBEE
Only 4 given in each district. CMV $60.

ALBEE AWARD 1987
Porcelain figurine given to Presidents Club Reps. Green dress. CMV $40.

ALBEE FIGURINE AWARD 1985
Hand painted porcelain. CMV $40.

ALBEE FIGURINE AWARD 1986
Fine porcelain. Special designed for Avon 100 Anniversary. For to reps only. **CMV $75.**

ALBEE FIGURINE AWARD 1984
Hand painted porcelain. Given to P.C. Reps. **CMV $40.**

ALBEE FIGURINE AWARD 1983
Purple dress lady given to all Presidents Club reps for top sales. **CMV $40 MB.**

(Left to Right)
ALBEE AWARD NO. 1 1978
Porcelain figurine 8 1/2" high in honor of the 1st Avon lady of 1886, Mrs. P.F.E. Albee. Given to top Reps. in sales in each district. Pink umbrella is also porcelain. **CMV $90 MB.**

ALBEE AWARD NO. 1 1979
Hand painted porcelain figurine of the 1st Avon Rep. of 1886. 2nd in a series. Given to President's Club Reps. for outstanding sales. Colors are blue and pink. **CMV $80 MB.**

ALBEE AWARD - CANADA 1979
Is the same as 1978 Albee issued in U.S. only the bottom printing is in French & English & dated 1979. **CMV $100 mint.**

ALBEE AWARD NO. 3 1980
3rd in the Albee series. Given to President's Club Reps. only. **CMV $60 MB.**

ALBEE AWARD NO. 4 1981
4th in the Albee series. Given to President's Club Reps. only. **CMV $50 MB.**

LADY OF ACHIEVEMENT TEST 1961
(Right) Pictured on right is smaller size original artwork test figurine for 1961 Lady of Achievement Award. Stands 7" high. Rare. Was not sold or given out by Avon. No price established. Used by factory only.

ALBEE AWARD 1982
5th in a series given to President's Club members for sales of $7,000 in 1 year. **CMV $30.**

WOMEN OF ACHIEVEMENT AWARD 1961
(Left) Painted ceramic figure of 1886 sales lady. One given in each district for highest sales. Came with stained walnut base & gold plaque inscribed "Avon Woman of Achievement Award". Printed on bottom of figure "Imported Expressly for Avon Products, Inc. Made in West Germany". **CMV $300., $325 MB.**

WOMEN OF ACHIEVEMENT AWARD 1969
(Right) White ceramic figure much the same as 1961 model. Base is tall & of white wood with gold trim. Printed on bottom of figure "Imported Expressly for Avon Products, Inc. Made in Western Germany Dresden Art". Brass plaque on base (not shown) says "Presented to. . .for Outstanding Contribution to the Better Way". **CMV $275., $325 MB.**

AWARDS & REPRESENTATIVES GIFTS

FIGURINE AWARD 1973
Awarded to each representative in district with greatest total sales increase. Made by Hummel, numbered & says "Made for Avon" on bottom. "Figurine 8" sits on white marble base with glass dome. **CMV $200., $225 MB.**

PRECIOUS MOMENTS CHRISTMAS MOUSE 1980
(Right) Given to Avon Reps. for signing up 2 new Avon Reps. **CMV $55 MB.**

PRECIOUS MOMENTS DISPLAY POSTER 1980
(Left) Used by managers C18-80. **CMV $5 mint.**

GOING AVON CALLING AWARD 1982
Yellow ceramic car with rabbit in pink, green base. Given to reps for Recommendation prize. **CMV $50 MB.**

FIRST LADY PORCELAIN FIGURINE 1976
Blue, white & pink porcelain made in Spain. Given to President's Club members only for outstanding sales in 90th Anniversary celebration. **CMV $45 MB.**

COLLECTORS CORNER FIGURINE AWARD 1982
Cherished Moments Collection mouse figurine. Given to 25 Reps. for top sales in Campaign 8, 1982 in each district. **CMV $25 MB.**

COME RAIN OR SHINE AWARD 1983
Ceramic Cherished Moments Rabbit with screw on ceramic umbrella. Given to reps for sales goals. 1st of 3 levels. **CMV $25 MB.**

LLADRO PORCELAIN LADY DIVISION MANAGER AWARD 1975
12 1/2" lady figurine made by Lladro in Spain. Comes with detachable porcelain umbrella. Given to division managers only. Dose not say Avon. Same figurine can also be purchased in fine stores. **CMV not eatablished**

PRECIOUS MOMENTS AWARD 1980
Rabbit figurine marked on bottom "President's Club Luncheon 1980". Given to Reps. at President's Club Luncheon only. **CMV $20 MB.**

PRECIOUS MOMENTS AWARD SET 1980
Set of 3 rabbit figurines given to Reps. for top sales. No. 1 is "Ready for an Avon Day". **CMV $25.**
No. 2 is "My first call". **CMV $35.**
No. 3 is "Which shade do you prefer". **CMV $60.**
Set of 3 CMV $110. Made in Japan only for Avon.

SMALL TREASURE CHERISHED MOMENTS MINI'S AWARD 1982
Pink box holds 3 mini rabbit ceramic figurines. Given to reps for Step 4 sales goals. **CMV $15 MB set.**

WE DID IT TOGETHER AWARD 1985
2 rabbit ceramic figurine in Cherished Moments Award series to Reps. **CMV $25. MB.**

PRESIDENT'S AWARD PERFUME 1963
Clear glass with stopper, silver 4A tag & string. Given to national winners in each division for President's Campaign, 1963. Box silver & white base with clear plastic lid. Bottom label on bottle says "Occur! Perfume Avon Products, Inc. N.Y., N.Y. contains 1 fl. oz.". **CMV $200 bottle only., $250 MB with label & tag.** Also came in 1/2 oz. size with gold neck 4A tag. Please write Bud Hastin if you know when and what the 1/2 oz. size was given for.

SMALL TREASURES CURRIER & IVES MINIS AWARDS 1982
Pink box holds mini ceramic Tea Set. Given to reps for Step 2 of sales goal. Made in Japan. **CMV $15 MB set.**

SMALL TREASURES ALBEE MINIATURES 1982
Pink box holds mini Albee figurines of number 2,3 & 4 Albee Awards. Given to Avon reps for 5th Step sales goal. **CMV $35 MB set.**

PERFUME - CIRCLE OF EXCELLENCE 1978
1 oz. glass stopper bottle, made in France. Paper neck tag says "Made Exclusively For You. Circle of Excellence 1978". **CMV $100 mint.**

SMALL TREASURE MINI ROSE AWARD 1982
Pink box holds small green leaf & pink ceramic rose. "The Avon Rose" on base, made in Taiwan. Given to reps for Step 1 of sales goal. **CMV $5 MB.**

OCTOBER 8 AWARD 1951
1 dram Forever Spring Perfume, smooth gold cap & bottle. Given to each representative sending an order in campaign 12, 1951. **CMV $40 MB.**

REPRESENTATIVE CHRISTMAS GIFT 1975
Clear glass in blue box. Reproduction of Trailing Arbutus Powder Sachet. **CMV $10. MB.**

CHRISTMAS GIFT PERFUME 1963
Given to Avon sales ladies for Christmas. The bottle at left is same as the one sealed in gold plastic container with green tassel & red ribbon. 4-10 oz. Christmas gift given to all representatives submitting an order in Dec. 1963. **CMV $40 complete., Bottle only $15.**

GOLDEN SLIPPER AWARD 1959
All gold metal slipper with red stone in toe & clear plastic heel. 1/2 oz. glass stoppered perfume bottle fits in slipper toe . No Avon name on shoe but has paper label on bottom of bottle saying "73rd Anniversary. Avon Products, Inc." Given to each representative in the winning group of each branch for top sales. **CMV $100 slipper & bottle with label., $150 MB.**

AVON 100 THOUSANDAIRE CLUB PIN 1986
Red, white & gold lapel pin. Came with numbers to hang below. Marked 1886-1986. **CMV $10. No numbers.**
AVON 100 THOUSANDAIRE CLUB PIN 1985
Same pin only blue border design. **CMV $10.**

MANAGERS GIFT PERFUME 1950
(Left) 1/2 oz. glass stoppered bottle in plastic case. Given to managers to help introduce To A Wild Rose. Paper label on bottom reads "Perfume Avon Products, Inc., Distributor, New York, Montreal, Vol. 1/2 oz.". Came with neck tassel. **CMV $250 mint, in plastic case.**
PRESIDENT'S AWARD CELEBRATION PERFUME 1955
(Right) 1/2 oz. perfume, glass stopper. Given to the winning team members for top sales. **CMV $75 BO mint., $100 MB.**

GREAT OAK CARD CASE 1987
(Left) Brass. **CMV $5.**
HONOR SOCIETY CARD CASE 1985
(Right) Brass card case. **CMV $10.**

PURSE OF GOLD AWARD 1948
Cardboard tube contained 8 samples of Golden Promise. CMV in packages shown. Given to each representative sending in an order at the close of campaign 3. **CMV $30.**

AVON 100 WATCH AWARD 1986
Black face quartz watch with Avon 100 on face - brown leather grain strap. Given to managers in Newark Branch. **CMV $65.**
AVON 100 PRESIDENT'S CLUB PIN 1986
Gold tone pin. Given to Reps. in black velvet Avon box. **CMV $15. MB.**
HONOR SOCIETY PIN 1986-87
Same as President's Club only came with Honor Society on bottom. **CMV $15.**

TASHA TEAM LEADER COLOGNE AWARD 1979
1.8 oz. spray cologne. Says "Team Leader 1979" in gold letters on front. Came in gold wrapped box with maroon color ribbon. **CMV $10 MB.**
TASHA "GO AHEAD AND DREAM" MANAGERS GIFT
Same bottle as above only "Go Ahead & Dream" in gold letters on face of bottle for managers at Christmas Conference. **CMV $20. MB.**

AVON 100 AWARD PINS 1986
Small gold tone on left with black letters. **CMV $7.** Small silver tone with black letters. **CMV $7.**
TRENDSETTER PIN AWARD 1984
Gold tone pin. **CMV $10.**

G.S.L. #1 PIN 1983
Red Pin. **CMV $10.**
AVON 100 TRENDSETTER PIN 1986
Blue, white & gold. **CMV $15.**
NIGHT MAGIC PIN 1987
CMV $2.
THOUSANDAIRE CLUB PIN 1985
Blue & white enamel. CMV with numbers up to 4. **CMV $10. Add $5 for each number up to 4.**
PEACH TREE PIN 1985
CMV $15.
AVON $1000 CLUB PIN 1986
CMV $10.
AVON LOVES ORDERS HEART PIN 1981
CMV $10.

AVON 100 GLASSES 1986
Set of 4 drinking glasses. Embossed Avon 100. **CMV $15. Set.**

AVON 100 DESK CADDY
Clear plastic with Avon 100 1886 - 1986 or caddy - white pen & note paper. Given to Managers. **CMV $15.**

AVON 100 ALBEE MIRROR 1986
13" x 17" gold tone frame mirror. 1886 - 1986 & 1st Avon Rep embossed on mirror. Given to managers at August Conference & also given for sponsorship. **CMV $45.**

AVON 100 CLOCK AWARD 1986
Clear lucite clock. Black face & letters. Given to Managers. **CMV $35.**

AVON 100 MANAGERS COMPACT AWARD 1986
Gold tone. Inscribed on back "Avon Centennial 1986 Dist. Sales Managers Conference." **CMV $25.**

AVON 100 BINOCULARS AWARD 1986
7 x 35 Binolux - Black. Given to Reps. Case says Avon 100. **CMV $75.**

AVON 100 TOTE BAG AWARD 1986
White canvas bag trimmed in blue & red. Given to people on trip to New York for 100 year celebration. **CMV $25.**

AVON 100 COFFEE CUP AWARD 1986
Blue ceramic cup. Avon 100 1886 - 1986 in gold letters. Given to representatives. **CMV $8.**

AVON 100 COFFEE MUG PASADENA 1986
White glass cup. Avon 100 on front. **CMV $10.**

AVON 100 PASADENA #1 AWARD 1986
Wood base, clear lucite Avon 100 plaque. **CMV $15.**

AVON 100 CALCULATOR 1986
Gold tone face Avon 1886 - 1986. Given to Managers. **CMV $10.**

AVON 100 BELL 1986
Clear glass bell, 5 3/4" high. Avon 100 embossed. **CMV $25.**

CENTENNIAL ARCH WATCH 1986
Enamelled arch stand with Avon face quartz pocket watch. Can be hung on chain around neck. Given to 10 top reps in each division for 100th anniversary. Comes in Avon 100 pink box & white Avon sleeve. **CMV $60.**

AVON 100 LEMONADE SET 1986
White plastic pitcher & 4 plastic Avon 100 glasses. **CMV $20.**

AVON 100 LIBERTY APRON 1986
Small red apron. White design from N.Y. Liberty Weekend. **CMV $25.**

AVON 100 HEAD BAND 1986
White head band. 100 years of beauty. **CMV $5.**

AVON 100 YEARS BAG CLOSER 1986
White plastic strip bag fastener. **CMV $1.**

AVON 100 CUP 1986
Plastic coffee cup. Look how good we look now. **CMV $1.**

AVON 100 LIBERTY WEEKEND T-SHIRT 1986
White T-shirt with collar. Given to workers on 4th of July Celebration in N.Y. **CMV $15.**

CENTENNIAL JEWELRY CASE AWARD 1986
8 3/4" square brass box. Given to Reps. **CMV $25.**

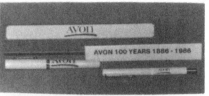

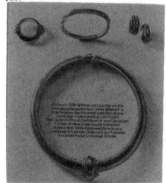

AVON NAME PLATE 1986
Gray & white plastic cork board. **CMV $2.**

100 YEAR ZIP LOCK FOR BAGS 1986
White & red letters. **CMV $1.**

PENS 1986
2 different. Both white, 1 Parker, 1 Shaffer. **CMV $15. ea.**

CENTENNIAL JEWELRY COLLECTION AWARDS 1986
All gold tone & rhinestones. Given to Reps.
Pin **CMV $10.**
Earrings **CMV $15.**
Bracelet **CMV $15.**
Necklace **CMV $20.**

AVON 100 LICENSE PLATE 1986
1886 - 1986

AVON LICENSE PLATE 1986
White & red letters. **CMV both $2.**

I LOVE AVON LICENSE PLATE FRAME
White frame given to Reps. **CMV $5.**

AVON 100 PLATE AWARD 1986
White porcelain plate. Back says C26 - 1985 Limited Edition. Pasadena Branch only. **CMV $25.**

CHECK BOOK COVER 1986
White plastic 1886 - 1986. Given to Avon Reps. **CMV $3.**

AVON 100 T-SHIRT AWARD 1986
White shirt, black letters, red trim. **CMV $10.**

NEWARK AVON FAMILY T-SHIRT AWARD 1987
White shirt, red design for Newark branch employees. **CMV $10.**

PRESIDENTS CLUB BIRTHDAY GIFT 1986
Chrome picture from "Avon 100" & note from James Preston Avon President. **CMV $8.**

MEDAL - 4A PENDANT AWARD 1980
Silver tone & black 4A design about 2 1/2" on red, white & blue neck ribbon. Given to managers only. Back says "You are a winner 1980" & name. **CMV $20.**

AVON 100 ROSE KEY CHAIN PENDANT 1986
Pink or gray Avon 100 box & sleeve has gold tone key chain & chain to use as necklace. Back says "Avon 1886-1986". Given to top 10 Reps. **CMV $15.**

"AVON 100" PILL BOX AWARD 1986
Small chrome box "Avon 100" on lid. Given at Presidents Club luncheon. **CMV $10.**

AVON 100 GOLD PIN AWARD 1986
14K gold. Small diamond. Given to Division Managers. **CMV $75.**
LIBERTY DIVISION PIN 1986
Blue & gold tone lapel pin. Status of liberty on face. Given to reps. **CMV $10.**

AVON 100 AWARD PINS 1986
Left is Newark branch Managers pins 14K gold. Has hook on back to wear as necklace. Back says Newark 1886-1986 14 K. **CMV $75. MB.**
Center is Newark branch. Gold tone. Larger in size. Very thin. **CMV $10.**
Right is Morton Grove Pin. Thicker gold tone. Design is different on all 3. **CMV $10.**

AWARD PINS MISC. 1986
AVON 2000 PIN
Black, white & gold. **CMV $10.**
AVON 100 PIN LARGE
1886-1986 - Black, red & gold. **CMV $10.**
AVON MEMBER PIN
Blue, black & gold. **CMV $10.**
AVON PIN
Black, red & gold. **CMV $10.**
AVON 100 PIN
Small black, red & gold. **CMV $10.**
AVON 100 PIN
Blue, white & red. **CMV $10.**
I LOVE AVON PIN
Black, red & gold. **CMV $10.**

AVON RAINBOW PIN 1986
CMV $15.
AVON BEAUTY ADVISOR PIN 1970s
CMV $15.
ARROW, APPLE PIN 1986
Red apple, white cross stick pin. **CMV $15.**
1-2 PIN 1970s
Gold tone. **CMV $25.**
AVON 100 PIN
Gold tone. **CMV $10.**

AVON100 DIVISION SALES MEDALLIONS 1986
Gold tone, siver tone & bronze tone medallions. Each say PC-Avon 100. Given in each division, 1 gold, 4 silver & 5 bronze.
CMV $75. gold
CMV $60. silver
CMV $40. bronze

PAPERWEIGHT CHRISTMAS IS FOR CHILDREN 1986
Avon - 1986 embossed clear glass. Given to Managers only at 6 places in U.S. **CMV $50.**

PAPERWEIGHT - GREAT OAK - AWARD 1981
Clear glass Avon, Kansas City #1-1981 etched on bottom. **CMV $50.**

GIVE N GAIN PRIZE 1970
10 3/4" high, 4" in diameter. A rose, butterfly and lady bug are etched in glass. Given to Avon ladies as prize. This was also sold in stores to public. Came in plain box with Avon stamped on it. Made by Abilities. **CMV $20 MB.**
RENAULT CAR GLASS 1971
(Right) Some sets came with this Renault car in set. Rare. **CMV $15.**

AVON 100 MIRROR 1986
Red plastic holder & Avon printed on mirror. **CMV $2.**
AVON 100 MATCHES 1986
Silver box. **CMV $1.**

RECOGNITION AWARD PIN 1974
About 1" size gold tone. Given to branch employees, rare. **CMV $35.**

REPRESENTATIVE OF THE MONTH PIN 1983-84
(Right) gold tone pin given to reps each month for meeting goals for the month. 2 in each district. Passed on to new rep each month. **CMV $10.**

45TH ANNIVERSARY VASE AWARD 1970'S
9 3/4" high x 4" across. Atlantis engraved "45th Avon Anniversary". Given for 45 years of Avon service. **CMV $200.**

PRESIDENTS DAY BOWL "LARGE" AWARD 1964
12 1/4" Oneida silver plate bowl. Center of bowl engraved with big 4A design & says "Presidents Day 1964 - Low Net." **CMV $45.**

PRESIDENTS DAY BOWL "SMALL" AWARD 1964
9 1/8" Oneida bowl as above. Center says "Presidents Day 1964 - Closest to Pin", 4A design. **CMV $40.**

SUBTLE REFLECTIONS HEART FLOWER VASE & FLOWERS 1982
Small heart shape lucite vase & silk flowers with Avon tag. Given to Presidents Club reps. Does not say Avon. **CMV $8.**

GOLDEN BELL COLLECTION AWARDS 1983
4 small brass bells given for meeting sales goals for C23, C24, C25, 1983. 1st bell has 4A design on top. 2nd bell has Acorn on top, 3rd bell has Avon door knocker. 4th bell was given if all 3 bells were won in all 3 campaigns as a bonus. 4th bell has a rose on top. **CMV 1st bell $10, 2nd bell $10, 3rd bell $15, 4th bell $20. MB. Add $5. to set if in plain boxes. For managers.**

CIRCLE OF EXCELLENCE CUP AWARD 1976
Polished pewter cup says "C of E 1976" engraved on side. Given to Circle managers only. **CMV $25.**

VALENTINE ATOMIZER AWARD 1980
Small clear crystal bottle, chrome top & red squeeze bulb. Given to team leaders & district manager. TL on bottom & DM. **CMV $10, TL bottle MB. CMV $20, DM bottle MB.**

ROSE ANNIVERSARY LUNCHEON PLATES AWARD 1980
Set of 4 clear glass 8" plates with engraved rose in center. Given to Reps. for selling $600 in C14-15 1980. **CMV $20 set of 4 plates.**

AVON LADY STEMWARE GLASSES AWARDS 1975
C-20 1975. Set of 6, 10 oz. & 6, 6 oz. glasses with 1st Avon Lady design. 1 set given to all Reps. in the winning district for top sales. **CMV set $50 MB.**

GREAT AMERICAN SELLATHON CHAMPAGNE GLASS 1981
Given to team leaders and managers. December 1981 on trip to Hawaii. **CMV $15.**

INITIAL GLASS AWARD 1970
Campaign 12 & 13, 1970. Reps. won the glasses and President's Club members won the goblets with initial of their choice for reaching sales of their choice or reaching sales goals in each campaign. The coasters were won by both for reaching sales goals both campaigns. **CMV on coasters $2, glasses $2, goblets $3 each.**

ULTRA CRYSTAL EVENT GLASS AWARD 1981
Tiffany & Co. box holds 2 engraved glasses. Given to Reps. who met sales goal by drawing for winner at sales meeting. **CMV $50 set MB.**

SALES ACHIEVEMENT AWARD 1979
Small gold tone trophy with wood base. Says "Avon Sales Achievement Award." **CMV $10.**
HONOR SOCIETY GOBLET 1987
Clear glass with black 4A design. Given to top reps. **CMV $15.**

1st DIVISION GLASS AWARD 1977
Lead crystal champagne glass given to No. 1 division Avon managers. **CMV $30.**
WINE GLASS FOR MANAGERS 1975
Yellow painted letters say "Avon Espana 1975". Came in 1975 Osborne Cream Sherry. Managers Gift Set on trip to Spain. **CMV $37.50.**

CIRCLE OF EXCELLENCE WINE GLASS 1979
Given to managers. Glass embossed "C of E 1979". Came in sets of 2 glasses. **CMV $25 each glass.**
CIRCLE OF EXCELLENCE CHAMPAGNE GLASS 1980
"C of E 1980" embossed on glass. Given to managers only in sets of 2 glasses. **CMV $25 each glass.**

GOLD PANNER TROPHY 1981
Metal gold panner. Plaque says "Sierra Division Achievement Break the Bank" 4A - 1981. Given to managers. **CMV $50.**

PASADENA BRANCH WINE GLASS 1974
No. 1 in sales. 429 given. "19 Avon 74 Pasadena Branch" on glasses. **CMV $15.**
CIRCLE OF EXCELLENCE GLASS 1974
Pasadena Branch No. 1 in sales C of E. Made by Fostoria, very thin glass. Only 30 given to managers. "C of E 1974" on side of glass. **CMV $25.** Same glass also came in 1973 & 1975. **Same CMV.**

TEAM ACHIEVEMENT AWARD 1977
Goblet given in 1st and 3rd quarters to top team in each district. Came in white embossed Avon box. **CMV $10. each quarter. MB.**

$100,000 TROPHY AWARD 1982
Glass dome holds $100,000 of chopped up U.S. money. Says $100,000 on dome. Wood base. Brass plaque from Avon 4A design given to 1 manager in Pasadena Branch. **CMV $50.**

AWARDS & REPRESENTATIVES GIFTS

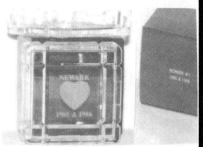

PICTURE FRAME RETIREMENT 1970s - 1980s
Sterling silver picture frame 8 x 10. Given to managers for retirement. Not marked Avon. Came with letters from Avon. **CMV $75.**

TRIBUTE VASE 1987
8" high clear glass vase. Embossed "Tribute 1987." Given to P.C. Reps only. **CMV $10.**

PRESIDENTS CLUB SILVER BASKET 1987
5 1/2" high silver plated basket. Has "PC Avon Presidents Club" tag attached. Given only to P.C. Reps only. **CMV $15.**

NEWARK #1 CRYSTAL BOX AWARD 1985-86
Lead crystal box with Newark with a heart 1985-1986 #1 embossed on glass lid. Given to managers in blue box. **CMV $25.**

AVON 100 CHAMPAGNE AWARD 1986
1886-1986 Avon 100 label. Given to Honor Society Reps. **CMV $25.**

FOSTERIA COIN GLASS BUD VASE AWARD 1970s
8" high in Avon box. **CMV $30. MB**

FOSTERIA COIN GLASSES SALT & PEPPER SHAKER AWARDS 1970s
Came with Avon literature. **CMV $15. set.**

CHRISTMAS GIFT TO REPS 1986
Lead crystal dish from France given to all reps at Christmas in green box. **CMV $10. MB** Given to Presidents Club Members in red P.C. box. **CMV $15. MB**

GLASS CASTLE AWARD 1984
Blown glass castle. **CMV $18.**

ALL YOU CAN BE CANDY DISH AWARD 1984
Clear glass full of candy. Given to managers 1984. **CMV $15.**

PRESIDENTS SALES CHALLENGE FLOWER AWARD 1983
Glass & brass box holds orchid. Label on top. Given to Reps for trip to Hawaii. **CMV $45.**

CIRCLE OF EXCELLENCE WINE AWARD 1981
Bottle of Abbey Chenin Blanc wine. Special black & gold label for Circle of Excellence 1981. **CMV $40. unopened.**

COMBOURG CRYSTAL AWARDS 1985
Each given to P.C. Reps for sales goals. Crystal made in France not just for Avon. **CMV Decanter $25.**
Set of 6 Champagne Glasses $20.
Set of 6 Wine Glasses $20.
Crystal & Chrome Ice Bucket $20.

REPRESENTATIVE X-MAS GIFT 1983
(Left) 3" ceramic box with dove on top. Bottom says "Holiday Greetings Avon 1983". Given to all avon Reps. **CMV $10. MB.**

REPRESENTATIVE X-MAS GIFT 1984
Heavy clear glass vase with snowflakes etching. Bottom says "Happy Holidays Avon 1984." Came in nice silver box & outter sleeve. **CMV $20. MB.**

MANAGERS CHRISTMAS GIFT 1959
Beige box with blue velvet lining holds French hand made bead purse & Majestic cultured pearl necklace. Given to managers at Christmas 1959. Very rare. Set not marked Avon, but valuable. **CMV not established.**

CERAMIC SAC AWARD 1986
White ceramic bag. Given to reps in U.S. & Canada. **CMV $20.**

SALES EXCELLENCE AWARD 1983
Lead crystal glass box. Inscribed "Sales Excellence Award 1983 Avon President's Sales Competition." **CMV $50.**

AVON 100 CERAMIC BOX 1986
White porcelain. Avon 100 front & back. 4A on top in red. **CMV $35.**

FRONT PAGE TUMBLERS 1971
14 oz. tumblers with Reps. name printed on "front page" of glass. Given for having a person reccommended as a Rep. appointed. **CMV $25 set of 8 MB.**

YOU MAKE ME SMILE GLASSES AWARDS 1978
Set of 6 glasses made only for Avon given to Avon Reps. for signing up a new Avon lady. **CMV $12 set MB.**

SPIRIT OF '76 CROCK SET AWARDS 1974
(Left) Multipurpose Pitcher - earned for $150 in sales. **CMV $7 MB.**
(Center) Bean Pot Casserole - earned for $200 in sales. **CMV $14 MB.**
(Right) Goodies Jar - earned for $300 in sales. **CMV $18 MB.**

CRYSTAL SALAD BOWL AWARD 1956
7 1/2" cut glass with silverplate edge. Comes with serving fork & spoon & card from Avon. Given to Reps. during 70th Anniversary Celebration in 1956. Made by Fina. **CMV $55 complete.**

SUGAR & CREAMER AWARD 1952
Sterling silver base and glass tops. Given to Avon Reps. in 1952. White and silver stiped box. Made by Fina. **CMV $55 set MB.**

CANDY DISH SET AWARD 1952
Sterling silver base by Fina. Glass screw on tops. Given to Avon Reps. in 1952. Came in plain white box. **CMV $55.**

PEOPLE WHO LIKE PEOPLE PRIZE PROGRAM AWARDS 1972
3rd level prize is a set of 8 10 oz. crystal and silver glasses. Won by Reps. for meeting 3rd level sales goals. Was not made only for Avon. **CMV $25 set MB.**

CRYSTAL CANDLE HOLDERS 1980
10" high clear crystal. Given to Reps. for 30 years continuous service. Base is inscribed "30th Avon Anniversary". **CMV $100 pair.**

MILLION DOLLAR INCREASE GOBLET 1978
(Left) Silver plated goblet given to all managers in top division for 1 million dollar increase in sales. **CMV $25.**

PORT O'CALL CANDY DISH & BAR 1977
(Right) China dish by Ilmoges - France & bar of French candy given to managers for meeting appointment goal. Box has gold label "Meet me at the lamp post, Port O'Call Pasadena". **CMV $10 MB.**

REPRESENTATIVE CHRISTMAS GIFT 1982
Small 4" porcelain dish made by Royal Worcester for Avon. Given to all Avon reps at Christmas 1982. Comes in green box with Avon card. **CMV $10 MB.**

WILD VIOLETS COLLECTION DESSERT BOWLS AWARDS 1984
Set of 6, 13.5 oz. dessert bowls. Clear glass with Violet flower design. Given to Avon reps for reaching level 3 of 4 sales goal levels. **CMV $15 MB set.**

ASH TRAY 1982
Used at Avon plants. **CMV $2.50.**

SMALL TREASURES FRAGRANCE BOTTLES IN MINIATURE AWARDS 1982
Pink box holds 3 mini size CPC reproductions with gold caps. Given to reps for Step 3 of sales goals. **CMV $15 MB.**

WILD VIOLETS COLLECTION PITCHER AWARDS 1984
Clear glass, Violet flower design. Given to Avon reps for level 1 of 4 levels. **CMV $12 MB.**

WILD VIOLETS COLLECTION WATER GLASSES 1984
Set of 6, 12 oz. clear glasss Violet flower design. Given to Avon reps for reaching level 2 of 4 levels. **CMV $12 MB set.**

JOLLY SANTA AWARDS 1986
All white & red ceramic.
Level 1 - Candy jar 7 1/2" high. **CMV $10.**
Level 2 - Set of 4 Santa mugs. **CMV $15.**
Level 3 - Santa Plate. **CMV $20.**

WILD VIOLETS COLLECTION TRAY & SALAD PLATES 1984
11" x 17 1/2" white plastic tray & set of 6 clear glass salad plates with Violet flower design. Given to Avon reps for reaching level 4 of 4 sales goal levels. **CMV $20 set MB.**

TOWNHOUSE CANNISTER & COOKIE JAR SET AWARDS 1983
Given to reps for sales quota. 1st level, small, **CMV $10.**, 2nd level, **CMV $20.**, 3rd level, **CMV $30.**. 4th level, Cookie Jar (right) **CMV $50**, or **CMV $90 entire set.**

CHRISTMAS GLASSES & TRAY AWARD 1985

Set of 6 12 oz. glasses with red & green X-mas tree design. **CMV $20.00 MB set.** Matching white ceramic 2 tier serving tray with brass handle. **CMV $15.00 MB.**

OSBORNE CREAM SHERRY MANAGERS GIFT SET 1975

Wine cask on box lid. Box holds 2 wine glasses with "Avon Espana 1975" painted in yellow, bottle of Osborne Cream Sherry with special label "Especially bottled for the 1974 members of the Circle of Excellence". This set was given to each manager on their C of E trip to Madrid, Spain. Only 200 sets given out. **CMV $130 set mint full.**

SALES ACHIEVEMENT MUG AWARD 1977

Pink rose on side and Sales Achievement 4th Quarter 1977 on other side. **CMV $10.**

ACHIEVEMENT AWARD MUG 1978

"1st Quarter 1978" on white ceramic mug given to team getting most new Avon ladies to sign up. **CMV $10.**

SPRINGDALE FOUNDERS CLUB COFFEE CUP AWARD 1979

(top) White glass cup given to all Plant employees who had worked from 1965 to 1979. Red letters. **CMV $10.**

COLOR UP AMERICA PEN 1979

(bottom) White, black & silver pen on brown leather neck cord. Given to managers. **CMV $10.**

PROSPECT COFFEE JAR & CUP AWARD 1977

Clear glass jar with green painted design on front says "1886-Avon 1977". Filled with coffee beans. **CMV $20 jar only.** Coffee cup-came with jar in white box as set. Has Avon district manager 1977 on cup & other writings. **CMV $10 cup only.** Both given to Avon managers only.

MERRY CHRISTMAS MUG 1977

Short glass mug with green lettering on front. **CMV $8.**

CIRCLE OF EXCELLENCE MUG 1970'S

Pewter mug inscribed C of E Avon on front. **CMV $25.**

GOBLET-CIRCLE OF EXCELLENCE AWARD 1975

(left) 7 1/2" high sterling silver goblet. Given to C of E managers who went to Madrid, Spain 1975. Base says "Circle of Excellence, Madrid, 1975" **CMV $60.**

TEAM LEADER MUG AWARD 1976

(right) White glass mug. **CMV $10.**

CIRCLE OF EXCELLENCE MUG AWARD 1978

Avon C of E District No. 1978 in red letters. Given to Reps. In winning districts. **CMV $10.**

QUEEN ELIZABETH CUP & SAUCER 1953

Avon 67th Anniversary celebration coincided with Queen Elizabeth Coronation. Awarded at a banquet for top organization. **CMV $80 mint.**

CURRIER & IVES SUGAR & CREAMER AWARD 1982

Set given to Avon Reps. for signing up 1 new Avon Rep. **CMV $10 set.**

AWARDS & REPRESENTATIVES GIFTS

AWARD COMPACT 1966
(left) Sterling silver compact. Engraved on back "National Champion, President's Campaign, 1966". **CMV \$17.**

AVON SUGAR BOWL CLUB 1960
(right) Awarded to sales ladies for getting new customers. **CMV \$50.**

CURRIER & IVES 5 PIECES PLACE SETTING AWARD 1981-82
Each set has dinner plate, salad plate, cup & saucer, and soup bowl. Given to Avon Reps. for signing up 1 new Avon Rep. **CMV \$25 set of 5 pieces.**

CURRIER & IVES 5 PIECES PLACE SETTING AWARD 1977-81 Same set only marked 1977-81 on bottom of each piece in set. Only 300 sets got out in Newark Branch. **CMV with 77-81 bottom date \$100.00 MB set.**

CURRIER & IVES TEA SET 1977-78
Set consists of plate, tea pot, sugar bowl & creamer. Avon Products, Inc. on bottom of each piece. Awarded to Avon Reps. for Distinquished Sales Achievement 1977. Plate - 1st step, **CMV \$6.50.** Sugar bowl & creamer- 2nd step, **CMV \$12.00.** Tea pot-3rd step, **CMV \$17.50.** Cup & saucer-4th step, Saucer 1st issue marked 1977 on bottom, 1978 issue has no date, **Add \$2 each piece for 1977 date. CMV \$35 set of 4. Add \$10 if writing on bottom is printed backwards for each piece.**

CURRIER & IVES COLLECTION AWARD 1977-78
Made only for Avon & stamped on bottom. Given to Avon. Reps. for meeting sales goals.
1st step - Dinner bell, **CMV \$6.50 MB**
2nd step - Butter dish, **CMV \$12.00 MB**
3rd step - Water pitcher 6 1/2" high. **CMV \$17.50 MB**
4th step - Cake plate 9 1/2" diam. **CMV \$32.50 MB**
Add \$10 each piece for bottom writing printed backwards.

MIKASA CHINA SET 1972
Candle holders & sugar/creamer set for reaching first prize goal, **CMV \$5 each MB.** Beverage server for reaching second goal, **CMV \$10 MB.** Eight cups & saucers for reaching third goal (to be won by President's Club members only), **CMV \$4.** For each cup & saucer set. **These items must be in Avon boxes with card or outlook as this set was not made just for Avon.**

FOSTORIA SUGAR & CREAM SET AWARD 1970
From Fostoria glass, box says "Avon Cosmetics". Given to Reps for sales achievement. Design is from the Henry Ford Collection. **CMV \$30 MB only.**

SILVER CANDLELIGHT SET GIFT 1972
Given to Reps. as a gift. Does not say Avon on set & was not made only for Avon. Can be bought in stores. Set has punch bowl & 2 goblets with silver rim. Box has Avon mailing label. **CMV \$35 in Avon box.**

PLATE AWARD "CPC" 1930'S
China plate about 9" has 2 deer on face, gold trim - "CPC Avon" on back. No information. **CMV \$100.**

5 YEAR ANNIVERSARY PLATE
8 1/2" porcelain plate, "The Great Oak" for 5 year service to Avon. 1st issued 1987. **CMV \$10 MB.**

10 YEAR ANNIVERSARY PLATE 1987 ON
8 1/2" porcelain plate. "The California Perfume Co." for 10 years service to Avon. 4 different plates issued starting in 1987. **CMV \$15.**

15 YEAR ANNIVERSARY PLATE
8 1/2" porcelain plate. "The Avon Rose" on plate. Given for 15 years service. 1st issued 1987. **CMV \$30 MB.**

20 YEAR ANNIVERSARY PLATE
8 1/2" porcelain plate. "The 1st Avon Representative" on plate. Given for 20 years service. !st issued 1987. **CMV \$40 MB.**

SPIRIT AVON AWARD PLATE 1986
7 1/4" clear glass plate. White lettering. 1 to a district. **CMV $35.**

25 YEAR SERVICE PLATE AWARD 1985 UP
8" Sterling Silver Plate. Inscribed "In Grateful Appreciation of Twenty Five Years of Loyal Service to Avon Customers. James Preston - President Avon Division." **CMV $75 in Tiffany bag & box.**

POSSET POT AWARD 1976
(left) 9" high stoneware. Bottom reads "Made in Brazil exclusively for Avon Products, Inc.". **CMV $25.**

PITCHER & BOWL RECOMMENDATION PRIZE 1975-77
(right) Given for recommending someone, if appointed as a Rep. Has Avon on bottom of both pieces. **CMV $50 set.**

DECORATORS CHOICE PITCHER AND BOWL PRIZE 1977
Ceramic pitcher 10" high & bowl 15 1/4" across. Made only for Avon. Given to Reps. for signing up 1 new Avon Rep. **CMV $50.**

SALAD SET GIFT 1972
Given to Reps. as gifts. Does not say Avon and was not made only for Avon. Can be bought in stores. Came in plain box with Avon mailing label. Set has large salad bowl & 4 small ones & silver plated spoon & fork. **CMV $35 in Avon box.**

DISTINGUISHED MANAGEMENT AWARD 1967
Glass plate with 4A design on bottom. Came in white box lined in red velvet. **CMV $45 plate only. $55 MB.**

BICENTENNIAL PLATES 1976
Blue & white. Given to Reps. that sent in order for campaign 1, 2, 3 totaling $100 or more.
(left) Independence Hall.
(right) Liberty Bell. Made in England. Has Inscription on back. **CMV $20 Independence Hall; $30 Liberty Bell.**

RECOMMENDATION GIFT SNACK SET 1973
Fostoria lead crystal dish & bowl. Came in set of 4 each. Given to Avon. Reps. for signing up new Avon ladies. **CMV $15 each setting. $60 for all 8 pieces.**

TENDERNESS COMMEMORATIVE PLATE 1974
9" diameter ceramic plate, pastel blue and greens. Awarded to Reps. for sending in orders for campaign 1, 2, and 3,, 1974. Inscription on back in blue letters "Tenderness Commemorative Plate Special Edition, awarded to Reps. in January, 1974". Plate is made by Pontessa Ironstone of Spain. Award plate has Pontessa in blue letters. Plate also sold with no inscription on back. **CMV $22 MB.** Red letter plate only.

77TH ANNIVERSARY QUEEN AWARD 1963
Awarded to 10 Reps. in each district that had greatest dollar increase in sales, were crowned Queen & also received Fostoria Crystal serving dish with Avon 4A in bottom. Tiara not marked Avon. Came with Avon Queen certificate - 2 different certificates were given. Also came with 1963 Queen Ribbon. 11 1/4" bowl. **CMV bowl only $50. CMV Tiara with ceritficate & ribbon $50. CMV complete set MB $100.**

CHRISTMAS BELLS-MANAGERS GIFT 1971
Red strap with 5 bells given to Avon managers at Christmas. Came with card with bells on it & "For you from Avon". Must have Avon card. **CMV $15 MB.**

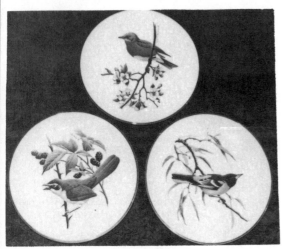

FOSTORIA COIN PLATE AWARD 1970
Does not say Avon. Must be in Avon box.
CMV $25 MB.

BIRD PLATE AWARDS 1975
Campaign 10, 1975. Available to Reps. for meeting product goals; serving specified number of customers and meeting goals at suggested customer prices. Bluebird was lowest goal, Yellow Breasted Chat second and Baltimore Oriole last. If total goals attained, Rep. received all three plates. **CMV Bluebird, $20 MB, Yellow Breasted Chat $20 MB, Baltimore Oriole $30 MB.**

LENOX CHINA PRESIDENT'S CLUB BOWL AWARD 1979
White box with gold trim & burgundy inside holds 4A inscribed china bowl. Bottom inscribed "For Avon's Very Best" given to all President's Club members for 1980. Box has Avon outer sleeve. **CMV $40 MB, bowl only $30.**

FOSTORIA LEAD CRYSTAL PLATES AWARD 1978
Given for top sales. 1st four plates won by Reps: Jeweled A, 1st Rep., Door Knocker, great oak tree. **CMV $30 set of 4 or $7 each.** President's Club Reps. & District Managers could win 1st 4 plus 4 more: 4A Avon Key, World of Avon Globe, Avon Rose Last. President's Club set had P.C. marked on Rose plate & D.M. marked Jeweled a plate for managers set. **CMV $100 D.M. set of 8, CMV $75 P.C. set of 8.**

WILD FLOWERS AWARD PLATES 1976-78
Each is 8 3/4". Southern Wild Flower plate for $195 in sales. Southern & Eastern given for $245 in sales & Southern, Eastern, Nothern & Western flower plates for $330 in sales. C-11, 1976. **CMV Southern $10 MB. Eastern $15 MB. All 4 plates MB $60 set. Northern & Western $20 each MB.** These same plates were reissued by Geni Products, a division of Avon in March, 1978, as awards to their sales reps.

COIN GLASS 1961-72
Coin glass in Avon boxes only are collectable. The same pieces are available in local stores with both 1886 and 1887 at low prices so get the box. Many pieces available at many different prices starting at **$10 up to $100 in Avon box.** 1st issue 1961.

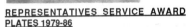

REPRESENTATIVES SERVICE AWARD PLATES 1979-86

Awarded for years of service. 1st issued in 1973 and some design changes in 1979. 1st 5 are white porcelain with decals. All are the same CMV as 1973 to 79 plates except the 25 year plate which is silver tone only and **CMV $40. CMV complete set $140 MB.**

CHRISTMAS GIFT PLATE 1971

(Top Left) Sent to Reps. at Christmas. Clear glass with frosted First Avon Lady. **CMV $17 MB. $12 no box.**

CHRISTMAS GIFT PLATE 1972

(Top Right) Sent to every Rep. at Christmas. Clear glass frosted rose. **CMV $15 MB. $10 no box.**

CHRISTMAS GIFT PLATE 1973

(Bottom Left) Sent to Reps. who had been with company less than 2 years. Clear glass frosted 4A. **CMV $15 MB. $10 no box.**

CHRISTMAS GIFT PLATE 1974

(Bottom Right) Sent to Reps. at Christmas. Clear glass with frosted Door Knocker. **CMV $12 MB. $8 no box.**

FRAGRANCE JAR AWARD 1924

American Beauty fragrance jar hand painted design in blue & gold. Pink & green flowers on lid. Pink ribbon. Given to Reps. for top sales. **CMV $350.**

REPRESENTATIVES AWARD PLATES 1973-79

Awarded for years of service. First 5, white with colored decals. Two years-Doorknockers **CMV $10.** Five years-Oak Tree with pink or brown acorns, **CMV $15.** 5 year "Factory Mistake Plate" marked as normal 5th Anniversary plate on back but same as 10th year plate on front. Rare.

Add $25 to 5 year plate. Ten years-California Perfume Co. **CMV $20.** Fifteen years-Rose **CMV $25.** Twenty years-First Avon Lady **CMV $30.** Twenty-five years-Sterling silver with message from Avon President. **CMV $100.** All Prices are mint & boxed. **CMV complete set $200 MB.**

NATIONAL CHAMPION AWARD 1966
Glass bowl with 4A design on bottom. **CMV $50 MB.**

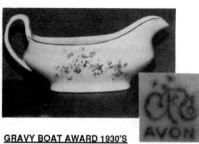

GRAVY BOAT AWARD 1930'S
CPC Avon on bottom. Given to Reps. for sales award in 1930's. Blue & green flowers on both sides. Gold trim. **CMV $75.**

COVERED DISH AWARD 1930'S
White ceramic bowl & lid. Gold trim with green & pink flowers. Bottom is stamped CPCo. Avon under glazing. Given to Avon Reps. for sales. **CMV $110 mint.**

GREAT SCENT EVENT TRAY AWARD 1980
9 1/2"x 17 3/4" gold tone mirror tray given to 15 Reps. In each district for selling the most Ultra colognes. Does not say Avon on tray. Came with & must have Great Scent Event card from division manager. **CMV$20 with card.**

CAKE STAND AWARD 1978
(Front) Given to top 50 Reps. in state. "Avon Division Top 50" inscribed in center. Silver plated. **CMV $25.**

IMPERIAL DIVISION AWARD TRAY 1979
(Back) Silver plated, inscribed "Avon Imperial Division Top 50, 1979 #29". **CMV $25.**

50 YEAR SERVICE PLATE 1976
Gold plated plate given to the late Mrs. Bessie O'Neal on July 27, 1976, by David Mitchell, President of Avon Products, for 50 continous years as an Avon lady. A letter from Avon & Mr. Mitchell came with the plate. The plate is 1 of a kind & priceless. The plate is made by Dirilyte. No value established.

SILVER SERVER AWARD 1977
(top) 11 3/4"x 18 3/4" silver plated tray & cover. Marked Avon Wm. Rogers on bottom. No information on why it was given to Reps. **CMV $45 mint.**

SILVER CREAMER AWARD 1950'S
(bottom) Avon Wm. Rogers on bottom. Silver-plate creamer. **No information on this as Avon award CMV $35.**

SILVER SERVICE AWARD TRAY 1957
Silver tray 13 1/2" long, "Avon-Wm. Rogers" on bottom. Awarded to Avon ladies in Anniversary Campaign. **CMV $30.**

HIGHEST SALES AWARD BOWL 1976
Silver plated fruit bowl was awarded to 10 different Reps. for highest sales in their category. Each bowl is engraved different from the other. The one is engraved with "4A" design. "Highest Percentage Increase Christmas 1976". **CMV $25, $30 MB.** Not awarded in all branches.

PRESIDENT'S CELEBRATION AWARD BOWL 1977
Over 40,000 were given as awards. 6 7/8" silver plated bowl given to Avon Reps. in 2 winning districts in each division for top sales. Inscription in center of bowl "President's Celebration 1977"; on bottom of bowl, "Awarded exclusively to Avon Reps." F.B. Rogers. Came in white box as shown. Red silk rose also given at same time with name tag. **CMV Rose only with tag, $5. CMV bowl $25 MB.** Bowl did not come with rose.

PRESIDENT'S AWARD SILVER BOWLS 1962
3 sizes silver bowls. 4A emblem and writing on outside. **CMV (left to right) $27.50, $32.50, $37.50.**

75TH ANNIVERSARY SALES CHAMPION SILVER TRAY 1961
Awarded to the top Avon district managers for best sales in campaign 9 & 10, 1961. **CMV $40.**

SILVER SERVER AWARD 1963
12 5/16" x 2" given to the top 4 established Reps. In each district for sale improvement over the previous year. 4A design engraved in the bottom. Small 9" servers were given to 3 newer Reps. for highest sale & 3 for outstanding sales ability. **CMV 9" $40, 12" $45.**

ACHIEVEMENT AWARD SILVER TRAY 1961
4A design in center of silver tray. **CMV $35.**

PRESIDENT'S CELEBRATION TRAY AWARD 1978
12" silverplated tray marked "Awarded Exclusively to Avon Reps." on back side. Given to 1 winning team Rep. In each division. **CMV $35 MB.**

DIVISION SALES WINNER TRAY AWARD 1975
17 3/4" long 13" wide silver tray. Inscribed in center 'Awarded to (name of manager) President's Program Best Wishes, David S. Mitchell'. Given to top district managers in sales. Came in blue felt bag & white box. **CMV $150 MB in bag.**

EL CAMINO DIVISION SUGAR & CREAMER SET AWARD 1977
Silverplated creamer & sugar bowl. Tray is engraved "Top 10 Sales-El Camino Division Campaigns 10-22, 1977". Made by Sheridan. **CMV $35 set mint.**

SILVER SERVER 1964
9" diameter. Same as 1963 server except no 12" bowls given and all are gold lined on the inside. **CMV $40.**

SILVER TRAY 1965
9 7/8" x 1" given to each Rep. from the winning group in each branch during the General Manager's Campaign, engraved "Honor Award-General Manager's Campaign 1965". **CMV $35.**

88TH ANNIVERSARY AWARD BOWL 1974
6" across and 3" high silverplated by Oneida. Paul Revere Silver. Given to top 5 sales Reps. in each district. **CMV $20.** Same bowl given to top 5 President's Club Sales Reps. and their award bowl says "President's Club" over 4A ensigna. **CMV $20.**

SALES EXCELLENCE AWARD 1977
Paul Revere, Jostens Pewter 5" bowl C26-76-C9-77. Awarded to top sales Reps. **CMV $20 MB.**

SILVER AWARD BOWL 1969
Silverplate bowl by Fina. Has 4A symbol and Avon in center of bowl. 2 3/4" high and 5" wide at top. Awarded to Avon Reps. **CMV $20.**

CHINA BELL REP. GIFT 1973
Christmas present to all Reps. that had been with Avon over 2 years. White China with pink roses. **CMV $10 MB.**

CHRISTMAS ORNAMENTS MUSICAL GIFT SET 1974

Given to Reps. for getting new Reps. Red & gold bell & green & gold ball. Both have music boxes inside. Made by Heinz Deichett, West Germany. Both came in red box as set. **CMV $30 each no box, $75 set MB.**

MANAGERS CHRISTMAS GIFT 1979

Blown glass in green leaves & red holly with red velvet ribbon. 2 pieces. Holly leaves ornament & candle holder. Given to managers for Christmas 1979. Does not say Avon. **CMV $15 set.**

REPRESENTATIVE AWARD BOWL 1956

Sterling silver Paul Revere Bowl was given to each Rep. in the top selling district in each division during President's Campaign 1956. **CMV $45.**

THE GREAT AMERICAN SELLATHON CHRISTMAS TREE AWARD 1981

Approximately 600 given out at Hawaiian President's Celebration in Hawaii. Has bottom Avon label & green & white gift box. **CMV $45.**

REPRESENTATIVE CHRISTMAS GIFT 1979

Ceramic tile picture frame made in Japan. Box says "Happy Holidays Avon 1979". Given to all Avon Reps. at Christmas. **CMV $10 MB.**

COMPOTE TALL 1960'S

Fostoria coin glass award. Must be in Avon box. Given to Reps for sales award. **CMV $45.**

MANAGERS CHRISTMAS TREE GIFT 1977

(Left) Hand blown glass Christmas tree in clear, green, red & yellow. Given to Avon managers at Christmas 1977. Does not say Avon. **CMV $25.**

MANAGERS CHRISTMAS TREE GIFT 1978

(Right) Brass Christmas tree ornament signed by "Bi Jan" on back. Given to Avon managers at Christmas 1978. Came in green box. **CMV $20 MB.**

FLOWER BASKET AWARD 1981

Small white ceramic flower basket. **CMV $25.**

91ST ANNIVERSARY COIN GLASS AWARD 1977

Footed compote on right won by Reps. for selling $270 in C8-9-1977. **CMV $7 MB.** Centerpiece bowl and footed compote won for selling $540 in C8-9-1977. **CMV $12 MB.** Centerpiece bowl. A pair of candle holders won by President's Club members only with P.C. embossed on bottom. This coin glass was made only for Avon, using Avon emblems in coins and 1886-1977 and the name Avon. Came with card on each piece from Avon and in Avon box. **CMV $17 candle holders, MB.** District managers received a full set of Coin Glass with D.M. embossed in center of each piece. **CMV $75 MB for complete D.M. set.**

"PICTURE FRAME" DREAM AWARD SEPTEMBER CONFERENCE 1979

Ceramic picture frame. White, pink & green flowers with white doves. Center is pink, says "Hold fast to your dreams, For if you do . . .Tomorrow you'll see More dreams can come true". **CMV $15.**

CAKE PLATE FOSTORIA COIN GLASS AWARD 1960'S
Fostoria glass cake plate given to Reps. for sales award. Comes in Avon box. Same piece was sold in local stores. Must be in Avon box as shown. **CMV $75 MB.**

APPLE PAPER WEIGHT AWARD 1978
Given to divisional managers for top sales. Clear crystal glass apple is engraved "You Made New York Smile", Avon, March 1978, on front side. **CMV $100.**

HEART TREASURE BOX AWARD 1976
Top sales teams in 252 winning districts won ceramic heart shaped box given in President's Celebration of 1976. Bottom says "Avon President's Celebration 1976". Made in Spain **CMV $20 MB.**

PRESIDENT'S CELEBRATION HEART AWARD 1979
Lucite heart marked "You're our number one- Avon 1979 President's Celebration". Made in Taiwan. Comes in white Avon box. **CMV $15 MB.**
MANAGER'S HEART "YOU'RE NO. 1"
(Right) Clear lucite, has smaller hole on top & heart is about 1/2" smaller. Came in red velvet bag. This one was given to managers only. **CMV $20 mint in bag.**

HEART PORCELAIN BOX AWARD 1980
Given to managers. Came in Tiffany & Co. box. Small porcelain heart box says "Bernardaud Limoges Made in France. Does not say Avon. **CMV $25 in box with card.**

TEAM LEADER BELL AWARD 1980
Fostoria bell inscribed "Avon Team Leader Re- cruit A Thon 1980". Only 1 in each district given. **CMV $30.**

LIMOGES FLORAL BOX AWARD 1980
Small white ceramic heart box with blue painted flowers. Given to managers. Does not say Avon. Must have Tiffany card for Avon Products. Was not made only for Avon. **CMV $25 MB with card.**

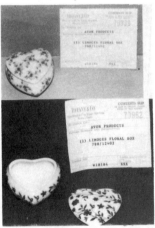

LIMOGES FLORAL HEART BOX AWARD 1979
Small heart shaped ceramic box made by Limoge of France. Given to Avon managers. Must have Tiffany & Co. card as shown for Avon Products. 2 different designs as shown. **CMV $25 with card.**

78TH ANNIVERSARY FOSTORIA AWARD SET 1964
Box marked Avon Cosmetics holds Fostoria salt & pepper, cruet & glass holding tray. Given to Reps. **CMV $45 in Avon box.**

MERRY MOODS OF CHRISTMAS ORNA- MENT 1960'S
Dark blue ornament for managers only. Other side says "Avon Presents" with 4A design. **CMV $35 mint.**

50TH ANNIVERSARY AWARD LAMP 1936
Made only for Avon "Lalique reproduction" lamp. 22" high, 19" wide shade. Frosted carved glass base. Pink ribbon on shade, clear beads around edge of shade. White painted base. Given only to 50 Reps. for top sales in nation. **CMV $300.**

SILVER FLOWER BASKET AUGUST CONFERENCE AWARD 1978
Sterling silver basket made by Cartier, hand made. "August Conference 1978" on top of handle. Yellow silk flowers, green leaves. Given to managers only. **CMV $100 mint.**

CANDLESTICK AWARDS 1952
Sterling silver candlesticks 2 1/2" tall and 2 3/4" wide at the base. They were given to Reps. for calling on 120 customers during the 66th Avon Anniversary campaign, 1952. Came in nice gift box. The candlesticks were not made just for Avon. Must be in box with Avon card as shown. **CMV $60 MB.**

ROSE PERFUME LAMP AWARD 1926
Pink rose colored frosted glass, rose shaped electric lamp with antique green metal base. Top of rose has a small indentation to put perfume to scent the air when lamp was burning. Lamp 4 5/8" across, rose 5" high. Given to only 8 Reps. for top sales. **CMV $200.**

TEAM LEADER JEWELRY BOX 1980
Silver tone box with blue felt interior. Mirror inside tray says "Team Leader-President's Celebration 1980". **CMV $20 mint.**

CIRCLE OF EXCELLENCE STEUBEN VASE AWARD 1970
9" high Steuben Vase, sits on Black wood base. Brass name plate says "Circle of Excellence Repeat Member-1970" plus name of winner. Comes in Steuben felt bag & box. Given to top C. of E. Managers only. **CMV $400 MB.**

NATIONAL DISTRICT SALES MANAGER PANEL AWARD 1980
Silverplated card case. Given to top managers only. Made by Reed & Barton. In box & blue bag. **CMV $50.**

GREAT OAK LAMP AWARD 1980
Electric light in wood base with solid hunk of clear glass with great oak engraved. Given to district managers at yearly conference. **CMV $75 mint.**

PRESIDENT'S CELEBRATION SILVER CHEST 1974
Silverplated, red lined. Embossed rose on lid. **CMV $47.50 MB.**

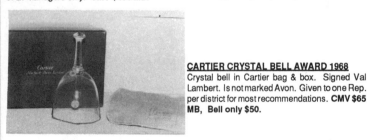

CARTIER CRYSTAL BELL AWARD 1968
Crystal bell in Cartier bag & box. Signed Val Lambert. Is not marked Avon. Given to one Rep. per district for most recommendations. **CMV $65 MB, Bell only $50.**

WE DID IT TOGETHER TRAY 1983
7 1/4" x 12" silver plated server tray. Given to Managers. **CMV $25.**

$1,000,000 DESK SET AWARD 1978
(Left) Wood base. Brass plaque. **CMV $50.**
DESK SET NATIONAL G.M. CHAMPIONS AWARD 1973
(Right) Marble base. **CMV $20.**

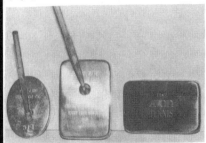

TOP RECRUITER PEN AWARD 1979
(Left) Sterling silver pen set. Engraved "Top Recruiter May 1979". **CMV $100.**
CIRCLE OF EXCELLENCE 8 YEAR PEN AWARD 1980
(Center) Engraved sterling silver pen set. **CMV $125.**
AVON TENNIS PAPER WEIGHT 1982
(Right) Heavy sterling silver paper weight engraved "1982 Avon Tennis". All are made by Tiffany & Co. **CMV $150.**

OPPORTUNITY UNLIMITED MUG AWARD 1981
Brass mug inscribed on side. **CMV $20.**
OPPORTUNITY UNLIMITED GLASS AWARD 1981
Champagne glass inscribed on side. **CMV $10.**

WINTER RECRUITING EVENT AWARD BOWL 1977
8" International silver plate. Side inscribed name - Gateway Division Winner 1977 - Winter Recruiting Event. **CMV $20.**
GATEWAY APPOINTMENT GOBLET AWARD 1975
Poole silver plate. Inscribed on side. **CMV 20.**

PAPER WEIGHT AWARD 1983
Square lucite with gold 4A center. Marked The Answer is Avon. **CMV $20.**
PAPER WEIGHT AWARD NEWARK 1983
Small round lucite, with 1979 Susan B. Anthony Dollar inside. **CMV $15.**

PAPER WEIGHT LOS ANGELES -1983
(Left) Clear & red lucite marked "Road to the Gold." **CMV $25.**
PAPER WEIGHT - SAN FRANCISCO 1982
(Center) Small clear lucite. Gold inner base. **CMV $30.**
PAPER WEIGHT - LONDON 1980
(Right) Clear & red lucite. Avon Marathon. **CMV $35.**

OAK TREE PAPER WEIGHT AWARD 1978
(Left) Lucite case holds oak tree coin with 4A design. Atlanta #1 - 1978. **CMV $20.**
READ LISTEN FOLLOW UP PLAQUE 1981
(Right) 4A design on sign. **CMV $10.**

VISION AWARD 1985
Clear lucite paper weight. Says "Avon Our Vision is Clear 1985". **CMV $15.**

MANAGER'S CONFERENCE CORSAGE 1960'S
Green & gold with red holly has Avon 7 dollar bill attached. Bill says "United States of Avon". Given to managers. **CMV $22.**

JEWELRY BOX AWARD 1968
10" long x 5" wide brocade & brass music box. Red lined. Given to Reps. for top sales. Does not say Avon. **CMV $60 mint.**

WOMEN'S INTERNATIONAL AVON "RUNNING" MARATHON AWARD 1979
Gold tone medallion in clear lucite with red background. Came on marble base with 22/9/79 plaque. **CMV $50.**
INTERNATIONAL WOMEN'S CHAMPIONSHIP MARATHON AWARD 1978 ATLANTA
Same as above only silver tone medallion with black background. **CMV $50.**

ARIANE NECKLACE & BOUQUET 1977
Wood basket & plastic flowers holds sterling silver necklace with August Conference 1977 on side. Given to Avon managers at August Conference Banquet. Necklace holds sample vial of Ariane perfume. **CMV $65 mint.**

HUDSON MANOR BUD VASE GIFT 1978
Avon silverplated bud vase & red rose in silver box. Bottom says "Team Leader, August 1978". Made in Italy. Same as regular issue only regular issue does not say Team Leader 1978 on bottom. **CMV $20.**
MANAGERS BUD VASE GIFT 1978
Same as above only says "August Conference 1978" on bottom instead of Team Leader. **CMV $30 MB.**

MANAGER'S FLOWER BASKET 1979
Basket of silk flowers with Avon tag to managers. In Avon box. **CMV $15 MB with tag.**
TEAM LEADER FLOWER BASKET 1979
Same flower basket only different box and different tag given to team leaders. **CMV $10 MB.**

SOUNDS OF SEASONS MUSIC BOX 1966
Given to managers only. Box holds green & gold Christmas Tree Pin, gold Key & Bell. Came from Cartier in New York. **CMV Music box only $65.00, Complete set $85 MB.**

SALES LEADERSHIP AWARD 1980
Large clear glass emerald diamond shaped paper weight. Engraved "Avon Sales Leadership Award Conference 1980". Tiffany & Co. on bottom. Comes in Tiffany box. Given to mangers only. **CMV $100 MB.**

OAK TREE PAPER WEIGHT AWARD 1980
Clear lucite with silver tone 4A design & oak tree. "Pasadena No. 1 - 1980" inscribed inside. Given to managers. **CMV $25.**

NO. 1 PAPER WEIGHT AWARD - CANADA
Chrome-plated No. 1, gold tone plaque says "You're Number One With Us". Given to Avon managers in Canada. **CMV $30.**

95th ANNIVERSARY CELEBRATION AWARD MUG 1981
(Left) White - Red letters. **CMV $10.**
WE'RE HOT MUG AWARD 1984
(Right) White mug - red & black letters. **CMV $10.**

PRESIDENT'S CLUB CUP 1986
Pinkish orange coffee cup. "Avon President's Club 86" on side in blue letters. **CMV $5.**
PEN "LOOK HOW GOOD YOU LOOK NOW" 1987
White pen. **CMV $2.**
PHYLLIS DAVIS ACHIEVEMENT AWARD 1985
Clear lucite 3" square with black background. C-26-85. **CMV $25.**

LIBERTY DIVISION PAPER WEIGHT 1978
Clear lucite has 4A design. "Liberty Division - Two Million Dollar Increase 1978". Given to top managers. **CMV $15.**
CIRCLE OF EXCELLENCE PINS 1979
(lower left) Small blue & gold tone pin says "C of E Winners 1979". Given to top managers. **CMV $10.**

OUTSTANDING IN FIELD CUP AWARD 1981
Ceramic cup with cow on other side. **CMV $10.**
CUSTOMER SERVICE AWARD MEASURING CUP 1982
By Fire King - Avon inscribed. **CMV $10.**

COFFEE CUP AWARDS 1984
Left to right.
WHITE GLASS - red letters, gold trim. **CMV $5.**
WHITE MUG - Avon in red letters all over. **CMV $5.**
SAY YES TO AVON MUG - White plastic, red letters. **CMV $5.**

TELEPHONE HONOR SOCIETY AWARD 1986
Red telephone given for $50,000 in sales. Engraved on top "PC Avon Honor Society". Comes in Unisonic box. **CMV $75.**

WE LOVE YOU MUG AWARD 1986
White ceramic cup. **CMV $5.**
AVON MARATHON AWARD, OTTAWA 1981
Clear lucite with white back. Dated 23 August 1981. Given in women's running circuit. **CMV $35.**

WONDER MUG AWARD 1987
White plastic mug. **CMV $5 MB.**

AVON TELEPHONE 1986 AWARD
White phone, wall or desk mount. Avon in black letters - red slash. Given to reps. **CMV $25.**
#1 TREND SETTERS WALL TILE AWARD - 1985
White tile given in Morton Grove branch. **CMV $25.**

P.C. COFFEE CUP GIFT 1987
Ceramic coffee cup given to President's Club members on birthdays. White, blue, orange & pink. Has ceramic lid. **CMV $6. MB.**

HOLIDAY GREETINGS GLASS AWARD 1971
Clear glass, red letters. **CMV $12.**
GOBLET 1971
Ruby coated glass says Lena - Avon 1971. **CMV $10.**
P.C. X-MAS PREVIEW CUP 1985
White plastic, red letters. **CMV $2.**
CHRISTMAS ORNAMENT AWARD 1984
White plastic, green letters. Teddy bear on back side. **CMV $5.**

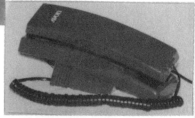

TELEPHONE AWARD 1986
Red wall mount or can sit on table. Says Avon in white letters. Given to reps. **CMV $20.**

SALES ACHIEVEMENT MUG 1977
White coffee cup, pink rose. Back says "Avon Sales Achievement Highest Percentage Increase Third Quarter 1977". **CMV $10.**

SHAWNEE DOOR KNOCKER IN LUCITE AWARD 1970's
Gold tone door knocker sealed in lucite - has Shawnee in blue. **CMV $20.**

TELEPHONE PRESIDENT'S CLUB AWARD 1983
Red plastic Touch Tone, given to top sales reps only. Made by Webcor. Outer sleeve says "Avon Calling" & Avon Calling on telephone. **CMV $25.**

DIVISION COMPETITION AWARD 1973
Clear lucite paper weight given in Springdale branch. **CMV $10.**

HEAT THERMOMETER AWARD 1981
Clear lucite, black letters & trim given to managers in 4 test areas only. **CMV $25.**

REP. CHRISTMAS GIFT BOWL 1978
Fostoria bowl with 4A design & 1978 on bottom. Given to all Avon Reps. for Christmas 1979. Box shown with red ribbon & gold tag & white & gold plastic bell given to managers. **CMV $10 Reps. MB, CMV $15 managers with ribbon.**

VALENTINE TEAM LEADER GIFT 1979
3 1/2" across crystal heart shaped glass dish given to all team leaders for Valentine's. **CMV $12.50 MB.**

CIRCLE OF EXCELLENCE CRYSTAL VASE 1980
Given to managers on trip to Spain. Box has "Avon Vase Soliflor." Was not made only for Avon. **CMV $40 in Avon box.**

SEASONS GREETINGS AVON REPS. 1977
5 1/2" high vase marked on bottom has 4A symbol. Given to all Avon Reps. at Christmas 1977 in special box. **CMV $10. MB.**

DIVISION MANAGER'S TROPHY 1966
Large pewter trophy given to winning manager in each division. **CMV $80.**

PRESIDENT'S CUP AWARD 1949
Sterling silver trophy engraved with top selling team in city & district in each division during President's Campaign during the late 40's & early 50's. Given to managers. **CMV $200 mint.**

JUBILEE ANNIVERSARY QUEEN AWARD 1977
Small wood base, gold top for division manager. **CMV $10.**

HOOSIER CUSTOMER SERVICE TROPHY 1975-76
(Left) Given to managers for most customers served. **CMV $22.50.**

PRESIDENT'S CELEBRATION TROPHY 1978
(Right) Marble base. **CMV $15.**

TRAVELING TROPHY 1972
Gold 4A with first Avon Lady over emblem on walnut base with engraved plate Team Honor Award. **CMV $20.**

35th ANNIVERSARY AWARD 1980's
Silver plate pitcher engraved on front. Given to Reps. for 35 years service as an Avon Rep. Comes with Avon card. In Avon box from Tiffany & Co. Engraved on side of pitcher "35th Avon Anniversary". **CMV $100 MB.**

ADDITION'S AWARD 1978
Black & clear plastic picture cube for recruiting new Reps. **CMV $25 MB.**

OBELISK COMMUNITY SERVICE AWARD 1979
8 1/4" clear lucite. 1 given to managers in each division. Has 4A design & message of Ralph Waldo Emerson in center. Came in 2 sizes - 1 is 2" shorter. **CMV $35 ea.**

PRESIDENT'S CLUB TROPHY 1977
Gold tone top. **CMV $8.**

PRESIDENT'S CELEBRATION TROPHY 1978
Given to Reps. for best increase over sales goal. Came with certificate. Marble with wood base. **CMV $20.**

KANSAS CITY BRANCH TROPHY 1969
"Number One" national sales increase. **CMV $17.**

LOVING CUP TROPHY 1961
Gold cup on white base. **CMV $20.**

BUD VASE AWARD 1954
(Left) 8" tall sterling silver vase awarded to each Rep. in winning district during President's Campaign. **CMV $45.**

PRESIDENT'S TROPHY 1954-56
(Right) 13 5/8" high, sterling silver trophy was given to top selling city & district managers in each division during President's Campaign each year. Trophy sits on black base. **CMV $125.**

ROYAL RIBBON TEAM LEADER AWARD TROPHY 1982
Wood base & silver toned cup. 1 given per district. **CMV $15.**

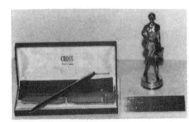

AVON CALLING PEN 1976
(Left) 14K gold filled. Made by Cross. In grey bag and red leather pen holder with rose design in gold. Pen is 5 1/4" long. Given to Reps. for recommendation prize. **CMV $20 MB.**

TOP 6 TEAM LEADER TROPHY 1977
(Right) Given for Top 6 Sales in Anniversary Celebration 1977. White marble base, gold statue. Blue plaque. **CMV $10.**

TOP SALES TROPHY 1966
(Left) Small 5" high gold trophy, wood base. C-11-13-1966. **CMV $15.**

ACHIEVEMENT AWARD TROPHY 1954
(Right) Avon in raised letters on the base of the metal figure. Given to top Reps. in each district. **CMV $20.**

PRESIDENT'S CELEBRATION TROPHY 1977
Inscribed to Top Selling Rep. for President's Celebration. **CMV $20.**

3 YEAR WINNER TROPHY 1971
Small wood base, brass plaque that says "Avon 3 Year Winner". Given to Reps. **CMV $15.**

DIVISIONAL SALES CAMPAIGN AWARD 1954-56
Only 20 black plaques with solid sterling silver rose, were given each year to managers in top selling district in each of the 20 divisions in U.S. **CMV $200.**

BEST SUPPORTING PERFORMANCE TROPHY 1965
(Left) This type trophy should not get too high in price as you can still buy the trophies & have brass name plate put on them. **CMV $15.**

ACHIEVEMENT AWARD TROPHY 1958-59
(Right) This type has Avon in raised letters on the base of the metal figure. These cannot be purchased & should be worth more. **CMV $25.**

KEY TO SUCCESS TROPHY AWARD 1978
Trophy floated to each winning manager in division till final winning manager won & kept it. **CMV $60.**

PRESIDENT'S TROPHY 1959-60
Sterling silver trophy given to managers in top selling district in each division. Given late 50's to early 60's. Trophy is inscribed with winning team & year. **CMV $150.**

NATIONAL DISTRICT PANEL PLAQUE 1974
Picture frame plaque-Sara Fleming. Gold & brown. **CMV $15.**

ANNIVERSARY QUEEN TROPHY 1978
Marble Base, Given to top Rep. in each division for top sales. **CMV $15.**

QUEEN'S TIARA 1978
Came with Queen's Trophy. Is not marked Avon. **No price established.**

STAR SPANGLED MANAGER PLAQUE 1970
Avon-Star Spangled Manager Summer 1970 on face plate. **CMV $14.**

DISTINGUISHED SALES MANAGEMENT PLAQUE AWARD 1977
Solid walnut base holds white ceramic tile center plaque & brass name tag on bottom. Given to top 10 managers in each division. **CMV $30.**

PRESIDENT'S CELEBRATION PLAQUE 1977
Engraved wood plaque with Cape Cod Water Goblet attached. Given to team leaders with highest sales. **CMV $15 mint.**

OUTSTANDING MANAGERS PLAQUE 1971
Wood base with gold plaque. Outstanding managers first quarter. **CMV $20.**

TEAM LEADER PLAQUE AWARD 1979
Given to team leaders in C of E winning division. **CMV $30.**

MILLION DOLLAR CLUB PLAQUE PASADENA BRANCH 1978
Walnut base with red front & gold trim. Presented to district managers for outstanding sales increase. **CMV $50.**

PRESIDENT'S CELEBRATION GREAT OAK PLAQUE AWARD 1980
Scrimshaw great oak on white plastic center, wood frame. Comes with Avon card also with or without brass inscription plate on face. Given to managers only. **CMV $35.**

BLUE RIBBON SOCIETY AWARD 1981
Wood & brass plaque. **CMV $25.**

MILLION DOLLAR SELECT GROUP AWARD 1977
(Left) Plaque with bag of money on front from Sovereign Divison. **CMV $75.**

OUTSTANDING ACHIEVEMENT AWARD 1975
(Right) Blue velvet on wood plaque, metal wreath with red, white & blue ribbon with 4A pendant with green stone in center. **CMV $100.**

AWARD PLAQUE 1971
Presented in campaign 1-26, 1971 for increased sales. **CMV $10.**

TOP 10 DIVISION TROPHY 1977
4 1/2" high 4A design inside lucite top on wood base & brass plaque. Given to top 10 sales Reps. in each division. Came in plain white box. **CMV $40.**

HONORABLE MENTION PLAQUE 1960'S
Green pearlessence plastic base with wood and brass plaque. **CMV $15.**

PICTURE GLASS FRAME PRIZE 1943
Etched glass frame holds 8x10 size picture. Given to Reps. for selling over $75 during campaign. **CMV $150.**

20 YEAR SILVER PICTURE FRAME AWARD 1981
Sterling silver picture frame from Tiffany & Co. given to Avon Reps. for 20 years service. Bottom of frame engraved "Avon 20 Years", & the initial of person winning frame. Comes in Tiffany felt bag. **CMV $100.**

AWARDS & REPRESENTATIVES GIFTS

CIRCLE OF EXCELLENCE HEART PICTURE FRAME 1981
Silver tone small picture frame with C of E card. Given to C of E managers. **CMV $25.**

MANAGERS DIPLOMA 1963
Certificate given to new Avon managers during the 1960's. Did not come in frame. **CMV $10.**

TEAM LEADER PICTURE FRAME AWARD 1978
Chrome picture frame marked on top of frame "Made Exclusively for Avon Team Leaders". Given for meeting sales goals. **CMV $10 mint.**

ACHIEVEMENT AWARD 1950
Pink & white with gold. Given for high sales during 64th Anniversary Celebration. This was celebrating new packaging & redesign of Cotillion. This matches packaging for this era. Approx. 10 x 14 inches. **CMV $25.**

PAUL GREGORY PLAQUE 1964
Silver plaque on black wood. Given to each manager in the winning division. **CMV $35.**

PAUL GREGORY PLAQUE 1965-67
Black & silver plaque given to winning division of Avon's Paul Gregory Trophy. **CMV $30.**

DIVISION CHAMPION PLAQUE 1965
Given for highest sales during general managers campaign 1965. **CMV $30.**

WHITE HOUSE PICTURE FRAME AWARD 1986
100th year signed by Ronald Reagan. **CMV $10.**

PICTURE FRAME "CERAMIC" AWARD 1984
Blue box holds small white ceramic picture frame with blue, green & yellow flowers. Given to Reps. for Sales Quota. **CMV $8.**

CHRISTMAS CONFERENCE AWARD 1985
2" deep wood frame with brass inscribed plaque with rose & 4A design & dated 1985. Given to managers only. **CMV $35.**

MANAGERS PICTURE FRAME AWARD 1986
Small oval brass tone frame with 4A design. Given at August conference. **CMV $15.**

THIS IS FOR YOU PEN & NOTE PAD AWARD 1984
White Avon Box holds note pads. **CMV $7.** White Avon light pen. **CMV $10., $20. for set MB.**

I LOVE NEW YORK GIFTS 1985
Note pad - blue plastic, apple rubber stamp & button. **CMV $5. all.**

SAN FRANCISCO RECORD 1980
Circle of Excellence envelope with Tony Bennet record. "I Left My Heart in San Francisco." **CMV $5.**

STICK WITH IT SOAP HOLDER 1973
Rubber soap holder given to Reps. Rare. **CMV $3.**

CARDS - PASADENA #1 1980s
Deck of cards. **CMV $8.**
CARDS - NEW YORK - LAS VEGAS - AWARD 1980
Deck of cards. **CMV $10.**
ICE SCRAPER AWARD 1984
White plastic - says "You're #1 with me - Avon" **CMV $1.**
FLASHLIGHT AWARD 1985
White plastic. Avon marked. Given to Reps. **CMV $8.**
KEY CHAIN AWARD 1983
Tan leather. Metal Avon tag. Given to Reps. **CMV $5.**

(Left to Right)
CIRCLE OF EXCELLENCE AWARDS 1977 NEW YORK - BERMUDA TRAVEL ITINERARY
Beige plastic cover & itinerary inside. **CMV $5.**
CANDY CUP
White plastic with gold covering. Rhinestone on front. **CMV $7.**
NAME TAG
White & blue plastic. **CMV $5.**

ORDER BOOK COVERS 1980s
Misc. order book covers used by Avon Reps. **CMV $1,$5 each.**

AVON 100 BOOK MARK 1986
Pocono Division leather book mark. Given to Reps. **CMV $5.**

SMALL TREASURE CABINET AWARD 1982
Small wood cabinet made in Brazil for small treasure figurines. **CMV $10.**

JEWELRY BOX MALE AWARD 1981
Fine wood box made by Buxton given to Male District Managers or Male Team Leaders. Brass label on front is only difference in both boxes. Same box can be bought in stores. Must have brass Avon name plate. District Managers **CMV $90,** Team Leaders **CMV $75**

CIRCLE OF EXCELLENCE BUTTON 1979
2 1/4" brown & white button. **CMV $2.**
CALCULATOR 1986
Pocket calculator, in Avon box. Brass & green face. **CMV $15.**
"YO YO AVON" 1986
White Avon yo yo. **CMV $5.**

LEFT- CALCULATOR AWARD 1983
Red canvas holds small Novus solar calculator. **CMV $20.**
CALCULATOR AWARD 1982
Black vinyl with 4A holds Casio battery calculator. **CMV $15.**

AWARDS & REPRESENTATIVES GIFTS

DIRECTOR CHAIR AWARD 1985
White fold up chair, red canvas. 5 given in each district. **CMV $35.**

DOOR MAT AWARD 1980s
Red door mat, white letters. Black rubber back. Bottom mat is 2" smaller and is red with black letters. **CMV $15. ea.**

PRESIDENT'S DAY FRISBEE BAG AWARD 1984
White nylon zipper bag given to Reps. **CMV $20.**

BLAZER JACKETS 1982-83
Blue blazer with 4A brass buttons & gold 4A ensignia or jacket for Reps. **CMV $75.**
Also came for Managers with <u>M</u> in center of 4A ensignia. **CMV $100.**

BASEBALL HAT 1978
White & black Avon cap. **CMV $5.**

TRAVEL BAG AWARDS 1985
Each is tax nylon & vinyl.
Flight Bag. **CMV $25.**
Overnight Bag. **CMV $20.**
Garment Bag. **CMV $25.**

PRESIDENT'S CLUB SCARF X-MAS GIFT 1985
White silk scarf with red & gold P.C. design in red box. **CMV $5.**
PRESIDENT'S CLUB BIRTHDAY PICTURE FRAME GIFT 1985
Red front paper frame with floral back. **CMV $5.**

SANTA'S SACK BY AVON 1986
Red canvas bag. White letters. Given to Reps. **CMV $5.**

AVON MENU SCARF 1976
White silk scarf with Circle of Excellence dinner menu in L.A. Calif. 1976 printed in blue letters. **CMV $25.**

INCENTIVE AWARDS 1985
Stocking hat, mittens & neck scarf. White knit with red letters. Given to Reps. **CMV $25 set.**

FUN SHIRT AWARD 1985
White sweat shirt. Red & blue design. Given to Reps. **CMV $10.**

SWITCH TO AVON TOTE BAG AWARD 1987
Beige canvas bag. Orange letters. Also came larger in size from Newark branch. **CMV $5.**

T-SHIRT AVON SUNSET AWARD
Light blue shirt - yellow sun. **CMV $10.**

T-SHIRTS AWARDS MISC. 1970s - 80s
ROSE BOWL SWEATSHIRT 84
Red - **CMV $20.**

FUTURES CIRCUIT TENNIS
Red t-shirt.

AVON CHAMIONSHIP TENNIS
Red t-shirt.

AVON T-SHIRT
Blue shirt.

AVON T-SHIRT CANADA
White with Avon on both sleeves.
CMV $10. all T-shirts.

CHRISTMAS IS FOR CHILDREN APRON 1986
White apron - green & red design. Given to workers only at 6 parties in U.S. **CMV $20.**

APRON AWARD 1979
Fruit on apron with red or yellow border & straps. Given at representatives meetings. **CMV $8. ea.**

T SHIRTS AWARDS MISC. 1970s-1980s
AVON WOMENS RUN - GREEN
AVON RUNNING CANADA - WHITE & RED
AVON MARATHON INT. WOMEN'S CHAMPIONSHIP - RED & WHITE
AVON INTERNATIONAL MARATHON TRAINNG 1983
White - red design - 2 girls running. L.A.
AVON RUNNING
White - red letters.
CMV $10. each.

CUSTOMER SERVING APRON 1987
Red apron, white letters & trim. Given to Reps. **CMV $5.**

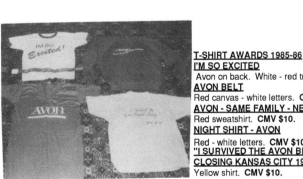

T-SHIRT AWARDS 1985-86
I'M SO EXCITED
Avon on back. White - red trim. **CMV $10.**
AVON BELT
Red canvas - white letters. **CMV $5.**
AVON - SAME FAMILY - NEW ADDRESS
Red sweatshirt. **CMV $10.**
NIGHT SHIRT - AVON
Red - white letters. **CMV $10.**
"I SURVIVED THE AVON BRANCH CLOSING KANSAS CITY 1985"
Yellow shirt. **CMV $10.**

APRON AWARDS 1986
"AVON" **CMV $5.**
"I LOVE AVON" **CMV $5.**
"I LOVE SUMMER WITH AVON" **CMV $7.**
All are white - red & black letters & trim.

AWARDS & REPRESENTATIVES GIFTS

WE'RE HOT T-SHIRT & SWEATSHIRT & BUTTON 1984
Red T-Shirt & Sweatshirt & We're Hot button. Given to Reps. **CMV button $5., T-Shirt $10., Sweatshirt $12.**

T-SHIRT AWARD - "WE CAN DO IT TOGETHER" 1984
Red T-shirt given to Reps. **CMV $10.**
YOU'RE HOT - HOT PAD AWARD 1982
Red & white glove hot pad. Given to Reps. **CMV $3.**

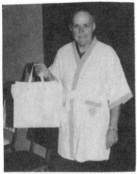

CIRCLE OF EXCELLENCE BEACH ROBE & BAG 1977
White terry cloth robe trimmed in light blue with C of E on pocket. White canvas bag C of E 1977. **CMV $15. Bag., $35. Robe.**

SPORTS BAG AWARDS - 1980s
AVON SPORTS
Silver & black bag. Avon sports red patch on both sides. **CMV $30.**
GIRL SCOUT AVON BAG
Silver & black bag. Girl Scouts Leadership today & tomorrow on back side. Avon on other. **CMV $30.**
AVON CHAMPIONSHIPS OF WASHINGTON TENNIS RACKET COVER
White, red trim. **CMV $25.**
AVON CORPORATE PRESIDENT'S DAY 1984
Frisbee shape blue & white bag unzips to make tote bag. **CMV $25.**

TOTE BAGS 1985 - 1986
AVON HAWAII
White. **CMV $12.**
AVON
White. **CMV $5.**
AVON LIFE
Red. **CMV $12.**
HAT AVON
White Avon Hat. **CMV $5**

TOTE BAG "AVON SPORTS" 1982
White canvas, red & lavender letters. Given to staff members of Avon Running Circuit. **CMV $15.**

TOTE BAG "HAWAIIAN" 1983
Turquoise canvas bag given to Top Reps on 1983 Hawaiian trip. **CMV $15.**

AVON RUNNING BAG 1983
White canvas bag with red & fushia color lettering. **CMV $20.**

ROSE PARADE AVON SEAT CUSHION 1984
Reddish orange plastic - white letters. Only 150 made & given to people at Rose Bowl game 1984. **CMV $50.**

LICENSE PLATE FRAME AWARD 1980s
White plastic, marked Avon. **CMV $2.**
MANAGER'S TAMBORINE 1970's
Wood frame, skin marked Avon. Made in China. **CMV $30.**

TOTE BAG 1987
Canvas bag with red handle & letters. **CMV $10.**

BEACH TOWEL 1987
29" x 60 " white beach towel. Red letters. **CMV $15.**

HORIZONS CLOTHES BAG GIFT 1977
Given to Avon managers. White plastic bag. **CMV $15.**

TIME OF YOUR LIFE BAG AWARD 1978
Beige canvas bag with red letters given to Reps. on trip to New York. **CMV $10.**

CIRCLE OF EXCELLENCE LOVE CAMERA 1985
Coke can size love container with top & side C of E labels. Holds small black & red love plastic camera in felt bag. Given to Managers for Hawaii trip. **CMV $15. MB.**

TRAVEL BAG - CIRCLE OF EXCELLENCE 1978
White leatherette bag given to 250 district managers. **CMV $50.**

ENVIRA VISOR HAT - AUSTRALIA 1980
Light pink visor hat given to Reps. at the introduction of Envira in Australia. **CMV $10.**

SELLATHON VISOR CAP 1981
(Left) Blue or red. **CMV $5.**

AVON TENNIS VISOR CAP 1981
(Right) White cap. **CMV $5.**

COLOR UP AMERICA NECK TIE 1979
(Top left) Given to male managers only. **CMV $10.**

COLOR UP FLAG
(Center) **CMV $2.**

COLOR UP HAT
(Bottom) **CMV $4.**

EMPRISE T-SHIRT 1977
Black t-shirt given to Avon managers to introduce Emprise line. **CMV $15.**

PYRAMID PAPERWEIGHT AWARD 1981
Clear lucite with gold 4A design on bottom & 2 sides on top. Given to district managers only. **CMV $50.**

H-E-A-T BAG AWARD 1981
Canvas bag. **CMV $10.**

H-E-A-T HAT
White hat. **CMV $8.**

YOU MAKE ME SMILE LUGGAGE TAG 1978
White plastic. **CMV $3.**
AVON CHAMPIONSHIP TENNIS HAT 1978
White hat, red letters. **CMV $7.**

QUICK STAMP 1982
Red Avon box has pink & white plastic name stamp. **CMV $3 MB.**

BASEBALL CAP 1978
Blue & white Avon Products Inc. hat. Used by plant employees. **CMV $12.50**
NECKTIE - AVON 4A 1970's
Used by Avon management. Tie has 4A design & is dark blue. Made of Dacron Polyester. **CMV $12.50.**

PRESIDENT'S CLUB LUNCHEON BANNER 1978
White canvas, red & gold letters. **CMV $20.**

MANAGERS BANNER 1976
White silk banner about 8 ft. long, gold braid, pink letters. Used by managers to encourage Reps. to call on new customers. **CMV $15.**

PRESIDENT'S AWARD PENNANT 1951-52
Royal blue pennant with gold trim & letters. Given to top selling city & district division managers during early 50's. **CMV $45.**

PRESIDENT'S CELEBRATION BANNER 1974
Small dark blue felt banner about 18" long, yellow letters & cord. Used by managers. **CMV $15.**

AVON CHRISTMAS TABLE CLOTH 1977
4x4 ft. blue satin, white letters, used at Christmas dinner 1977 for Avon Reps. in Atlanta branch. **CMV $15.**

PRESIDENT'S AWARD BANNER 1961
Small banner given to top sales team in each division. Each winning division had their name on banner. **CMV $25.**

OUR BANNER YEAR 1966
Used during district sales meetings. **CMV $20.**
There are many different banners of this type.
CMV will range $15 to $20 on most.

COLOR UP AWARDS 1979
Blue & red backdrop used at sales meetings "Color Up America", **CMV $5.**
Color Up Plastic Bag, **CMV .50.**
Color Sale Paper Bat, **CMV .25.**
Color Never Looked So Good On Glasses-set of 6, **CMV $10 set of 6.**
Color Up Scarf, **CMV $2.**
Clutch Bag, **CMV $3.**
Make Up Bag, **CMV $6.**
File Folder, **CMV $6.**
Table Cloth & 4 matching napkins, **CMV $15 set.**
Colors are red, white & blue striped.

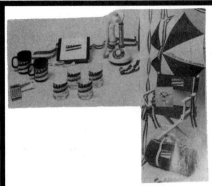

GREAT AMERICAN SELLATHON AWARDS 1981

Given to Avon Reps. for meeting top sales goals in C18-81.
T-Shirt, **CMV $5.**
Calculator, **CMV $20.**
Coffee Mugs, set of 2, **CMV $10.**
Drinking glasses, set of 4, **CMV $12.**
Hot Plate, **CMV $20.**
Telephone, antique, **CMV $75.**
Travel beach bag, **CMV $15.**
Clock, **CMV $35.**
Directors chair, **CMV $35.**
Umbrella, **CMV $25.**
Poncho in bag, **CMV $10.**
All are red, white & blue decoration.

KEY CHAIN "RECORD BREAKER" 1979

Yellow, green, white or pink plastic. Has 4A design & says "I'm an Avon Record Breaker". Given to reps for getting new reps. **CMV $5.**

MATCHES-PRESIDENT'S CELEBRATION 1979

Blue foil top box. **CMV $2**

LUGGAGE TAG 1970'S

White plastic with gold 4A emblem & The Better Way. **CMV $5.**

MOISTURE SECRET MANAGERS GIFT SET 1975

Pink box holds pink plastic jars of creme gel 4oz., enriched freshened 5oz., and night concentrate 3 oz. C-8-75. **CMV $15 set MB.**

WHAT'S COOKING RECIPE BOX 1975

Given to Reps. for drawing their name at sales meetings. Avon on the bottom. **CMV $5.**

NAME TAGS LATE 1970'S

3 different stick on name tags used by Reps. **CMV .50¢ each.**

AVON SMILE SALES PROMOTION ITEMS 1978

Are all red and white.
Silk Scarf, **$6**
Ballons, 2 different, **.25¢ each**
Hat-paper, **$1**
The Smile Lips, red paperlips, **.50¢**
Record, Avon Smile, red small record, **$2.**

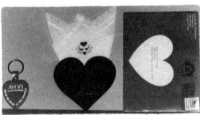

VALENTINE-PRESIDENT'S CLUB 1980

Given to President's Club Reps. Red valentine and white, red and green lace hankercheif, **CMV $5 mint in envelope.**

KEY CHAIN HEART 1978

Red plastic heart given to managers. **CMV $2.**

TEDDY BEAR CANDLE AWARD 1980

Small plastic bear candle holder. Given to Avon Team Leaders. Neck tag says "From Avon with Love". Red candle. **CMV $15.**

DISTINGUISHED MANAGEMENT AWARD LUGGAGE TAG 1966

Plastic name tag for luggage on white strap. **CMV $7.50.**

POCKET ADDRESS MEMORANDUM 1966

2"x3" white w/gold lettering. **CMV $8.**

TRAVEL SURVIVAL KIT 1982

(Top) Given to managers March, 1982. **CMV $7.**

AVON CALLING KEYCHAIN AWARD 1980

(Bottom) Clear lucite with blue letters. Given to Avon Reps. **CMV $5.**

MOISTURE SECRET PRESIDENT'S CLUB GIFT 1975

Sent to President's Club members to introduce Moisture Secret. **CMV $6. MB.**

I KNOW A SECRET PIN 1975

For President's Club members. Pink pin. **CMV $1., $2. on card.**

TEDDY BEAR TEAM LEADER GIFT 1981
White ceramic heart shaped box. Given to Team Leaders for 1981 year end party. Can also be bought in Hallmark stores. Does not say Avon . **CMV $10 MB**

POLLY PROSPECTING BIRD AWARD 1977
Stuffed toy by Possem Trot. Tag has Avon Products on it. Given to Avon managers for recruiting new reps. Came with 2 large cards as shown. **CMV $25 with Avon tag. Add $1 each card. Came in Avon mailer tube & letter. CMV $35 MB all.**

AWARD BANK 1980
Black & gold tin bank. Given to Avon managers in Springdale branch. Special hold label on front says "Fifth National Bank & Trust Co. Springdale Branch. Assets 367 Managers, R. Manning President". Bottom marked "Made in England for Avon". **CMV $30.**

TEDDY AWARD 1979
Black base with plaque. Brown top & bear has red shirt with Avon in white. Given to one Team Leader for recommendation support in each district. **CMV $35.**

TEDDY BEAR COOKIE JAR AWARD 1979
Tan & red ceramic bear cookie jar. Given to Team Leaders at Christmas. **CMV $25.**

SALES AWARD SACHET 1962
Cream sachet in blue glass with blue, gold & white lid. Gold metal stand. **$12 jar only, $15 in box.**

CABLE CAR MUSIC BOX AWARD 1981
Only 100 given to Circle of Excellence Managers at San Francisco C of E meeting. Was not made for Avon. **CMV $35.**

TED. E. BEAR TEAM LEADER GIFT 1978
Tan teddy bear with red shirt was given to all team leaders at end of year party Nov. 1978. Fold out Teddy Bear card was on each table at party. **CMV $4 card, CMV $25 bear mint.**

MONTE CARLO BRASS BOX AWARD 1981
Brass box with burgundy velvet lining. Lid inscribed Casino Monte Carlo. Given to Avon managers eligible to win a free trip to Monte Carlo. **CMV $40.**

TEMPO MANAGERS GIFT 1978
(Left) .33 oz. splash cologne. Given to district sales managers at August Conference 1978. Came with red felt belt. **CMV $15 in bag.**

TEMPO SPRAY ATOMIZER GIFT 1978
(Right) Given to avon Reps. for advanced orders of Tempo fragrance. Silver color container red letters. "Tempo Fall 1978" printed on bottom of case. Came in beige velvet bag, red pull string in special issue box. **CMV $10 MB.**

PRESIDENT'S CAMPAIGN COMPACT AWARD 1966
Case marked sterling silver & back marked "Branch Champions President's Campaign 1966". Came in white & gold Avon box in felt bag. **CMV $35 in silver case MB.**

ANNIVERSARY HONOR AWARD PURSE 1966
Red leatherette purse given to Reps. for high sales. 4A design on snap & Avon Anniversary Honor Award in gold letters on purse. Came in Avon box. **CMV $15 purse only, $20 MB.**

SURPRISE GIFT 1960
Silver and Gold box contained one Deluxe Lipstick. Given as a Christmas Gift to all representatives. **CMV $22.50 MB.**

CIRCLE OF EXCELLENCE TOTE BAG 1976
Tan & brown tote bag with C of E on front. Given to Avon managers on Hawaii C of E front. Given to Avon managers on Hawaii C of E trip. **CMV $16.**

AWARD PURSE 1960'S
Avon marked box holds beige vinyl clutch purse trimmed in brass. Made by St. Thomas. Given to Reps. during President's Campaign. Purse does not say Avon. **CMV $9 mint in Avon box.**

PURSE AWARD 1951
Egg shell off white purse with clear plastic closure. Given to Avon Reps. for best sales. Came in Avon box. Purse not marked Avon. Must be in Avon box. **CMV $27.50 MB.**

ANNIVERSARY CAMPAIGN AWARD PURSE 1961
Same purse with deluxe lipstick & compact as Champagne Mood Set. In Avon award box. **CMV $20 MB.**

TRENDSETTER CARRY ALL BAG 1975
Made of tan burlap & brown leatherette. Given to managers only. **CMV $45.**

CIRCLE OF EXCELLENCE TOTEBAG 1972
About 18" across, black plastic. For trip to Mexico. Aztec calendar design. Given to C of E managers on Mexico trip. **CMV $30.**

FOAMING BATH OIL SAMPLE GIFT 1975
Given to President's Club members. 1/2 oz. bottle, white cap. President's CLub label on bottom. Came in introductory envelope. **CMV $3.50 in envelope.**

PORTFOLIO BAG AWARD 1935
Red two tone brown leather bag with suede inside. CMV with matching key case, billfold, change purse, 2 way mirror. Given to top 77 Reps. in U.S. for top sales during Mr. McConnell birthday celebration. **CMV $75 complete.**

CIRCLE OF EXCELLENCE BAG 1981
White canvas bag, red line around bottom. Given to managers in San Francisco C of E trip. **CMV $15 mint.**
CIRCLE OF EXCELLENCE MAP 1981
Map of San Fraancisco given to C of E managers on trip. **CMV $3.**

GREAT OAK BAG AWARD 1980
Canvas bag. **CMV $10.**

PRESIDENT'S CAMPAIGN AWARD PURSE 1965
Bone beige coin & bill purse with 4A design on flap. Given to each Rep. in 2 top sales teams in each branch for greatest sales increase over year before period. **CMV $15.**

CIRCLE OF EXCELLENCE TOTEBAG 1979
Khaki color bag. Says "Circle of Excellence". Given to top 250 managers. **CMV $15.**

PRESIDENT'S SERVICE AWARD PURSE 1963
Given to all Reps. who called on 35 or more customers during President's Campaign 1963. Egg shell color vinyl coin purse with 4A design on snap. Box says "Avon Fashion First". **CMV $20 MB.**

PURSE - AVON PLANT TOUR GUIDE 1970
Gray plastic purse with heavy silver chain. 4A silver button on purse. Used by tour guides at Avon Plants. **CMV $20.**

TOTE BAG 1977
White canvas with black nylon straps. Came from Avon in New York. Was not issued to Reps. in U.S. **CMV $25.**

SWEET PICKLES BAG GIFT 1978
Green canvas bag given to district managers on introduction of Sweet Pickle products. **CMV $12.50 bag only.**

TASHA STOWAWAY BAG 1980
Purple shoulder bag given to Reps. Avon tag inside. Pink inside bag. **CMV $15.** Managers also got the same bag without the brass snap on the outside. Same color inside as outside. **CMV $20.**

SALES MATES PRIZES PRESIDENT'S CLUB 1978
All are tan & beige in color, covered with "A" design. Umbrella, Beauty Showcase handbag and jewelry demonstrator given to President's Club Reps. for selling $975 worth of Avon in C4-5-6 1978.
Umbrella, **CMV $20.**
Jewelry Demo Case, **CMV $7**
Handbag, **CMV $7.**

TASHA UMBRELLA "I'M NUMBER ONE" 1980
Tan silk umbrella given Reps. on Flight to Fantasy Trip to Monte Carlo. **CMV $75.**

LIBERTY WEEKEND UMBRELLA 1986
Red & white umbrella. Marked Avon Liberty Weekend. Rare N.Y. Liberty Celebration. **CMV $150.**

APRIL SHOWERS UMBRELLA GIFT 1976
(Left) Beige canvas, wood handle. Avon in blue letters. Given as recommendation prize. **CMV $27.50.**

ADVERTISING UMBRELLA 1977
White Avon box holds brown plastic handle umbrella. Has the names of Avon & magazines & TV shows Avon advertises on. Given to district managers. **CMV $30 MB.**

PRESIDENT'S CELEBRATION UMBRELLA 1977
Marked New York. Given to winning teams. **CMV $35.**

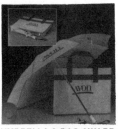

UMBRELLA & BAG AWARD 1980
Tan & brown Avon bag comes with Avon umbrella. Given to Reps. for selling $425 of products in C16-17 1980. **CMV $18.**

DEVOTEE TREASURE BOX AWARD 1986
Brass & glass box mirror bottom. Given to Reps. in black box. **CMV $25 MB.**

AVON TENNIS UMBRELLA 1980
Only 50 silver nylon with fine wood handle umbrellas were given to press & promoters of Avon tennis matches. Comes in matching silver pouch. Rare. **CMV $125.**

AVON TENNIS CLOTHES BAG 1980
Red & white patch on silver & black nylon travel bag. Comes in small carrying pouch. Given to players of Avon tennis matches. **CMV $50. Rare.**

AVON TENNIS WRISTS BANDS 1980
Pair of white cotton wrist bands used by players in Avon tennis matches. **CMV $4.**
AVON TENNIS HAND TOWEL 1980
White cotton, used by Avon tennis players. **CMV $10.**

EMPLOYEE GIFT 1939
Blue box with Avon's Suffern Plant on box. Holds Tulip label and gold cap of Cotillion Toilet water. CPC label & Cotillion powder sachet. Rare. **CMV $125 MB.**

DESK SET ACHIEVEMENT AWARD 1979
Black plastic note pad & pen. Given to district managers for sales achievement. **CMV $15 with pen.**

CHRISTMAS CAROL CANDLE SET 1959
Red velvet box with green lining holds 4 red & white angel candles with blue eyes & blond hair. Candles made by Gurley Novelty Co., label on bottom. Outside of box says "An Avon Christmas Carol". Given to Avon managers at Christmas 1959. **CMV $130 MB.**

UMBRELLA LIPSTICK AWARD 1981
White nylon, black & red trim, red plastic handle. Given to Team Leaders. **CMV $25.**

58th ANNIVERSARY GIFT BOX 1944
Holds heart shaped sachet pillow. Given to all Reps. on Avon's 58th anniversary. **CMV $100 MB.**

ANNIVERSARY ALBUM AWARDS SET 1942
Book type box opens to show 2 satin pillowettes with 56th Anniversary on back of each. One is blue & one pink. Given during Anniversary campaign. **CMV $125.**

56th ANNIVERSARY AWARD 1942
Satin Sachet pillows given to each Rep. who worked her territory for 56 hours during the Anniversary Campaign. Came 2 to a box, in blue & pink. **CMV $30 mint.**

BETSY ROSS RED GIFT SET 1941
Set given to employees of Avon's Suffern Plant as Anniversary campaign gift. Rare. Came with handwritten gift card. **CMV $100 MB.**

DOOR BELL - DOOR KNOCKER AWARDS 1979
Redwood box with brass Avon Calling door knocker on front, door bell on back side. Given to 5 managers in each division. **CMV $75.**

MANAGER DESK SET AWARD 1972
Has 4A emblem, marble base, 14K gold plated pen. Set made by Cross. **CMV $60, $75 MB.**

DESK SET PRIZE 1973
Brown plastic came with paper & pen. Given to Reps. for meeting sales goals. **CMV $10.**

AVON CALLING DOOR BELL 1950's
(Left) Used at Avon meetings. Has button on back to ring door bell. **CMV $85 mint.**
PERFUME CREME ROLLETTE CHRISTMAS GIFT 1962
(Right) .33 oz. gold cap, 4A embossed bottle & box. Given to Reps. at Christmas 1962. Came in Here's My Heart, Persian Wood, To A Wild Rose, Topaze, Somewhere, Cotillion. **CMV $12 in box shown.**

INKWELL & PEN SET AWARD 1977
Blue & gold display box holds wood base with old glass ink well & 3 feather quill pens & plastic bottle of ink. Avon card about pen set. Avon brass plaque on base. Given for recruiting new Reps. **CMV $45 MB.**

88th ANNIVERSARY DESK SET 1974
White marble base. Black pen. Turquoise & silver 4A says "Avon 88th Anniversary". Given to Reps. for selling $125 worth of Avon. **CMV $10, $15 MB.**

REPRESENTATIVE GIFT CIGARETTE CASE 1961
Siver colored metal case. 4A design & Christmas 1961 on lid. **CMV $47.50.** Also given to managers in gold tone case. **CMV $70.**

DESK VALET - CPC AWARD 1922
Solid bronze. Marked CPC 1922. Awarded to CPC Reps. **CMV $100.**

TOCCARA PINS 1981
3 different pins. Same design on face, edges are different. **CMV $10 each.**

TOCCARA NECKLACE AWARD 1981
Toccara design on one side & Avon Toccara 1981 K.C. on back. Sterling Silver pendant & chain in Tiffany bag & box. Given to Division Managers. **CMV $100 MB.**

STEAK KNIFE & CARVING SET 1972
C-12, 1972. In Avon box. **CMV $20 each set MB with sleeve.**

SPOON - PRESIDENT'S CLUB AWARD 1979
(Left) Silver plated serving spoon marked "Avon President's Club 1979". Came in Avon box. **CMV $10 MB.**

CAKE SERVER AWARD 1978
(Right) Silver plated serving spatula. "Avon 92nd Anniversary - President's Club 1978" on spoon. Given to all President's Club members. Special box & card. **CMV $10 MB.**

WINNING TEAM DESK SET AWARD 1976
Given for best sales team in district in 1976. White marble base, silver color pen. **CMV $8.**

IMARI 1ST EDITION COLOGNE AWARD 1985
1.2 oz. spray cologne marked First Edition 1985 on bottle. Given only to Reps. **CMV $15.**

LETTER OPENER MANAGER AWARD 1975
Red & black box holds wood handle letter opener. Brass Avon lady insignia & K.C. No. 1, 1975 on hand. **CMV $20 MB.**

PRESIDENTS CLUB FRUIT JARS AWARD 1988
Set of 3 glass jars marked Avon Presidents Club on side. **CMV $20.00 Set**

50th ANNIVERSARY SPOON - 1936
Gold spoon engraved "Compliments Mr. & Mrs. D. H. McConnell - Anniversary 50". The gold on these spoons does not stay very well so many are found silver. **Spoon in box gold CMV $100 mint., Silver spoon only CMV $50., Spoon with gold CMV $75. mint.**

CIRCLE OF EXCELLENCE LETTER OPENER 1976
Given in Indiana only to C of E Reps. Only 25 were given. Brass plaque & door knocker pin is embedded in black plastic handle. **CMV $40.**

DOLLAR INCREASE CLOCK AWARD 1978
Dark amber lucite clock stand with pen set & 4A. **CMV $20.00**

CPC SPOON "STERLING SILVER" 1915

Sold as souvenir at the CPC exhibit at the Panama-Pacific International Exposition. Front reads "Palace of Liberal Arts - Panama-Pacific Exposition Tower of Jewels". Back of spoon reads "CPC 1915 Court of Four Seasons". **CMV $100 with card shown, $75 spoon only.** Was also given to Reps. for selling 12 CPC talcum powders, 1 free for each 12 talcs.

WINDBREAKER 1980

Blue jacket, red & white trim. Sold to Avon employees in Springdale branch for $15. Modeled by Dwight Young. **CMV $15.**

CANDID BLAZER & TIE 1977

Off white blazer with CA on left pocket. Given to division managers only. Came in both male & female sizes. Tie is Candid color with CA on it. Very few of these blazers around. Modeled by Dwight Young. **Blazer CMV $75., Tie CMV $10.**

AVON AWARD SPOONS 1969

6 silver plated demitasse spoons. Each engraved with a design signifying a different fragrance: Occur, Rapture, Unforgettable, Regence, Brocade & Charisma. Each spoon was given in this order for progressively higher sales. A seventh spoon was given to each Rep. in the winning district of each branch. It was engraved "1886-1969" and had a picture of the 1886 Sales Lady. **CMV $45 set MB with sleeve or $5 each spoon. 7th spoon $12.50 in silver envelope.**

AVON RUNNING RAIN COAT 1981

Shown front & back side. Given to people helping in Avon Running Tournament. Red plastic. Modeled by Vera Young. **CMV $10.**

BLAZER JACKET 1977

Blue blazer with 4A design buttons. Inside label says "Made exclusively for the Avon Representative by Family Fashions". Sold to Avon Reps. Red Avon sewn on patch for pocket. **CMV $35.**

SILVERWARE AWARD 1938

Made only for Avon. Each piece marked on back Simeon L. & George H. Rogers Co. Ltd. X-tra. Given for meeting sale goal during Avon's 50th Anniversary. 55 piece set. **CMV set in box. $125 mint.**

CPC SILVERWARE 1920-30's

Used in CPC fatories for employee eating areas. CPC stamped on back of knife, fork & spoons. **CMV $5 each piece.**

AVON REP. BIRTHDAY GIFT 1982

Box says "A birthday gift for you". Satin & lace heart pincushion. Comes with Avon card. Given to Reps. on their birthday. **CMV $5.**

MANAGERS CHRISTMAS GIFT 1980
Red & white scarf and mittens given at Christmas time. **CMV $30 set.**

TOCCARA AWARDS 1981
(Sweater) Dark navy blue with Avon tag. Given for 1st level sales achievement. **CMV $10.**
(Caftan) Lavender & white with Avon Toccara label. Given to 2nd level sales achievement. Came in shiny silver plastic Toccara bag. **CMV $25 in bag.**

AVON SMILE HAT 1978
White hat given to Avon collectors at Houston, Texas, 1978 National Association of Avon Club Convention by Avon Products. Modeled by the late Charlie Crawford. **CMV $15.**

CIRCLE OF EXCELLENCE TOWEL 1979
Given to top 250 managers. **CMV $20.**

I'M GOING TO MONTE CARLO MAGNET 1981
(Center) Given to managers. White, red & gold. **CMV $4.**
VALENTINE SUCKER 1981
(Left) Red heart shaped sucker with red tag. Given to Avon managers. **CMV $10.**
NUMBER ONE SCARF AWARD
(Right) Given to team leaders. **CMV $4.**

CIRCLE OF EXCELLENCE AWARDS 1979
Each item given to managers on C of E trip to Paris 1979.
TRAVEL ALARM CLOCK
(Lower right) Plaque on top says "Circle of Excellence 1979". **CMV $25.**
TOTE BAG
(Upper right) Dark navy blue. Circle of Excellence on front. **CMV $15.**
CIRCLE OF EXCELLENCE YEAR BOOK
(Center) Blue & gold cover shows all C of E winners. **CMV $10.**
FRAGRANCE & FASHION BINDER
White plastic. **CMV $25 with contents.**

ODYSSEY AWARDS 1980
(Bathrobe) Pink bathrobe given to Reps. for meeting 2nd level sales goals. **CMV $25 in Avon bag.**
(Nightgown) Pink nightgown matches bathrobe. Given to Reps. for meeting 1st level sales goals. **CMV $15 MB.**

TOCCARA PILLOW AWARD 1981
Dark blue satin pillow with Avon card. Given to managers at August Conference. **CMV $15 with Avon card.**

AVON REP. CHRISTMAS GIFT 1981
Red box says "Happy Holidays Avon 1981". Tapestry design address book. Managers book says "District Manager" on front. **CMV $15 MB.** Reps. same except plain on front. **CMV $10 MB.**
HOSTESS APRON
Cotton tapestry design apron given to team leaders who met requirements. **CMV $15.**

TOWEL RACK PRIZE AND MILK GLASS SOAP DISH 1972
An exclusive Avon prize. **CMV rack, $5. Soap dish $10.** White glass dish, 2 white hand towels, gold initials, black & brass stand.

AWARDS & REPRESENTATIVES GIFTS

AVONS BEST BANNER 1982
(Top) Red & white banner. **CMV $5.**
AVONS BEST SCARF 1982
(Bottom) From Morton Grove branch. Red & white scarf given to managers at Atlanta Conference. **CMV $15.**

CIRCLE OF EXCELLENCE BEACH TOWEL 1976
White & brown towel given to managers on C of E Hawaii trip. **CMV $20 mint.**

T-SHIRT - AVON RUNNING 1979
Red t-shirt given to each runner in Avon marathon race. **CMV $10.**

PRESIDENTS CAMPAIGN GLACE AWARD 1967
Managers is in script writing with white lined box. **CMV $22.50 MB. $18.50 compact only.**
Representatives is in block writing on Presidents Campaign with blue felt lined box. **CMV $10. $12 MB.** Both came in Hawaiian White Ginger box.

FOUNDERS CAMPAIGN ACHIEVEMENT AWARD SCARF 1941
Blue & white folder holds blue border, white pink & green silk scarf. Shows 1st CPC factory & 1st Avon lady with "The doorway to loveliness" marked under her. Given to reps in 1941. Very rare. **CMV $75 in folder mint, $50 scarf only mint.**

SYMPHONY SCARF 1952
Blue background with pink rose & parts of letters in French. Pure silk. Purchased from store in New York & awarded for selling 36 products in the Prelude to Spring campaign. **CMV $30 mint.**

SILK SCARF AWARD 1970
Beige & brown silk scarf. 4A design. Given to Avon reps. **CMV $20.**

AVON CURTAINS 1960's
Used to decorate in offices & Avon plant. **CMV $35.**

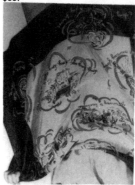

64TH ANNIVERSARY SCARF 1950
Silk scarf was made only for Avon. Given to representatives for selling 64 pieces of Avon in campaign 9, 1950. Silk scarf has blue border, white center with sketches in turquoise & rose. Some words on scarf say "Long, long ago"; "A thing of beauty is a joy forever"; "The doorway to loveliness". **CMV $50.**

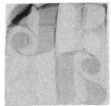

AVON SCARF 1972
All silk pink, orange & white scarf with 4 big "A" on it. Avon in corner. Made in Italy. Came in silver box. **CMV $12. mint.**

CANDID SCARF GIFT 1976
Silk scarf designed by S.M. Kent in Candid folder. Given to Avon President's Club members. **CMV $7.**

TASHA AWARDS 1980
Monte Carlo scarf, **CMV $20.**
Tasha picture of the late Princess Grace of Monte Carlo with Tasha card. **CMV $20.**
Tasha matches - box & book matches, **CMV $1 each.**
Items were won by reps on Avon trip to Monte Carlo.

4A QUILT 1971
Reversible, ruffled edged, cotton filled comforter in gold, avocado or blue. Given for having a person recommended a a representative appointed. **CMV $150 mint.**
4A QUILT 1969
Pink quilt with white 4A design. **CMV $150 mint.**

4A WALL PLAQUE 1960's
Used at sales meetings. Large size. **CMV $25.**

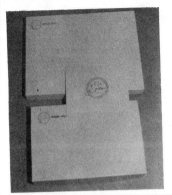

CIRCLE OF EXCELLENCE STATIONERY ROME 1983
2 boxes given to all managers on trip to Rome in 1983. **CMV $25 MB set.**

GREAT AMERICAN SELLATHON PRIZES 1981
Name tag, **CMV $1.**
Luggage tag, **CMV $2.**
Menu Presidents Celebration, **CMV $2.**
Portfolio, **CMV $2.**

ORDER BOOK & CALCULATOR 1983
Red Avon box has red Avon order book cover with order book, calculator & calendar. 5 reps in each district won them. **CMV $17.50 MB.**

AVON APRON 1948
Aqua in color with white center. Avon in center & pictures of Avon products of 1948. Given to Managers only for sales demo. **CMV $50 mint.**

WALL PLAQUE 1960's
Used at sales meetings. Blue & gold cardboard. **CMV $25.**

TOTE BAG (WHO COULD SELL AVON) 1983
Beige canvas hand bag, red letters. Given to reps. **CMV $5.**

JAM GIFT SET AWARD 1980

Set of 16 small jars of jam with front label "Especially for You from Avon". Given to managers. Was not made only for Avon. **CMV $10.**

AFTER CONFERENCE MINTS 1979

Pink box of fifty 1979 Susan B. Anthony dollar coins with card for Avon managers for Outstanding Recuiting. **CMV $100 MB with all 1979 coins mint.**

VALENTINE GIFT TO REPRESENTATIVES 1976

Whitman Sampler went to all reps. with Avon card. **CMV $3 with card only.**

VALENTINE CANDY 1978

Red and gold heart box. Holds 4 1/2 oz. of chocolates by Bartons. Back of box says "This candy heart selected by Avon and packaged especially for you. Given to Avon reps. **CMV $5 box only., $10 MB full.**

GENERAL MANAGERS HONOR AWARD 1960

(Top) Order book cover in blue. **CMV $8 mint**

HONOR AWARD ORDER BOOK COVER 1959

(Bottom) Red plastic with gold trim, also had gold pen. **CMV $10.**

ORDER BOOK COVERS 1980-81

Blue plastic. Avon pen inside. Given to all new Avon reps. Gold Avon stamped on face. **CMV $2.** Also came wtih Avon stamped upside down. **CMV $5.**

TREND SETTERS ORDER BOOK AWARD 1976

(Left) Yellow plastic with 4A design and Avon Trend Setters on front. Given to Avon Trend Setters Reps. **CMV $5.**

TEAM LEADER MIRROR GIFT 1977

(Right) Mirror in red plastic, holder with white star and letters. Given to Avon Team Leaders at Avon luncheon, Dec. 1977. **CMV $4.**

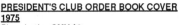

PRESIDENT'S CLUB ORDER BOOK COVER 1975

Blue plastic. **CMV $3.**

ACHIEVEMENT AWARD ORDER BOOK COVER 1960'S

(Left) Light blue cover. **CMV $7.**

ORDER BOOK -CANADA 1977

(Right) Dark blue plastic. Used by reps in Canda. Came with blue and gold pen and order book. **CMV $5.**

ORDER BOOK COVER 1973

Blue and green design matches delivery bag. Has turqoise and gold pen. Earned for prize points. **CMV $5.**

75 YEAR HONOR AWARD ORDER BOOK 1961

Red with gold letters. **CMV $8 mint.**

PRESIDENT'S CLUB ORDER BOOK COVER 1960

CMV $7.

PRESIDENTS HONOR AWARD ORDER BOOK COVER 1977

Blue plastic with gold trim. **CMV $8.**

REGENCE ORDER BOOK HONOR AWARD 1966

Green plastic with gold trim to match Regence packaging. **CMV $3.**

ALBEE STATIONERY NOTES 1980
Box of 1st Avon lady notes with outer sleeve given to President's Club Reps. **CMV $5 MB.**

PORTFOLIO 1974
Red plastic, 4A design for Avon Reps. **CMV $3.**

PRESIDENTIAL WINNERS AWARD 1957
Blue felt booklet given to winning district Avon representatives upon touring district Avon plant. **CMV $30.**

DISTRICT MANAGERS ORGANIZATION GUIDE 1970'S
Dark blue & gold loose leaf binder, contains guide material. **CMV $10.**

LADY DESK FOLIO 1971
Pink cover holds calendar to be used as a plan guide for sending orders and making appointments. Given for sending a $75 or larger order in. C1-71 **CMV $7.50.**

MANAGER-REPRESENTATIVE INTRODUCTION BOOK 1952
Turqoise & silver booklet. Used by managers to train new Avon Reps. **CMV $10.**

CHRISTMAS GIFT FOR AVON REPS. 1980
Ceramic base & green note pad holder signed by William Chaney, Avon President. Given to all Avon Sales Reps. at Christmas 1980. **CMV $10 MB.**

CELEBRITY AUTOGRAPH BOOK 1965
Not marked Avon. Only in box. **CMV $5., $8.50 MB.**

CIRCLE OF EXCELLENCE PASSPORT HOLDERS 1969-80
Given each year. Each marked Circle of Excellence. Given to top managers only for annual C of E trip. Different color each year. **CMV $5 each.**
CIRCLE OF EXCELLENCE PROGRAM
Given to C of E managers at annual C of E celebraion. **CMV $5 each year.**

SUEDE ORDER BOOK COVER AWARD 1977
Brown plastic suede order book cover holds 4 Avon order books. Given to Avon Reps. for reaching sales goals. 1886 Avon lady embossed on front. Was not awarded in all branches. **CMV $10.**

MANAGERS SALES MEETING NOTE BOOK 1961
Campaign 15,16,17,18 sales meeting plans. Inside front cover says "# so & so of a limited edition for the Management Staff Only". Cover is red satin 12"x20", comes in white box. For you from Avon on cover. **CMV $75 mint.**

NOTE PAD TRENDSETTERS 1976
Clear plastic, Avon on top holder. Trendsetter note pads. Given to managers only. **CMV $20.**

DIAMOND DECADE HONOR ROLL AWARD 1960-70
Silver with blue 4A booklet. Given to managers for outstanding service. **CMV $12.**

CLIP BOARD MANAGERS GIFT 1979
Front says "Thank you for making us number one". Avon on bottom. Given to managers only. Made of Lucite. **CMV $10.**

AVON COSMETICS MARKETING HIGH-LIGHT BINDER BOOKLET 1970'S
Used by managers. **CMV $5.**

TEAM LEADER CARDS 1978
4 different cards given to team leaders, with bears on them. **CMV $1 each.**

AUGUST CONFERNCE PICTURE HOLDER 1978
Tan cover. Given to managers at August conference. **CMV $15.**

NICE KRISPIES BOX 1980
Small size cereal box given to team leaders. **CMV $6.**

PARIS PICTURE GIFT 1978
French print scene by Bernard Picture Co. given to each manager with French printed Avon circle of excellence card & ribbon. **CMV $7.50. Must have Avon card as shown.**

DATE BOOK 1979
Rust color date book given out by Avon managers. Inside cover says "A gift from your Avon manager". **CMV $2.**
PENCILS-AVON
1979 Blue marking pen-fine point. **CMV $1.**
1979 Color Up America-red pencil. **CMV $1.**

CIRCLE OF EXCELLENCE MATCHES 1977-79
Given to managrs on trip to Paris 1979. White, gold letters. Matches are gold heads. **CMV $5. Also given in 1977.**
GO AHEAD & DREAM MATCHES 1979
White, red letters. Given to managers at September conference. **CMV $2 mint.**

CHECK COVERS 1973
Red & green plastic check book covers given to Reps. **CMV $3 each.**

PORTFOLIO & CALCULATOR 1984
Red canvas zipper portfolio with small NSC calculator & 1984 calendar & note pad & Avon red pen inside. Given to Reps. **CMV $30.** Calculator also given by itself in red canvas folder. **CMV $15.**

CARD CASES AWARDS 1970'S
President's Club. Pink & turqoise; vinyl, **CMV $2.50.** Top one Foreign, **CMV $5.**

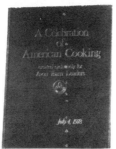

COOK BOOK FOR TEAM LEADERS 1978
Red cover 96 page book given to Team Leaders July 1978. **CMV $10 mint.**

AVONOPOLY 1978
Game used by managers at Avon Rep. sales meeting C12-78. Also came with Avon play money of 25 & 50 green notes. **CMV set $12.**

BROCADE HONOR AWARD ORDER BOOK COVER 1967
Given to Reps. for calling on customers during introduction of Brocade. Came with Avon pen also. **CMV $5., With pen $8.**

TASHA FLIGHT TO FANTASY VASE 1980
White porcelain vase given to Reps. on Monte Carlo trip. **CMV $40.**
TASHA PASSPORT HOLDER 1980
Given to Reps. on Monte Carlo trip, held luggage tag & misc. Tasha paper items, program, etc. **CMV $20 for all.**

PRESIDENTS CELEBRATION ORDER BOOK COVER 1977
Red plastic. **CMV $3.**
PERSONAL POCKET DIARY 1976
Blue plastic cover with Avon pocket diary and calendar inside. **CMV $3.**

TEDDY BEAR AWARD PLAQUE 1980
Certificate in black frame. Given for high sales. **CMV $10.**
TEDDY BEAR RECRUITING AWARD PLAQUE 1980
Ceritficate in black frame. Given for recommendation. **CMV $10.**

PRESIDENT'S CLUB THANK YOU NOTES 1979
White box with outer sleeve. Both has "President's Club, Avon's Very Best" on lid. Holds 25 thank you notes. Given to President's Club Reps. only. **CMV $5 MB complete set.**

PICTURE ALBUM AWARD 1966
White Avon box holds large and small picture album and picture frame in brown and gold. Cover says "For you, from Avon". **CMV $45 MB.**

AVON QUEEN CERTIFICATE 1964-65
78th & 79th Anniversary Award Certificates. One red and others blue border. Given to top selling Reps. only. **CMV $10 each.**

MANAGERS INTRODUCTION BOOK 1945
Blue cover, 28 page book, used by Avon Managers to sign up new Avon Reps. 11" x 14" size. Came with clear plastic cover. **CMV $35 mint.**

AVON CHRISTMAS CARD 1976
Green & gold Christmas card. Inside says "From your Avon Representative". Box of 75 cards given to Avon Reps. for recommendation of new Avon lady. **CMV $20 box of 75 mint, .25¢ each card mint.**

PLACE MAT AWARD 1966
Plastic place mat showing Avon Daily Need Products. Given to Reps. for meeting sales. **CMV $5.**

PASADENA BRANCH DEDICATION BOOKLET 1947
Gold spiral bound booklet given at opening of Pasadena Branch, Sept. 22-27, 1947. Front says "Avon Serves the Golden West". **CMV $25.**

BEAUTY & FRAGRANCE CALENDAR 1978
Punch out calendar given to special good customers in C24-77 by Avon Reps. Made only for Avon. **CMV $5.** Only given in certain states for test marketing.

TENNIS OFFICIAL BUTTON - 1977
Red futures circuit Avon official button. **CMV $5.**
AVON FUTURES SPONSOR 1980 BUTTON
White - red letters. **CMV $5.**
ROSE PARADE FLOAT DECORATOR BUTTONS
1982 white, 1984 gold. **CMV $10.**
PRESIDENT'S DAY CORPORATE MEDALLION 1983
3" brass medallion with red, white & blue ribbon. **CMV $20.**

BUTTONS
GOING FOR THE GOLD BUTTON 1984
TENNIS CHAMPION SPONSOR 1982
GOOD BYE CHARLIE 1984
100 YEARS BEAUTIFUL AVON
CMV $2. each button.

AVON 100 CUSTOMER SERVICE PIN 1986
Gold & black pin.
AVON 100 YEARS OF BEAUTY PIN 1986
White & black.
WHO'S THE BOSS PIN 1985
Red & white.
WHO COULD SELL AVON PIN 1985
Tan & black.
CMV $2. each.

MUSIC BOX TEAM AWARD 1978
Red painted wood music box made in Japan only for Avon. Brass plate on lid says "You Made Avon Smile". Given to winning team for selling most lipsticks. **CMV $20.**

BUTTONS 1983-85
Misc. buttons given to Avon Reps.
CMV $1., $2. each.

BUTTONS 1983-85
Misc. buttons given to Avon Reps.
CMV $1., $2. each.

BUTTONS 1981-85
Misc buttons given to Avon Reps. **CMV $1., $2. each.**

AVON AWARDS MISC. - 1985-86
ROSE PARADE BUTTON
THE SMILE STARTS HERE BUTTON
LOOK HOW GOOD YOU LOOK KEY CHAIN
AVON ICE SCRAPER
WE THINK YOU'RE BEAUTIFUL MIRROR.
CMV $2. each.

BOWLING AVON PATCHES 1981-82
Cloth patches from Baltimore & St. Louis Avon Bowling Tournaments. **CMV $20. ea.**
AVON TENNIS CHAMPIONSHIPS BADGES 1981
1 red & 1 yellow badge. **CMV $20. ea.**
AVON DOUBLE PEN AWARD
White & black & white & blue double pen.
CMV $10.

CUSTOMERS SERVICE FILE 1969
Turquoise paper box holds file envelopes for Avon lady sales. **CMV $5.**

FILE BOX 1961
(Left) Turquoise cardboard file box with 4A design on lid. **CMV $6 mint.**
DESIGNERS DREAM SWEEPSTAKES AWARD 1971
(Right) C7-1971. White lace handkerchief with note from Avon for sales accomplishments.
CMV $6.50 mint.

JUNE 15 BUTTON PIN 1971
Bright green to remind customers June 15 was Father's Day. **CMV $3.**
HELLO 1970 BUTTON PIN 1970
Black background with red, yellow & blue letters & numbers. Given to all representatives to tell the world she welcomes successful seventies. **CMV $3.**

EARLY TEAM LEADER RIBBON BADGE 1970's
Yellow badge and ribbon used by Team Leaders at sales meetings. **CMV $5.**
I GOT IT PIN 1978
Gray and white pin given to Reps. at Avon sales meetings. Measures 2 1/4". **CMV $1.**

ZANY BUTTON 1979
Given to Avon Reps. on introduction of Zany Products. **CMV $1.**
TEAM LEADER BUTTON 1979
Given to Avon Reps. **CMV $1.**

I'M THE HEART PIN 1974
Given to Reps. as being the heart of Avon.
CMV $2.
HI, I'M BUTTON 1981
Says "I'm going to make you feel beautiful".
CMV $2.

AWARDS & REPRESENTATIVES GIFTS

BUTTON - PINS
1978 Top Horizon 50 pin. **CMV $2.**
1976 Say Yes Yes To No No's. **CMV $1.**
1978 The Smile Starts Here. **CMV $1.**

POSTCARD GREATEST HOMECOMING 1978
CMV .50¢.
GREATEST HOMECOMING PIN 1978
CMV $1. Both are yellow & blue. Used for President's Celebration.

AVON 91st BUTTON & RIBBON 1977
(left) Red and white button. **CMV $1. button,
CMV $2. button & ribbon.**
"ASK ME ABOUT THE LOVE OF MY LIFE" BUTTON 1979
(left) White and red button. **CMV $1.**
LUGGAGE TAG 1977
(right) Round white plastic, back side says "The Magic of Avon". **CMV $2.**

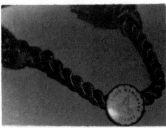

CONFERENCE PIN MANAGERS 1946-47
On gold braided rope. **CMV $50 mint.**

4A NAME PIN 1960
Used by Avon Reps. at meetings. 2 1/2" in diameter. **CMV $3.**
COLOR WORKS MAKEUP BUTTONS 1977
Given to Reps. for sales meeting attendance. **CMV $1.**

TEAM LEADER BOOK MARK 1974
Gold & red Book Mark. For Avon Reps. use. **CMV $8.**

ROYAL RIBBON AWARDS 1980
Given to Reps. for sales achievements. Yellow or red ribbon. **CMV $2.** White & blue given with certificate. **CMV $5 each with certificate.** Some dated 1980 and some not.

AVON CARDS AWARD 1980
(right) Silver faced playing cards say 1980 - Avon New York - Las Vegas. Given to Division Managers at Las Vegas conference for Pasadena Branch **CMV $15 MB.**
FRISBEE - AVON 1980
(left) White plastic, blue and red letters. **CMV $10.**

FACE POWDER GOLD KEY 1936
9 1/2" long key is gold on one side with large tulip A & Avon. Back side holds silver face powder sample. CMV label. Given to Reps. only. **CMV $25 mint as shown.**

AVON COASTERS 1981
Plastic sheet of 8 white plastic coasters. Had to be cut out. Given to managers. **CMV $5 for sheet of 8.**

FRISBEES - GIFT TO REPS. 1976
White plastic with red letters. **CMV $6.** White with red & green letters. **CMV $8.**

MANAGERS TOOTHBRUSH 1976
Given to managers. Came in different colors. "Avon" on one side; "Prospecting is a habit, too" on other side. **CMV $5.**

CAMEO VANITY SET PRIZE 1965
Made by Syroco only for Avon. Set consists of Cameo brush, 2 combs, vanity mirror, and hand mirror. Given to Reps. for selling 40 cameo lipsticks or compacts for brush and comb. **CMV $7. 76 total for vanity mirror. CMV $13. 100 for hand mirror.**

CHARGE CARD MACHINE 1977
Red plastic, marked Avon. Used by Reps. to take charge cards for Avon Sales. Used only for a short period. **CMV $10.**

McCONNELL FAMILY REUNION COASTERS 1980
Package of 4 white Fiesta Coasters. Center says "James McConnell Family Reunion 1980". Were given at 1st family reunion of David McConnell ancestors since 1948. Very rare. **No price established.**

WHAT'S COOKING AVON GIFT 1974
5 yellow plastic scoop, strainer, funnel, egg separator, measurer. Given to Reps. for sales meeting attendance. Made by Geni, a division of Avon. **CMV $2 each.**

ORDER BOOK COVER & PEN 1976-77
Given to only new Avon Reps. Blue plastic cover and blue and gold pen. **CMV $3.**

WACKY MONEY BAG 1980
Silver tone bag with red tie string & red $ design. Used at sales meetings. Does not say Avon. **CMV $15.**

LIVE-LAUGH-LOVE TEMPO AWARDS 1979
Given to Reps. on cruise to Caribbean. Red T-Shirt-**CMV $15**
(Left) Picture Cube 1978-Says"New York-Bermuda-Circle of Excellence" **CMV $15.**
(Right) Bahama Stick Pin-In brown felt bag given to Reps. on cruise. Does not say Avon. **CMV $2.**
(Center) Cruise Program -Feb.2-5, 1979. **CMV $2.**

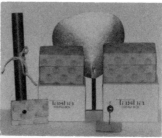

TASHA AWARDS 1979
All are pink and purple. (center) Wishing box given to Reps. **CMV $5 MB.**
(right) Dream box with Tasha pin & tray inside given to Managers. **CMV $10 MB.**
(left) Key Chain. **CMV $2.**
(back right) Fan. **CMV $1.**
(back left) Scroll Dream Test. **CMV $1.** All were given to Reps, except Dream box.

CPC SALES MANAGERS GIFT 1909 -1912
4" x 4" size, pressed crystal glass jar with Rogers Silver Plate lid. Given to each Rep. selling $50 in sales in December 1909 & 1912. The silver lid has an embossed floral design. **CMV $200 mint.**

71ST ANNIVERSARY CAKE 1957
A real cake with 71 on top with Avon card given to managers. Made by Schraffts. **CMV $50.**

AVON DUNCE CAPS 1964-65
Came in several different colors of plastic. Used at sales meetings. 4A design on top and bottom. **CMV $10 each.**

RECORD-HAPPY BIRTHDAY 1980
It's a most unusual day on cover. Given to President's Club Reps. on their birthday. **CMV $5 mint.**

CASTINET AWARD 1975
Given to Circle of Excellence managers only on trip to Spain. Comes with Circle of Excellence orange award card as shown. **CMV $25 MB with card.**

FLIGHT TO FANTASY RECORD 1979
(left) Given to Reps. in C20-79 to introduce Fantasy fragrance. **CMV $3 record and cover mint.**

BON APPETIT COOK BOOK 1979
(right) Given to managers on Circle of Excellence trip to Paris. Avon on front, **CMV $5.**

TEAM LEADER & MANAGERS CHRISTMAS GIFT 1981
Wood case jewelry box with mirror inside says "Avon Team Leader 1981". **CMV $65.**
Same thing given to Avon managers only says "Managers 1981". **CMV $85.**

DOOR KNOCKER RING DISPLAY BOX AWARD 1979
Black ring box with gold tone door knocker on cover. Given to Avon managers. **CMV $30 mint.**

TRAINING RECORDS-FILM STRIPS
Used by managers to show new products at sales meetings. Box came with record and 1 film strip for each record. Have been used for many years by Avon. Many different varieties. **Record only CMV $2., $5 set MB.**

AVON RECORDS 1970's
Christmas Records, given to Reps. at Christmas. **CMV $3.**
Campaign 21, 1974 Sales Meeting record. **CMV $3.**

AVON CHRISTMAS RECORD 1970
33 1/3 RPM record in blue holder with letter from Avon President Fred Fusse. **CMV $5.**

RECOMMENDATION PRIZE 1976
Blue plastic case holds 2 order books and an Avon book calculator made by Arizona. Warranty card says "Made for Avon". Given to Reps. for getting 2 new Avon Reps. **CMV $25 mint in working order.**

ROOSTER AWARD 1968
Rooster shape leather covered green glass bottom on wood base. Brass plaque says "Rooster Highest Percent Increase, 4A design & all 7 Avon branches". Given to disrict supervisor. **CMV $45.**

CURRIER & IVES COASTERS 1977
Pack of 6 given to Team Leaders at Christmas. Also given to Reps. for recommendation prize. Marked Avon. **CMV $5 pack of 6.**

ROSE PARADE JACKETS AWARD 1981-83
Avon Products issued 100 Rose Parade jackets in red to people working with Avon float in '81-'83 parade, rare. Same inscription on front. **CMV $100 each.**

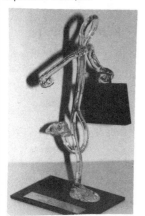

GATEWAY SPRING COMPETITION AWARD 1977
Lucite man on plastic base & nameplate. Given to managers in Morton Grove branch. **CMV $35.**

PARKER PEN AWARD SET 1982
2 gold tone Parker pens. Says Avon on side. Given to managers. **CMV $35 MB.**

MUSK FOR MEN TRAVEL KIT AWARD 1983
Travel kit bag & 2.8 oz. Musk Cologne for men. Comes with Avon letter to reps for meeting sales goals. Bag does not say Avon. **CMV $15 MB with letter.**

TEAM CAPTAIN AWARD 1972
Awarded to all Team Captains in each district. Thick plastic over lettering with gold frame. **CMV $12.**

RAIN GEAR COLLECTION AWARDS 1983
Made only for Avon & given to Avon reps for meeting sales goals in 3 levels.
LEVEL 2 WEEKENDER BAG & ACCESSORY BAG
Tan color cotton. Both have Avon Rain Gear tags. **CMV $15 set.**
LEVEL 3 RAIN GEAR RAINCOAT & UMBRELLA
Tan matching coat & umbrella. Avon tags. Raincoat, **CMV $25.** Umbrealla, **CMV $25.**

PASADENA SUNGLASSES 1982
Blue sunglasses says "Pasadena '82". Made in the shade. **CMV $5.**
C OF E SALES GROWING BUTTON 1983
Yellow button. **CMV $2.**
PASADENA NO. 1 BUTTON 1982
White button with red , white & blue ribbon. **CMV $2.**

AWARDS & REPRESENTATIVES GIFTS

FOOT HILL DIVISION HIGHEST DOLLAR SALES INCREASE AWARD PLAQUE 1982
Wood base plaque given to managers only. **CMV $40.**

JEWELRY BOX AWARD 1965
White box has 2 lids, blue inside, 4A design & says "Bleding Corticelli" inside lid. Given to managers. **CMV $15 box only mint.**

PRESIDENTS HONOR SOCIETY AWARD 1983
Plaque in gold tone glass picture frame. Given to reps for top sales. **CMV $10.**

FEEL LIKE A STAR BUTTON 1981
3" blue & white button. **CMV $2.**

JEWELRY BOX PRESIDENTS SALES COMPETITION AWARD 1983
Black lacquer music box made only for Avon. Bottom says "President Sales Competition 1983". 8"x 4 3/4" size. Given for sales goals. Comes with Avon card. **CMV $25.**

DIRECTOR'S CHAIR AWARD 1980
White folding chair with green seat & back. Back says "You never looked so good". Given to reps for signing up new Avon reps. **CMV $30.**

BEAR PRIDE OF NEWARK AWARD 1982
Small 6" bear hobo name tag with gold tone chain & pendant around neck. Says "Thanks for making us No.1 & 4A design" on 1 side & "District managers are the pride of Newark" on the other side. Bear must have Avon pendant. **CMV $30.**

KEY CHAIN NEW YORK AWARD 1982
I Love Avon's New York on front. Given to group sales leaders at Leadership Circle Celebration in N.Y. **CMV $15.**

NECKTIE 1980'S
Blue necktie with "Avon" in red, white & blue design. Label says "Neatwear Tie London, The Club Tie Specialist". Given to Avon Executives. **CMV $25.**

AVON BEAR SMALL TEDDY AWARD 1979
About 6" high brown bear. Made in Korea, given to managers. **CMV $50.**

CALCULATOR-COLOR UP AMERICA AWARD 1979
(Left) Avon color never looked so good on face of calculator. Came in Avon leatherette case & matching box. Given to Reps. for sales awards. **CMV $22.50 MB.**

COME COLOR WITH US ANNOUNCEMENT 1979
(Right) Inside has crayola & invitation to meeting. **CMV $2.**

AVON'S SPRING FEVER 1968
Green felt board with 6 tin painted flowers pins. Managers gave a pin to each representative for recommending a new Avon representative. **$35 complete card mint. Each pin $4.**

KEY CHAIN YOU NEVER LOOKED SO GOOD 1982
White plastic, black letters. Never issued to reps. **CMV $5.**

MERRI RAT AWARD 1982
(left) White stuffed rat with pink ears & feet, red hat has wood sign around neck "To the best from your N.Y. Buddy". Given to Avon managers just for the hell of it. **CMV $20.**

TEDDY BEAR SWITCH TO AVON 1982
(right) Small brown & white stuffed bear. Red Avon banner, made by Ruso. Given to winning team in each district. **CMV $7.50.**

RECOMMENDATION CASIO PRIZE 1980
Casio LC 315 calculator in 4A design black case. **CMV $20.**

REPRESENTATIVE CHRISTMAS CARD GIFT 1976
White Avon embossed box holds hand screened fold-out glass Christmas card given to all Reps. in 1976. **CMV $10 MB.**

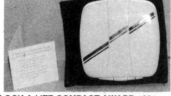

LOOK A LITE COMPACT AWARD 1981
Lavender and silver trim. Made only for Avon. Given to Reps. & Managers in blue bag. Card came with it. **CMV $15 in bag.**

SWITCH TO AVON BUTTON 1982
Blue pin. **CMV $1.**

AVON OPPORTUNITY UNLIMITED BUTTON 1982
Yellow button. **CMV $1.**

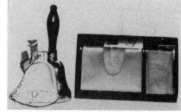

RING THE BELL-MANAGERS GIFT 1963
(Left) 6 1/2" tall brass bell, black handle. Used by Avon managers at sales meetings. Came with red ribbon & 7 bell shaped cards with Avon on each one. Must have Avon bell cards for value. **CMV $60.**

WALLET & KEY CASE-MANAGERS GIFT 1976
(Right) Leather wallet & key case given to Avon managers with Avon card on top of box. **CMV $15.**

KEY CASE AWARD 1971
Blue case with large 4A design. **CMV $10.**

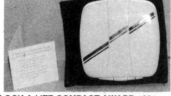

PICTURE YOURSELF MIRROR 1970
Two sided mirror with antiqued gold. Awarded for selling 7 body lotions during campaign 7. **CMV $7., $9 MB.**

AVON TENNIS BALLPOINT PEN 1980
Gold tone pen says "Avon Tennis" & has tennis racket on side. Given to Avon tennis match players. Comes in tan suede Avon tennis pouch. **CMV $20 mint.**

DAISY CHAIN JEWELRY & PIN 1971
White and gold earrings, 2 different pins or a daisy topped pen could by chosen by a representative for each person recommended as a representative. Only one gift for each name. **CMV $6 each. Daisy display card $7.**

YOU'RE THE HEART OF AVON AWARD 1986
Calculator, black & silver color. Given to managers. **CMV $35.**

ARIANE VASE AWARD 1978
Clear lucite with Ariane Avon on side. **CMV $15.**

CUSTOMER SERVICE PENCIL 1980
Red & white large pen. **CMV $4.**

PRESIDENT'S CLUB CANDIDATES PEN SET AWARD 1980
Red & gold Avon box holds gold tone pen & pencil set. Inscribed on side of pens, "President's Club Candidate". **CMV $25 MB.**

DIVISION MANAGERS TRIBUTE PEN 1969
Silver pen with 4A on clip. Came in blue flannel sleeve & white box. **CMV $35 MB.**

PEN FOR LEADERSHIP AWARD 1969
Silver, black top with olive leaf on top. Garland Pen. Given to Avon Reps. **CMV $15 MB.**

KEY CASE AWARD 1967
Blue case with gold 4A emblem. Given to Reps. for reaching sales goal in campaign 12. **CMV $10.**

KEY CASE FLASHLIGHT 1970
Red key case with flashlight inside. Not marked Avon. Made only for Avon. Given to Reps. for meeting sales goals. **CMV $5., $8 MB.**

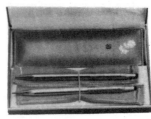

15 YEAR PEN SET AWARD 1976
2 Cross 14K gold filled pens engraved "Avon 15 Years" & person's initials. Both pens are in gray felt bags & pink leather pen holder with gold. 4A pen with red ruby in center & gold rose embossed. **CMV $75 MB.**

FORUM MONEY PEN AWARD 1977
Clear plastic pen full of chopped up money. **CMV $10.**

STERLING CLOCK PEN AWARD 1979
Sterling silver pen with digital clock & calendar inside. Inscribed "Number 1 in $ Inc.", plus name of division. Given to managers only. **CMV $50 MB.**

TEDDY BEAR PEN AWARD 1979
Cross chrome pen with small bear marked TL for Team Leader. Avon bear sleeve fits over box. **CMV $27.50 MB.**

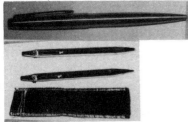

PRESIDENT'S CLUB PEN AWARD 1979
Parker 75 silver & gold pen. Inscribed on side, "President's Club 1979". Comes in blue felt Parker case. **CMV $20.**
DIVISION MANAGER'S PEN & PENCIL SET AWARD 1969
Sterling silver pens. 4A emblem on pens. Came in blue brocade Cross pen box. Given to managers only. **CMV $50 set MB, each pen only $20.**

AWARD PENCIL 1950
Deluxe Eversharp, gold color. Given to Reps. for writing 50 or more orders in campaign 2, 1950. 5 inches long with "Avon Woman of Achievement on pencil. **CMV $40 pencil only, $50 MB.**

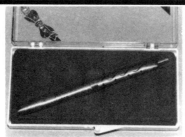

TOP REPRESENTATIVE PEN GIFT 1975
Brass & black design ball point pen. Small size. Came in red velvet lined, plastic display box & gold sleeve. Given for meeting sales goals. **CMV $10 MB as shown., Pen only $5.**

AVON PEN AWARD 1940'S
Yellow & black plastic, "Avon "on clip. Fountain pen on one end, lead pencil on other end. No information. **CMV $40.**

AVON PENS 1970'S
Blue & silver "Diamond Quarter 1977". **CMV $2.**
Red pen says "Get Write to the Point-Sell Avon". **CMV $2.**

RAIN HAT 1972
Plastic rain hat in pink & white case. Given at Beauty Salons only. **CMV $2.**
DING-DONG AVON CALLING PEN 1974
Given at Christmas. Black & white pen. **CMV $3.**

RADIO AWARD 1985
White, plastic battery powered Blue face. AM-FM in blue sleeve Avon Box. Given to Reps. **CMV $35 MB.**

CHRISTMAS MAGIC PENCIL 1960'S
White pencils from Avon. **CMV $1 each.**

CIGARETTE HOLDER AWARD 1934
Made of solid ivory in velvet lined custom made blue & gold box marked "Avon" inside lid. Green & silver center band. **CMV $75 MB.**

WORLD OF CHRISTMAS-FLOWER PEN AWARD 1970
Small white pen with red, yellow & green holly flower on cap. Given to Avon Reps. **CMV $3.50 mint.**

AVON BRASS MOLD STAMP 1936-53
2" brass mold stamp in reverse says "Avon Products Inc". "Tulip A" in center-New York-Montreal. Rare, **CMV $150.**

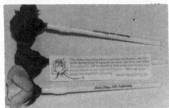

84TH ANNIVERSARY FLOWER PENS 1970
Given for sending in an order C-12 84th anniversary. White barrel with red printing with yellow, pink, red, orange or white rose. **CMV $2 each, $3 in cellophane wrapper with card.**

SUGAR 'N SPICE CANDY JAR AWARD 1980
(left) Glass jar full of red candy drops. Yellow neck label. Red Avon sleeve fits over white box. Given to President's Club members. **CMV $6 MB.**

ULTRA WEAR DEMONSTRATOR 1980
(right) Box holds clear plastic box with steel ball to test Ultra Enamel to customers. Given to Avon Reps. in C10-80. **CMV $5 MB.**

UNSPOKEN PERFUME VIAL 1975
Blue box holds small 1-5/8" vial Unspoken perfume. Given to Managers only. Outside sleeve on box. **CMV $10 box.**

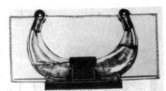

WESTERN CHOICE (STEER HORNS) "MANAGERS" 1967
Managers received the steer horns in a special box with "Avon" embossed all over the box. Was used to show at meetings on introduction of Steer Horns. Rare in this box. **CMV $45 MB as shown.**

ZANY RADIO 1979
Orange and pink Zany bottle shaped AM radio made in Hong Kong for Avon Products. Given to Avon customers in a drawing. Came in pink bag and certificate. **CMV $25 MB, $20 mint in bag complete, radio only $15.**

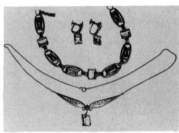

TOPAZE JEWELRY AWARDS 1960
Awarded for sales of Topaze products. 12 carat gold filled with imported Topaze stones. Necklace **CMV $40, $50 MB,** Bracelet **CMV $60, $70 MB,** Earrings **CMV $30, $40 MB.**

RADIO AWARD 1980
Red and white plastic AM-FM Avon radio given 1 to each district manager to give at a drawing. Made by ISIS, in box. **CMV $60 MB.**

CHRISTMAS CUP 1969
White glass mug. Avon on bottom. Given to district managers for Christmas. **CMV $30.**

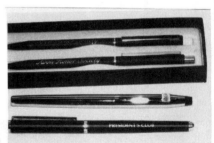

HONOR SOCIETY PEN SET AWARD 1990
Box holds 2 black & gold tone pens with Avon Honor Society on side of each pen. **CMV $25.00 MB**

PRESIDENTS CLUB PEN AWARD 1990
Chrome pen with PC on it. **CMV $10.00**

PRESIDENTS CLUB PEN 1989
On bottom is black & gold with Presidents Club on side. **CMV $10.00**

PRESIDENT'S CELEBRATION CANDLE HOLDERS 1980
Blue candles in clear glass base. "Avon" on bottom label. Given to all Reps. at banquet. **CMV $10 pair.**

CIRCLE OF EXCELLENCE PEN SET AWARD 1990
Grey box holds 3 black Quill pens with C of E on top of each pen. **CMV $35.00**

TIMELESS ULTRA COLOGNE MIST FOR PRESIDENT'S CLUB ONLY 1974
2 oz. size, gold cap. 1st issue to Avon President's Club members only, had 4A design on bottom under label. Regular issue had Avon on bottom. Box also came with special card saying it was collectors edition, fall 1974. **CMV $6 MB shown.**

TIMELESS MANAGERS GIFT SET 1975
Gold box holds perfume rollette, cologne mist & creme perfume. Given to Avon Mnagers only at introduction of Timeless. **CMV $35 MB.**

SONNET AWARDS 1972
(all earned for selling Cologne Mist)
VANITY TRAY
10" white plastic, gold trim. **CMV $10.**
VANITY BOX
White plastic, gold tirm. **CMV $18 MB.**
THREE PANEL MIRROR
White and gold. **CMV $24 MB.**
HOSTESS ROBE
White satin, gold trim. (won by Presidents Club members only) **CMV $30 MB.**

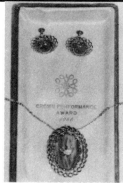

REGENCE EARRINGS AWARDS 1966
Gold with truqoise settings. Customer service award campaign 14-18, 1966. Has green velvet box. **CMV $60 in box.**
REGENCE NECKLACE AWARDS 1966
Crown performance award. Gold with turqoise setting & gold crown set in center, can also be worn as a pin. Has green velvet box. **CMV $50 MB.**

RAPTURE PIN 1964
(Right) Silver gray in color. **CMV $7. Pin only, $10 on Avon card pictured.**

RAPTURE AWARD BOWL 1965
Fostoria glass bowl with Rapture doves etched in bottom. Given to each Representatives in the winning district during the 79th Anniversary campaign. **CMV $35, $40. MB**

MOONWIND ORDER BOOK COVERS 1971
Dark blue with silver trim. President's Club cover earned for entry into President's Club. Honor Award earned for sales goal. Each came with pen. Honor cover with pen, **CMV $4,** President's cover with pen, **CMV $6**

SALES EXCELLENCE AWARD CUP 1977
6 1/2" high pewter cup. "4A design, Avon Sales Excellence Award 1977" on side of cup. Given to top 2% of sales Reps. in each division. Same cup also in 1979, only dates are different. **CMV $15 MB.**

ROSES ROSES AWARDS 1972
ROSES ROSES HOT PLATE 1972
6" square, white Corning Ware with pink and green rose. Given for selling Mist of Roses Cologne. **CMV $12 MB.**
ROSES ROSES GOBLET 1972
Gold trimmed goblet with bouquet of pink artificial roses. Came with card of congratulations. Given for selling Mist of Roses Cologne. **CMV $15 MB.**
ROSES ROSES CLOCK 1972
3" clock by Hamilton, 4 small roses on front. Given for selling Mist of Roses Cologne. **CMV $18 MB.**
ROSES ROSES GOWN 1972
Pink floor length gown with sash. Given for selling Mist of Roses Cologne. **CMV $20 mint. $25 MB.**

ROSES ROSES ORDER BOOK AND PEN 1972
Redesigned size is larger than older Order Books, pink with darker pink rose and green leaves. Given to all President Club members. **CMV $5 mint.**

PATCHWORK CANNISTER AWARD 1972
Level 3. Earned for selling cologne mists. White glass 3 piece cannister set with Patchwork decals. **CMV $25 set MB.**

PATCHWORK BINGO CARD 1973
9 1/2" paper bingo card used by Reps at meetings. **CMV $2.**

PATCHWORK REFRIGERATOR AWARD 1972
Level 1. Earned by selling cologne mists. White plastic with orange, green, red & yellow patchwork decals. **CMV $10 set, $12 MB.**

PATCHWORK COOKER AWARD 1972
Patchwork design. Level 4. Earned for selling cologne mists. **CMV $30, MB $35.**

PATCHWORK COOKIE JAR AWARD 1972
Level 2. Earned for selling cologne mists. White glass with orange, green, red & yellow. **CMV $15 MB $20.**

IMPERIAL GARDENS AWARDS 1973
Earned for selling certain numbered Cologne Mists for each level.
Level 1 BUD VASE
White china with orange and gold trim. **CMV $8 MB.**
Level 2 TRAY
White plastic with orange and gold trim. **CMV $10, $15 MB.**
Level 3 GINGER JAR
White china with orange and gold trim. **CMV $25 MB.**
Level 4 ROBE
Beige with orangish pink trim and floral sash. **CMV $25 MB.**

FIELD FLOWERS ORDER BOOK COVER & PEN 1971
President's Club. One was given for being eligible for membership. Honor award was earned for sales goal. Cover on left-Canadian President's Club Honor Award. Each came with Avon pen. **CMV $5 each with pen.**

IMPERIAL GARDEN TEA SET 1973
White Bone China with Imperial Garden design. Given to one Representative in each district when her recommendation name was drawn at the Christmas Party. **CMV $175 MB.**

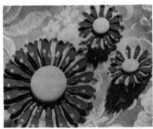

HANA GASA HAPPI-COAT AWARD 1970
Yellow with orange and green flowers. Given when someone a Representative recommended was appointed as a Representative. One size fits all. **CMV $10 mint.**

HANA GASA JEWELRY AWARDS 1970
Enameled pin and clip on earrings are deep red and purple. Given when someone a Representative recommended was appointed as a Representative. **CMV $15 set.**

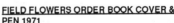

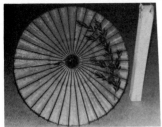

HANA GASA UMBRELLA 1970
Bamboo painted in Hana Gasa colors. Used at sales meetings at introduction of Hana Gasa. Came in Avon box. Very rare. **CMV $100 in box.**

EMPRISE NECKLACE GIFT 1977
Gold double E necklace given to Avon Team Leaders to introduce the new fragrance. T.L. on back side and it came in an Avon box. **CMV $10.** District Managers also got one marked D.M. on back and in D.M. Avon box. **CMV $15 MB.** Was also given to Division Managers. **CMV $15 MB.** Emprise money clip for male Reps. **CMV $15 MB.**

ELUSIVE PINK & GOLD SCARF AWARDS 1969
Given to Avon sales ladies on first Elusive sales campaign. White box has 4A design & signed by S.M. Kent, designer. **CMV $7.50 MB.**

FIELD FLOWERS UMBRELLA AWARD 1971
(Left) 18" spring green nylon umbrella has cream colored floral-relief handle. Given to Reps for making sales goals. **CMV $10.**
FIELD FLOWERS RAIN CAPE AWARD 1971
(Center) Given to Pres. Club Reps only for making sales quota. Beige with floral sash. **CMV $20.**
FIELD FLOWERS TOTE BAG AWARD 1971
(Right) Cream colored wet looking vinyl tote bag. Field Flowers pattern inside. Given to Reps for achieving sales goal. **CMV $12.**

ELUSIVE CLUTCH PURSE AWARD 1969
(Left) Pink leather with gold trim. Awarded for selling cologne mists. **CMV $10.**
ORDER BOOK COVER 1969
(Right) Pink plastic with gold "Avon Honor Award" on cover, came with pink & gold pen. **CMV $7.50**
ELUSIVE BALLAD 1969
(Back) Small black record marked Avon in pink sleeve. **CMV $6.**

CHARISMA JEWELRY AWARD 1968
Red & gold necklace, bracelet & earrings. Given for meeting or exceeding a prize goal. **CMV $37.50 set MB, $12 each MB.**
CHARISMA ORDER BOOK COVER 1968
(Back) Introducing Charisma. Came with red pen. **CMV $5, With pen $6.**

EMPRISE PURSE AWARD 1977
Black satin purse with jewel snap. Has gold carrying chain inside. Purse does not say Avon on it. Given to Reps for top sales of Emprise products. Came in clear plastic bag marked Avon. Designed by S.M. Kent. **CMV $10 MB.**

ELUSIVE BLOUSE & CUFFLINKS AWARDS 1969
Blouse light lavender silk with label with S.M. Kent signature & Avon. Cufflinks are gold with pink sets. Awarded for selling Elusive cologne mists. **CMV $10 Blouse, $7.50 Cufflinks.**

CANDID SALES LEADER TROPHY 1977
Wood base with brass plaque with bottle of Candid cologne mist glued in base. Given to 1 Rep in each district who sold the most Candid cologne mists on its introduction. **CMV $12.50.**

CANDID BAG FOR MANAGERS 1976
Maroon and white canvas bag. Back side says Avon, New York, London, Paris. **CMV $10.00**

CANDID TOTE BAG 1977
Light colored canvas bag given to Reps for going to C-10 sales meeting. **CMV $3.00** They could also win a Candid matching purse organizer. **CMV $3.00**

BIRD OF PARADISE ROBE 1970
Blue terry cloth robe given to Reps for selling 24 Bird of Paradise 3 oz. cologne mists in C-19-1970. Came in S-M-L sizes. Bird of Paradise on pocket. **CMV $35.**

BIRD OF PARADISE ORDER BOOK COVERS
(Left) Canadian. Presidents Club earned for eligibility into Presidents Club. Honor Award earned for sales goal. Each came with pen in matching design. **CMV $5 each with pen.**

BIRD OF PARADISE ORDER BOOK COVER 1970
Blue & turquoise, awarded for qualifying for Presidents Club, has matching pen. **CMV $7.50.**

BIRD OF PARADISE SCARF 1970
Awarded for selling cologne mists. Blue and turquoise silk. **CMV $10.**

AVON 100 DEVOTEE PERFUME AWARD 1986
.33 oz. glass stopper perfume given to Managers. Same as public issue only inscribed on bottom of gold tone container "100 years of Beauty 1886 Avon 1986". **CMV $15 MB.**

ARIANE ADDRESS BOOK 1977
Red velvet booklet with note pad and address book. Chrome pen has no markings. Given to team leaders. **CMV $6.**

ARIANE "INCH" NECKLACE 1977
Silver container holds small vial of Ariane cologne. 3 different ones, came in red velvet bag, 1 for Avon Reps with black pull cord on bag. **CMV $10 in bag.** 1 for President's Club members with PC on back of necklace and silver pull cord, **CMV $15 in bag.** 1 for Managers, sterling silver, back side says "August Conference", has red pull cord, **CMV $50 in bag.**

MOONWIND TRAY 1971
(Top Left) Blue glass tray trimmed in silver emblem of Diana in center. Given for selling 10 Moonwind cologne mists during C18-19. **CMV $22, MB $25.**

MOONWIND JEWELRY BOX 1971
(Bottom Left) Blue & silver. Emblem of Diana on top in silver. Given for selling 20 Moonwind cologne mists in C18-19. **CMV $25, 30 MB.**

MOONWIND ROBE 1971
(Right) Blue, zipper front with silvery trim. Zipper pull is emblem of Diana. Given to President's Club representatives for selling 35 Moonwind cologne mists. **CMV $30.00, MB $45.00**

BIRD OF PARADISE AWARD JEWELRY 1970
Gold pin, bracelet and earrings with turquoise stones. **CMV pin $12, bracelet and earrings $20 MB.**

STAR PC TRIBUTE PLATE AWARD 1989
5" Blue & silver porcelain plate. Marked PC Star Tribute 89. **CMV $5.00**

PC TRIBUTE PLATE AWARD 1988
6" chrome plate marked PC Tribute 1988. **CMV $5.00**

MRS ALBEE "Spring Magic Splendor" AWARD PLATE 1990
7" porcelain plate. 1st is series of 4. Given for $50.00 sales increase. **CMV $20.00 MB**

ALBEE FIGURINE AWARD GOLD & SILVER 1989-90
Metal figurines given to reps in silver for recruiting & gold for total sales. Both have blue base in red bags. **CMV Silver $85.00, CMV Gold $125.00**

C OF E IMARI BOWL 1987
Porcelain bowl given to Avon managers on 1987 Japan C of E. trip. Not marked Avon. Must have C of E. Avon Card. **CMV $75.00 MB with card.**

MRS ALBEE "Summer's Soft Whisper" AWARD PLATE 1990
7" porcelain plate. 2nd in series of 4. Given for $50.00 sales increase. **CMV $20.00 MB**

ALBEE AWARD 1987-88
1st in District in sales volume & sales increase is gold tone. **CMV $90.00**
2nd thru 5th in sales in District in volume & sales increase is silver tone. **CMV $60.00**

MOOSE AWARD PLATE 1930'S
White ceramic plate with green edging trim with 2 moose in brown on face. Back of plate is marked CPC Avon. **CMV $150.00 Mint**

MRS ALBEE "Autumn's Bright Blaze" AWARD PLATE 1990
7" porcelain plate. Given to Presidents Club Reps for top sales. 3rd in series of 4. **CMV $35.00 MB**

SSTARR DOLL AWARD 1989
Only 12 dolls given in U.S. 17 inch porcelain doll face, hands & feet. White satin dress, pink roses, blue ribbons. Given at Night of Avon Stars National Celebration. **CMV $350.00 in Avon Box.**

MRS ALBEE "Majesty of Winter" AWARD PLATE 1990
7" porcelain plate 4th in series of 4. Given for top sales. **CMV $35.00 MB**

ALBEE FIGURINE AWARDS 1988-1990
(left) 1990 yellow & white porcelain figurine. Given for $8500.00 in Sales. **CMV $100.00 MB**

(right) 1988 Albee is rose & pink color porcelain figurine. **CMV $100.00 MB**

ALBEE AWARD 1989
Rose pink color coat dress with detached cart. Given to Star Presidents Club Avon Reps. **CMV $100.00 MB**

STAIN GLASS ALBEE AWARD 1988
Blue glass, silver trim Albee given at Presidents Celebration only 2 given in each division. Not marked Avon - plain box. **CMV $45.00**

PRESIDENTS CAMPAIGN BRACELET AWARD 1976
Chrome chain & red letters on heart pendant. **CMV $10.00**

ACAPULCO CHARM BRACELET AWARD 1990
Sterling silver sombrero charm. Marked Avon on back. **CMV $25.00 MB**

STARS SYSTEM PIN 1989
(left) silver tone star & blue inlay given for $4500.00 in Sales. **CMV $3.00 MB**

TRIPLE CROWN NECKLACE 1988
(center) 14k gold pendant with 3 crowns on it & chain. Given to managers. **CMV $40.00 MB**

PRESIDENTS CLUB MANS TIE TAC AWARD 1988
(right) gold tone tie tac with small red stone. **CMV $15.00**

PRESIDENTS CLUB PIN 1988
Gold tone pin - "PC 88". 4 levels.

#1 Pearl	CMV $10.00
#2 Cintron "Topaz color"	CMV $15.00
#3 Ruby	CMV $20.00
#4 Sapphire	CMV $25.00

SPONSORSHIP LAPEL PIN MEN'S AWARD 1986-88
Gold filled pir s given to male Avon Reps for signing up new Avon Reps.

1 Sapphire	CMV $35.00 MB
2 Ruby	CMV $60.00 MB
3 Emerald	CMV $85.00 MB
4 Diamond	CMV $110.00 MB

HONOR SOCIETY AWARD PINS 1988-89
Gold tone pins "HS 88" or "HS 89". With:

Ruby	CMV $20.00
Sapphire	CMV $25.00
1 Diamond	CMV $30.00
2 Diamond	CMV $35.00
3 Diamond	CMV $40.00

ROSEBUD PEARL NECKLACE AWARD 1990
20" strand of pearls with 14k gold rose clasp. Given to Reps for 45 years service. Made only for Avon. Does not say Avon. **CMV $300.00 MB**

HONOR SOCIETY KEY CHAIN AWARD 1988
(bottom right) Gold tone key ring with H-S in red letters under clear Lucite. Given to top Reps. Came in Maroon box. **CMV $8.00**

SPONSORSHIP CHARM AWARDS 1986-88
Gold filled charms with colored stones.
Step 1-Lapel Pin .... CMV $10.00
Step 2-Sapphire .... CMV $25.00
Step 3-Ruby .... CMV $50.00
Step 4-Emerald .... CMV $75.00
Step 5-Diamond .... CMV $100.00

SIGNATURE COLLECTION AVON PIN 1990
Gold tone pin for Avon Peps. Has simulated Diamonds & Rubies. **CMV $8.00**

EXCELLENCE ROSE PIN AWARD 1990
1" gold tone pin. Red enamel rose. Excellence on edge. Does not say Avon. **CMV $7.50**

PRESIDENTS CLUB STAR PIN AWARDS 1989-90
Gold tone pin with gold star ... CMV $10.00
Blue & white star charm .... CMV $15.00
Red star .... CMV $15.00
Green star .... CMV $20.00
Blue star .... CMV $25.00
White star .... CMV $35.00
Star charm with pearl .... CMV $20.00
Gold star in circle charm .... CMV $15.00

DISTRICT ACHIEVEMENT AWARDS 1989
Blue Lucite stand holds one quarter oz. sterling silver Avon coin. 4 Steps - Volume, Customers, Recruiting, Sales Increase. **CMV $12.50 ea.** Also came in gold over silver "Best of the Best" in same 4 Steps above. **CMV $25.00**

HONOR SOCIETY QUARTZ CLOCK PICTURE FRAME AWARD 1987
Brass & maroon frame. **CMV $15.00**

COLOR WHEEL WATCH AWARD 1988
Color Watch - Avon on back. Gray strap. Given for sales incentive. Came in Avon Plastic box. **CMV $30.00 MB**

ROSEBUD PEARL BRACELET AWARD 1990
Double strand pearl bracelet with 14k gold rose clasp. Given to Reps for 40 years service. Not marked Avon. Made only for Avon. **CMV $250.00 MB**

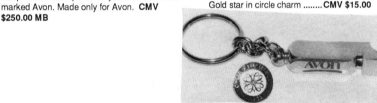

CIRCLE OF EXCELLENCE PIN 1988
4A red & white or blue & white pin. **CMV $3.00**

WHISTLE KEY CHAIN AWARD 1989
Brass whistle key chain says Avon in red letter. **CMV $6.00**

ROSEBUD PIN 30 YEAR SERVICE AWARD 1990
14k gold rose pin with diamond chip center. Given to Avon Reps for 30 years service. Made only for Avon. Not marked Avon. **CMV $100.00 MB**

ROSEBUD EARRINGS 35 YEARS SERVICE AWARD 1990
14k gold rose earrings with diamond chip. Given for 35 years service. Does not say Avon. Made only for Avon. **CMV $125.00 MB**

CLOCK CIRCLE OF EXCELLENCE AWARD 1988
Gold & brass tone Seth Thomas clock. Has "1988 Circle of Excellence District" on face. Comes in white box marked Circle of Excellence. **CMV $125.00 MB**

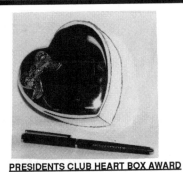

PRESIDENTS CLUB HEART BOX AWARD 1990
White satin lining says Avon PC 1990. Chrome heart box with gold ribbon on lid. **CMV $15.00**
PRESIDENTS CLUB PEN AWARD 1990
Black & gold Chromatic pen. Says PC Presidents Club. **CMV $3.00**

KISS WATCH AWARD 1990
Gold tone watch, Avon & red lips on face. Given to Reps. **CMV $50.00 MB**
HUNDRED YEAR MANAGERS WATCH AWARD 1986
Back says "1886-1986 Avon" gold tone band & case has 3 diamond type stones & says Quartz. **CMV $100.00**

PEARL BRACELET WATCH AWARD 1990
Gold tone watch made in China. Pearl face marked "Avon 1990". Given for top sales. **CMV $35.00**

TOWNHOUSE CANISTER AWARD SET 1989
5 ceramic canisters. Not marked Avon but lady on second canister has bag marked Avon. **CMV $10.00 ea., $25.00 for large one on right.**

PRESIDENTS CLUB CHRISTMAS GIFT 1987
White porcelain box with Music box in lid. Pink rose on lid. **CMV $15.00**

ALBEE WATCH AWARD 1990
Gold tone watch with brown strap & picture of 1990 Albee on face. **CMV $25.00**

RING THE BELL AWARD 1949
Metal inscribed bell given to reps in 1949 for sales goal. **CMV $75.00**

ALBEE JEWELRY BOX AWARD 1989
Wood box with Mrs. Albee etched in glass top. Not marked Avon. **CMV $25.00**

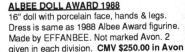

ALBEE DOLL AWARD 1988
16" doll with porcelain face, hands & legs. Dress is same as 1988 Albee Award figurine. Made by EFFANBEE. Not marked Avon. 2 given in each division. **CMV $250.00 in Avon Marked Box.**

WATCH INCENTIVE AWARD 1989
Gold tone case Avon on Face. Made in Clina. Brown Strap. **CMV $25.00**
WATCH PSST AWARD 1989
Quartz gold tone watch. PSST on face. Beige leather skin strap. **CMV $50.00**

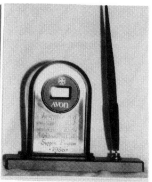

STAR AWARDS 1989
(left) Small Tribute chrome picture frame. **CMV $3.00**

STAR PAPER WEIGHT
(center) Sstarr Tribute PC 89 on clear glass paper weight. **CMV $5.00**

STERLING STAR PIN
(right) Comes in blue box. Sterling silver pin marked on back side (National Star Event 3/19/90). **CMV $75.00 MB**

SUPPORT PROGRAM DESK SET CLOCK AWARD 1986
Black plastic set says Avon 1986. **CMV $20.00**

SALES EXCELLENCE AWARD 1988
Wood plaque with brass Avon lady design, came with brass stand. #1 Division is gold. **CMV $100.00**
#2 thru 5 is silver tone. **CMV $75.00**

STAR BEST OF BEST PAPERWEIGHT AWARD 1989
Glass paperweight given to top Manager in each division. 1 ea. given for Best Percent increase, Best $ Dollar increase & Best Sales increase. **CMV $50.00 MB**

SUPPORT PROGRAM AWARD 1986
Small maroon & gold trim picture frame & clock. Given to group sales leaders. **CMV $5.00**

DESK SET AWARD 1985
Brown marblized plastic. Given to Avon Reps. **CMV $5.00**

AVON CALLING AMERICA PHONE AWARD 1990
Blue, white & red telephone given to Reps. **CMV $40.00 MB**

DIAMOND JUBILEE PAPERWEIGHT AWARD 1986
Clear glass marked C-12-15-1986. In grey box & Diamond card. **CMV $30.00 MB**

MANAGERS CHRISTMAS GIFT SPOON
Small silver spoon has Christmas tree & Rejoice 1977 inscribed. Came in red & white felt boot bag. **CMV $15.00**

1988 STARS OF CHRISTMAS RECORD AWARD
Framed Platinum tone record in silver & blue frame. **CMV $40.00**

PRESIDENTS CLUB BIRTHDAY GIFT 1989
Small white porcelain picture frame with pink & green flower decoration. Comes in Avon green PC box. **CMV $10.00 MB**

PRESIDENTS CLUB CHRISTMAS GIFT 1988
Gold tone metal trivet. Came in green & red PC Avon box. **CMV $10.00 MB**

STAR CLOCK AWARD 1989
2 3/4" high clear Lucite quartz clock says Avon. **CMV $10.00**

AVON TENNIS BALL KEY CHAIN AWARD 1986
Small yellow, red & white tennis ball. **CMV $2.00**

WHEEL OF FORTUNE CLOCK 1990
Wall clock. White plastic with glass face, says Avon. **CMV $25.00**

HONOR SOCIETY POCKET MIRROR AWARD 1987
Brass inscribed small pocket mirror given to Reps. Came in Red felt sleeve & white box with flower & yellow ribbon. **CMV $10.00 MB**
CALCULATOR AWARD 1987
Small white mini calculator given to Reps. Red design on face. **CMV $5.00**

PEN & KEY CHAIN SET AWARD 1989
White pen & key chain. **CMV $2.00 set MB**

C OF E AWARDS 1987
(left) Wood paddle, hand painted Yukata. Must have C of E Avon card. **CMV $20.00**
C OF E CHOPSTICKS
(right) Set of 2 hand painted chopsticks. Must have C of E Avon card. **CMV $5.00 MB**
Both items given to C of E Avon Managers on 1987 Japan trip.

SUNGLASS AWARD 1990
Avon marked sunglasses in red Avon case. Given for recruitment. **CMV $20.00**

CHRISTMAS GIFT TO AVON REPS 1987
Avon note pads in green book box. Red pen. **CMV $3.00**
Matching address book was also given to Reps. **CMV $3.00**

PANDA BEAR AWARD 1990
9" tall panda bear with red Avon shirt given for recruitment. **CMV $20.00**

ALBEE CHRISTMAS ORNAMENT 1989
Clear glass ornament with 1989 Albee etched on glass. Dated Avon 1989. Given to Reps. **CMV $10.00 MB**

FRAGRANCE 50 CLUB FIFTH AVENUE BOWL AWARD 1986
Clear glass bowl with blue lettering given to Reps on Intro of Fifth Avenue products. **CMV $20.00**

CUP & SAUCER 1980'S
4A marked ceramic dinnerware use in Avon Plant cafeterias. **CMV $1.00 ea. piece.**

CERAMIC JAR AWARD 1988
Off white ceramic Jar with gold 4A on front. **CMV $15.00**

COIN GLASS
HANDCRAFTED BY FOSTORIA

By Ogreta Simmons

The Fostoria Glass Company began operations in Fostoria, Ohio on Dec. 15, 1887. This site was chosen because of a promise of very low cost for natural gas for their furnaces. However, the gas field was short-lived and in 1891, Fostoria moved to Moundsville, West Virginia, its present location.

During the first 10 years, Fostoria made pressed ware. About 1897, oil burning lamps were added to the line and soon became a major part of the production. Today, the lamps are highly prized by antique collectors. As electric lights replaced the oil burning lamps, other handmolded items were created, such as dresser sets, table sets containing tumblers, spoon holders, sugar and creamers and upright celery holders.

Early in the century Fostoria realized the importance of fine quality blown stemware along with crystal service. They began to concentrate more on glassware for the home. This was, and still is, produced in the "much higher than average" quality of glassware.

When Coin Glass was first produced, the date of 1887 on coins was used, being the year that the Fostoria Company was founded. On the original pieces of coin glass production, real coins were reproduced. Since this was contrary to law, the U.S. Government quickly stopped production and ordered the molds destroyed. Today, the antique flavor of the stimulated coins and the lovely old shapes produce collectors items to grace contemporary living. Fostoria Coin Glass is now produced in crystal, amber, olive green, blue and ruby. Fostoria for Avon has only been produced in crystal.

Like collectors of Avon coming together and forming the National Association of Avon Clubs, likewise, there is a Fostoria Glass Society of America, Inc., a non-profit organization, which furnished much of the information for this article. Fostoria, like Avon, has a colorful past history and is a story all of its own. The plant covers 8 acres of ground and has over 450,000 square feet of floor space. About 420 persons are presently employed and there are 90 employees who have been with Fostoria from 25-40 years. Most employees are highly skilled craftsmen that take great pride in their work.

As traditional with Avon wanting to offer their customers only the best, in 1961, Avon selected Fostoria to produce Avon's 75th Anniversary year memento of the founding of the CPC Company. This was the first Fostoria Coin Glass piece offered by Avon and was the Coin Glass Wedding Bowl. In 1977, for 91st Anniversary of Avon, the Fostoria Company revised the date to 1886 for Avon. This brings up a highly controversial subject about the dates on Coin Glass. Information from Fostoria states that no exclusive items are made for Avon and that Avon does select pieces which are available to Fostoria Dealers around the country. However, for the items selected by Avon, the molds are revised to show the 1886 date. Then, since the molds are owned and retained by Fostoria, the 1886 dates can be found in retail stores on some pieces as Avon does not "own" the 1886 date. For this reason, the cartons and boxes that Fostoria is shipped to Avon Representatives is definite proof that the item is an Avon issue, the collectors should retain the packing box to prove its authenticity status. Each white cardboard box has "Avon" inscribed on it and is your proof that the item came from Avon. However, on the "Coin Glass type" of Fostoria where the Avon motifs are used in lieu of the dated coins, it would appear that these items were made exclusive for Avon you don't need a box to prove that they are Avon.

This article furnished by
Mid America Avon Collectors Club
Ogreta Simmons, Editor
Kansas City, Missouri

Following are some Fostoria Awards given by Avon. There may be others.

1961	Coin Glass Wedding Bowl
1961-72	Coin Glass Covered Compote
1961-72	Coin Glass Oval Center Bowl
1961-72	Coin Glass Candle Holders
1960's	Coin Glass Cake Plate
1960's	Coin Glass Tall Covered Compote
1963	Crystal 77th Anniversary Queen Award (11 1/4" bowl with 4A design)
1964	Coin Glass 78th Anniversary Salt & Pepper, Cruet and Tray
1970	Crystal Creamer and Sugar, Henry Ford Design
1971	Coin Glass Plate
1971	Coin Glass Short Bud Vase
1971	Coin Glass Handled Nappy
1971	Coin Glass Creamer & Sugar
1971	Coin Glass Salt & Pepper
1973	Lead Crystal dessert plate and bowl, set of 4 each
1977	Coin Glass Footed Compote with AVON emblems
1977	Coin Glass Round Center Bowl, AVON emblms
1977	Coin Glass Candle Holders, AVON emblem
1978	Lead Crystal Plates, came in 2 sets of 4 each
1978	Crystal Candy Dish with 4A design. (Christmas gift)
1980	Crystal Team Leader Recruit-A-Thon Bell

Some of the Fostoria items sold by Avon are as follows: (there may be others)

1969	Salt Cellar w/small silver spoon
1973	Perfumed Candle Holder
1974	Covered Compote w/Skin So Soft bath oil capsules
1975	George Washington Goblet Candle Holder
1975	Candlelight Basket Candle Holder
1976	Martha Washington Goblet Candle Holder
1977	Mount Vernon Sauce Pitcher Candle Holder
1977	Hearts and Diamonds, Soap Dish w/soap
1977	Crystal Egg Soap Dish w/egg-shaped soap
1978	Hearts and Diamonds Loving Cup Candle Holder
1978	Hearts and Diamonds Candlestick for 2 sizes of candles
1979	Crystal Pool Floating Candle
1980	Crystal Bud Vase w/scented carnation
1980	Ring Holder
1982	DAD Paper Weight
1983	Images of Love Picture Frame, Paper Weight
1983	MOM Paper Weight

SILVER PHOTO FRAME AWARD 1916
Solid sterling silver frame 4 1/2" high by 3 1/2" wide. Oval band is 1/2" wide, velvet back. Given to Reps. for selling $50 at Christmas. **CMV $350.**

PERFUME ATOMIZER AWARD 1927
Peacock blue opaque crystal bottle with embossed gold top. Silk net over bulb. Given to six Reps. In each district for top sales of gift sets in December, 1927. **CMV $125. BO mint, $165. MB.**

MISSION GARDEN PERFUME AWARD 1923
8" tall cut glass bottle with sterling silver trim, glass stopper. Given to Reps for top sales. Very rare. **CMV $250.**

SILVER TOILET WARE AWARD 1915-1917
Silver plate handle whisk broom made by International Silver Co., and two glass jars with silver plate lids of same design. Hair receiver jar shown with hole in center of lid. Puff jar is same only no hole in lid. Set was given to Reps. for selling $75 order in four month period. **Whisk Broom, CMV $75., Jar, CMV $125.**

DIAMOND JUBILEE PEARL AWARD 1933
18" long strand of Coro pearls. 14K white gold clasp with diamond inset. Satin lined box and silver metallic cloth outside. Given to 75 top Reps. in U.S. in July, 1933. **CMV not established.**

PENDANT LAVALLIERE AWARD 1916
Pure gold pendant and chain. Diamond in center of pendant with pearl above. Given to Reps for $150. Wholesale order. **CMV $400.**

PRESIDENTS CUP AWARD 1932
81/2" tall silver plate, gold lined. Given to only twenty Reps. in U.S. Engraved on side-winners name, from D.H. McConnell, President California Perfume Co., Inc., July 18, 1932. **CMV $300 mint.**

ELEPHANT CRYSTAL JAR AWARD 1928
6" long and 4" high, wrinkled glass to look like skin. Came filled with Vernafleur Bath Salts. Glass top of elephant lifts off. Given to 36 Reps. for highest sales. This will be considered the 1st decanter Avon ever issued. Very rare. **CMV $300.**

SILVER FRUIT COCKTAIL SET AWARD 1932
Silver plate tray and six silver cocktail bowls. Given for $250. order. **CMV $75. set.**

LAMP AWARDS BY STAFFORDSHIRE 1936
Imported pottery lamps, ivory color with flowers. Shades are shell pink or rose trimmed in rose or gold. Base is gold tone. Given as a pair to top 50 Reps. in U.S. for top sales. **CMV $125. each.**

SILVER TEA SET AWARD 1906
Rogers quadruple silver plate tea set given to CPC reps for selling $100 order. **CMV $300 set.**

TEA SET AWARD 1907
4 piece Rogers quadruple silver plate serving set. Given to Reps. for selling $125 in three months. **CMV $350 set.**

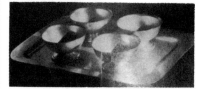

SILVER SHERBET SET AWARD 1932
Silver plate tray and four sherbet bowls. Given for $200 order. **CMV $60 set.**

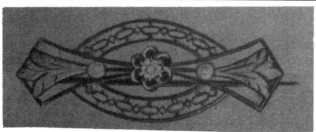

BROOCH AWARD "GOLD" 1916
Solid gold with one full cut diamond and two pearls. Given to Reps. for $150. wholesale order in four months. **CMV $400.**

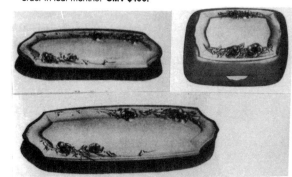

SILVER CLOTH BRUSH AWARD 1917
Silver plate back. **CMV $125.**
SILVER HAT BRUSH AWARD 1917
Silver plate back. **CMV $125.**
SILVER JEWEL CASE AWARD 1917
Silver plate jewel box. **CMV $20.**
Each piece has the Butler Grey Flower pattern. Each piece was given to Reps for selling $60. in four month period.

TEA SET AWARD 1907
4 piece Rogers quadruple silver plate tea set. Given to Reps. for selling $75. in three months. **CM V $300 set.**

OLIVE DISH CUT GLASS AWARD 1916
8 3/8" long by 4 3/4" wide. Genuine crystal cut glass. Given to Reps. for $30. wholesale order. Made only for CPC. **CMV $200.**

SUGAR & CREAMER AWARD 1913
Glass decorated with sterling silver. Sugar bowl is 3 1/4" side by 2 3/4" high. Creamer is 4" high by 2 3/4" side. Given to Reps. for selling 40 packages of Laundry Crystals and Starch Dressing. **CMV $100. each piece.**

POCKET WATCH AWARD 1907
14K gold filled watch with either Elgin or Waltham movement. Given to Reps. for $200. order in three months. **CMV $300.**

FLOWER VASE AWARD 1913
Glass vase decorated in sterling silver. Given to Reps. for selling 75 packages of Laundry Crystals and Starch Dressing. **CMV $300.**

CLOCK AWARD "8 DAY" 1913
Eight day Ormuler clock from New Haven Clock Co. Gold plate finish beveled edge glass. 10 3/4" high by 9 1/2" side. Given to Reps. for $100. in sales in three month period. **CMV $750.**

SILVER TOILET SET AWARD 1917
Set holds beveled edge hand mirror of silver plate back and matching silver plate brush and comb. Flower design is Butler Grey pattern. Given to Reps. for selling $96. in four month period in 1917. **CMV $300. MB set.**

CANDELABRA AWARD 1912-13
Heavy Rogers silver plate. Given to Reps. for selling $75. in four months. **CMV $500.**

CLOCK AWARD "1 DAY" 1913
Ormuler gold plate clock with 2" porcelain dial, 10 3/4" high by 6" side. From New Haven Clock Co. Given to Reps. for $60 in sales in three month period. **CMV $600.**

COMB & BRUSH SET AWARD 1912
Box holds two silver plate brushes and matching comb. Given to Reps. for $75. order in three months. **CMV $300. set MB.**

WATCH AWARD 1906
14dK gold filled case, heavy engraved. Choice of Elgin or Waltham jeweled movement. Choice of small ladies or larger mens watch. **CMV $350. each.**

PUFF & HAIR JAR AWARD 1917
Real cut glass jars with cut glass lids given to Reps. for $50. in sales in January 1917. Given as sets only **CMV $200. each.**

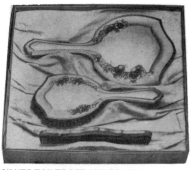

SILVER TOILET SET AWARD 1908
Box holds Rogers silver plated mirror, brush and comb. Given to Reps. for $75. order in three months. **CMV $300. set MB.**

SILVER CANDLESTICK AWARD 1932
Set of two silver plate candlesticks. Given for $50. order. **CMV $40. set.**

CUT GLASS SUGAR & CREAMER AWARD 1917
Real cut glass set given to Reps. for sales of over $50. in February 1917. **CMV $150. each piece.**

237

LOYALTY BIRTHDAY CELEBRATION AWARD 1934
Three piece W.A. Rogers silver plate tea set given to top 76 Reps. in U.S. during Mr. McConnell's birthday celebration. **CMV $85. set.**

SILVER SUGAR & CREAMER SET AWARD 1932
Silver plate tray and sugar & creamer. Given to Reps. for $85. order. **CMV $75. set.**

SALT & PEPPER AWARD 1931
Chrome plated salt and pepper shakers. Given to Reps. for selling eight jars of Rose Cold Cream in January, 1931. **CMV $30. set MB.**

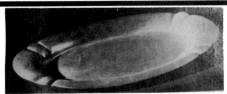

SILVER PLATTER AWARD 1932
Designed only for Avon. Gold lined center. Given to Reps. for $35. order. Silver plate. **CMV $35.**

CLUTCH POINT PENCIL AWARD 1914
5" long gold filled lead pencil. Given to Reps. for $30. order. **CMV $100.**

ARMY NAVY PEN 1918
Made by Salz Bros. N.Y. Made of Para rubber with 14K gold pen point. Shaped like a bullet. Given to Reps. for $50. order in September, 1918. **CMV $50.**

DINNER DISH SET AWARD 1906
Limoges China, 100 piee set. Given to Reps. for $200. order in three months. **CMV not established.**

DINNER DISH SET AWARD 1905
Made only for CPC. 100 piece set of Limoges
fine china dinnerware. Given to Reps. for a
$200. wholesale order in three months. **CMV
not established.**

CHINAWARE AWARD 1933
A complete set of china dishes could be won
by Reps., a few pieces at a time. Pattern was
made only for Avon. **CMV not established.**

NAAC CONVENTION BOTTLE & BELL 1988 SAN DIEGO, CA.
5 1/2" high porcelain, brown & tan dress. 800 made with brown trim on hat. **CMV $18.00**
100 CLUB SAMPLES
Made with blue trim on hat. **CMV $25.00**
400 BELLS
Made with dress color reversed. **CMV $22.00**

NAAC MRS. ALBEE COMMEMORATIVE BOTTLE & BELL 1988
1200 made of porcelain 5 1/2" high. Black hand bag. **CMV $18.00**
100 CLUB SAMPLES
Made with brown hand bag. **CMV $35.00**
400 BELLS
Were made with dress color reversed. **CMV $22.00**

CLUB BOTTLES-PLATES-CONVENTION BOTTLES-BELLS

What are they? Where did you get them? Club bottles were made for Avon collectors and sold thru any of the more than 100 Avon Collectors Clubs throughout the United States and Canada. These clubs are all members of the National Association of Avon collectors (N.A.A.C.). Club bottles or plates were sold for a period of 60 days only and only the amount sold in that time were made. At the end of the sale period, the order was placed with the factory. Each bottle is numbered with the quantity made. All club bottles are hand painted porcelain of the finest quality. If you do not have an Avon Club in your area belonging to the N.A.A.C. we invite you to join the Avon Times. $17.00 yearly membership ($20.00 for Canada, U.S. funds money orders only from Canada).

Send to:

AVON TIMES
Box 9868
Kansas City, Missouri 64134

All N.A.A.C. Avon club & convention bottles & bells 1972 to 1986 were designed, created & manufactured by Bud Hastin. Bud has created over 100 different hand painted porcelain bottles & figurines. They have become very collectable over the years. All are very limited editions.

NAAC CONVENTION BOTTLE & BELL 1988 - INDIANAPOLIS
5 1/2" high, all are yellow dress, green trim. Indianapolis Avon Convention 700 made. Brown hair, yellow fan. **CMV $18.00**
100 CLUB SAMPLES
Made with red fan. **CMV $35.00**
100 CONVENTION DELIGATE BOTTLES
Made with blonde hair. **CMV $35.00**
CONVENTION BELL
Is reverse color dress, with green fan. 400 made. **CMV $22.00**

2nd NAAC McCONNELL CLUB BOTTLE 1973
2nd annual Club Botle issued by the NAAC Clubs in honor of Mr. & Mrs. D. H. McConnell, founders of Avon. Registration certificate goes with the bottle. 5,604 bottles were sold & numbered. **OSP $11.95. CMV $50.**

1st ANNUAL NAAC AVON CLUB BOTTLE
1st AVON LADY 1972

7" high, hand painted porcelain bottle. Made for Avon Club members only belonging to the National Association of Avon Collectors. 1st NAAC Club bottle issued. Made in image of first CPC saleslady. Each bottle is numbered. Released in June 1972. Total issue was 2,870. Bottle made and issued by National Association of Avon Collectors. OSP $10.95. **CMV $200.** 18 made with red hair & green purse. **CMV $600. for a redhead.** No registration certificates were issued with the '72 Club Bottle. 4 bottles had blue lettering on bottle. All others had black letters. **CMV blue letter bottom $700.** 1972 factory sample of 1st lady sold by mistake. Same as above only no lettering on bottom & neck is flush where cork fits top of bottle. No raised lip for cork as regular production was. Bottle has letter from Bud Hastin as 1 of a kind sample. **CMV $500.**

NAAC MINI McCONNELL & CPC FACTORY 1978

(Left) Miniature size figurines of the 1886 CPC Factory and Mr. & Mrs. McConnell the founders of Avon. Issued by the National Association of Avon Clubs. Only 1,200 sets were sold. OSP $16.95. Original set came with McConnell & factory 2nd from right. Factory was too large so issued a second smaller factory on left. 1,200 small factories made. **CMV set with 1 factory & McConnell $35. CMV with both factories in center $55.**

NAAC CPC FACTORY CLUB BOTTLE 1974

(Right) 3rd annual club bottle issued by the NAAC Clubs in honor of the 1st California Perfume Co. Factory in 1886. Came with a registration card. 4,691 bottles were made, the mold was broken at 3rd annual NAAC Convention June 22, 1974 in Kansas City. OSP $11.95. **CMV $30.**

5th ANNUAL NAAC AVON CLUB BOTTLE 1976

(Left) In the image of the 1896 CPC Avon lady. Blue dress, black bag, and blue feather in hat. Black hair. 5,622 were made. Came with registration card and numbered on the bottom. OSP $12.95. **CMV $25.**

BLOND AVON LADY 1976

(Right) Of the 5,622 regular issue 1896 lady, 120 had blond hair. **CMV $175. on blond, rare.**

NAAC CLUB BOTTLE 1906 AVON LADY 1977

6th annual club bottle issued by the National Association of Avon Clubs. Made of porcelain and hand painted in the image of the 1906 Avon lady. She stands 7 1/2" high with yellow dress, brown hat and carrying the CPC Avon sales case of the period. Only 5,517 were made & sold for $12.95 each. Came with NAAC registration certificate and is numbered on the bottom. **CMV $25. MB.** 100 sample bottles were given to each NAAC Club and are the same only they are numbered and marked club sample on bottom. **CMV $50. sample bottle.**

NAAC CLUB BOTTLE 1978

7th annual club bottle made in the image of the 1916 CPC Avon lady. She stands 7 1/2" high with a rust colored hat and coat. Brown hair. Only 5,022 were made. The bottle is numbered on the bottom and comes with a registration certificate. Made of hand painted porcelain. OSP $13.95. **CMV $25.** Club sample was marked on bottom of 125 club bottles given to each club in the NAAC. Sample bottles are same as regular issue only marked club sample. **CMV $50.**

4th ANNUAL NAAC CLUB BOTTLE 1975

The modern day Avon Lady is the 1975 Club bottle from the NAAC. Blue hand painted porcelain. Each bottle is numbered on bottom & came with registration card. 6,232 were made. OSP $12.45. **CMV $20.** Club sample bottles. **CMV $50.**

NAAC CLUB BOTTLE 1936 AVON LADY 1980
(Left) 9th annual club bottle. Purple dress, black bag. 7 1/2" high. 4,479 were made & sold & numbered on the bottom as total sold. Did not come with certificate. Bottom cork. OSP $14.95. **CMV $25.** Same bottle came with blue bag & marked club sample on bottom. 155 club samples were made & given to to NAAC clubs. **CMV $50. blue bag club sample.**

NAAC CLUB BOTTLE 1946 AVON LADY 1981
(Right) 10th annual club bottle. Only 3,589 sold and made. Green dress, black bag, cork in bottom. OSP $15.95. **CMV $25.** 140 sample club bottles made and marked club sample on bottom. **CMV $50.**

NAAC 1st CONVENTION BOTTLE 1980
Sold only to NAAC club members. 1st in an annual series of NAAC Convention bottles to commemorate the annual NAAC Convention held in Spokane, Washington in 1980. 7 1/2" high, lavender dress of 1890s style. Hand painted porcelain. This bottle is the only one in the series that the cork is in the head, and 7 1/2" size. All rest are 5 1/2" size starting in 1981. The rest of the series will have a cork in the bottom to present a prettier bottle. Only 3,593 were made & sold. OSP $14.95. **CMV $25.**

NAAC CLUB BOTTLE 1984 AVON REPRESENTATIVE 1984
13th annual club bottle 7 1/2" high, hand painted porcelain. Gray pants suit, pink blouse, red hair. Brown bag says Avon. Bottom cork. Choice of a white or black representative. SSP $20. 1,133 white rep bottles were made. 1,070 black reps made. **CMV $25. MB each.**

NAAC CLUB BOTTLE "MR. AVON" 1985
7 1/2" high porcelain bottle. 14th & last in club bottle series. Only 1,800 made. SSP $20. **CMV $25. MB.** 100 club sample bottles made. **CMV $50.**

NAAC CLUB BOTTLE 1926 AVON LADY 1979
8th annual club bottle. Purple & black. Brown hat & shoes. 4,749 were made & numbered on bottom. Came with certificate that says 4,725. Actual count is 4,749. OSP $14.95. **CMV $25.** 150 club samples were issued to NAAC Clubs. Bottom is marked club sample. **CMV sample $50.**

NAAC CLUB BOTTLE 1956 AVON LADY 1982
(Left) 11th annual club bottle for NAAC club members. 7 1/2" high, red dress, bottom cork. Only 3,000 made & sold. OSP $17. **CMV $25.** 150 club sample 1956 lady bottles made & marked on bottom. **CMV $50. for club sample.**

NAAC CLUB BOTTLE 1966 AVON LADY 1983
(Right) 12th annual club bottle. 7 1/2" high, hand painted porcelain bottle made only for the National Association of Avon Collectors in the image of dress of the 1966 Avon lady. She wears a black & white striped dress. Blue bag. 2,350 made, bottom cork. OSP $18. **CMV $25.** A new club bottle is issued each year to NAAC members only. 100 club samples made. **CMV $50.**

7th NAAC CONVENTION BOTTLE & BELL 1986
5 1/2" high porcelain bottle. Black dress, red hair on 100 club samples. **CMV $50.** Regular issue has red dress, black trim. Only 1,800 made. SSP $18. **CMV $25.**

7th NAAC CONVENTION BELL 1986
Same as regular issue bottle only bell with dress colors reversed. Only 500 made by Bud Hastin. SSP $20. **CMV $30.**

NAAC CONVENTION BOTTLE & BELL 1987

5 1/2" high porcelain bottle. 8th in series. 750 made for Chicago Avon Collector Convention. Hand painted porcelain, light blue, dark blue trim. SSP $20. **CMV $25.**

CONVENTION BELL

Same only dress color reversed. Only 300 made. **CMV $30.**

NAAC 2nd CONVENTION BOTTLE 1981

Long Beach, CA Convention. 5 1/2" high hand painted porcelain bottle. Yellow & green dress of the 1800s style. Second in a series of 11 bottles of the 1800s style. Only 3,128 were made & sold to NAAC club members. SSP $15. **CMV $25.**

CONVENTION CLUB SAMPLE 1981

140 club sample bottles were made for NAAC clubs. Each marked club sample on bottom & numbered 140 edition. **CMV $50. club sample.**

5th NAAC CONVENTION BELL 1981

Same as bottle only has green dress. 500 made & sold in 1984. SSP $20. **CMV $25.**

NAAC 4th CONVENTION BOTTLE 1983

5 1/2" high, bottom cork. Rust & brown color hand painted porcelain. 4th in a series of Avon ladies of the 1800s to commemorate the NAAC Avon Collectors Convention in Wilmington, DE in June 1983. Only 1,875 made. Total number sold marked on bottom. SSP $15. **CMV $25.** 150 club samples made & marked club sample. 1 of 150 on bottom. **CMV $50.**

2nd NAAC CONVENTION BELL 1983

Same as 1983 Convention bottle only dress colors are reversed and bottom is open as bell. Bottom label, only 500 made. SSP $15. **CMV $25.** Bells created and sold by Bud Hastin.

NAAC 1st CONVENTION BOTTLE RE-ISSUE 1982

Same as 1980 bottle only is 5 1/2" high to match rest of series in size. Only 1,775 reissue bottles made. Reissued bottles sold in 1982. Cork in bottom. OSP $15. **CMV $25.** 150 club sample bottles were made & marked in the bottom of the 5 1/2" size. **CMV $50.**

4th NAAC CONVENTION BELL 1980

(Left) 5 1/2" high porcelain bell same as bottle only dress colors reversed. Issued in 1984. Only 500 made by Bud Hastin. SSP $20. **CMV $25.**

6th NAAC CONVENTION BOTTLE & BELL 1985

(Right) Seattle, WA. Avon Convention. 5 1/2" porcelain bottle. Pink dress with dark pink trim. 1,800 made. SSP $18. **CMV $25.**

NAAC CONVENTION BELL 1985

Is same as bottle only dress color reversed. Only 500 bells made & sold by Bud Hastin. SSP $20. **CMV $25.** 15 bells were painted same as convention bottle by mistake & came in bottle boxes. Some have no inside labels. Rare. **CMV $125.**

NAAC 3rd CONVENTION BOTTLE 1982

(Left) 3rd in a series of 1800s style dress. Blue dress,pink bag & hat rim, blond hair.5 1/2" high porcelain. Only 2,205 bottles were made & sold to NAAC convention was held in Las Vegas, Nevada. SSP $15. **CMV $25. mint.** No club samples were made.

NAAC CONVENTION BELL 1982

(Right) 1st issue - only 500 bells made in the same shape as the 1982 convention bottles. Only the dress colors are reversed. Pink dress & blue trim. You had to attend the 11th Annual NAAC Convention in Las Vegas, June 22-27-1982 to get a bell. SSP $12. **CMV $35.**

NAAC 5th CONVENTION BOTTLE 1984

5 1/2" high porcelain bottle, bottom cork. Brown dress, yellow and black umbrella. 1,650 made. 5th in a series of 11 convention bottles to be sold thru NAAC clubs of the Avon ladies of the 1890s for NAAC Avon Collectors 13th Annual Convention in Kansas City, MO June 1984. SSP $15. **CMV $25.** 100 NAAC Club Samples made and marked Club Sample on bottom. 1 of 100. **CMV $50. club samples.**

3rd NAAC CONVENTION BELL 1984

Same as 1984 NAAC Convention bottle only dress & umbrella colors reversed & bottom is open as bell. Bottom label. Only 500 made for Kansas City, NAAC Convention. Bells created & sold by Bud Hastin. SSP $16. **CMV $25.**

NAAC PLATE 1983
9" porcelain plate of the 1946 Avon Lady on face. Only 1,125 made. Label on back. SSP $25. **CMV $35.**

NAAC BOARD MEMBER PLATE 1983
Same as regular issue only back has special label marked "NAAC Board Member Sample". Only 7 made with each board member's name on back. **CMV $100.**

NAAC PLATE 1974
1st in an annual series of plates. Clear crystal thumb print plate with blue & red background. Only 790 plates were made. OSP $12.95. **CMV $40.** Factory sample plate had decal instead of painted logo. **CMV $100.**

NAAC BOARD MEMBER PLATE 1974
Same as regular issue only have Board Member on plate. **CMV $100.**

3rd ANNUAL NAAC 5 YEAR AVON COLLECTORS PLATE 1976
9 3/8" porcelain plate showing the 1st 4 NAAC club bottles. 1755 were made. OSP $13.95. **CMV $35.**

NAAC CONVENTION PLATE 1975
Only 250 made for 4th annual NAAC Convention, Anaheim, Calif. OSP $12.95. **CMV $25.**

NAAC SAMPLE PLATE 1975
(Left) Sample plate never issued to general public. 84 were made and sent to each Avon Collectors Club in NAAC, numbered on the back. **CMV $50. each.**

2nd ANNUAL NAAC PLATE 1975
(Right) General issue plate Mr. & Mrs. McConnell founders of Avon in center, gold 2 inch band around edge. OSP $12.95. **CMV $35. MB.**

NAAC PLATE 1984
Limited edition 9" porcelain plate 1956 Avon Lady. 8th in series. SSP $26. **CMV $35.**

NAAC 6 YEAR PLATE 1977
1886 Avon lady on plate. Made by AVON Products for the National Association of Avon Clubs. A beautiful china plate. Total of 5,000 were made with 1,500 gold rimmed, and numbered. **CMV $35. MB.** 3,500 were silver rimmed and not numbered. **CMV $30.** 7 plates marked board member. **CMV $100. MB.**

PLATE - NAAC BOARD MEMBER 1975
(Left) 2" wide gold edge marked board member. Only 7 were issued, This was a general issue plate. **CMV $100.**

PLATE - NAAC BOARD MEMBER 1975
(Right) White plate with small gold edge marked board member. Only 7 were made. This plate was never issued to public. **CMV $100. MB.**

NAAC PLATE 1985
9th in series. 9" plate of 1966 Avon Lady. Limited edition. SSP $26. **CMV $35.**

NAAC ROSE BOWL PLATE 1987
9" porcelain plate. 1st in a series of Avon Floats in the annual Rose Bowl Parade. Floats in the annual Rose Bowl Parade. Less than 2,000 made. No NAAC plate was made in 1986. SSP $25. **CMV $35.**

NAAC 7 YEAR PLATE 1978
Made by Avon Products for the National Association of Avon Clubs. A beautiful china plate with a decal of the 1906 Avon Sales Lady. Only 5,000 were made. OSP $14.95. 2,310 were gold rimmed plates. **CMV $35. MB.** 2,690 are silver rimmed plates. **CMV $35. MB.** 7 made for board members. **CMV $100. MB.** Rare issue plate with backward printing on back. **CMV $60. MB.**

NAAC PLATE 1926 AVON LADY 1981
Limited edition of 2,000. Gold rim. Marked on back. OSP $20. **CMV $35. MB.**
NAAC BOARD MEMBER PLATE 1981
Same plate as above only back is marked 1981 board member sample. Only 7 were made this way for NAAC board of directors. **CMV $100. MB.**

NAAC CUP PLATES 1984-86
Sold at Annual Avon Convention. 1st issue 1984 in Kansas City. Light yellow glass. 2nd issue 1985 - Seattle, Wa. Green glass. 3rd issue 1986 - Nashville, Tn. Red glass. All under 500 issued. **CMV $15. each.**

NAAC PLATE 1896 AVON LADY 1979
Limited edition of 5,000. Made by Avon Products exclusively for the NAAC. Came with gold edge & numbered back. **CMV $35 MB.** Silver edge and no number. **CMV $25 MB.** OSP $14.95 sold only by NAAC clubs. 7 plates made - marked board members. **CMV $100.**

NAAC CONVENTION GOBLETS 1976-83
Different color goblet sold each year at NAAC Convention. 1st year, red, 1976, 276 made. **CMV $60.** 1977, blue, 560 made. **CMV $30.** 1978, smoke, 560 made. **CMV $20.** 1979, clear, 576 made. **CMV $15.** 1980, purple, 576 made. **CMV $15.** OSP was $4. to $6. each. 1978-83 a special marked goblet given to each NAAC delegate. **CMV $25.** Less than 100 delegate goblets made each year. Special marked goblets were made for each 7 NAAC board members. **CMV for board member goblets $100. each year.** 1981 - 684 goblets made. **CMV $15.** 1982 - 700 made. **CMV $15.** 1983 - 322 made. **CMV $25.** 1983 is last year goblets made.

NAAC PLATE 1916 AVON LADY 1980
Limited edition of 4,000. Came with gold edge & number on the back. 2.060 made. **CMV $35. Or silver edge, 1,940 made & no number $35. MB.** Made by Avon Products exclusively for the NAAC. OSP $14.95. 7 plates made marked board members. **CMV $100.**

NAAC PLATE 1982
Only 2,000 made and numbered. 6th in a series of the 1936 Avon lady. SSP $25. **CMV $35.**

NAAC CONVENTION BANQUET MIRROR
1974
(Left) Yellow and black, mirror on back.
Convention held in Kansas City, Mo. June 22,
1974. **CMV $15.**

NAAC CONVENTION BANQUET MIRROR
1975
(Right) Blue and black, mirror on back.
Convention held in Anaheim, Calif. June 21,
1975. **CMV $10.** Both were given to each
person attending the annual NAAC Avon
Convention Banquet.

NAAC CONVENTION MIRROR & BUTTON
1984-85
1984 - yellow - Kansas City, Mo. Convention.
1985 - green - Seattle, Wa. Convention.
Both less than 350 issued. **CMV mirror $10.
each. CMV buttons $3.**

NAAC CONVENTION BANQUET MIRROR
1980-82
Only 500 of each made for annual NAAC
Convention Banquet. 1980 - Spokane,
Washington, 1981 - Queen Mary, Long Beach,
Ca. 1982. - Las Vegas, Nevada. **CMV $10. ea.**

NAAC CONVENTION BANQUET MIRROR
1976
(Left) 5th annual Avon collectors convention
mirror in white with blue letters. Held in
Cincinnati, Ohio, June 25-27, 1976. Mirror on
back. **CMV $10.**

NAAC CONVENTION BANQUET MIRROR
1977
(Right) 6th annual Avon collectors convention
mirror in blue with yellow letters. Mirror on
back. Hollywood, Florida, June, 1977. **CMV
$10.**

NAAC CONVENTION BANQUET MIRROR
1983
Only 500 small mirrors for the 12th annual
Avon Collectors Convention in Wilmington, De,
1983. **CMV $10.**

NAAC CONVENTION MIRROR 1972
Only 300 made. given at banquet, also some
were made with pins instead of mirrors. These
were dealers badges. **CMV $25. each.**

NAAC CONVENTION BANQUET MIRROR
1978
(Left) Purple with mirror on back. Given to
over 500 who attended the Avon Collectors
Convention Banquet in Houston, Texas,
June 1978. **CMV $10.**

NAAC CONVENTION BANQUET MIRROR
1979
(Right) White & red, mirror on back. Given
to over 500 people attending the annual
Avon Collectors Convention Banquet in St.
Louis, Mo, June 1979. **CMV $10.**

NAAC KEY CHAIN 1983
Red & white with black pen insert. Given to
Delaware convention attendees from Avon
Products. Only 500 made. **CMV $5. each.**

NAAC NASHVILE CONVENTION MIRROR
1986
Only 400 made. Red buttons with white letters.
Mirror back. 15th Annual. **CMV $10.**

NAAC CHICAGO CONVENTION MIRROR
1987
400 made. White button, red letters, blue
design. Given at 16th NAAC Convention
banquet. **CMV $10.**

GOLD COAST ("BUD HASTIN") CLUB BOTTLE 1974
Issued in honor of Mr. Bud Hastin for his contribution to the
field of Avon collecting. 1st in an annual series. Only
2,340 bottles were made. Bottle is 8 1/2" high, white pants,
maroon coat, black turtle neck shirt, black shoes. Few
were made with white shirt. Rare. OSP $11.95. **CMV
black shirt $25. CMV white shirt $75.**

PRESIDENTS GOLD SET 1980
Set of six different U.S. Presidents Bust, with antique brush gold finish. Only 250 sets made & issued by Bud Hastin Avon Club. OSP $70. set. **CMV $100. MB set.**

AVON ENCYCLOPEDIA COVER SHEET REJECTS 1976
30,000 covers for the 1976 Avon Encyclopedia were printed with the word Encyclopedia spelled encylopedia. The covers were never used but about 200 sheets were given to collectors with 4 covers and backs printed on a sheet. These sheets are rare. The rest of the covers were destroyed. **CMV $15. each sheet.**

AVON LADY MINI SET NO. 2 1977
1,265 sets of 11 miniature Avon ladies of the 1886-1900 period. Issued by the Bud Hastin National Avon Club (now called Avon Times) in 1977. Set came in special display box. Came with numbered registration certificate. Sold only to Bud Hastin's National Avon Club members. OSP $60. set. **CMV $125. MB.**

CLINT GOLD COAST CLUB BOTTLE 1977
7-5/8" tall. Blue pants, shirt, jacket. Black shoes, brown hair. 1,264 made & numbered on the bottom. Came with registration card. 4th Annual Club bottle. OSP $13.95. **CMV $25.**

BICENTENNIAL MINI AVON LADY SET NO. 1 1976
10 exact replicas in 3" high miniature figurines of the larger NAAC Club bottles. Issued by the Bud Hastin National Avon Club (now called Avon Times). 1775 sets were made and came with a numbered registration certificate. OSP $60. for set of 10. **CMV $125. MB.**

PRESIDENTS 1978
A set of 6 3" high bust figurines of the 1st five presidents of the United States, plus Lincoln. Only 1,050 sets made. Hand painted porcelain and came with a numbered registration card. Sold only to members of the Bud Hastin National Avon Club. OSP for set of 6 $40. **CMV $85.**
PRESIDENTS ALL WHITE 1978
Same set as painted presidents above only all white porcelain. Only 150 sets made. OSP $40. **CMV $125.**

MINI REDHEAD SET 1977
965 sets of Something Old - Something New made. Issued by Bud Hastin's National Avon Club with registration card. 3 1/2" high, 1886 Avon lady on left has green purse and red hair. 1975 Avon lady on right has red hair & Avon Calling is misspelled on base of figurine. OSP $12. set. Sold as set only. **CMV $25.**

WORLD WIDE JO OLSEN AVON CLUB BOTTLE 1975
(Left) Light blue dress, black hair. 1,102 bottles sold. Made in the image of Jo Olsen for her contribution to Avon collecting. OSP $12.95. **CMV $25.**
GOLD COAST RON PRICE CLUB BOTTLE 1975
(Right) Green suit, brown hair and shoes. Holding book "Testing 1-2-3". 1,096 bottles sold. Made in the image of Mr. Ron Price for his contribution to the field of Avon collecting. Mr. Ron Price was a member of the Board of Directors of the NAAC. Mr. Price passed away in 1977. OSP $12.95. **CMV $25.**

GOLD COAST MINIS 1976
A set of 3 miniature figurines 3 1/2" high in the image of Bud Hastin, Jo Olsen and Ron Price. 914 sets were sold at $18. per set. **CMV $30. per set.**

BUD HASTIN NATIONAL AVON CLUB BOTTLE 1976
2nd issue. Hand painted porcelain made in the image of Mr. Dale Robinson, past director of National Association of Avon Clubs. 1,000 bottles made & numbered. OSP $14.95. **CMV $30.**

AVON ENCYCLOPEDIA HARD BOUND COLLECTORS EDITION 1974-75
Only 1,000 special limited collectors editions were printed. Blue hard bound cover with gold stamped letters on front. Each is signed and numbered by Bud Hastin. OSP $20. **CMV $32.50 mint.**
AVON ENCYCLOPEDIA HARD BOUND 2nd COLLECTORS EDITION 1976-77
Only 500 special limited collectors editions were printed. Maroon hard bound cover with gold stamped letters on front. Each book is numbered and signed by Bud Hastin. OSP $20. **CMV $30. mint.** 6 hard bounds were found with all pages upside down. Each was signed by Bud Hastin as 1 of 6 rare upside down books. Very rare. **CMV $40.**
AVON ENCYCLOPEDIA HARD BOUND 3rd COLLECTORS EDITION 1979
Only 350 special limited hard bound covers with gold letters on front. Each book was signed and numbered by Bud Hastin. OSP $22.50. **CMV $30.**

BUD HASTIN NATIONAL AVON CLUB BOTTLE 1974
1st issue club bottle by Bud Hastin Avon Club (now called Avon Times) is a 3-piece Avon Family Scene. 3 separate bottles showing the Man, Child & Woman Avon Collectors. 1,091 sets sold. OSP $45. per set. Sold in sets only. **CMV $100.**

MID AMERICA NAAC CONVENTION PLATE 1972
(Left) Clear glass with frosted lettering, 134 were made for the 1st annual NAAC Convention in Kansas City, Kansas, June 1972. This plate was not made until 1975. OSP $12.95. **CMV $20.**
CENTRAL VALLEY NAAC CONVENTION PLATE 1973
(Right) Clear glass, frosted lettering. 124 were made and sold for 2nd annual NAAC Convention at Sacramento, Calif. This plate was not made until 1975. OSP $12.95. **CMV $20.**

NAAC CONVENTION DELEGATE PLATE 1977
White china plate with the date & place of 6 NAAC Annual Conventions. Given to each NAAC Club delegate attending the convention "85 plates". **CMV $25.** 7 board member plates were made the same only marked Board Member. **CMV $100.**

NAAC CONVENTION PLATES 1975-83
Made by Mid-America Avon Club as the official
NAAC Convention souvenir plate each year.
Very low issue on each. All are etched clear
glass & signed by the artist. OSP was $12.95
each. 1975 Orange County, CA - 1977
Hollywood, FL - 1978 Houston, TX - 1979 St.
Louis, MO - 1980 Spokane, WA - 1981 Long
Beach, CA - 1982 Las Vegas, NV - 1983
Wilmington, DE - **CMV $20. each.**

**MID-AMERICAN NAAC CONVENTION
PLATE 1974**
(Left) Crystal plate with frosted inscription
made in honor of the 3rd NAAC Convention by
Mid-America Club. 225 were made. OSP
$12.95. **CMV $20.**
**QUEEN CITY NAAC CONVENTION PLATE
1976**
(Right) Clear glass with frosted letters. OSP
$12.95. **CMV $20.**

BETSY ROSS MOLD 1976
(Left) Very rare steel mold given to Avon
Collectors at 1976 NAAC Convention. Mold
was cut into 5 pieces. Must have a letter from
Avon Products stating it is 1 of a kind. **CMV
$300. with letter.**
**ANNIVERSARY KEEPSAKE MOLD BASE
1976**
(Right) Steel base of Avons anniversary
keepsake mold given to National Association of
Avon Clubs by Avon Products and auctioned
off to Avon collectors. The numbers (17) and
5,215 on bottom. **CMV $300.**

**CALIFORNIA PERFUME ANNIVERSARY
KEEPSAKE MOLD 1975**
This is the actual steel mold Avon used to
make the 1975 Anniversary bottle. Mr. Art
Goodwin from Avon Products, Inc. New York
presented this mold cut into 5 separate pieces
to the National Association of Avon Clubs at
the 4th annual NAAC Convention banquet at
Anaheim, Calif. June 19, 1975. The mold was
auctioned off bringing several hudreds of
dollars on each piece. This is the 1st time an
Avon mold has been destroyed & given to the
general public. Very rare. **CMV $300. each
piece.**

ST. LOUIE BLUE PERFUME 1979
Small glass bottle, white cap. Special perfume
made & given by Mid-America Avon Club &
NAAC at NAAC Convention in St. Louis, June
1979. 231 bottles with registration card &
envelope. **CMV $20. mint & about 120
bottles only given without envelope & card.
CMV $10. BO.**

**BETSY ROSS NAAC CONVENTION
SOUVENIR 1976**
Given by Avon Products to all collectors touring
Avon plant in Springdale, Ohio, June 24, 1976.
Special NAAC label on bottom. **CMV $17.50
with special label.**

THE KING II "FOR MEN" 1975
(Left) Special label reads "Souvenir, June 19,
1975 NAAC Tour Monrovia Avon Plant". Given
to each male taking the Avon plant tour at
NAAC Convention, Monrovia, California. Only
150 bottles have this label. **CMV $17.50.**
SKIP-A-ROPE "FOR LADIES" 1975
(Right) Same special label given to all ladies
on same tour. **CMV $17.50.**

NAAC AVON CHESS BOARD 1975-76

21 1/2" square plastic chess board made for the Avon chess pieces. Silver & brown checker top with black rim border & back. NAAC logo in center, silver over black. 105 were made for sample to each NAAC club with center gold logo over black. 1,500 are numbered & last 1,000 are not numbered on back. **CMV gold logo $200. MB, regular issue silver logo with number $70. MB., black border no number $50. MB.** OSP $19.95 MB. Also came brown border with large black logo in center. **CMV $40. MB.** Last one to be issued had brown border & small logos in center, brown back. **CMV $40.**

NAAC CONVENTION MIRROR 1988-89-90

88 - San Diego, CA
89 - Indianapolis, IN
90 - Canton, OH
CMV $10.00

NAAC COLLECTABLES
PLAYING CARDS 1978
CMV $4.
CONVENTION TRAY 1984
Glass tray given by Avon Products to NAAC Convention. Marked "Avon Welcomes NAAC to Kansas City, Mo. Convention, June 19-24, 1984". **CMV $10.**
CONVENTION CARD HOLDER 1985
Brass business card holder given by Avon Products to NAAC Convention in Seattle, Washington, marked "Avon Welcomes NAAC Convention, July 1-7, 1985. **CMV $10.**
NAAC CHRISTMAS ORNAMENT 1985
1st in series. Clear glass center, brass chain rim. Marked "NAAC 1985". **CMV $10.**

CONVENTION DELEGATES RIBBON 1973

(Left) Red ribbon with a red rosette was given to all delegates. Gold printing reads "Official Delegate National Association Avon Clubs Convention Sacramento, California, June 22, 1973". **CMV $8.**

CONVENTION BOARD MEMBER RIBBON 1973

(Not Shown) Same as the delegate ribbon only in blue instead of red. Board Member replaced the Official Delegate on the ribbon. **CMV $15.**

CONVENTION NATIONAL CHAIRMAN RIBBON 1973

(Right) Same as the Delegate ribbon only in maroon instead of red. Only one of these ribbons was made. It is owned by Mr. Bud Hastin. No value established.

NAAC CONVENTION SOUVENIR BADGE 1972

(Center) Round, light blue background with first CPC Lady in center. Has pin back. **CMV $10.**

NOTE: Each ribbon & badge above was issued each year in a different color with the city & date from 1971 up to present date. All have same CMV as shown.

Dear Avon Collectors,

Certain Avon Items Have Been Removed From This Book. Avon collecting has changed many times since 1967 when collectors first started saving Avon Decanters. Many Avon items and even complete categories of items that were once very popular can not be given away today. You will find this true with almost anything in life.

What this new Avon Collectible book does is show you what are the hottest and most popular of all Avon Products in the 1990's. This includes all figural type items in Men's, Women's and Kids. Almost anything in these categories are popular and we hope we have covered all items that fall under these sections.

Remember, if its a household kitchen or decorator item and not marked Avon on the product we do not feel it is a true Avon Collectible. It must be marked Avon on the product. We have removed all Christmas Tree ornaments and hanging ornaments, that do not have the Avon name or logo or the year or date on each item. Collect only ornaments that can be identified as Avon.

Avon Plates are still very popular, but most collectors only want porcelain, ceramic or glass plates. Pewter plates are not desirable and most collectors will not want them.

Candles are popular in Glass, Ceramic or in Wax, only in Figural type design. The wax candles must have Avon on them. Do not collect taper candles of any kind, they are not marked Avon and will not stand and display on their own. All taper candles have been removed from this book. We have included all candles made by Avon that are now collectible.

Soaps of all kinds are very popular in the Avon line. Soaps must not be damaged in any way. If they are, we suggest not buying them. All Soaps must be in New Mint Condition.

We have used the Inflation Index method to reprice many older Men's and Women's Decanters, Candles and Plates. The new products now issued by Avon are much higher in original issue cost. They cost more than similar, much older items we had priced in past books. We feel if you will pay the price to get a new item from your Avon Representative that is plentiful, you should be willing to pay the same price for older and much harder to find Avon Collectibles in Mint Condition.

Avon Representative Awards and Gifts are still very popular with many collectors. We have removed some items in the Award section. Many Paper items, Purses & Bags, Clothing, Scarfs and Award Plaques that are not national level awards, and trophies have been removed.

We have weeded out many items in each of these categories and left many in. Most of this type of item is becoming less popular over the years. If you have any of these items and they are not pictured in this book, just use a item in this book that is similar to get a price for the current value.

Most of the avid Award collectors tell me they are now only interested in Awards that are given on a National level. They must fit on a shelf or hang on a wall and display well. If they don't fit this description, they will not appeal to the next collector when you decide to sell your collection.

A word of warning! I know how excited many collectors get to get a new item or award and pay a big price to get it, then find it much lower in price in a few months. This is particularly true with the Albee Figurine Awards. I have seen this happen on every Albee Award to date. Have patience. Wait a few months and you will save a lot.

National Association of Avon Clubs are no longer issuing Club Bottles, Plates or Convention Bells. There will be no new items of this type in the future in NAAC collectibles.

I hope this information helps guide you in your Avon Collecting.

Bud Hastin

NOTE: Bud Hastin now lives in Ft. Lauderdale, Florida but all book orders are processed in Kansas City, Missouri.

When writing to Bud Hastin, Box 9868, Kansas City, MO 64134 for information of any kind please send a self addressed stamped envelope.

Alphabetical Index

Typesetting by:

Contemporary Type Design

P. O. Box 15327, Kansas City, MO 64106

(816)822-0123

Owners: Carla Grant
          Sharon McNulty

Photograph Paste-up and Layout by: Bud Hastin

A New Book For Avon Collectibles –1st Edition

AVON *Collectibles Price Guide* ORDER FORM

5000 Avons Priced & Pictured to 1991

All books sent FOURTH CLASS MAIL. Allow 4 weeks for delivery. Order books only from Bud Hastin.

Money Orders - Your order is filled immediatley. Personal Checks - Order is held till check has cleared your bank.

DISCOUNT TABLE - U.S. ONLY

The following discounts are for Avon Ladies, book and bottle dealers, Avon Clubs, and anyone else who feels he or she can sell my books to other collectors.

Volume Discount Price	
Book Cost	**Postage & Handling Cost**
7-14 ....$12.00+P&H	1st Book $2.75
15 and up ....$10.00+P&H	**For:** **Add:**
Volume Discount Begins	2nd-4th ....$1.00 ea.
with 7th book	5th and up ....50¢ ea.

U.S.A.   **Canada**

$14.95+   **$15.95+**

Postage & Handling   Postage & Handling
$2.75 per book $3.50 per book

U.S. Funds - Money Orders Only
From Canada

Sorry - No COD's
No Credit Cards Accepted

Quantity Ordered ⌞_ _ _ _⌟

Mail to (please print)

Name _____

Address _____

City _____ State ___ Zip _____

ORDER FROM:
  BUD HASTIN
  P.O. Box 9868
  Kansas City, MO 64134

All books sent 4th Class Mail

ALL PRICES SUBJECT TO CHANGE WITH NOTICE - ALL SALES FINAL

A New Book For Avon Collectibles –1st Edition

AVON *Collectibles Price Guide* ORDER FORM

5000 Avons Priced & Pictured to 1991

All books sent FOURTH CLASS MAIL. Allow 4 weeks for delivery. Order books only from Bud Hastin.

Money Orders - Your order is filled immediatley. Personal Checks - Order is held till check has cleared your bank.

DISCOUNT TABLE - U.S. ONLY

The following discounts are for Avon Ladies, book and bottle dealers, Avon Clubs, and anyone else who feels he or she can sell my books to other collectors.

Volume Discount Price	
Book Cost	**Postage & Handling Cost**
7-14 .... $12.00+P&H	1st Book $2.75
15 and up .... $10.00+P&H	For: Add:
Volume Discount Begins with 7th book	2nd-4th .... $1.00 ea.
	5th and up .... 50¢ ea.

	U.S.A.	Canada
	$14.95+	**$15.95+**
	Postage & Handling $2.75 per book	Postage & Handling $3.50 per book

U.S. Funds - Money Orders Only
From Canada

Sorry - No COD's
No Credit Cards Accepted

Quantity Ordered ☐ ☐ ☐ ☐

Mail to (please print)

Name _____

Address _____

City _____ State ___ Zip _____

ORDER FROM:
BUD HASTIN
P.O. Box 9868
Kansas City, MO 64134

All books sent 4th Class Mail

ALL PRICES SUBJECT TO CHANGE WITH NOTICE - ALL SALES FINAL

Send SASE for Price of 1987 11th Edition Avon Encyclopedia. This book covers all Avon Products (13,000) 1886 to 1987. The Avon Encyclopedia will not be updated till 1993.

A New Book For Avon Collectibles –1st Edition

AVON *Collectibles Price Guide* ORDER FORM

5000 Avons Priced & Pictured to 1991

All books sent FOURTH CLASS MAIL. Allow 4 weeks for delivery. Order books only from Bud Hastin.

Money Orders - Your order is filled immediatley. Personal Checks - Order is held till check has cleared your bank.

DISCOUNT TABLE - U.S. ONLY

The following discounts are for Avon Ladies, book and bottle dealers, Avon Clubs, and anyone else who feels he or she can sell my books to other collectors.

Volume Discount Price	
Book Cost	**Postage & Handling Cost**
7-14 .... $12.00+P&H	1st Book $2.75
15 and up .... $10.00+P&H	For: Add:
Volume Discount Begins with 7th book	2nd-4th .... $1.00 ea.
	5th and up .... 50¢ ea.

	U.S.A.	Canada
	$14.95+	**$15.95+**
	Postage & Handling $2.75 per book	Postage & Handling $3.50 per book

U.S. Funds - Money Orders Only
From Canada

Sorry - No COD's
No Credit Cards Accepted

Quantity Ordered ☐ ☐ ☐ ☐

Mail to (please print)

Name _____

Address _____

City _____ State ___ Zip _____

ORDER FROM:
BUD HASTIN
P.O. Box 9868
Kansas City, MO 64134

All books sent 4th Class Mail

ALL PRICES SUBJECT TO CHANGE WITH NOTICE - ALL SALES FINAL